SEDUCED BY
MADNESS

ALSO BY CAROL POGASH

*As Real As It Gets: The Life of a Hospital
at the Center of the AIDS Epidemic*

SEDUCED BY MADNESS

THE TRUE STORY OF THE SUSAN POLK MURDER CASE

CAROL POGASH

WM

WILLIAM MORROW
An Imprint of HarperCollinsPublishers

Photo Insert Credits: Courtesy of Sheila Byrns: 1, 2, 9, 14, 16, 17, 23; courtesy of Evelyn Polk: 3; courtesy of Helen Bolling: 4, 5, 7; courtesy of Valerie Harris: 6, 10, 11, 12, 13, 15, 18, 22, 27, 28; courtesy of Barry Morris: 8; courtesy of author: 20, 21, 29, 30, 33; courtesy of Contra Costa County District Attorney's Office: 24, 25, 26; sketches by Joan Lynch: 31, 32; photo by Paul Chinn, the *San Francisco Chronicle:* 34.

HarperCollins books may be purchased for educational, business, or sales promotional use. For information please write: Special Markets Department, HarperCollins Publishers, 10 East 53rd Street, New York, NY 10022.

FIRST EDITION

Designed by Kris Tobiassen

Library of Congress Cataloging-in-Publication Data has been applied for.

ISBN 10: 0-06-114770-2
ISBN: 978-0-06-114770-8

07 08 09 10 11 * / RRD 10 9 8 7 6 5 4 3 2 1

CONTENTS

Part IV. In the Court of Susan Polk

In memory of
not *a* Jim Wood
but *The* Jim Wood

PART I

PRELUDE TO MURDER

1.

"AREN'T YOU HAPPY HE'S GONE?"

IN OCTOBER, SOIL IN THE BAY AREA IS PARCHED FROM MONTHS OF NO RAIN. A snap fire could wipe out communities overnight. Wooden signs warn residents that the fire hazard is "EXTREME." As the autumn air begins to cool, locals talk about earthquake weather, even though everyone knows cumulus clouds have nothing to do with the shifting of tectonic plates deep inside the earth. But there's this: the Loma Prieta earthquake, which registered 7.1 on the Richter scale, occurred on October 17, 1989. The Berkeley-Oakland firestorm, which killed twenty-five and destroyed 2,886 homes, occurred on October 20, 1991. Many Bay Area residents find the month of October unsettling.

Fifteen-year-old Gabriel Polk, the youngest of the three ruggedly handsome Polk boys, was not thinking about those historical markers on the afternoon of October 14, 2002. He was apprehensively waiting for his father, Dr. Felix Polk, a popular and respected psychotherapist, to drive up to their $1.8 million home in the upscale hamlet of Orinda, twenty minutes west of San Francisco. The home was more a compound really, with numerous buildings dotting the wooded hillside. Graceful old live oaks formed a canopy over the spacious pool, the pool house, the weight room, and the sprawling Arts and Crafts style main house.

With his wide face, pronounced cheekbones, and amiable smile, Gabe resembled his father. While the boy was still waiting for his adolescent growth spurt, he kept his hair like that of his brothers—marine short. Having missed months of classes, he was enrolled in a continuation school. His mother had encouraged his truancy, telling him that he was special, that the rules that applied to other kids didn't apply to him. Despite trouble at school, Gabe carried himself with confidence, possessing a vocabulary that more closely resembled an educated adult's than a high school student's.

Felix had told Gabe he would see clients in the morning and be home around three. His dad had promised to take him to a playoff between the Giants and the St. Louis Cardinals at the new Pac Bell Park in downtown San Francisco. It would be a good night for the Bay Area. The Giants would score a run in the ninth inning to clinch the playoff and head to the World Series, but Gabe and his father would not be there to see it.

Gabe had spent the warm morning at Del Oro High School in Walnut Creek, a public school designed for kids with problems. He left school at 12:30 PM, after which he and his mother lunched at Baja Fresh, an upscale Mexican chain in the neighboring town of Lafayette, and then ran to the drugstore to pick up some acne medication. Though other teenagers might shun being with their mother in public, Susan's sons appreciated her company, enjoying her beauty, intelligence, and love. When things were going well, she was literate and charming; she lavished her sons with her attention.

As soon as they arrived home, Susan stood in their kitchen and announced, "I'm going to run some errands," a statement which Gabriel found odd. If she had other stops to make, he wondered, why hadn't she done them when they were together? Leaving Gabe at home, she drove back to Lafayette, where she stopped at Blockbuster to pick up the movie *Scooby-Doo*. While she was gone Gabriel and his dog, a sweet yellow Lab named Dusty, went for a quick swim in the pool before heading to the exercise room, a freestanding building next to the pool house, where he lifted weights and anticipated his father's return from work.

As the autumn sky darkened, Gabriel looked at the lower driveway where Felix normally parked his black Saab. Considering the bitter fights he had recently witnessed between his parents, Gabriel took his father's delay as an ominous sign.

To an outsider, the Polks made a handsome couple. Even at seventy, the charismatic Felix had an air of accomplishment about him. A sturdy, muscular man who maintained his physique, he had European bearing with a crown of dark, graying curls and an empathetic expression that made patients want to confide in him. His tanned face was rounded and carved in curves, whereas his wife's porcelain profile was angular. Susan Polk, twenty-five years younger than her husband, had the perfect features of a woman in a soap commercial, before

Dove discovered average women. Her nose was small, her eyes the color of morning toast. She wore classic clothes that were too big for her thin frame, which was slender and coltish like a young Katharine Hepburn.

Before the difficult years, Gabriel's parents had had a loving relationship. They shared a passion for news, politics, culture, and literature. His parents' prized library contained over a thousand books, including numerous first editions. They were completely devoted to each other. When marriages fail, more often than not a third party is involved, a mistress, a yoga instructor, or someone from the high school reunion who drives a wedge in an already fragile relationship. But that was not what happened to the Polks. Felix and Susan were so entwined that there was no oxygen left for anyone else.

A few years ago, his parents' fragile relationship began to splinter. His mother courted Gabe's allegiance in her crusade against her husband. She told Gabriel that his father was their malevolent controller, whispering that she wasn't sure she could escape the marriage—get out from Felix's control—by any other means than to kill him. He had heard her say it; he heard his mother threaten to blow his father's head off with a shotgun. In fact, during the past few months his mother had talked to her youngest about killing his dad so often that her comments about drowning, drugging, or driving over him had lost much of their meaning.

Gabriel had come to believe the evil stories his mother told about his father. It had been his mother who had always been there for him, not his dad. While his father often seemed distant and unreachable, there was never any doubt that Susan loved him and his brothers. But recently he had started spending more time with his father, and his perception was changing. As the boy and his father enjoyed each other's company, Gabe found his mother's portrait of his father eroding, revealing a man who, though flawed, loved his son and his family very much.

AFTER WRAPPING UP HIS HOUR-AND-A-HALF-LONG WORKOUT, GABRIEL LEFT the weight room and padded across the brick patio to his bedroom in the main house. Mindlessly, he watched TV and played video games to dilute his growing anxiety. He had called his father's Berkeley office four or five times during the afternoon and early evening, yet all he heard was his father's soothing voice on the answering machine. It failed to soothe Gabe's fears. Resigning himself to his father's absence, Gabriel had dinner with his mother, and shortly after, at 7:00 PM, with the baseball game in San Francisco getting under way, he again retreated to his room, where he called his father's office once more, this time leaving a message.

The situation gave Gabe an uneasy feeling. Felix had never been the most attentive father, but when he made a plan with one of his sons, he came through. Because his father's car wasn't home, Gabriel hadn't actually looked around the property for him. He wondered whether his father might be in the pool house, but he was afraid to check. He promised himself that in another hour he would call the cops to ask if they knew anything about his missing father.

He went to the kitchen and asked his mother, "Where's Dad?" partly to see if she knew and partly to gauge her reaction.

"I don't know. Maybe he got in an accident," his mother said. "Why don't you call the highway patrol and see if there's been a problem?" Gabriel thought her voice sounded phony, and her eyelids fluttered when she spoke, a tic Gabe had come to recognize as a sign that she was lying.

"No," he told his mother, "I'm gonna handle this." By then he was pretty sure there was something wrong. He thought his father wasn't just late; something more malicious had occurred.

The hot sun was long down and the night had grown cool. His mother was washing dishes. He left the house. With dim lights illuminating the path, he walked to the other side of the property. Reaching the cottage, he pressed down on the wrought-iron handle of the thick wooden door. It was locked. He didn't really want to open it; he was afraid of what he might find. There were two other entrances. He didn't try them. It was dark, and there were dead light switches on the walls. Whenever he went there at night, he stumbled around.

Returning to the main house he found his mother still in the kitchen, where she was scrubbing up. Again, he confronted her. "Where's Dad?"

"He's gone and aren't you happy?" she said. "I am."

"Where is he?" Gabriel repeated.

"Aren't you happy he's gone?" she said, as she busied herself putting dishes away.

"Nope," he responded.

"I guess I didn't have a shotgun, did I?"

Gabriel didn't understand what his mother was saying. As smart as she was, he knew well that sometimes she uttered the most nonsensical remarks.

He returned to his room and punched in 911. He asked for the nonemergency number for the Orinda police. The emergency operator advised, "We don't give nonemergency lines," but depending on what he needed, "We could help." The operator learned he was fifteen. But when asked for details, Gabe hung up. No sense talking with the operator about his fears, since they could be unfounded or even alarmist. If he returned to the cottage and there was nothing there, he'd feel like a complete idiot.

Twenty minutes passed. Dressed only in gym shorts, the barefoot Gabriel made himself do what he dreaded; he grabbed a flashlight and strode through the living room to the front door, "Gabe, what are you doing?" his mother inquired.

"Nothing."

"What are you doing?"

"Nothing," he answered, not suspecting that that might be the last civil conversation he might hold with his mother.

It was 9:00 PM, six hours after he expected his father home. Gabriel hiked to the top of the property, where he examined the family's silver Volvo station wagon for clues about his father's whereabouts. He was relieved to find no trace of blood, no signs of a struggle, and nothing belonging to his father. Gabriel climbed down the steps from the upper driveway and crept to the pool house. This time he went to the kitchen door, and with a turn of the knob, the door swung open. Edging his way along the narrow kitchen corridor and from an elevated level, he shone a sharp light down on the snug living room.

There he found the still body of his father lying faceup on the tiled floor. He was wearing only black briefs, with brown blood pooled on his chest and thighs. He lay on his back, his arms slightly outstretched like a blood angel in a pond of his own fluids. His scalp was caked in blood that had trickled down his face like tributaries on a topographical map.

Gabriel was horrified. He looked, but only for a moment. He spun around and raced back to the main house, where he dashed to his room, grabbed his cordless phone, and fled. He took cover behind the garbage cans, and at 9:09 PM he called 911 and told them his mother shot his father, who was dead in pool house.

Overhearing his conversation, his mother rushed outside. He could hear her enter the pool house and call out, "Gabe, where are you? Hey, did you see that?" as though she were viewing Felix's body for the first time. He knew it was not the reaction of a wife who had just discovered her husband's blood-soaked corpse.

He couldn't help but be fearful of her.

From behind the garbage hutch Gabe yelled, "You killed him!" Within moments firemen, who'd been alerted to the incident, roared up to the front of the property in their fire truck from a station house less than half a mile away. Gabriel ran down the hill to safety. He knew his mother loved him. He didn't think she might kill him too, but now he couldn't be quite so sure.

AT 9:11 PM, CONTRA COSTA SHERIFF'S SERGEANT KENNETH HANSEN HEARD over the radio that there was an injured man at 728 Miner Road in Orinda and that the suspect was barricaded in the house. Orinda's crime rate was so low that police were often left to deal with vandalized mailboxes and identity theft. For several years, an officer from the department spent the noon hour at the high school, where he tried to prevent kids from cutting in line.

As he listened to the report, the twenty-nine-year veteran could feel his pulse quickening. He tried to tease information out of the mobile data computer next to his seat, but the aged computer was characteristically sluggish. Hansen flipped on his wailing siren and raced along the freeway at ninety miles an hour to the village of Orinda.

Knowing how easy it is to get lost along the town's unlit winding roads, Hansen took the longer but more easily traversable way up the hill. As he drove, he barked orders at the deputies already on the scene to set up a perimeter as best they could on the large property and to block the driveway to avoid sudden flight. That Monday night of Columbus Day, the department was spread thin. Sergeant Hansen placed all deputy sheriffs in the area on priority one: forget petty crime and head for the hilltop estate belonging to Dr. Felix Polk and his wife, Susan. As he drove, he switched to channel one and heard another report: the 911 call had come from the son, who said that his father was dead in the pool house and that his mother had shot him.

The boy had said she was still in the house. Sergeant Hansen worried that she might still be armed.

As he approached the wooded compound, Hansen shut down his siren and flashing lights. Over the years he found that the calmer the environment the easier it was to subdue a suspect. Checking himself, he made sure to be mindful that his adrenalin rush wouldn't give him tunnel vision, a dangerous tendency for a cop at a crime scene. At 9:29 PM he reached the foot of the property. He promptly drew his 9-mm weapon—loaded with fifteen rounds. To the three deputies already on the scene he announced, "I'm going to see if the guy is still alive up in the pool house."

He climbed the brick steps to the pristine, rustic home. Through the bay window of the gourmet kitchen the sergeant noticed "a female subject" moving toward him. He rapped on the door and confronted a slender, graceful woman of forty-four dressed in a white long-sleeved jersey and faded Ralph Lauren jeans.

"Are you Mrs. Polk?" Hansen inquired. "I'm here to check on the welfare of your husband. I'm told he's injured in the pool house. Have you seen him?"

"Not since earlier this afternoon," she said as she stood framed in the doorway, her small body backlit by light from her kitchen.

He sized her up. Mrs. Polk hardly looked like a killer. He determined she presented little threat and treated her accordingly. She spoke in a calm, nonchalant way. Funny, he thought, there was no tone to her voice. Playing it safe and following the standard procedure he told her, "I'm cuffing you, for your safety as well as mine." Before handling Mrs. Polk, he shoved his gun back in its holster to avoid any chance that she might make a grab for it.

The eerily calm Mrs. Polk did not protest. She placed her hands at the base of her back while the sergeant clamped the handcuffs on her bony wrists like a silver bracelet designed for a much larger woman. He told her to sit on the wooden bench that abuts the house, and he assigned Deputy Shannon Kelly to watch over her while he searched for the victim.

Sergeant Hansen's eyes swept the property. He walked past the lilting Japanese maples, the bonus-size barbecue, the rough-hewn picnic table and benches. He passed under the old oak trees next to the pool, which had been the focal point of many noisy teenage parties since the Polks first moved onto the property.

As he stepped along the brick path, Sergeant Hansen focused on the dark outline of the pool house. He had a single goal: "to find this guy and see if he's alive."

The sergeant opened a door on the side of the cottage and passed through the narrow kitchenette. Shining the beam of his twenty-thousand-candle-power flashlight around the small cottage, the light settled on the corpse of Dr. Felix Polk.

After working for two and a half years for the county coroner, Sergeant Hansen knew what a dead body looked like. Dr. Polk's eyes were open and fixed. His skin was pallid. His chest was still. Gravity had pooled his blood to the lowest parts of the body—something that occurs three hours after death. A lake of dried blood surrounded the body. Blood splatters stained the floor and furniture. The scene told the sergeant that there had been a horrific struggle and that Susan Polk's husband "did not die immediately." Had the heart stopped shortly after the wounds were inflicted, the blood would not have continued to pour across the terra-cotta floor.

Not wanting to contaminate the crime scene, the sergeant stopped three feet from the body. He examined the scene for two minutes before carefully backing out of the cottage. He contacted police dispatch, telling them to invoke homicide protocol—contacting the crime lab, the district attorney's office, the police chief. Then he followed the brick path back to the spot where he had left Deputy Kelly and Mrs. Polk.

Meanwhile, Gabriel was being placed in the back of a black-and-white—deputies thought he too might be a suspect. Returning to the handcuffed Susan Polk, Sergeant Hansen somberly gave her the news: her husband was dead, and it appeared to be from unnatural causes.

In the course of his career, Sergeant Hansen had notified maybe twenty people of the death of their loved ones. He had heard people scream; he'd seen them twitch and shiver uncontrollably, seen them collapse, and even bolt and run for three blocks. He had never seen anyone as devoid of emotion as this woman.

After a minute, she spoke.

"Oh, well," she said, looking up from her seat on the bench, "we were getting a divorce anyway."

2.

IN LOVE WITH HER THERAPIST

SUSAN BOLLING, NINETEEN YEARS OLD, LAY IN BED ON A SUMMER'S NIGHT, the shadow of twigs dancing on her bedroom ceiling. She was happy in the way a girl approaching womanhood is when she feels enchanted by herself and the world's reaction to her. Still in a dreamlike state, she felt her life was in harmony. She wanted to examine it like a child does a cat's-eye marble, but as she did, it dissolved, and all that remained was the memory of it and the pleasure the dream had given her. She hugged herself with satisfaction that was both strange and new.

Her life was not that of a normal teen. She spent her days absorbed in reading the great novels of Western literature with a passion beyond her years and receiving an intense form of psychotherapy from a brilliant forty-three-year-old therapist with whom she had fallen in love. She was scheduled to see him later that day in his new office. She counted the hours.

Not even her itchy scalp could drag her down. She blamed it on her mother, who had exiled the dog and cat to the backyard, leaving behind a colony of ravenous fleas that had found Susan to be a juicy alternative. She had tried to wash them out, but nothing worked. And she had thought they didn't like human blood.

To distract herself she counted her prized collection of books. She had filled a new bookcase in just a couple of weeks and had recently gotten another. When she finished counting she was disappointed. She thought she'd read thousands of books, but she only counted one hundred and ninety. After that, she cataloged the rest of her things: her plants, her new carpet, her quilt, her seashells, and the posters of marine life tacked to her paneled walls. There was so much color: blues, greens, reds, and yellows. The richness and colors of the objects in her room, she felt, reflected the depth and complexity of her own mind.

She pulled on white gym shorts, admiring her mirrored reflection. Her body was slender. She had smooth olive skin and a head full of dark, bouncy curls. That she was a very special and a precocious young woman was one of many things on which she and her therapist agreed. He had even recently asked her to share her wisdom with his graduate students, who were studying the treatment of adolescence. He had told her she could teach them a lot. And she knew that to be true.

After four years of deep and difficult psychotherapy with him, discussing her therapy with grad students turned out to be painless. She remembered with relish telling them that therapy had unleashed a remarkable power inside her. It was a feeling she had on dark starry nights and sometimes, like now, on sunny days as well. She could literally feel the power flowing out her fingertips like electricity. It was a type of power with which she was sure she could shape her destiny.

Susan knew the students had understood her, and in fact, she was certain that they were awed by her. She imagined that they could almost see the electricity emanate from her body. "No doubt about it," she wrote, she was a kind of "wonder woman. . . . There had never been and never would be again, anyone quite like [her] in the whole world."

Susan looked at herself again in the mirror. She was sensual and yet something of a prude, at least around boys her own age. That was remarkable given that this was the 1970s, the high-water mark of the sexual revolution and she was a rebellious teenager living in the center of it all, northern California. This was the era of free love, fueled by easy access to birth control pills and cheap and plentiful marijuana. Sex among friends and acquaintances was not much more than a handshake in previous times.

Yet, when it came to physical contact, Susan remained as reticent and high-minded as the aristocratic young women in the Russian novels she so adored, except for when she thought about *him*. During their sessions together, Susan tried to commit his image to memory. Later she would write down the details, remarking on the warmth of his bronze face and his fine tanned hands, capable and reassuring.

THE TROUBLES THAT BROUGHT SUSAN INTO TREATMENT HAD COME TO LIGHT a few years before in 1972 when she was just fifteen years old. She had been miserably unhappy. At a parent–teacher conference, her mother learned that she had habitually been skipping school and staying home, where she escaped into the world of fiction. Susan's mother, Helen Bolling, was not at all pleased. The principal told her Susan needed the help of a trained psychotherapist. She recommended a prominent Berkeley therapist who specialized in adolescence.

Up to that point, Helen Bolling, who herself had quit school at fourteen, had thought she had been doing well raising Susan and her older brother, David. As a single mom working full-time at the Oakland army base at the lowly level of a GS-3, it wasn't always easy making ends meet or raising her kids. Her daughter was born willful, ready to do battle over the smallest of incidents. While that caused difficulties, Helen was quietly proud that her daughter would never be a pushover, unlike Susan's brother, David, a year and a half older, who was more pliable. When brother and sister fought, usually over something trivial, the fight dragged on because Susan refused to give ground. Helen would have to convince the more easygoing David to give in, just to end the dispute.

Susan was the second child born to Helen and Dick Bolling. Though her birth had not been planned, Susan's father was more accepting of the new red-faced infant than Helen was. After Susan's birth, Helen suffered from postpartum depression. Susan was a cute, precocious child who started crawling at six months and walking at eight. When she began to speak, she favored what her mother called "those upper-class words." Susan learned to read before entering kindergarten. Her mother was always lugging home books from Goodwill or the public library for her children. Both offspring were gifted, a fact which, when verified by teachers, pleased their mother. Helen herself read to them from the great Russian authors, though she was selective, choosing only those books that had a quality translation.

"I told her there was this great literature the Russians had made. The Russians are the ones you can't beat," Helen remembered later. As a young woman, Helen socialized with other people who were well read, and she expected as much from her children. Helen was self-educated. She had loved school and wished she could continue, but one morning when her mother went on her daily milk run—they could not afford an icebox—Helen found her beloved father in her bed. That prompted Helen to run away from home, abruptly ending her formal education.

Although she never tried to push her literary taste onto Susan, her daughter also gravitated toward the Russians. Early on, she expressed special interest in Dostoevsky's *The Idiot*, the story of a Christ-like man in a corrupt society coping with love, madness, betrayal, and murder. Her mother encouraged her, despite a friend telling Helen that Susan was too young to deal with such themes. Years later, Helen would be haunted by that warning.

Susan's fondest memories are of jumping rope or sitting in an almond tree in the front yard, where she once spotted a white owl. Because Dick Bolling was working while attending law school for seven years, he had little time to frolic with his children. Her mother assured the young Susan that after her father graduated, he would make up for lost time. But that's not how it worked out.

Shortly after he received his law degree, Dick Bolling fell for another woman, a temptress, according to Helen, whom he met in community theater. When Susan was five, Dick sought a divorce. Helen says that at first she told her husband she would see a lawyer, but she delayed. He complained, "You're never going to let me go."

According to Helen, one evening when he came home full of rage, they had an altercation which Helen said made her fearful of him. A practical woman, Helen says that after that she decided, "Hey, wait a minute, damn it! If he wants a divorce, I'll give him a divorce!" She attributed her ex-husband's wayward heart to what she calls "penisitis." Men, the practical Helen Bolling exclaimed, "are controlled by their penises. They're not logical. Not reasonable. Not rational, which is unfortunate."

Susan says she remembers witnessing this incident and not knowing what to do. (Helen Bolling says she has no recollection of her daughter having been there.) Regardless, Susan's image of marriage was never going to be anything as simple as a couple living "happily ever after."

AFTER DICK BOLLING REMARRIED, HE TRIED TO WIN CUSTODY OF HIS CHIL-dren, an effort that set off a series of events that no doubt affected Susan as well. Losing her children was Helen's worst nightmare. Her own mother had lost her children from a previous marriage and had fallen into a deep depression from which she never emerged. Helen was fearful that the same fate would befall her.

She was so distraught by the prospect of losing her children that she suffered a nervous breakdown and had to be hospitalized. For weeks afterward, she cried uncontrollably. But she must have pulled herself together when a county official came to Helen's home and spoke to both children, because it was determined that the children would remain with their mother.

Helen wanted a better life for her kids than she had had. She taught her daughter that education "was the only way to lift yourself out of the mud and become at least middle class." Money was so tight that after the divorce, they rented their suburban house in Concord, California, and moved into a cheaper flat in Oakland, where mother and daughter shared a bedroom and David slept on the living room couch.

Over the years, Helen encouraged her ex-husband, for whom she somehow managed not to hold a grudge, to spend time with his children. But when he did, Susan used the occasion to reaffirm her ties to her mother. In a poignant letter the young girl wrote that she missed her mother so much tears were streaming down her face.

As Susan and David grew older, their father, who had remarried again, lost interest in his children. By the time Susan was eleven, he was rarely around, a situation that worried her mother greatly. She felt that their father's absence would cause her children to have permanent heartbreak. In the summer of 1969, Helen Bolling wrote a letter pleading with her former husband to give his children some attention. She said she understood that the demands on his time must be great. She begged him to "some how, some way" see their children. But by then, Dick Bolling was immersed in his other life.

"I would not ask you Dick. . . . but I sense a need, a need I hope you will find in your heart to alleviate."

BEFORE THE ONSET OF ADOLESCENCE, SUSAN HAD SEEMED CONTENT RUN-ning with her brother and the neighborhood boys. After school each day, brother and sister would run down to the corner playground, a gathering place for Chinese, Japanese, and African American kids. Susie, as she was then called, felt comfortable there and accepted in the homes of her friends. This was the 1960s, when California cities were generally prosperous and city councils considered it their civic duty to provide playground supervisors and camp counselors for the underprivileged. Under the watchful eye of these park supervisors, she played dodge ball and other games, and when bored with playing, Susan Bolling would skip around the neighborhood, scooping up empty glass bottles to be exchanged at the supermarket for pocket money with which to buy Starbursts and Life Savers.

Summers she attended a free camp in the eucalyptus-covered hills of Berkeley's Tilden Park, where park rangers served as naturalists and counselors. One summer, Susan even tried out for a part as one of her favorite literary characters, Alice, in a production of *Alice in Wonderland*. The play was to be produced at Fairyland, a children's fantasy park in downtown Oakland. Susan's heart sank as she surveyed the competition: she was up against a crowd of blond girls. It didn't matter that she understood the book in a way they never could, the girl with the curly black hair did not get the part.

As Susan grew, Helen noticed that her daughter lacked the desire or skills to socialize with other children. "She didn't know how to smile and make someone feel accepted," her mother noted. Susan saw herself as a social child, but her mother thought otherwise. Helen's view of Susan's sociability was reinforced when the family moved from Oakland back to their home in Concord around the time that Susan was fifteen. A sleepy suburb full of middle-class people with Midwestern attitudes, Concord was twenty-one miles east and many cultures away from the more liberal cities that bordered the San Francisco Bay. In Concord, Susan hated her two-mile walk to school and resented the growing chorus of catcalls from the older boys. Some days when she heard the whistles, she sensed danger, pivoted around, and headed home. Another part of her was just plain offended by their immaturity and obnoxiousness. Men did not act like that in the novels she read.

The days that she managed to make it to school weren't much better. She found the social world of middle school and high school upsetting. The girls were boy crazy and pairing off. Friends were already having sex. She felt she didn't belong.

"High school was so boring," she later said. "I didn't want to play the game. I did not want to submit to all the authority required in the high school experience." As for many precocious teens, the social world of school seemed beneath her. The longer she stayed away, the further behind she fell in math class and the harder it became to catch up. Besides, none of her classmates and few of her teachers had read as much as she had of Tolstoy, Jack London, Steinbeck, Dickens, Faulkner, Hemingway, and Lewis Carroll.

She also felt disconnected in another, more disturbing way. In an essay her mother would read aloud years later, Susan wrote, "I floated into class and floated out in a dream. I had the experience of never communicating with anyone or being understood. . . . I was on another plane, in another dimension. My thoughts were different. I felt I spoke an inner language which could not be communicated."

Taking refuge in a life of make-believe, Susan liked nothing more than reading a book, beginning to understand it, and "then starting over and decoding it." Since she wasn't communicating with many people, she didn't bother trying to tell other people about her interior world. "I talked, but not of what was essential to me," she later wrote in the essay her mother found. "I did not feel what I spoke of had real meaning. I spoke of only what was superficial to me, what was not important to me. I ceased to communicate what was the content of my thoughts."

HELEN RESPECTED AUTHORITY AND CREDENTIALS. SHE DIDN'T QUESTION the school's recommendation that her daughter see a psychotherapist. Given her limited station in life, Helen gladly took the principal's referral. Driving Susan to Berkeley for her first appointment, Helen worried that her daughter might not like the therapist. Susan had shown mostly contempt for authority figures. She was so stubborn. Once Susan decided that someone wasn't worthy of her respect, there was no appeal, and there weren't many people she liked.

The therapist's office was in a converted house on Ashby Avenue, one of the main thoroughfares and next door to the home of former Black Panther leader Eldridge Cleaver. Much of the street was lined with physicians' offices in converted houses and with the sprawling gray institutional buildings that made up Alta Bates Hospital. Susan and her mother entered through the first of two double doors designed to prevent a waiting patient from overhearing what another client might say. The waiting room was dark and comfortable.

When the therapist ushered the pair into his office, Helen was impressed. Dr. Felix Polk conveyed warmth and kindness. He was a psychologist with a PhD, and an air of confidence and authority. Helen Bolling sat with Susan for the first session, which both agreed at the time had gone well.

Driving back home to Concord after the first meeting, Susan consented to see Dr. Polk a second time. Her mother smiled in relief. Her daughter would receive the help she needed.

Within weeks, Susan was enjoying her therapy sessions. With pride, she remembers Dr. Polk asking, "What do you like to read?" She knew he probably expected a fifteen-year-old to say something like "Nancy Drew." She looked him in the eye and said with seriousness, "Dostoevsky."

And Helen Bolling was pleased as well. Her little girl, who "grew up with a hole in her heart," finally had a father figure who cared about her.

UNDER HER THERAPIST'S CARE, SUSAN'S LIFE DID NOT IMMEDIATELY improve. In fact, during her first year of treatment her behavior seemed to spin out of control. She still refused to attend school, a situation that Dr. Polk inexplicably accepted and supported. Not long after she started therapy, she was caught shoplifting a dress and was sentenced to a month in juvenile hall. She ran away from the facility and hitchhiked to a friend's house in Oakland, where she holed up for a month. Her distraught mother had no idea where she was until Susan called and asked to come home, prompting Helen to telephone her therapist to make sure it was legal. He arranged with the courts for Susan to avoid juvenile hall if she attended continuation school and remained in therapy with him.

Not surprisingly, Susan despised continuation school. Classes in the trades were unsuitable for a brainy girl like herself. She recalls feeling despair. "I was forced to attend a school for morons. It was very upsetting. They didn't have the same goals I did. There were girls with lots of substance-abuse problems. They didn't have the same academic interests I had. These girls were very promiscuous and some were not very smart at all."

The bright spot in Susan's life became her weekly trips to therapy. She thought Berkeley, with its great university, enormous bookstores, and its libraries, was a wonderful cosmopolitan city, remaining relatively oblivious to the sex and drugs that were a central part of the counterculture.

And yet, while she did not embrace the loosened mores of post–1960s California, she did not reject them entirely. As she developed into a graceful and lithe young woman, she stopped wearing the buttoned-down shirts and skirts over the knees. She slipped into more fashionable clothes, including miniskirts that were so short they made her mother wince. She let her wavy hair, which she hated because it seemed to have its own agenda, grow to a sexy shoulder length. She saw that boys and men were attracted to her, but she remained aloof to their advances.

There was only one man she wanted to be close to. From the very beginning of therapy, when he had admitted his own passion for literature, she agreed with him, they were remarkably alike. Nobody could understand her the way he could. He admitted things to her, like the fact that he too was painfully shy when he was young. He equated reading all the time with withdrawing from the world, something he had done as well. They shared the same liberal values. They understood one another when so many other people seemed not to. At times if she felt disconnected, he said he had felt that too. And when she was depressed he not only empathized, he told her he had gone through such a stage as well.

Their physical relationship started slowly when she was in her late teens.

When she told her mother she had a boyfriend who was a doctor, her mother was pleased until Susan explained the boyfriend was her therapist. As furious as Helen became, she never thought about turning the psychotherapist in to the authorities. She was never one to make trouble. What did she know about psychotherapy anyway? The therapist seemed to be just what Susan had needed, and it wasn't her role to object. Helen visited Felix to talk about the liaison. "He was sheepish," she recalled. Certain that the affair would wither, Helen Bolling told him: "When this is over, I hope you will be kind to her. Wean the child away from you. Let her down easy." He promised he would, and she believed him.

AFTER SUSAN COUNTED HER BOOKS AND TOOK STOCK OF EVERYTHING IN her room, she headed out for a run to help kill the time before she would be in his presence. She drove her car through parched pastures, parking on a narrow road, where her tires left crevices in the soil. She liked that: leaving her mark on the earth. As she jogged along the roadway waves of warm air engulfed her. Today was unlike any other; today she would not analyze her life. She'd accept it for what it was, a glorious day. Driving home she still felt like a wonder woman. After her jog she dressed in new clothes, knowing he would appreciate her small waist in her wide skirt.

A few hours later, she was finally at his new office. She had loved his snug old wood-paneled one. His new suite was beige, airy, and spacious with colossal windows that overlooked the Berkeley campus. The room was so big that she immediately asked in a tiny voice if he would sit close to her.

As she looked around at the potted plants, she warmed to the new place. She was proud to think that he'd done it all himself, that he was not only brilliant, perceptive, and loving but he also knew how to design his room and make it whole.

She glanced from his Wallabees to her own. He too noticed that they were wearing the same style of shoes. "We're twins," he said.

But he could tell there was something different about her that day. She told him about the fleas. Another day she might have been irritated. Today, she just laughed. Then she asked if he liked her new clothes, knowing all along what he'd say. He told her she looked beautiful. He asked what she was reading. She told him she was rereading *War and Peace,* one of his favorite books. As she spoke, he stroked her hair.

She remembered the electric excitement of the first time she had sat beside her therapist, before it had become part of their ritual. Then she was sitting on his lap, which was more intimate. The hour went by in a flash. Her favorite part was the lingering hug at the end of each session. She snuggled in the nappy wool of his rust-colored sweater. She wished the moment would last forever. Neither one spoke of love. Instead she said as she laughed through her nose that she was giving him fleas.

Back home she was glad that her mother wasn't there and that she had the house to herself. Suddenly, she had the strange certainty that she had somehow willed the house to be empty. For the first time since she could remember, she felt like herself. It had really been a good day.

She picked up *War and Peace,* knowing that she would finish it late that night. Absorbed, she soon forgot her fleas. She didn't hear her mother come in because she was with Prince Andrei and Natasha in Russia. She had forgotten to eat. She felt like she was dying with Andrei and mourning with Natasha. And by the time she had finished the book it was nearly dawn.

Before going to sleep, she thought again about the hour she had spent with her therapist. He was the only person who seemed as real as the characters in the books she read. She drifted off to sleep.

3.

THE MAKING OF DR. POLK

FOR MANY, INCLUDING FELIX POLK, THE LATE SIXTIES AND EARLY SEVENTIES were a time of unlimited possibilities. A hairdresser could reinvent himself as a goat farmer. A banker could become a street poet. A used car salesman could become a self-awareness guru. A professor could become an advocate of free love—with his students.

Changes wrought by the 1960s, plus the fact that more Americans were delaying marriage, led to other cultural shifts. For the first time, a majority of the American public approved of premarital sex. Some began to consider marriage just a government-sponsored convention for uptight couples. Shacking up was part sexual and part political. People talked about a political revolution—and meant it literally—willfully ignoring that Richard Nixon was elected president in 1968 and reelected in 1972. The idea was that whatever life one had before had little to do with what one might do next. The past was a bland prologue; one's future would be in Technicolor. The young shared beliefs about themselves, their social connections, and their responsibilities that were radically different from those taught them by their parents. A revolutionary new age was dawning, or so people thought. The old rules no longer applied. The new order was simple: there were no rules.

In northern California, the human potential movement was in full bloom. By 1960, Esalen Institute in Big Sur, California, operating in a grove overlooking the rocky coastline, was organizing encounter groups for the socially adventurous to join in a merging of minds and (nude) bodies. Human awareness workshops sprouted like orange poppies across the region.

The Bay Area became a mecca for the nationwide counterculture. Young people migrated west, where neither relatives nor traditions could keep them from sampling new freedoms. People didn't just want to change the political scene; they wanted to alter human nature. From 1950 to 1970, California's population doubled to nearly twenty million. Young people came to re-create themselves, and if that didn't work, some reasoned, they could always jump off the Golden Gate Bridge.

In 1960, Felix Polk and his young wife, Sharon Mann Polk, an accomplished concert pianist, came to California so that he could attend graduate school at Berkeley. He told new friends he picked California because he wanted to get away from his family. In the parlance of the time, he had a lot of emotional and psychological "baggage" to leave behind. He came to California for the same reason that young people had migrated west for generations: to start fresh and leave the detritus of his previous life behind. Yet he remained an uptight East Coast transplant, at least for a while. All around him, students were demonstrating in support of the Free Speech Movement and against the Vietnam War and were experimenting with free love. Felix Polk never did. He was a family man, a serious student who had retired from the military, a repressed academic. On special occasions, he sometimes wore his dress whites—in Berkeley. He was ripe for changing.

By 1971, when Felix Polk began treating fifteen-year-old Susan Bolling, he appeared to have managed a remarkable metamorphosis. Justifying the wildest claims of the human potential movement, he had transformed himself from an anxious and self-destructive young man to a confident and respected psychologist. At thirty-nine, Felix Polk was handsome in a warm, craggy way that made strangers feel safe when confiding their deepest fears and insecurities. His hazel eyes drew people in and set them at ease, inspiring their trust in him. Although he was only five foot nine, he seemed imposing; he was fit, the result of weekend hikes, skiing, and a daily ten-mile jog. His hair was kinky, but shaped and styled. His posture was erect.

He believed in himself as did others. Felix Polk would go on to manage a program for drug-abusing adolescents in the Berkeley schools and, most impressively, he would serve for three years as chief psychologist for Mental Health Services of Alameda County (which includes Berkeley and Oakland). He was in charge of psychological services for the county's hospitals and clinics. He produced a pamphlet on how to interpret test results from the Minnesota Multiphasic Personality Inventory. While working with adolescents, he developed useful classifications, stressing that often the cause of delinquency is the environment, not the kid. Many probation officers he trained employed his classification system. Felix Polk was trusted by his patients and by many, if not all, his peers.

At home Felix was also leading a successful family life. "The outward appearance to everybody, and I mean everybody, was that they were the idyllic couple," said Stephen Pittel, a forensic psychologist who was Felix's closest friend when the two were in graduate school. "They presented themselves to the world as being loving, affectionate, and kind to each other. I never heard a cross word," Pittel recalled. "On the surface, it was a beautiful marriage," he added. The couple was raising their two young children, Andrew and Jennifer, and while Felix loved them both, he favored his son. "Jennifer was not the shining star that Andy was. She was never the life of the party and Andy was," Pittel recalled.

Felix was working in a time, place, and profession where almost everything was being questioned. During the years when he was coming into his prime, the line between patient and therapist was increasingly questioned and blurred, not only accidentally but deliberately. The early seventies was a time when progressive West Coast therapists were known to socialize with their clients. Dr. Polk found this perfectly natural and could not see the harm that befriending his patients might cause, especially in Berkeley where one might encounter a patient at the food co-op or at a party. Or one might trade services with them. Felix belittled the concept of the exalted analyst in his tower or the therapist only comfortable in his office and feeling exposed outside. He and his colleagues imagined that they were participating in a specialty, which was questioning all its assumptions and would come up with something new and improved.

The lines that Felix would cross with his beautiful young patient, however, would not be so blithely transgressed. For what he was about to do with young Susan Bolling, there would be consequences beyond what he could have imagined.

FRANK FELIX POLK WAS BORN ON JUNE 30, 1932, IN AUSTRIA, TO JEWISH parents who played four-hand piano compositions and encouraged their children to lead the life of the mind. As the second born of fraternal twins, Felix would always suffer from insecurities resulting from his birth order. "The firstborn is always more comfortable in the world," Felix's older sister, Evelyn, said. His brother, John, would be the more social, more athletic twin, and he always did a little better than Felix at school, although both boys were at the top of their class. Felix was the smaller and weaker of the two. He was also more inquisitive, the more thoughtful, more brooding, more sensitive, and more imaginative twin. They were not the sorts of twins who form a whole; they were competitors, though John was less aware of it than Felix. His parents often held John up to Felix as the model child.

Felix otherwise had an idyllic childhood—including a toy-size steam engine in the yard that was wide enough for a child to mount—in Hietzing, where the Habsburgs' Schoenbrunn summer palace is located. In the summer, the Polk children vacationed in the mountains with their governesses; their parents joining them on weekends. In the winters, the children were taken skiing before there were ski lifts. Despite their heritage, the family was Jewish only in name. They never went to temple, and at Christmas they did what Austrian Christians did, they decorated a tree with lighted candles and homemade cookies.

In Vienna, the family lived on the first floor of a stone house with a garden, and as with many well-to-do families of that time, they had a cook, a maid, a chauffeur, governesses, and nurses. As Felix would say frequently during his life, his mother lacked maternal instincts, delegating much of the actual parenting duties to others. Because of his absentee mother, Felix became extremely attached to Katya, his *kindermadchen,* or nursemaid. She in turn was so devoted to him that when the local postman asked to marry her, she refused, unwilling to give up her boy. According to a family history that Felix's mother wrote, the postman approached her and asked her to intervene on his behalf, but still Katya could not be swayed.

Much of the family's success was due to Felix's grandfather, who began his career as a pushcart peddler of secondhand clothing. From those humble beginnings he built a men's clothing store on Ringstrasse, the broad boulevard built in the late nineteenth century, which encircles Old Vienna and is the focal point of city life. The elegant store sold lederhosen, jackets, and custom and ready-made suits.

When Felix's cultured father married his equally cultured mother, he was expected to work in her father's store. She, too, began working there; she believed her presence would soften her father's autocratic attitude toward her husband. Together the family worked six days a week, eventually opening a second store, also on Ringstrasse.

The good life ended in 1938. While Evelyn and John remember very little from that time, much of the details were seared in Felix's memory. He would remember "the skies dark with German airplanes" and "the thunderous sound of soldiers marching in the streets." The twins were six when Nazis arrested their father, releasing him from custody only after he promised to hand over his businesses and his home and flee Austria.

Before they could leave, the family had to find a country willing to take them in. Felix and his brother were baptized in hopes that would facilitate their acquiring exit visas for France. While awaiting visas the Nazis began raiding their block. To avoid arrest, the family hid in plain sight every morning from six until noon at a park that encircled the former imperial summer residence. Twice, while they were gone, the Germans scoured their street for Jews. The lines in front of consulates for countries that would accept Jews were long. Using whatever connections they could muster, and with a newly established business in Paris, the Polks managed to acquire French visas. Felix felt the constant fear of the grown-ups. His mother believed the experience was devastating for them, that the months of insecurity and terror had a lasting influence on their lives.

When the family left Vienna, Felix was not only leaving his sweet-smelling home, he was also separating from the only woman who had mothered him. Katya, whom he later called his "nurse mother," was at the gray, barren train station to see them off. She wore a worried expression. Fierce-looking Nazi soldiers policed the tracks. Felix remembered the cautious, tight, and alarmed sound of his father's voice. And he felt his own unspent tears, the stiffness of his body erect against the seat and his heart thundering in his chest. He was frightened and confused and felt emptiness, "a sense of impending doom and an enormous rage," he would later write. As the train hissed down the tracks, he sat in a musty compartment with his family. His mother ordered him to stare straight ahead. Using his peripheral vision, he sneaked a peek at his nursemaid . . . and never saw her again. For the rest of his life, Felix would play that scene over and again in his mind.

In Paris, Felix's father established himself while Felix and his siblings were briefly shuttled off to boarding school. In retrospect, Felix's mother thought that "this too must have increased their sense of displacement and insecurity." At school Felix suffered from nightmares and would call out for his "Katya." The staff could not comfort him; they couldn't even understand him. They spoke no German, and he did not yet know French. He desperately needed Katya, but there was nothing his older sister, who was with him, could do. A few times, Evelyn was allowed to call their parents in the middle of the night and tell them that he was crying for Katya. He was so unhappy that he willed himself into sickness, developing a fever, which had the anticipated result of drawing his mother to him.

When Paris was no longer safe, the Polks sought refuge in the ancient walled city of Saint-Malo, where a sympathetic family harbored them. Felix's father joined the French army. Felix, John, and Evelyn briefly attended public school. While there, Felix's mother became a translator for the French to communicate with German soldiers. With their mother distracted by such matters, Evelyn, who was three years older than her brothers, became their surrogate mother. When the Germans marched through town, villagers provided cover for the Polks, convincing the Nazis they had come from Alsace-Lorraine.

While Evelyn recalled mostly happy times with her brothers, jumping over huge log piles at the lumber mill, Felix would later say their living conditions were "appalling, restricted, and desperate." He would recall that as darkness descended, the children were told to stop talking and become very still. He would say they lived "the Anne Frank existence," although that is not the way his siblings remember it. They did, however, worry whether their father was alive. There were, in fact, times in Paris when the children were sent with empty saucepans to beg for fresh milk from a nunnery and other times when in Marseilles, they subsisted on turnips, parsnips, and other root vegetables and occasionally a bit of horsemeat. To fall asleep, Felix imagined drilling through the earth and emerging in his own bedroom in Vienna, where he played with toys. The family was reunited after his mother put a classified ad in a newspaper in southern France. Another Viennese refugee who had seen the ad and kept the information in his pocket spotted Felix's father near the Spanish border.

Together, family members returned to Paris, where they had to dispose of most of their possessions, keeping only some linen, dishes, music, and books. Concerned their money might be confiscated during their journey out of France, they ingeniously carved out the insides of two French breads, deposited their cash in the cavity, pressed the pieces together with dough, then baked the breads shut. While they waited for visas to America, the family lived in a fifteenth-century house and ate whatever spoiled potatoes farmers had left in their fields. Felix remembered being hungry and living on cabbage soup. They made their way to Portugal, where John remembers that fish—which he hated—was the favorite food. Eventually the family emigrated to the United States, sailing on the *Siboney,* a cargo ship that felt like paradise to the Polk children. Food was plentiful and Felix and his siblings could at last run free. In November 1941, they arrived in New York harbor, and the family began to reestablish themselves, first in New York City and later in Harrison, New York.

Felix's father was gentle; his mother was the powerful force in the family. Her attitudes prevailed. After coming to this country, the Polks never looked back. Although Felix had been deeply scarred by his early experiences, no one in the family talked about it.

As they started their lives over again, Felix resented his family's new low socioeconomic status. His sister's recollection is more positive: "We were delighted to be here, safe and sound." She and her brothers "were not so delighted by having to work hard with the family to set up another successful life, which happened in a short time. It wasn't life like the lives of other kids we knew in school. It was a matter of pride for all of us to do very well in school, and we were exceedingly well received by the community of Harrison, in school, in public life, and at the store. My parents made many friends through their business and were very well liked by the people who worked for them and who later showed their friendship after my parents had given up the store, coming to visit if either of them was ill."

All three children excelled at school, although because John always did a bit better, he was held up as an example for Felix to follow. He and his brother socialized with the kids they walked to school with. But Felix remained uncomfortably shy. If both liked the same girl, Felix would let his brother ask her out, but he would tell friends later that if he had *really* wanted the girl, he could have had her. Felix buried himself in literature and became remarkably well read. On a scholarship, he attended St. John's College in Annapolis, Maryland, the Great Books School, based on a curriculum of direct study in the basic texts of Western civilization. John, who excelled in math and science, went to MIT, also on a scholarship.

In college, Felix was a sullen and passive loner, though he retained dreams of greatness. When he wrote letters home he said little of college life, writing instead about cosmic issues and esoteric philosophy. He engaged in self-analysis. He dated infrequently, becoming involved with an older well-to-do would-be actress named Winnie, who, according to his medical records, infected him with gonorrhea.

After graduating from college, both Felix and his brother joined the military. His brother became a second lieutenant in the army, serving in Korea. Felix joined the navy, attending Officers Candidate School in Newport, Rhode Island, in the summer of 1953. He disliked the routine but completed the courses and was commissioned an ensign in November of that year.

By now, Felix was withdrawn, anxious, and depressed, but he kept his feelings to himself. He received training in amphibious warfare and communications at Little Creek, Virginia, before being shipped off to Japan. Aboard ship he served as store officer and gunnery officer. When on leave he went home, which only exacerbated his emotional state. He consulted a psychiatrist. He admitted feeling deeply guilty about masturbating and that he'd been preoccupied by incestuous fantasies involving his sister since adolescence.

He became excruciatingly lonely and frightened for his future. He was pathologically self-conscious; unable, for instance, to attend a naval dance because he knew the evening would have been painful. When out on a date, he was so uncomfortable that he couldn't speak. "The more I tried to relax, the more self-conscious I became until it became almost unbearable . . . I was near collapse," he wrote in a letter. Friends called him an idealist for living in a world that does not exist. "I deny that my world is unrealistic and yet I am tormented by my inability to communicate in the 'real' world," he wrote. When a friend tried to fix him up for the captain's surprise party, he assented, but later had to renege. He couldn't tell his friend the reason why. "This is what I would have had to say: how impossible my existence is."

The twenty-three-year-old spent what might well have been the last weekend of his life in New York with the would-be actress Winnie. He had often mentioned the possibility of killing himself to his on-again, off-again lover, inquiring about her brother who had killed himself. Strangely, he said these things with a smile, so she didn't take him seriously. On a weekend in mid-October of 1955, that assumption would change.

Saturday, Felix drove to New York City, where he and Winnie went to the theater to see *La Ronde*, a once controversial play written in 1897 about the transience of love and the spreading of syphilis throughout Viennese society.

The next day, perhaps looking for something lighter, they took in a matinee performance by the French mime Marcel Marceau.

The show did little to cheer him. That evening, according to what Winnie later told police, Felix became inconsolably depressed and drove back to his parents' home. At 7:00 PM, he called her to say that he had arrived safely. The sadness in his voice increased her concern. She called back a few hours later to find him even more miserable. When she tried to console him, he repeated over and over: "It was too late . . . too late for the world."

After they hung up, she became wild with worry and had her mother call the Harrison Police Department. Near midnight, officers discovered Felix's unconscious body in the garage, which was filled with carbon dioxide from car exhaust. He'd climbed in his father's car and, with the garage door shut, had turned the engine on.

It had been a serious suicide attempt. Had he not been found, he almost certainly would have died. Felix's suicide note poetically expressed his feelings of hopelessness:

> I have done what for a long time I have known I must do. When a rock is thrown into the water it sinks. It must sink as now must I. My mind is so heavy with wretchedness, with utter loneliness, with an unknown past, a frightening future and an intolerable present that no choice remains.
>
> I don't fear death at all. What is it but non-life and what is life but continuous torture?
>
> This final act is not sudden or impetuous. I have known that some day it would take place. The question has only been where, when and how. Until a few weeks ago there has always been some spark, some hope which prevented me from the obvious. This night there is no hope. There is nothing . . .
>
> I say goodbye to a hateful world with a smile. In life I hated pity and in death I want none. I have forgotten the world and now the world must forget me.

Naval doctors diagnosed Felix as suffering from "schizophrenic reaction," a term more commonly used then than now. Felix was hospitalized in a mental ward for a year. He begged his sister to get him out. She wanted to help, but the doctors told Evelyn he was still depressed and that he could not yet be released.

His twin heard about Felix's problem but never inquired about it. As with their harrowing experiences during World War II, the subject was nothing his parents talked about.

IT'S HARD TO RECONCILE THAT DISTURBED AND SUICIDAL YOUNG MAN, locked up in a mental ward, with the prominent therapist he became. Outwardly, at least, he had made a remarkable turnaround and he would always say his own experience made him a better healer.

Some gave the credit to Sharon Mann, whom he met on a blind date set up by his brother's wife. Sharon, then attending Juilliard, was a beautiful, dynamic, and accomplished pianist. His brother's wife, Barbara Polk, also a student at Juilliard, selected her because she was looking for someone who was fun and outgoing to complement her introverted brother-in-law.

After being discharged from the navy, Felix married Sharon. He would tell friends that she nursed him back to health. At Yeshiva University (Albert Einstein), he studied social work, receiving his masters degree in 1959. He decided, however, that social workers weren't influential enough; they lacked the power to improve lives that a therapist had. He'd been in analysis, a powerful experience that led him to seek a PhD in psychology. At the beginning of the new decade, the couple moved to California, where, over the course of the next six years, Felix earned a PhD in psychology from the University of California at Berkeley.

By the time Felix was setting up his private practice, Sharon was working part-time as a concert pianist and teacher—Felix's equal and then some. Outspoken, funny, bubbly, dynamic, and charming, Sharon was a joy to be around. The two were handsome, cosmopolitan, and when they entered a room people gravitated toward them. Often, Felix would invite friends over for a spaghetti feed, a step up from their meager grad-student existence. With their small children, Andy and Jennifer, the Polks went on picnics and on outings to the zoo and to concerts. Despite what appeared to be a loving relationship, in conversation with his sister Felix confided that he was not happy. To friends he began to complain that at home his wife ran the show, leaving him feeling like "a schlemiel." Five years before he met Susan Bolling he had decided to leave his wife. He filed for divorce, but he was so emotionally dependent on Sharon he couldn't leave her.

Despite his insecurities, Felix soon became a well-known member of the psychotherapeutic community. He built a burgeoning practice specializing in troubled adolescence, though he was not averse to treating patients who were considerably older. He lectured at the University of California at Berkeley and taught at many schools, including at Holy Names College in Oakland, where he was so trusted that the Catholic Archdiocese sent him wayward priests and troubled nuns. On a National Institute of Mental Health fellowship, he also studied under R. D. Laing at the Tavistock Clinic in London. Laing argued that the mentally ill were expressing alternative views that they could not express in other ways.

Felix developed his own brand of therapy. He was not wedded to the severe Freudian style. He saw nothing wrong with offering whatever thoughts his instinct prompted or in talking about himself, which he did a lot, especially with patients who, at least initially, were uncomfortable talking about themselves. Unlike more traditional therapists, Felix didn't believe in neutrality; he didn't subscribe to the concept that a patient should know almost nothing about him. Felix didn't think that he should be a transparent sounding board on whom the patient could project qualities that could help him. Rather, he saw himself as a friend who talked about himself and involved many of his patients in his life. He was convinced that his warmth and love could help wounded clients, and if their friendship hampered therapy, Felix would never acknowledge it.

Although on the inside Felix was neither a happy man nor a secure one, as a therapist and professor he was able to project himself as a charismatic problem solver. He had about him an air of grandiosity that may have masked feelings of worthlessness he had felt in his youth. From his patients and students, Felix Polk drew strength and a greater sense of his own worth. "He loved being adored," said one of his former students. To many peers and patients he was their guru. It was as though their adulation confirmed that he truly was who he wanted to be.

Felix Polk and many other therapists, especially those in California, were vulnerable to the psychological fads of the times. He became a convert to est, short for Erhard Seminars Training. Est offered a grab bag of theories for needy subjects, including CEOs, pop stars, university presidents, and well-known psychiatrists and psychologists; at least, those who were willing to be mocked, berated, locked in a ballroom, and not allowed to use the bathroom for twelve hours. Those who refused to participate were dismissed as too uptight to take the plunge. Est promised participants that if their egos, which were ripe for bruising, endured the training, they could be reshaped to reach a higher level of consciousness. The founder, Werner Erhard, born John Rosenberg, had been a used-car salesman before leaving his wife and children to create his own profitable niche in the human potential movement. Felix found est irresistible. He recommended it without reservation to his colleagues, students, and patients.

Erhard flattered Felix and his fellow psychologists, offering them a discount, because each was considered a *distinguished therapist.* Est members were enticed with the promise of true understanding and control over their lives; they would "get it," though no one defined what "it" was. That, in fact, was the point of "it": the essential state of being-in-the-world could not be defined. If one truly accepted that, one could relax and create for oneself "whatever you really want." That they had their own peculiar vocabulary gave est seekers a sense of superiority over outsiders.

Followers didn't just attend seminars; they became devotees, urging their friends to join. "Go do it," therapist friends would tell one another. "You want to ask questions. You want to say, 'Why?' " one of Felix's friends recalled. The response he received from Felix was fast and iron shut: "Because I said to do it!" And many of them did. Some became Erhard acolytes and, to this day, still wax nostalgic about their early est experience. "I loved it, I hated it, I loved it!" said Felix's friend Robert Wilk. While est damaged the most vulnerable seekers and left others unimpressed, for Felix and thousands of others it was both mind-blowing and life-affirming. They learned they were not doomed to the life they thought they had but could shatter old patterns and take greater control over their lives.

Felix and other followers came away convinced they were able to see themselves in new ways. "Anytime you get to look at your own ego or are encouraged to examine your life in ways you haven't before, in terms of what you're doing with it, what you want to do with it, you get a lot more out of it," Wilk recently said. Est was not for the meek. "People like Felix and me are therapists. We think we have big balls!" he declared. "And we'll stand up, you know; we'll take on these guys."

Even when some of his patients balked, having found est practices too degrading to endure, Felix coaxed them to try it one more time.

Leaders of est encouraged followers to change their names to suit their new selves. By 1972, Frank Felix Polk had dropped his first name and became just simply Felix Polk, *felix* being the Latin adjective meaning "fortunate." Felix also insisted that his musician wife, with whom he had reconciled, join him at est meetings. Sharon took the name Sha, which stayed with her for years.

When Felix told his old grad school friend Danny Goldstine that he had learned more in one est weekend than in all of graduate school, Goldstine shot back: "This is hokum, Felix. This guy's a con man." Felix looked at him as though Danny had shot him through the heart.

Felix had no reservations about est. Estians believed that the individual is responsible for everything that happens to him and, in a variation of positive thinking, that a person has the power to be what he or she wants to be, guilt free. His involvement with est made it that much easier for him to disregard convention and ignore taboos. Est allowed Felix to follow his feelings.

Soon thereafter, he subjected himself to painful psychodrama, reenacting the train scene of his youth. Participants volunteered to be Nazi guards, Katya, and his family. Felix attacked his "adversaries" with a foam rubber bat. For two hours, he would later tell friends, he battled his "enemy," tossing people bigger than he like matchsticks. Later, he would claim not to have any recollection of the reenactment. In an essay, he wrote that participants later told him that he was enraged, violent, and inconsolable. He thrashed about, roared with grief, and raged. When it was all over, he looked around and said, "I could not take care of it all. And then I returned to my customary consciousness." Whether his account was true or apocryphal, it was one that he repeated many times to patients and friends, and it always ended with his saying that the catharsis made his childhood pain bearable.

MANY EARLY PATIENTS RAVED ABOUT THE EXPERIENCE OF BEING IN TREAT-ment with Felix Polk. "He understood my world and the difficulty of it," explained Joel Tepper, a pianist who was twenty when he threatened his mother with a knife. He met Felix when Tepper was holed up in a psychiatric hospital and diagnosed with schizophrenia. Dr. Polk was brought in as a psychological consultant. The first thing that Joel Tepper remembered about Felix was that the therapist intended to give him a Rorschach test, often used to determine if someone is psychotic, but forgot to bring the inkblot cards. Joel's first reaction was, "How human he was." What Felix told him was reassuring at a time when the young man desperately needed reassurance. Felix said, "I think I understand the nature of your problem and I think I can help you." And he said it in such a way that it gave Joel hope.

"God knows I needed some hope at that time," Joel said. "He was terrific, empathetic, sensitive, and a very kind man and learned in his field."

Eventually, Felix did the testing determining that Joel was not schizophrenic but a borderline personality, "for whatever that's worth," Joel said. "Then he came to the conclusion that the psychiatrist who was seeing me (at the hospital) was definitely not the right person for me. As it turned out, according to Felix, the man was gay and was not going to be a good role model for the particular problems I had. So Felix made an attempt to make sure that when I got out I would be seeing Felix with my family."

Tepper, a clasically trained pianist with a nine-foot piano in his sparsely furnished living room, saw Felix from 1967 until 2002, more or less consistently, "which I'm sure makes me the longest-running patient he had," Tepper said. He felt that Felix was without pretense. Tepper said what many of Felix's patients would say: "He was authentic. I had the feeling I was with someone who was a friend."

Another early patient, Lee Steinback, was working and going to school while suffering from the demise of an early marriage. Friends told her to talk to Felix Polk. "I didn't have much money," but Felix didn't care. "I paid him a little bit when I could," she said. "He was the ultimate emotional reader of people. He could tell you exactly what was going on with you *and he was right*." Steinback thought she was afraid of rejection. With Felix's assistance, she had one "Aha!" session in which he pointed out that she was afraid of love and connections. His insight, she said, made a difference in her life.

Lee Steinback joined one of Felix's therapy groups, which in the '60s and '70s had become a popular way for shrinks to bring various patients with problems developing or sustaining relationships together once a week to apply what they had learned in individual therapy. Felix provided gentle guidance. Steinback remembers spending the first few sessions wrapped in a heavy coat. Several weeks into the process, she unbuttoned the coat as she came to feel more comfortable. Sometimes the meetings took place in Felix's office. On other occasions, the group would rotate among members' houses. Because personal relationships between patients outside of the group would affect their therapy, some therapists might frown on the development of such friendships; however, Felix had no such concerns. Participants became so close that eventually four, including Steinback, moved in together. Two of Felix's group therapy patients married one another. In honor of their therapist, another couple named their cat "Felix." He was never just a facilitator. Everyone wanted to please Felix.

During group sessions, Felix would jump-start a discussion, then bow out. He tried to keep the subject matter on course while leaving the session unstructured. Participants were expected to help one another. When a woman complained that she was too nervous to talk to the group, Felix would say, "You're talking right now." And one of the "helpy helpers," as a member of the group called them, might add, "You don't talk very much, but when you say something it's very interesting." Steinback thought Dr. Polk was "a fine therapist, and as far as I knew, a total professional."

Another patient, a depressed nun, found Dr. Polk to be a caring and loving therapist. It was not until years later that she learned his practice of befriending patients was unorthodox. Babysitting for Felix's children, she said, was a healthy distraction for her. She baked cookies and crocheted Christmas stockings for them. When she was down and out and had overdosed on drugs, he visited her in the hospital. And when her large family had a "conference," Felix flew to Southern California to facilitate.

When a patient couldn't afford his services, Felix would work out a deal. One of his clients, for example, built a sauna in Felix's backyard as payment for his therapy.

"He was a wonderful clinician," said Sheila Byrns, who also was his student and patient. "He knew what people needed and he could provide it." Her issue was abandonment. In therapy, Sheila had a tendency to arrive fifteen minutes early. "He was always three minutes late. I had to deal with the thought that he was not coming, over and over and over again," Byrns says approvingly. She believed he was trying to teach her that despite her anxiety, he would not abandon her. She became so close to her therapist that when she was going through hard times, such as during her divorce, she liked arriving an hour early or staying an hour afterward in her car in the parking lot. Just being near his aura, she said, made her feel better. Long after she quit therapy, Sheila Byrns and Felix Polk would remain close friends.

Despite their closeness, when Sheila Byrns was forty-three and suffered "a traumatic experience" requiring therapy, Felix's response was uneven. Concerned she wasn't responding properly and wanting her to pass through an anger stage, he abruptly quit seeing her. "It didn't affect me in a negative way nearly as much as the wonderful, positive things he did for me," she said recently. She had been a mound of clay and he had molded her "into a good human being. Not only that," she said, "he allowed me into his life, as he did many people," which made her feel special. He once told her that he always fell in love with his patients. That he had a very real relationship with the people he saw, she said, made him "so magical, but it also is what got in the way."

To Felix Polk, the connection he had with his patients overrode the rules of engagement. When he invited his patients over for holiday meals, for example, he was demonstrating how important they were to him. He was giving them something their families never did. But he also risked treating his clients differently because they were his friends and there was the additional risk of their becoming dependent on him. Unlike most therapists, he gave his patients his home number, and when on vacation he told them how he could be reached. He allowed himself to become a major player in their psyches, which he no doubt found gratifying, but there was no way he could satisfy all their demands. A more conventional therapist would not have become so involved with his patients, believing that the overriding purpose of therapy was to instill in them qualities that would have enabled them to move on, independent of his therapy and friendship.

4.

THE THERAPIST
AND HIS PRIZE PATIENT

"I DREAMED THAT I WAS THE GIRL IN THE MOVIE . . . BEING [HELD] CAPTIVE," Susan wrote for Felix early in her therapy. As part of treatment Felix had asked his young patient to write down her dreams and nightmares so that he could analyze them during their weekly sessions. The implications of her dreams were obvious. Her captor fell in love with her and locked her in a room where he alone could have her. Susan enjoyed the dream and felt there was something familiar about it.

It does not require a Freudian stretch of the imagination to suppose this dream may have reflected Susan's feelings about her burgeoning relationship with her therapist.

In another dream she was alone at the beach, dusting her feet in the sand, when a man who may have been her captor approached. "I felt that I was sick and crazy, and I sort of liked it," she wrote. She felt stuck in her dream, destined to remain there. A man approached who understood her, and liked her strangeness. She stood at the water's edge alone with him and she felt comfortable. She thought he must be a seer or a soothsayer.

Susan believed she and her therapist shared a way of thinking and of seeing the world. This sort of idolization of the therapist (especially by a young patient of the opposite sex) is quite normal. It is, in fact, central to many theories of how therapy works. The patient looks up to the healer, while the healer leverages that influence to encourage the patient to make positive changes in her attitude and behavior. However, in order to encourage independence and self-determination in the patient, the therapist must eventually decline the exalted role that the patient is offering. All the evidence indicates that Felix was not inclined to make this critical sacrifice. And in the case of Susan Bolling, Felix Polk was returning those feelings. Most likely Felix was aware that his relationship with the girl was something apart from that with his other patients, but he must have found it so pleasurable that he convinced himself that he could manage the danger. Instead of developing a stronger sense of self and a better understanding of how to cope, Susan became increasingly invested in her role as a devoted patient. Not only did Felix allow her to idolize him, he told her how fundamentally alike they were, that he too had felt a youthful alienation and disconnection from people. At times when he spoke, he also felt as though he were standing apart, listening to an echo. Susan and Felix began keeping one another's secrets, although the exchange was hardly one of equals.

She reveled in the idea that she was akin to the man she both admired and was falling in love with. He told her things that he didn't tell his other patients, such as the story of his attempted suicide.

Whether Susan Bolling had heard her therapist's suicide story and was influenced by it when she was sixteen cannot be confirmed. Whatever the circumstances, shortly after her 1974 arrest for shoplifting, Susan, upset about being caught up in the legal system and frustrated with her life, tried to commit suicide by swallowing a fistful of Diazepam, her mother's sleeping pills. Helen Bolling arrived home with a friend to find red lipstick scribbled on the mirror, loud music blaring, and her daughter sprawled semicomatose on the bed. It's not clear whether Susan had taken a fatal amount of the drug, but the music and lipstick make it pretty clear that she hoped to be saved. Helen rushed her daughter to the hospital, where doctors pumped her stomach. She was briefly placed in a mental ward.

Therapy was supposed to make Susan better, not worse. Helen was understandably upset. She didn't know whom to turn to or what to do other than to rely on her daughter's therapist, the expert, who knew what was best for Susan.

If Felix felt any culpability he didn't admit it. Instead, he blamed other authority figures in her life. He wrote a letter to officials stating that her only salvation lay in more psychotherapy. Dated March 1974, Dr. Polk wrote the director of the girls' center:

> As you know, Susan Bolling recently made a serious suicide attempt, as a result of which she was psychiatrically hospitalized at Kaiser Hospital, Richmond.

It must be stressed that this was a most serious suicide effort and not a suicidal gesture.

Susan Bolling is a severely disturbed girl with strong depressive features. As I indicated in my last report to the Court, it is my very strong opinion that she requires therapeutic rather than correctional attention.

Further, Susan cannot be expected to matriculate as a normal child in a public school setting. In spite of what appears to be a hard exterior, she is terrified and acutely self-conscious in any group of peers. This is the principal [sic] reason for her truancy.

This evaluation of Susan was provided to the Contra Costa County Juvenile Court on a prior occasion and ignored. Susan was then sent through the probation process, which, in my judgment, contributed to her mental deterioration and suicide attempt.

Should there be further questions regarding this case I would be pleased to answer them.

Sincerely,

F. Felix Polk, PhD

Clinical Psychologist

The authorities in charge of Susan's case apparently agreed. Susan would not have to serve anymore time, nor would she be expected to attend school. She was released to the custody of her mother *and her therapist*. Susan now devoted her weeks to literature and therapy.

Felix's therapeutic techniques were eclectic and unconventional even by the laissez-faire standards of California at that time. Sometimes he told rambling stories about his life. Other times he sat quietly. Often he would ask Susan directly: "What do you want from me? Do you want my feedback? My feelings? Do you need my direction?" He was also fond of employing guided visualization techniques he cribbed from his est training. He would tell her to close her eyes and imagine a room with a television set. On the TV, he told her, she could flip the channels and view different periods of her life. Then, Susan later claimed, he would have her bring him into the fantasy room, where he could take over her TV set. Other times she would lie down on the floor and at his request visualize her big toe. Then he'd tell her to find a place on her little toe and visualize that. He would go up and down her body over every part telling her to find a place on her head, her neck and visualize her center.

As Susan was creating an identity for herself as Felix's prized patient, her mother saw that Susan was happier. She seemed to be creating a more grown-up life for herself, and Helen was encouraged. It looked as though her daughter would survive her horrendous teenage years, not unscathed but intact.

Susan had become the chosen one: the special patient of a man who was the focus of many devoted patients. She had exclusive access to a ready-made god. He encouraged her—along with his other patients—to call him Felix, and the two began to do things together—outside of therapy. He even took his young patient along to one of his wife's piano concerts.

By the time she was eighteen or nineteen, Susan idolized Felix in a way she had never been able to idolize her own father or any other man. She never attended a high school prom or ever went on a date with anyone. She entered Felix's world, and he entered hers.

THE AFFECTION THAT SUSAN AND FELIX SHOWED FOR EACH OTHER WAS OBVI-ous to those who observed them, sometimes embarrassingly so. Felix and his colleagues at the California Graduate School of Family Psychology (over the years, the school went through many name changes) in Marin County frequently brought patients to class to demonstrate—in a specially built room with sound equipment and one-way mirrors—how to conduct therapy. "It was a wonderful part of the school," marveled one colleague. "That's what we did in the school so students could experience therapy and learn how it works."

Felix Polk was a tremendously popular professor, although his habit of playing favorites meant that some students often felt shunned. Still, he was admired for his openness, which he extended to include his patients. Because the patients participated willingly, Felix and other professors didn't consider it a violation of their confidentiality, even when, as in the case of Felix Polk, the patients were adolescents. The therapists considered it a growing experience for their clients. They believed their school was full of the best and brightest professors and that the work they were doing was cutting edge.

Felix Polk taught several courses in adolescent psychology. In his Adolescent III class he interviewed relatively normal kids and followed that with interviews with his young clients. It was in that context that the professor brought to his class a young Susan Bolling. She would come numerous times. According to several people who were there, she was probably in her late teens when she and Felix began their very public therapy sessions. He presented her as a girl he had masterfully "cured" of schizophrenia.

He told the students that Susan came to see him after she ran away from home and had been placed in a detention center. Sheila Bryns, Felix's former student and patient who became his close friend and teaching assistant, remembers his telling the class that Susan had been smart to run away because it extricated her from her mother, with whom she had had a stultifying, symbiotic relationship.

Felix enjoyed showing Susan off. That she was young and beautiful seemed to add to his pride. Students noticed that Susan was constantly looking at Felix, which "is not so unusual for a teenaged girl in a classroom full of students," one of those students recalled. That Susan idolized her mentor was obvious.

Felix was so proud of his successful therapy with Susan that he invited other professors, including his own mentor, to attend. (His mentor agreed to share his recollections as long as he remained anonymous.) Observers, including the mentor, remained skeptical: "When I hear the word *cure* in psychiatric medicine, I don't believe anything," he scoffed. "No one is ever cured. They keep getting involved in the same old patterns." A good therapist, he explained, can help a patient develop coping mechanisms.

"Nobody but Felix would say he had cured her of schizophrenia. That's so self-aggrandizing," said a psychiatrist who knew Felix well.

When Felix brought Susan for psychological show-and-tell, he revealed much more than he had intended. Students could see her thought process was a little off. They also couldn't help but notice that Susan and her therapist wore similar soft, comfortable clothes and identical Wallabee shoes. They wondered if such deliberate twinning symbolized something more. The students listened, and after awhile, some squirmed; they whispered to one another, "What's going on here?" Felix and his patient seemed too familiar, too intimate. Their one-hour session went over the allotted time. "There was something weird about the interview," the mentor recalled. "Everyone noticed it. It was too seductive."

Felix's mentor intervened, "I said, 'You've got to stop it.' " The semipublic "intensive" therapy session ended. "People in the class said 'he loves her,' " said Sheila Byrns. Felix's mentor might have pushed things further, he might have insisted that Felix break off treating Susan altogether, but nothing happened, and their dangerous liaison continued.

SLOWLY BUT STEADILY, FELIX WAS CROSSING MORAL, ETHICAL, AND POSSIBLY even legal lines with his young patient. Susan claimed that during therapy, Felix would have her walk around his office, with the supposed goal of making her less self-conscious about her body.

"He would stare at me," Susan said, speaking of it now. "I was just so embarrassed. He would comment on my anatomy. He would ask, 'Did I feel men watched my bottom when I was walking?' " Felix Polk rarely consulted other therapists. "He thought he was capable of handling situations himself," an old therapist friend recalled. He failed to consult anyone about his growing intimacy with the young Susan Bolling until much later in their relationship.

As their relationship progressed, and they continued sitting together they started holding hands. The physical nature of the relationship only escalated from there. Sometimes their legs touched. At the end of each session their lingering hugs were punctuated with kisses. Susan says that by the time she was eighteen or nineteen she and her therapist had fallen in love and were having sex during therapy on the floor of his office.

Helen made an impassioned plea to her daughter and attempted to pry Susan away from Felix by exposing her to more age appropriate men. Although she had invested in real estate and grown affluent, Helen didn't live that way, always loathing the thought of spending money. Nevertheless, she took her daughter on vacation to Santa Barbara, where the girl might meet young men her own age. Helen "wanted to introduce her to the opposite sex." But the balmy weather, swaying palms, and the young men who looked longingly at her had no effect. Susan was "glued in," her mother said. Which is exactly the term that Felix's friends would use to describe his affinity for her.

Felix began to teach Susan about what true love meant. Love, he told her, meant two people coming together as one. "My body as his body," Susan remembers. "My breast as his breast." Felix believed there was nothing more profound in the world than an intimate relationship. He convinced his patient to believe that too. By settling on Susan, Felix had found a young woman as dependent on him as his wife was independent. And unlike Katya, his nurse-maid and first love, he thought she would never leave.

Part of Felix's love must have relied on his belief in his ability to heal her. She was the victim and he her rescuer. That was part of his wishful idealism, his dream that likely led him to overestimate his own powers. He became the guardian of Susan's sanity and life. The more she needed him, the more special he was to her and to himself. Because of their unique relationship, Felix never did what good therapists do; he never prepared her for the fall, when she would discover that the center of her life, the key to her transformation was not a god.

WHILE FELIX HOPED HE COULD KEEP THE AFFAIR A SECRET, HIS OFFICE mates were not as oblivious as he hoped. A female psychiatrist who, along with her husband, shared an office with Polk during 1977 and 1978, recalled telling her husband: "Felix is fucking his patient." Susan Bolling would have been twenty or twenty-one by then.

"Oh, you don't know that," her husband said. But the signs were every-where. She observed what she described as the flirtatious stage of an early romance; an ethereal Susan gliding into the waiting room with a bouquet of flowers—for her therapist. Another time Felix was peeping through the crack of his barely open door, coyly whispering to Susan. Alone in the waiting room, Susan could be seen perched excitedly on a seat, squirming in anticipation. His colleague found Felix's actions to be "very inappropriate." By now, Susan "was not a child. She was a young thing. It wasn't like pedophilia, but I thought it was just terrible. It was terribly unethical," the psychiatrist said.

Most likely because of their affair, Felix quit seeing Susan one-on-one, sending her to see a female therapist for individual counseling. Amazingly, the therapist was a close friend of his wife's, and according to Susan, Felix was upset with her when she confessed the affair. Meanwhile, Susan continued to attend Felix's weekly group therapy sessions.

Their affair might have continued to be cloaked in secrecy had Sharon Mann Polk not gone public with her husband's transgressions. On November

27, 1978, the day that San Francisco's mayor and the city's first gay supervisor were gunned down by a former elected official, the Polk-Bolling affair became painfully public. Susan had turned twenty-one two days before.

During days of great public stress, troubled people, already on edge, often fall overboard. The psychiatrists who shared office space with Felix Polk were braced for trouble. The three officemates—minus Felix—were gathered in the coffee room discussing the shocking city hall murders when Felix's wife, Sharon, whom they all liked and respected, shoved open the door and entered in a state of consuming fury. She had known about Felix and Susan for some time, but today she had spotted Susan while lunching with a friend and lurched into a rage.

"What kind of doctors are you?" she screamed at the group. "What kind of colleagues are you to be associated with this? How can you be decent people when your colleague is [having sex with] his patient?"

Sharon Polk's friend was trailing behind her. She herded Sharon out of the coffee room and through the building. Chagrined, Felix shamefacedly entered the room and in collegial tones he announced: "I want to apologize for Sharon, for exposing you to that tirade. I'm really sorry." He turned to go back to his office.

His female colleague, who had spotted the affair months before, agitatedly chased after him: "You don't need to apologize for Sha. You need to apologize to everyone you exposed to this dreadful thing!"

"Everybody was asking what in the hell is he doing?" said his former patient and friend, Bob Wilk, also a therapist. "He had so many people that loved him, adored him; they'd wanted what was best for him. I think it was only people like me and others that could say, 'What the hell is he doing?' "

As the relationship continued, Felix's colleagues at the graduate school followed the scandal. Some were uncritical. He had not been a womanizer, some pointed out. This was the only patient he had ever had an affair with. Others thought it was inexcusable, even dirty. They felt guilty about knowing yet not having done anything about it.

Many of Felix's friends were remarkably tolerant. "I'm rather nonjudgmental," said Felix's friend Ernst Valfer, a fellow therapist who occasionally sought therapy with Felix. "I always thought that Sharon was more attractive, more lively. Sharon, whether I agreed with her or not, was a real presence while Susan was more mousy."

"There are times I've had trouble keeping my own life together. I'm not judging," said Wilk, the therapist. "I don't tell people what to do."

Susan's mother, Helen, objected to Felix's being so much older than Susan—two years older, in fact, than Helen was. Worst of all was that her daughter was going with a married man. She had lost her husband to a woman who had no such reservations, and in Helen's mind, that was "a no-no." Helen's closest friend encouraged her to go to the police: "I was horrified," the old neighbor said. "I would have turned him in." But what could the police have done anyway? At the time a therapist having sex with his patient was not a crime in California; it wasn't even an official violation of professional ethics.

Although she disapproved of their love, Helen Bolling had thought that Dr. Polk was rational and reasonable and a father figure for a girl who didn't have one. Susan's brother, David, thought, "She could have done worse."

THE TABOO AGAINST SEX BETWEEN DOCTOR AND PATIENT DATES BACK TO THE fourth century BC, when the Hippocratic Oath was written. It reads: "In every house where I come I will enter only for the good of my patients, keeping myself far from all intentional ill-doing and all seduction and especially from the pleasures of love with women or with men, be they free or slaves."

Freud recognized the harm that could come to patients who become intimate with their analysts, yet in the early days of psychotherapy there was no outrage attached to great psychotherapists having sex with their patients. Carl Jung had affairs with numerous patients, including an affair with Sabina Spielrein, his first patient, after she was no longer under his care. Sandor Ferenczi had an affair with a young female patient whose mother had been both his patient and his mistress. While analyzing the daughter and sleeping with her, Ferenczi wrote Freud: "I know, of course, that by far the greatest part of her love for me was father transference, which easily takes another as an object." Ferenczi later married the young woman's mother.

In the 1960s and 1970s, rules governing therapist-patient relationships were not established. "It was a time of dethroning of power," explained Danny Goldstine, chief psychologist at Berkeley Therapy Institute and Felix's old friend. Some doctors had sex with their patients, teachers with their students, lawyers, their clients. Despite that, Goldstine said that a therapist engaging in sex with his patient "is totally wrong under any standards, any time, no matter what." Yet back then, there were schools of thought—especially in California—that held that sex between therapist and patient was beneficial—and not just for the therapist but for the patient as well.

Concern was raised by two very unlikely sources. In researching their books *Human Sexual Response* and *Human Sexual Inadequacy,* the famed sex researchers William Masters and Virginia Johnson were shocked to discover how many women had been in sexual relationships with their therapists. From their interviews, Masters and Johnson came to believe that the aftereffects of sex between a therapist and a patient damaged the patient severely. "We feel that when sexual seduction of patients can be firmly established by due legal process, regardless of whether the seduction was initiated by the patient or the therapist, the therapist should be sued for rape rather than malpractice, i.e., the legal process should be criminal rather than civil," they wrote.

It was not until 1992 that the California Psychological Association declared sex with a patient to be unethical. Today, the American Psychiatric Association prohibits sex between doctor and patient or former patient: "A therapist who gratifies his or her own needs by exploiting a patient's vulnerability destroys the trust essential to treatment." The American Psychological Association is more forgiving, prohibiting sex during therapy but permitting it "under the most unusual circumstances" if two or more years have elapsed since the end of therapy.

Gary Shoener, a therapist and expert witness who has handled an estimated two thousand cases of sexual abuse in therapy, says the real issue is not sex but intimacy, a position that was reinforced in the oft-quoted decision of *Zipkin v. Freeman.* In that suit, filed in Missouri in 1968, a Mrs. Zipkin went to see a Dr. Freeman to help eliminate her persistent headaches. Over the course of treatment, she fell in love with Dr. Freeman, who responded by taking her on overnight trips and to nude swimming parties. The two had sex, and he convinced her to leave her husband and buy a farm for him, where she worked the land. The court found Dr. Freeman guilty of negligence for "mishandling the transference phenomenon." The court wrote that, "it is pretty clear from the medical evidence that the damage would have been done to Mrs. Zipkin even if the trips outside the state were carefully chaperoned, the swimming done with suits on and if there had been ballroom dancing instead of sexual relations."

Which is to say, a doctor should not conduct a social relationship with a patient, but if he does, he should be held responsible for the damage that may ensue. Once the relationship ends, patient-victims often experience isolation, emptiness, guilt, suppressed anger, and an inability to trust A study of a thousand patients who had sex with their therapists found that 3 percent married their therapist, 11 percent were hospitalized, 14 percent tried to commit suicide, and 1 percent succeeded.

Berkeley psychologist Dr. Margaret Singer, a national expert on brainwashing and cults, was firmly in the camp that believed in a clear separation between a therapist and patient. Singer taught Felix Polk when he was a graduate student at Berkeley. Her views were plain and simple: "You don't have a dual relationship," Singer warned. "The therapist doesn't become the landlord or the lover, because a person puts onto therapy all the most positive hopes they can gather. Then, when a therapist lets the patient down or violates them, it's terrible. It's worse than a brother stealing money out of your purse."

The collateral damage from Felix's relationship with Susan spread to Felix Polk's other patients. Joel Tepper was in an evening therapy group with Susan, whom he considered, "of all the people there, probably the most troubled." He thought she seemed detached. All along, he felt that Felix had skewed the group experience to protect her, at the expense of others in the group. One evening, as the participants sat on the floor of Felix's office, Susan Bolling and Joel Tepper, his two prized patients, began arguing about some long forgotten point. In the heat of the moment Susan blurted out:

"You don't know all the details. You don't know what's really going on." Then she followed with the explosive news, "Felix and I are lovers!"

"I was just so tired of seeing my therapist and pretending he wasn't my lover," Susan said. "I just told everyone in group therapy."

Although they had kept it a secret, Felix's attitude, Susan says, was that they had done nothing wrong. "Why shouldn't we?" he seemed to say. Sex was just an extension of the love they felt for one another.

Her revelation shattered the group. Members felt betrayed and unloved by their therapist. Of all his female patients, Felix had chosen Susan, which meant he had not found his other female patients as worthy as she. Some thought what Felix was doing was unethical and wrong, others just felt uncomfortable. They had been in this together; they were revealing themselves to one another. Honesty was essential. Except that the therapist and his prized patient had engaged in a conspiracy of silence. Their affair must have influenced how Felix behaved toward other group members. Susan's well-being, not theirs, must have been his prime concern. The subject was too hot for calm discussion. Almost immediately that evening the meeting broke up.

Joel Tepper had a decision to make: though the therapy had brought him benefits, he stopped seeing Felix. "He lied to all of us," Joel said. For months, he remained upset with Felix, but in time he would return to the fold.

Despite the debacle, Susan retained one friend from the group. Kathy Lucia remembers her therapist and Susan were very much in love. "You can't even call what Felix and Susan had 'closeness,' " Kathy said. "They were one."

Susan relied on Felix for all her important decisions. At the age of nineteen, after having skipped high school but taken a few courses at a local junior college, she applied to a four-year school. Her mentor-lover-therapist recommended she attend Mills College—a private all-girls school in the Oakland hills. As part of her application she was asked for a page of self-analysis.

"Have there been any special circumstances which may have affected your performance in school? If so, please explain (illness, family problems, etc.)."

She could have written about her alienation from normal life, her being sent to a therapist, her depression, her brush with the juvenile system, her attempted suicide, and her running away from home. She might have written that she fell in love with her therapist and he with her. Instead, she provided a starchy account of her situation:

"Yes. In my early high school years I was surrounded by serious family problems resulting from the breakup of my parent's marriage . . ."

Asked to describe herself, she wrote that she had "a fertile imagination" and that she was interested in literature, history, and human psychology. The young Susan Bolling was very different from the adult Susan Polk. She wrote that while she believed she was intelligent, she knew she was also shy and lacked confidence. She told the admissions officer she hoped to become a professor of psychology or literature and that she was also interested in music, philosophy, religion, and ancient and medieval history.

On her SATs, Susan scored an impressive 740 in English. Her math score of 530 wasn't bad for a girl who had never attended a high school math class. In 1977, she began attending Mills College on a partial scholarship from the state of California.

Once at school, she adopted the free-spirited style of the times. She now wore Berkeley clothes: jeans and sweaters, no makeup. Kathy Lucia recalls that Susan was beautiful, and though she was not interested in anyone other than Felix, she also wasn't pleased with their relationship.

"I think it was a father thing. She was mixed up," Kathy said. "Women and men fall in love with their therapist. She had issues about it. Susan had resented it when Felix had designated an older woman in their therapy group to take Susan under her wing. She thought he was controlling." Susan told her friend she wanted to end the relationship, but it was hard. She didn't want to hurt Felix. Plus, Kathy Lucia said, Susan was also dependent on him in lots of ways. She didn't want to let go of all that support and advice.

There was something else that bothered Susan. She strenuously objected to his use of cocaine, which he had snorted during his grad school days and continued to use years afterward. Cocaine had a long history of abuse among therapists. One prominent example was Freud, who penned some of his best-known theories about the unconscious mind while high on cocaine. But Felix's reaction to the drug was less fruitful. Susan complained that when he was high, Felix sometimes hallucinated and became impotent.

THEIR LOVE AFFAIR CONTINUED UNTIL SHE WAS TWENTY-ONE, AT WHICH point Susan left him. Felix told his friend Sheila Byrns that *he* had actually wanted to break with Susan but had orchestrated it in such a way so Susan would leave him, giving her some sense of control. It's not clear if he was truly that controlling or if he was simply a shunned suitor trying to save face.

In 1978, after a six-month break, they started the affair again. With the promise and the vision of Susan to buoy him, Felix was finally able to separate from his wife for good, announcing to Sharon and his children that he was leaving the marriage.

Before the divorce was finalized, Susan says that Sharon Mann Polk wanted to meet "the other woman." (Sharon Mann refused to be interviewed, so there is no way of verifying Susan's account.) The three met in Felix's office near the Berkeley campus. "I was just a kid," Susan recalled. Felix sat back in his chair and let the two women talk. Susan remembers Sharon warning: " 'You have no idea what you're getting yourself into. You have no idea what he's like.' " Felix looked embarrassed.

"I couldn't even take it in because it completely conflicted with the illusion," Susan said. Before she left, Susan said that Sharon looked at her and said, "Okay, you can have him."

When she was twenty-two, Susan transferred to the less expensive San Francisco State University. Susan's mother rented her an apartment near campus, which she shared with a meandering cat and a Muslim girl who converted to Judaism. Susan saw her lover once or twice a week. She loved attending San Francisco State. She adored living on her own. She slept on a mattress of straw and wrote in her diary that this was the happiest time of her life. She liked the students she crossed paths with, although she never went out on a single date.

Susan says she talked to Felix about breaking up again. She claims that he grew despondent, first becoming cold and angry and then reminding her that in his youth he had tried to commit suicide. "He started crying. He reminded me I could never leave him." He told her what he had told her many times before, that he was vulnerable because he had lost his beloved Katya when his family fled Vienna.

"I felt I had this responsibility," Susan said. "This man had had such a traumatic childhood. He had lost everything, including the woman who raised him. I thought, he's my responsibility. I made my bed; I have to lie in it. He had left his wife. He had given everything up for me."

Despite her reservations, which she talks about in retrospect, people who observed the two at the time could tell how much she loved him. Felix's old friends recall Susan following Felix around like a puppy dog, transfixed by his every thought.

"She was a child under the wings of her protector," said forensic therapist Stephen Pittel, once Felix's closest friend. Felix had been best man at Pittel's wedding. And Pittel had guided Felix through his PhD thesis. In one sense, Pittel thought Susan suited Felix well. Felix had a big ego, Pittel said, and "needed to be in control."

Soon the two moved in together. Felix Polk went from a home where he felt he received no respect to a relationship where his patient-lover worshiped him. He went from a relationship in which he needed Sharon to one in which Susan needed him. Felix told friends he had never been attracted to younger women before, though a number of people who knew him noticed he had a covey of attractive—and needy—young female students as well as patients who spent longer in therapy than they otherwise might have. He told Sheila Byrns, his patient and friend, "There's something about Susan." He fell in love with her mind, he told Sheila, but that would be something a man who fell in love with a beautiful young woman might say to his female contemporary.

Felix felt he was in love with everything about Susan. She was just the sort of girl who wouldn't have given the teenage Felix, competing with his twin, a glance. But he was older now, and had his warmth, worldliness, and sophistication to offer . . . and a young patient of his could fall in love with him for all of that.

Sometimes he appeared shocked by her love, though perhaps he should not have been. If she was frightened of the real world, if she needed to feel safe, he was her omnipotent therapist. "My God," he told Sheila Byrns, "she adores me!" And in those days, Susan was loving, no matter what she said years later. She was optimistic, encouraging, and interested in others. Some thought of her as a young flower. Sheila Byrns believed that Susan was a replacement for Katya, his nursemaid, all softness, sweetness, and youth.

When Felix was married to Sharon, he was involved with music because she was a musician. When he took up with Susan, he followed more literary pursuits, as suited Susan. "Both were real parts of him," his old friend Sheila said.

Felix once confided to a friend that "I know it's not going to work," but the friend chalked that up to Felix's natural pessimism. Susan and Felix briefly lived at the home of Felix's friend Steve Pittel, who recalls Susan as a waiflike, ethereal young woman. He said she was "very fey." She was fifteen degrees off center.

Pittel once overheard Susan speaking to Felix in bed—his room was next to theirs. "You've taken something precious from me," she told Felix. "I'm giving you the greatest gift of all." Pittel thought her remarks were "bizarre, preadolescent nonsense." But what was upsetting was the fact that his middle-aged friend "fell for it."

Felix and Susan spent hours holed up together working on what Felix thought would be his breakthrough book on juvenile delinquency. He was going to teach the rest of the profession how to understand troubled adolescents like the many he treated, including Susan. Felix dictated his thoughts to her, but the manuscript, which Pittel says was little more than a mishmash of concepts, never found a publisher. Shortly after that, the two friends drifted apart. Pittel came to see Felix as an unoriginal thinker who was prone to glom onto whatever trend wafted his way. Felix was a Zelig of popular psychology. Eventually that characteristic would lead to twisted and tragic consequences.

During those years, Susan and Felix kept mostly to themselves. She had no close and enduring friendships, though when she socialized with Felix's other patients they found her "sweet and loving," an inquisitive charmer. Sometimes she had a way of being interested in other people, of asking questions, which drew them out and made them feel comfortable. Others admired her inner brightness that caused her to sparkle when she smiled.

At other times they found it impossible to get close to her. Sometimes she was inexplicably phlegmatic. Sometimes Susan would encounter Felix's friends and rather than charm them she would be cold, distant, or strange. They came to realize it wasn't something they had done; it was just Susan. If he was aware of her odd behavior, he never mentioned it to anyone.

A few colleagues who knew about his involvement with his patient quit referring patients to him, but he retained a loyal following. At the California Graduate School of Family Psychology he was still adored by his students and his mentor, who ran the school.

He must have been embarrassed by his relationship, because in 1981 Felix is said to have burst into the graduate school faculty room gleefully announcing: "The good news is that I'm getting married! The bad news is that I'm marrying a twelve-year-old!" He didn't need to tell them he was marrying his former patient; by then, they knew.

Helen Bolling remembers talking to Felix about the impending marriage. The blunt-talking but curiously uninvolved mother told him, " 'I never envisioned you as my son-in-law.' I was trying to say, 'Hey, I don't want any trouble. Let's do this as free of trouble as possible.' "

Shortly before they wed, Felix briefly saw a therapist. He must have sensed what he was getting into, yet he couldn't resist. He told the therapist that he was worried because he was about to marry a disturbed young woman who had been his patient. He was going in with his eyes open. The therapist asked him, "Why are you marrying her?" Felix's answer was simple: "I can't not."

By marrying Susan, Felix thought he was making a bad situation better. Had word spread further about his involvement with Susan, it could have ruined his practice. He felt both cornered and in love. In part it may have been the times: the unethical had become acceptable. Est had given Felix permission to do what he wanted even though he knew it was wrong. The therapist who was full of sage advice for others rarely adhered to it when it came to the ex-patient he loved.

They were married the day after Christmas in 1981 at the chapel on the Mills College campus. He was forty-nine and she was twenty-four. Her wedding ring was a diamond her mother had been given by a wealthy friend. "He reset it in silver, rather than platinum," Susan later sniffed. As Felix had had quiet reservations, so Susan did too. "There I was about to get married. I supposedly had what I wanted: this man." She wanted to halt the wedding, she later said, but she lacked the courage to flee. And so she stayed with the shaman who had guided her through her late childhood. By coming together, each became more of what they were: she the undeveloped, troubled, lost self and he the important all-knowing authority.

They had a Jewish wedding, which amused Felix's friends, most of whom were Jewish. Felix wouldn't know what the afikomen (the piece of matzo that children search for during Passover,) was even if he found it. A cantor chanted in Hebrew, and at the conclusion of the ceremony, Felix shatttered a wineglass with his shoe, an expression of sorrow at the destruction of the Temple in Jerusalem, as well some say, as a symbol of the fragility of relationships.

Susan wore a diaphanous white dress with a delicate garland of wildflowers in her long, curly hair. Felix's family accepted Susan as one of their own. "My house became her house," said his brother's wife, Barbara Polk. They wanted Felix to be happy, and Susan seemed to make him that.

While Barbara thought that Susan's mother, Helen, was fun, Helen remained critical of the union: "This was not what I wanted," she said. She knew Felix's family was full of pianists and intellectuals, but she added, "They're Jews. I'm not a Jew. There was no reaching out." Felix's sister, Evelyn, didn't try to make sense of it. She felt badly about the split with Sharon, but she knew Sharon had moved on. Felix and Susan "seemed happy, so I was happy," she said.

"Felix was a vibrant man," said his patient and friend, Joel Tepper, who attended the wedding. "I could understand why he was attracted to Susan but not why he built his whole life with her."

The honeymoon was a Polk family affair. Susan, Felix, his mother, his brother and sister-in-law, his son Andy and daughter Jennifer rented a cabin near Tahoe. After the wedding reception they drove up past the site of the famed Donner Party, the unlucky wagon train of migrants who got stuck in an early winter and resorted to eating their dead. A few days later, as the Polk family celebrated the close of 1981 and made resolutions for the New Year, a massive storm was rolling in off the Pacific and heading toward the Sierra.

5.

A RISING FEAR

IT DID NOT TAKE LONG FOR SUSAN AND FELIX TO SETTLE INTO MARRIED LIFE. With the help of her mother, they bought a huge and stately Walter Ratcliff home with cabled windows and hand-hewn beamed ceilings in Berkeley's quiet Elmwood District near a hardware store, a drugstore with an old-fashioned soda fountain, and a toy shop. The neighborhood of old Berkeley brown-shingle houses was home to young professors, aging hippies still living in communes, political activists, journalists, part-time nudists, and small-time marijuana growers. That same year, 1982, Susan graduated magna cum laude from San Francisco State University with a degree in creative writing.

Felix moved his practice into a study in their house. While he told his ex-wife, Sharon, that he did it to save money, the main reason he moved his office into their house was to be close to the woman he loved. During breaks between patients he liked nothing better than to spend a few minutes with Susan. At that point, he was working six days a week, often ten to twelve hours a day, not only to support two families but also because he was much in demand and because his clients gave his life greater meaning.

As she developed her own sense of taste, Susan refurbished their home. She taught herself to cook organically; she wanted to be sure with a husband so much older than she, that he remain healthy. She began investing in real estate just as her mother had done. They soon bought a couple of properties. She improved them, rented them out, or resold them and bought more. She felt as though everything she "touched turned to gold." She took over billing her husband's clients, a task which occasionally included her fishing uncashed checks from his office wastebasket. Other bills were never paid, because, having befriended his patients, Felix was loath to remind them about overdue payments. That Susan was good with money pleased Felix. "He loved it. He didn't know what to do without me," she said. "He needed me emotionally and he couldn't handle business."

While Felix had his colleagues, his students, and his patients, many of whom became his friends, Susan relied on herself for much of her entertainment, as she devoted hours every day to reading fiction and poetry and writing in her diary. Felix told friends he encouraged her to find a job. She briefly worked at a boutique that sold handmade clothes around the corner from their house, but she preferred to stay at home and write. Later she would claim that it was she who wanted to work outside the home but that he discouraged her.

Susan took on neighborhood causes, spearheading a fight to keep a local ice-cream shop from building a factory in the neighborhood; but despite her involvement, Susan made few friends. Though she and one older neighbor bonded, others thought she was a little odd, and they kept their distance. They saw Felix as a warm older father, more relaxed than his wife and more solid. Yet Susan knew how to be cordial. Once a month, when the faculty at Felix's graduate school met at their house, Susan would be the gracious, if shy, hostess. The couple shared an abiding interest in music, literature, and history. They subscribed to the *New York Times,* the *Wall Street Journal,* and the *San Francisco Chronicle.* Both read books voraciously.

Together, Felix and Susan made a stunning couple. Felix's natural warmth, his enthusiasm, his hospitality, and his muscular fitness made him appear younger than his years. Susan seemed to slide into the role of the young wife whose appearance was part Saks Fifth Avenue and part *Sunset* magazine. She convinced Felix to spend money on himself, to buy quality suits and jackets. As Felix grew to rely on Susan's sense of taste and style, his appearance improved.

Susan considered herself a loving person. She very much wanted to be a good wife. "I was trying to make him happy," she said. She found pleasure in their life together. Her husband composed almost the whole of her social and emotional world, at least until the children came along. Felix's sister, Evelyn, recalls that "they were exquisitely happy."

ON JANUARY 3, 1983, TWO YEARS AFTER THEY MARRIED, SUSAN GAVE BIRTH to Adam, the first of their three sons. Felix told friends he always knew Susan would be a good mother; he just hadn't realized how devoted she would become to their peaceful child. Susan had found her life's calling, and a bona fide reason to settle into domestic life. But the arrival of Adam also raised fears in her.

Any mother of a small child worries about his safety, and in those years there seemed to be special reasons to be concerned. In 1980, a blond-haired five-year-old referred to in the media as "little Timmy White" was kidnapped from his home in Ukiah, California. A year after Adam was born, in 1984, Kevin Collins, a freckle-faced parochial school fourth grader, was kidnapped outside a playground near his Haight-Ashbury home in San Francisco. (Timmy White was eventually rescued. Kevin Collins has never been found.) Parents across the nation, but especially in northern California, reacted with appropriate concern; they became more vigilant, rarely letting their children out of their sight.

Susan Polk took this vigilance to the next level when she tried to form a neighborhood group to respond to the threat. But other moms were not interested in checking out every parked car on their street. Other mothers tamped down their fears, proceeding with their lives. Susan's suspicions festered and grew.

For the first few months, Susan and the baby were inseparable—she even went so far as to strap him to her back when she gardened. To one of Felix's patients who babysat Adam and spent time in the house, it seemed as though Susan was more attracted to her baby than to her husband. Felix felt that as well and at times was jealous of the attention his wife paid their son. Eventually Felix suggested Susan look for child care. In a local child-care newsletter, she found parents who wanted to share the cost of an au pair. They were upper middle class, and the references for the fifty-year-old au pair checked out. Over the next few months when Susan had real estate business to conduct, she dropped Adam off with the babysitter. Those hours when Adam was away from her, Susan worried obsessively about his safety.

The headlines of the time only exacerbated her fears. That year, 1983, Susan and Felix began to hear of another threat to children. The McMartin Preschool abuse scandal in Manhattan Beach, California, became news across the nation. Sparked by a mother who had a history of false accusations, parents and children were soon accusing the caregivers at the McMartin Preschool of sexual, physical, and psychological torture—all done under the guise of satanic worship. The story was cheered along by *20/20* and the *Los Angeles Times*. In 1987, the young and enthusiastic TV personality Geraldo Rivera reported on TV: "Estimates are that there are over one million Satanists in this country. . . . The majority of them are linked in a highly organized, very secretive network. From small towns to large cities, they have attracted police and FBI attention to their satanic ritual child abuse, child pornography and grisly satanic murders. The odds are that this is happening in your town." (Eight years later Geraldo, who was not alone but was the most outspoken of town criers, stated that he had been "terribly wrong" about the satanic day care abuse.) The McMartin name became a synonym for sexual abuse of children. Soon there were similar accusations and stories in other cities.

So many stories were published about satanic abuse in day care centers that even normally skeptical people suspected something was going on. Nervous mothers, especially working moms who had little choice but to put their children in day care, were especially susceptible. For Susan Polk such stories merely fed into her roiling paranoia. There would be no gatekeeper—her therapist was now her husband—no one to reason with her, although that might not have made a difference anyway.

Shortly after Adam's first birthday, Susan and Felix began to notice what they believed were troubling signs. Felix claimed that Adam bit the family dog. They wondered what would make a toddler act so violently. Adam also began expressing fears. At night he sometimes woke up with nightmares. Although Susan had left Adam in the care of the au pair only about twenty times for a total of about a hundred hours, she and Felix began wondering whether something horrible had happened while Adam was out of her sight. She suspected that he, like the children at the McMartin Preschool, had been a victim of ritual abuse. Although there was no outside corroboration, from these simple observations they made the giant leap that their son Adam had become a McMartin-like victim of satanic abuse.

As Adam began to string together his first sentences, Susan quizzed her eighteen-month-old about what the "bad people" had done to him. Jennifer, Felix's daughter from his first marriage, lived with the family during this period while she was in high school and watched these interviews with amazement. Susan not only thought that her toddler could provide verbal clues to what had happened while he was in child care, but she also believed he was capable of identifying the individuals who were responsible. Adam would babble to his mother and when she heard something that sounded like a name, she would leaf through the phone book and ask: "What name did you say? Did you say this name?" Adam would babble some more. Once she was certain Adam had identified a suspect, she would then look up the person's address, drive to his home, and follow the person around. Sometimes Susan drove Adam around town asking him to point out familiar locations. She claimed that he picked out "the picture taker's house," a family friend recalled. That was the home of a nationally recognized nature photographer.

As Susan drew more and more information out of her son, Felix became equally convinced that Adam had been sexually abused; however, it was vague just how much of Susan's claims Felix actually believed. Early in the hysteria, Felix consulted his old professor Dr. Margaret Singer because he didn't know how to respond to Susan's claims that their son had been abused. If he opposed Susan, if he challenged the veracity of her claims, he knew she would peg him as the enemy. He understood how important it was to be on her side. Yet he certainly seemed to be more than just a supporter of Susan's growing paranoia. Felix also asked his son questions, scribbling down his utterances, which he took to be proof that something horrible had happened. Consumed by their fears, the Polks repeatedly interviewed the young boy. From these interviews they constructed a shocking narrative of abuse that would shape their lives for many years.

The Polks came to believe that after they dropped Adam off at the upper-middle-class house with the seemingly responsible au pair, he, along with other children, was shuttled in a school bus to a warehouse with cement floors, where they were placed in cages. Audiences would gather to watch the obscene satanic performances. Onstage, adults dressed in red and wearing triangular masks ritually raped Adam and other children. There were large, studio-quality television cameras to record the crimes.

That wasn't the worst of it. From Adam's responses to their questions, they came to believe that children were actually killed in the rituals. They believed Adam told them about a baby put in a plastic bag and hammered to death and that he had witnessed children being burned, drowned, and buried alive. He supposedly told them that the group feasted on children's flesh, feces, vomit, and urine. Nothing, it appeared, was beyond the pale for these homicidal, pedophilic, and cannibalistic Satanists.

Despite their outlandish-sounding nature, in truth, stories like those elicited from Adam were not unusual at that time. As parents across the country watched TV stories and read newspaper accounts of allegedly widespread satanic abuse, they too began to quiz their children. Sure enough, more stories came to light and more accusations against child care workers were leveled. In all, there were over forty satanic scares across the country, many involving day care.

For years, both Felix and Susan became obsessed with the abuse they contended Adam had suffered. Was Felix gullible, bordering on delusional, or did he just catch a wave and surf it? He was not alone. Therapists around the country fueled the paranoia by asking anxious-to-please children leading questions. When Susan gave birth to their other sons, she and Felix came to believe that they, too, were victims of satanic abuse. Eli, the second child was born June 2, 1985, two and a half years after Adam. A year and a half after that, on January 10, 1987, Gabriel was born. During all this time, the Polks continued to quiz Adam about the satanic abuse that they believed he experienced not only at the day care center but also later on when he visited a therapist

IN THE MINDS OF FELIX AND SUSAN—AND OTHERS WHO PROMOTED SATANIC abuse stories—there was a simple answer to the fact that no credible evidence for large-scale satanic conspiracy existed. They argued that the underground satanic conspiracy was so extensive, well funded, and connected within law enforcement and government that it could operate with impunity. The audacity of the abusers who supposedly were busing their victims around town and filming their grotesque crimes only proved how effectively they operated their secret society.

Asked at the time why no evidence had yet surfaced, Felix explained: "It's clear . . . that satanic groups are highly organized and that their people are well placed in key parts of our system. That includes some in law enforcement, some in the judiciary. Some in quite high places. Cases are mysteriously closed down, evidence disappears. That is not a random matter. I suppose as time goes on it will become clearer and clearer."

Shocked by what they had "discovered," Susan and Felix dedicated themselves to stopping the satanic abuse of children. As fear gripped the country, the couple founded an organization called Enough!, a grassroots group of angry parents and distraught sympathizers who believed they were at the forefront of a national movement. The two spoke at rallies and vigils, becoming minor celebrities in the burgeoning movement. Felix, because of his prominence in the Bay Area mental health establishment, gave keynote speeches, while Susan was relegated to lesser roles. Enough! demanded that the federal government take action. They had people with credentials fighting for their cause, including a child psychiatrist who was president of the authoritative-sounding California Professional Society on the Abuse of Children.

According to news accounts, the Polks' concerns reached the desk of then attorney general Edward Meese. Composed by Felix and Susan, their organization's manifesto included such statements as "CHILDREN HAVE THE FUN-DAMENTAL RIGHT TO TELL THEIR STORY TO A JURY. The failure of the prosecutor to press charges in the majority of child abuse cases creates a false impression in the public consciousness: an impression that the accused is inno-cent, when the reality is too often that the child is deemed too young to testify. If a child is too young to testify, but old enough to be raped, does he/she have any legal recourse? . . . Those who molest, rape, mutilate, or kill a child must know that they will be prosecuted and that they will go to prison.

"THE PUBLIC HAS THE RIGHT TO KNOW. The extent of the problem of child pornography must be made public. Child pornography is a $3 billion a year industry in the United States alone. Yet acknowledgment from the legislature and the U.S. Department of Justice of the scope of the problem has not been forthcoming."

Felix, who never had any compunction about discussing his personal life with his patients or students, spoke openly with them about his son's abuse. He told Joel Tepper that Adam had been driven in a van to a warehouse, where he had witnessed murders.

"And Felix assumed that was true. I'm convinced he thought that was true. He clearly believed it," Tepper said. Tepper was so concerned for Felix Polk and his family that he held a benefit piano recital to raise money for Enough!

At school, Felix raised the issue with his grad students: "I need to let you know this is the place I'm in," he told his class, which was just the sort of attitude that endeared Felix to his students. His account of Adam's abuse was so upsetting that one of his graduate students, Patricia Topsmiller, an upper-middle-class mother and a patient of Felix's, bolted from the classroom weeping. Someone followed her and asked if "that brought up something in my past. It hadn't, but I had been pretty naïve when I went into this. I was unaware of pornographic child photo rings."

Felix's students printed and distributed brochures and helped organize meetings. Together, they searched the east bay for the facilities where the crimes supposedly occurred. "Adam had always talked about a tunnel near water and we were never able to find it," Topsmiller recalled years later. "Kids were threatened by holding them upside down close to the water."

On November 8, 1987, Enough! held a meeting and press conference at the posh Mark Hopkins Hotel on Nob Hill in San Francisco attended by some four hundred supporters. Their story made the local nightly news and Page One headlines the next day. With dozens of other angry parents Felix declared, "I'm here because of what happened to my son. I'm here because there's something wrong. Our justice system is failing the children and that's not tolerable." He called what was happening "an American holocaust" . . . strong words for a survivor of Nazism.

In a news story published in the *San Jose Mercury* on December 9, 1987, entitled "Abused Kids' Parents Cry 'Enough!' " the reporter wrote: "Saying their children 'have had enough,' parents from throughout California vowed Sunday to seek justice for their sons and daughters, mainly preschoolers who, they said, were sexually abused in rituals." A black-and-white photo of a paternalistic Felix with his arm around a very young Susan accompanied the news story. They looked both serious and depressed. Susan was then twenty-seven years old, the mother of three, and Felix was fifty-two.

A month later, on December 20, Susan and Felix organized a candlelight vigil in front of the state capitol in Sacramento, where letters from children were placed at the governor's door. A letter from four-year-old Adam supposedly dictated to his father read, "Governor: Make me not have any more bad dreams, please." The front page story in the *San Jose Mercury* the next day read, "Their noses red from the cold, their eyes often filled with tears, more than two hundred parents and children—many of them victims of abuse—held a candlelight vigil Sunday night for missing and abused children."

Taking advantage of the fact that they were at the forefront of a growing movement, Felix began lecturing frequently on the subject. In February 1988, he spoke at a conference in Alameda County. He said he only wanted to be

introduced as "the father of a ritually abused child." Early in his speech, however, in what was supposed to seem like an offhand remark, he said, "I want to
identify myself very briefly. I'm a psychologist, a clinical psychologist. I used to
be chief psychologist for this (Alameda) county. I've taught at UC Berkeley
among other places." His tone was somber. In a phrase he had established his
credentials. He was not to be questioned.

In the same speech, Felix said that because of the abuse, Adam was now suffering from multiple personality disorder: "He's a girl. Why is he a girl? Because
he was dressed as a girl, professionally made up, then raped onstage in front of
an audience. So he's a girl. He's a killer. He has the eyes of a killer . . . less so
now, much less so now. He has a wonderful therapist and I like to think that he
has Susan and I [sic] as well. He's a killer because he was looked at by people
who were killers. And he's . . . he has their glance. He's also seen killings. And he
has himself. And he's a wonderful little boy."

Although he and Susan were gaining support to fight satanic abuse, Felix riled
at the notion that public exposure was a motivation. "Our group has had some
exposure now in the media," he said in the speech. "Some people think we're interested in fame and fortune. That couldn't be less true of us. Susan and I would love
nothing better than to be peaceful with our family and just go on with life. We
can't do that and we won't do that until something else has happened for us."

He believed that if they could express enough public outrage against
the satanic abusers, they could change the laws and stop the brutalization of
children. "What we hope for is to get so many voices shouting at people to
act—legislators—people who are equipped to have influence—the clergy,
police—that they cannot be ignored. And we won't stop short of that. We'll up
the ante to whatever extent we have to until something happens. We're committed to that." He sounded as though he meant it.

Unwavering belief in the stories of the children was central to the movement. Felix's own daughter ran afoul of that principle when she accused her
father of falling for Susan's fabrications. She also suggested that her father
might be reveling in his role as the head of a movement. In response, Felix
wrote a stinging letter that showed a side of him his acolytes rarely saw.

"It is a lie that I need to hang onto a cause, that I need something to be upset
about," Felix wrote his only daughter. "I don't need causes. YOUR USE OF
'LATEST CAUSE' TO REFER TO ADAM ENRAGES ME. I want to shove those

words down your throat. My son ADAM was brutalized and I, his father, have not been able to protect him or see that something happens to the people who raped and did all those other things to him."

He told Jennifer that he was not taking up Adam's cause to make a name for himself. "I will have a very hard time ever forgiving you for saying that . . . I think you must be jealous about all the energy I am devoting to Adam, child abuse, etc. You probably want that attention instead. You probably want to be treated as if you had been abused. When I read about your 'disgust' I picked up the phone. I could barely contain myself . . . You have never bothered to talk to anyone about what really happened to Adam. I have invited you to talk to . . . anyone who, unlike you, is informed.

"It is a lie that you do not know what really happened to Adam. What happened to Adam is what Susan and I have told you happened to him. He was raped, photographed, witnessed the ritual murder of other children, etc. Why don't you talk to his therapist about that. Why don't you read the articles about this sort of thing having happened to other children across the country. Why don't you attend one of the meetings we or others have held so that you can be informed. The answer is that you want to maintain the lie that you don't really know what happened so that you don't have to leave family center stage . . . PLEASE STOP PROJECTING THAT SHIT ON ME. I will simply throw the shit back at you if you project it on me."

It's hard to comprehend how a father could write something like that to the daughter he loved. In retrospect, a few of Felix's closest friends believe he must have viewed Jennifer's criticism as a threat to his relationship with Susan.

Susan continued their campaign through the media, contacting various outlets—including then *Washington Post* California reporter Cynthia Gorney (currently vice chairman of the University of California at Berkeley Graduate School of Journalism), who was in the midst of writing a series on the aftermath of the McMartin case. From her experiences in Southern California, Gorney was accustomed to encountering otherwise rational parents who believed their children had been whisked away by plane while at day care and taken to a location where they had been exposed to ritual stabbings, animal sacrifice, and satanic abuse. Gorney would come to believe these parents had fallen victim to some sort of person-to-person psychosis. Susan Polk was calm, articulate, and presentable when she told Gorney she knew her story was hard to believe; and yet the tale she wove was even outside the realm of the normally bizarre accounts Gorney had heard. Susan claimed, among other things, that her son had been taken by plane to a secret location by one of the greatest wilderness photographers in the country. Although Susan was utterly sincere, after half an hour, Gorney quit taking notes. There would be no story; Susan Polk, she concluded, was deranged.

IN ADDITION TO THE MEDIA'S FIXATION ON THE SITUATION, THERE WAS A RAP-idly growing body of mental health professionals that was leading the charge against the supposed Satanists. Therapists, like Felix, who professed an expertise in ritual abuse appeared on talk shows. They published popular books, taught about satanic abuse in college courses, and held accredited training seminars on the topic.

In organizing Enough! Susan had found her voice. She gave speeches on behalf of their cause. At a demonstration in San Francisco she told the assembled crowd: "It's not enough to write letters. Our legislators won't change the laws that need to be changed until there's enough public pressure to do so. We need people who are willing to come out for the kids. We've had enough violence against children!" Felix's friends wondered how his wife's newfound confidence might change the marital equation. "She started speaking out, getting power," said a former patient, friend, and student of Felix's, "and I wondered what would happen to their relationship now that she had become more independent."

Though at the time many of his clients said that Felix continued to be a wonderful therapist, some worried that he had suspended his sense of reality. His old grad school friends, a skeptical lot, might have tried to talk sense into him, but those friendships had fallen away. Most of his new friends, many of them fellow therapists, some of whom he had trained, believed that there was at least some truth behind the accusations and stories.

Dr. Sheila Byrns, Felix's friend, patient, and colleague, was initially skeptical: "It can't have happened. It was just too extreme." But then she weighed what she thought was credible evidence: "I saw Adam when I was babysitting for them, he would want me to tie him up. I saw him goose-stepping," Dr. Byrns says with a heavy sigh. "Here is this little tiny tike . . . He said something about 'bang, bang dead.' " When it was pointed out that that's what little boys say, Sheila Byrns responded that until then, she had not known that snuff films existed. "So I don't know. How would Susan know? How would she know to make this stuff up?"

Felix's friend, Dr. Jerrold Lee Shapiro, currently the chairman of the department of counseling psychology at Santa Clara University, who Felix's friends say saw Susan Polk as a client (though he has not acknowledged that), believed that the episodes stemmed from Susan's concerns as a protective mother, which he said, "went awry. How much she was right? I just don't know."

In an attempt to gain support and continue momentum for Enough! Felix called many of his psychologist and psychiatrist friends to seek their advice and enlist their help. Some empathized. Others, including one who had shared an office with him, concluded Felix had gone crazy. Some thought it was obvious that Felix and Susan Polk were engaged in a folie à deux. "They melted together," said Felix's mentor. "There was no longer any definition of who he was and who she was."

Years later, it would be Adam, the eldest, alone in the family who would come to an understanding of what had happened. In retrospect, Adam suspected that his father was so in love with his mother he could not face the truth that she was paranoid and delusional. Instead, he was sucked into her world, and deciding to believe, he willingly spearheaded a very public campaign to end the supposed satanic abuse. Referring to their long-term relationship, Adam said, "My parents went to a crazy place together."

Although he has no memory of the ways his mother and father elicited the satanic abuse accusations when he was only a year and a half old, by the time Adam was a little older he knew what was going on. He remembers when he was four that he wanted to stay home rather than attend Temple Beth El preschool in Berkeley. He recalls standing in the kitchen in Berkeley on the left side of the island when his mother asked: "Do you like going to preschool?"

"I said, 'No.' I liked being home," Adam recalls.

His mother asked, " 'Did somebody touch you? If you were touched by somebody, you don't have to go to school anymore.' I remember telling her 'Yeah,' because I didn't want to go to school."

When this interaction took place, he knew what he told her wasn't true, and later he came to believe that this dialogue was probably similar to others that occurred when he was younger. He never believed the satanic tales, and by the age of six, he understood what had happened better than his parents did. He went through a similar interrogation when he wanted to stop seeing a therapist. Again, his mother told him that if he had been molested, he would not have to return, so Adam said he was molested. The accusation led his parents to file a police report about the alleged incident, eventually prompting the therapist, who maintained his innocence, to flee the state.

Most shockingly, years later, Felix would confide in his mentor that he had never believed his or Susan's stories about satanic abuse. He had participated, he claimed, as a marketing ploy to make himself a sought after expert in the burgeoning new field.

BY THE EARLY 1990S, THE NATIONAL HYSTERIA OVER THE SATANIC CULTS HAD waned, and the public had forgotten it like a fevered dream. To date, there is not a single scrap of compelling evidence of an organized satanic cult in the United States that held meetings in which they raped or killed children.

Susan and Felix's campaign disappeared as the public interest in the topic faded. There were no more vigils or conferences—no more reporters showing up on their doorstep. Enough! ceased producing flyers and manifestos. Felix told friends that he and Susan had been threatened by shadowy forces. He said that Susan had seen signs in the garden and on the front porch that the Satanists had left as warnings. He told them "It's time to shut it down."

PART II

NO EXIT

6.

THE BUBBLE YEARS BURST

GIVEN THAT BOTH SUSAN AND FELIX CLAIMED THEIR FIRST CHILD HAD been the victim of a pervasive satanic conspiracy, it's surprising how normal much of the 1990s seemed to be for the Polk family. In the warmth and security of their home, Susan strove to provide a noncompetitive, cultured environment for her boys. Every morning she woke up wondering what she could do to make her boys happy. She adored her sons and had "an enormous amount of fun" with them.

Adam, who was Felix's favorite, was highly intelligent, testing off the charts. He never had to be taught to read; he simply knew, and he spent much of his time in his room with his books. Gabriel, the youngest, was his mother's favorite, while Eli, the wild middle son, was always in trouble. His parents worried about him and thought he was hyperactive, leading Susan to shop at specialty stores for foods without sugar. In spite of her culinary efforts, he remained a difficult child.

At home, Susan promoted a regimen in which creativity was paramount. She was always making sure that the boys had "a huge amount of art supplies" at their disposal. Every day she set up an easel in the kitchen, and summers, she carted all the materials outside, watching as her sons painted and colored for hours. When they weren't engaged in artistic endeavors, she enlivened their worlds with elaborate stories. In a diary entry from those days she described young Adam saying, "Tell me a story about ponies that fly," and with her vivid imagination, she made one up. Thinking there was nothing wrong with having his patients be a part of his personal life, all three boys took piano lessons from Felix's talented patient Joel Tepper. At night, Susan read books to them about fantasy worlds like *The Lord of the Rings* trilogy and the *Narnia* series.

"We were at a point in our lives when everything was perfect. Everything was like a fantasy," Adam would comment years later. "It was almost like we were living in a bubble."

Though she remained concerned about her children's well-being, Susan did not keep the kids locked in the house. She and her sons went on daily outings, strolling to the park or dropping by the library, only a few blocks away. Sometimes they stopped at Nabolom Bakery, a worker collective with hearty pastries, located on a shaded side street. Other days they wandered down to Noah's Bagels on College Avenue and sat on the wooden bench out front, nibbling the doughy treats. Occasionally, they visited La Farine, a small pastry shop full of lemon and berry tarts and artistically painted chocolate tortes. Susan and her three sons would sit at the communal table, with its crocheted tablecloth, and sip tea with dessert.

As they grew older, the boys traipsed to soccer, football, baseball, and rugby, collecting dozens of trophies that cluttered their bookshelves. Felix introduced Susan and the boys to outdoor adventures. As a family they regularly hiked in Yosemite and Mount Tamalpais, the spectacular mountain in Marin County that descends into San Francisco Bay. Felix, an excellent skier, enjoyed heading to the slopes of the Sierra with his sons. When he wasn't watching his San Francisco Giants or other sports on TV, Felix filled their house with Bach's Mass in B, Mozart's "Requiem," and Beethoven's 9th Symphony.

On weekends, each boy was allowed to invite one friend to sleep over. Susan delighted in knowing that as they grew up, her sons were popular with their peers. It was as though having missed out on high school she was living vicariously through her boys. Years afterward, she would still point with gusto to Gabriel's fifth grade coed karaoke birthday party as "the party of the year!"

In many respects, the Polks led a traditional family life, observing the sort of fixed schedule that was becoming increasingly rare. The family sat down to dinner promptly at six each night. Susan became a fine cook, stirring fried tomatoes with sesame seeds, baking tangy lasagna, and cooking a hearty pea soup. Each year they took a family vacation, visiting Canada, Europe, Mexico City, or Hawaii, and they would also venture back East to visit Felix's family. Felix taught his sons by example to appreciate both Mozart and the San Francisco Giants. Felix's sister and brother recalled that Susan and Felix behaved as though they were very much in love. Susan was quiet and responsible, always running after one of her sons. On the few occasions when she did not accompany Felix, he made sure to find a gift for her, stopping at Bloomingdale's to purchase something special.

Felix may have been the patriarch, but their son Adam recalls, his mother made most of the day-to-day decisions—particularly those that involved raising their sons. Felix had little time for his children, rarely helping with their homework. Although he was a loving father, "He didn't do anything with us," Adam once admitted.

Felix always made time for his wife, though. When he heard the jangle of Susan's car keys he'd pop out of his office to inquire where she was headed. He often asked her to wait for him before going food shopping. When they passed one another in the hallway, they often embraced. They liked to share quiet moments together or when the boys were around, speak French to one another, their secret language. Susan looked up to her husband. On holidays, she drew beautiful cards and wrote loving poems. For his birthday, she would whip up a cake with homemade vanilla icing and fresh strawberries and decorate the dining room table with streamers and confetti.

Given how their relationship had started, Susan and Felix appeared to have beaten the odds. Felix thought Susan was brilliant, loving, and kind, and even after all these years, his love continued to grow. While female friends of the family sometimes found Felix's behavior toward Susan paternalistic and thought he treated her as though she were his beloved child, they also noticed how much he loved her and enjoyed being by her side. Sometimes they compared their husbands to Felix and found their mates wanting. Not only was Felix a charmer, but he also professed strong moral values. When friends and neighbors sought advice about their wayward adolescents, Felix recommended tough love.

IN 1992, THE POLKS MOVED FROM BERKELEY TO A HALF-MILLION-DOLLAR house a few miles away in the posh enclave of Piedmont, with its stately homes set back from the street, wide lawns, and old shade trees. A community of only ten thousand and two square miles, Piedmont once had more millionaires per square mile than any other community in the country. Susan liked to say that her family moved to "Baja" Piedmont, the poorer side of a very rich town. While that was true, there was no doubt that they had moved into a magnificent home. Their new house became a work in progress for Susan, who redid the kitchen and the floors and then repainted the house and pasted up new wallpaper. Moving on to the exterior, she cut down small trees and mowed the lawns. On her own, she furnished the inside with dark Mission-style furniture accented by amber Arts and Crafts lights. Many of the rooms in the house were cavernous with high ceilings. The fifty-by-thirty-foot library, where Susan spent many hours reading, was lined with books; Susan favored fiction and poetry, Felix, history and psychology. Once again, Felix had his office in their house, not only to save money but also to be closer to his wife.

Susan gave numerous reasons for their departure from Berkeley. At times she had loved the political turmoil of The People's Republic of Berkeley. However, she also complained that the community was "weird" and that her boys, who were attending a Jewish preschool, were being deprived of a broader education. A move to Piedmont allowed her sons to attend a top public school.

Yet there was another, more troublesome, reason; in Berkeley, Susan often suspected she was being followed. As she walked to the library and the local produce store—only a block from their house—she caught glimpses of shadowy figures tailing her. She told her boys and they believed. She told her husband and he too believed, suspecting that her pursuers were nefarious opponents of their satanic abuse campaign several years before. As always, Felix backed up his wife, even when her perceptions of the world seemed questionable.

Initially, Susan tried to fit into the community of Piedmont, becoming a classroom mom and baking cookies for the school bake sale. She drove the requisite Volvo station wagon, attended her sons' soccer matches, and, when it was her turn, supplied the snacks, water, and sliced oranges. But unlike other parents watching their children on the playing field, when Susan or Felix attended, they rarely chatted in the bleachers, choosing instead to stand alone at the edge of the field.

Susan thought Piedmont residents were smug and uninterested in outsiders.

She believed that her sons were dumped into the B soccer league because she and Felix weren't part of the in-crowd. There may have been some truth to it. Once Adam was recognized as a great athlete, the family gained greater acceptance. Still, the Polk sons had a wildness about them that concerned other parents. Even on the sports field, dads noticed that the Polk boys were overly aggressive.

SUSAN LIKED HANGING OUT WITH HER BOYS, BUT SHE HAD TROUBLE DEAL-ing with teachers, administrators, and parents. In the beginning, she might like a person, but in time, she would find fault with him or her. It would begin as a speck of information, a negative rumor, or a remark uttered carelessly or, more often, misunderstood. Soon, she would become convinced that the person was out to harm her and her family. The only people she trusted were her boys and Felix.

For many neighborhood children, the Polk house was an irresistible arena trafficked by kids, dogs, and pet birds. Some parents didn't want their kids hanging out there because they thought Susan sometimes behaved more like a child than a parent. Once, she even took her boys and their friends to have their ears pierced, not thinking to call the other parents to ask permission.

Never much of a disciplinarian, Susan appealed "to a child's reason, honor, integrity, and sense of fairness," trusting that was how her sons would develop good values. Few of these progressive beliefs were shared by area parents.

Susan still looked up to Felix as older and wiser than she. Sometimes when she'd express herself Felix might respond paternalistically, saying things like, "No Susan, that's not the way it is." If the family was going on a trip Susan might say, "We need to arrive an hour early," and Felix might counter, "You don't know what you're talking about. We need to arrive *two* hours early." He would explain his reasoning and Susan would demure, "I didn't know that. I'm so glad you're here to tell me," but rather than being passive aggressive, she actually meant it.

Susan was a pushover. Her boys could say anything to their doting mother. "Make me some food," one might demand, and she would oblige without protest. Susan was sufficiently distressed that she consulted a therapist, who advised her to become more assertive. Still, when she tried to tell her sons what to do, they often ignored her. When her boys wanted their way, they would yell, which would bring her husband stomping out of his office. He would tell Susan he needed quiet, and as a result, she says, she felt compelled to give in to her sons' demands.

"I found myself in a pickle," she said, employing her trademark fifties slang. "They were quite good at working the system. It was hard for me to set limits. I trusted their love for me would override that . . . and it did." Susan and Felix encouraged their sons to challenge authority and defy convention. When the boys weren't invited to parties or celebrations, Susan was proud that they crashed the events anyway. She liked telling the story of how Adam reacted when he was not invited to bar mitzvahs. "He'd dress up in his sports coat and khakis and gate-crash every single one!" she said with amusement. "Adam was his own man. He would finagle a ride—often from me. When he arrived, everyone would cheer, 'Yeah, Adam!' He would have a wonderful time . . . it became the wonderful saga of Adam."

Not surprisingly, Susan's in-your-face behavior failed to endear her to her new community. She engaged in a bitter fight with other parents when she ordered that asbestos shingles be removed from a rental property she owned— right next to the boys' elementary school. Although she acquired the proper permits, parents were infuriated that a cloud of asbestos fibers might waft over the school and into their children's lungs. Susan was indignant, as she often was. It was not possible for any of the other mothers to talk things over with her. She was right; everyone else was wrong. Susan's temper and her practice of finding fault at the slightest offense became common knowledge among Piedmont parents.

IN NOVEMBER OF 1997, SUSAN TURNED FORTY. HER HUSBAND THREW HER A surprise birthday party and delivered a loving tribute. As he spoke their eyes met. Guests remarked that they saw the pair smiling their secret smile at each other.

What Susan now says she was seeing though when she looked at her husband that night was far from loving. Doubts about their marriage, which she would later say she had always harbored, were mounting. Her living room was full of Felix's patients and fellow therapists. "I thought, My God, what am I doing with this guy who is twenty-five years older than me? He's the age of my Dad. . . . He had been my therapist. I didn't think it was right that I married a married man. The man I married was willing to marry his patient . . . that's not something I agree with." And she didn't like that many of her guests were her husband's patients, she said. She surveyed the room and wondered, "What am I doing with my life?"

She began to bridle when Felix commented on her behavior or choices. She had a short Anne Klein jumper that Felix said was too provocative to wear around the boys. "My boys were always proud of me that I looked good," she said "There was nothing sexual there." Normally she would have laughed off his prudishness, but she began to think that such comments were proof that Felix was far too controlling. Similarly, she claimed Felix wouldn't let her wear a Ralph Lauren outfit because he thought its flower print was "hippie stuff." Acting like a rebellious teenager with a strict father, Susan bought a pair of hippie Birkenstocks.

She grew angry about his demands. "He was wanting to be catered to about food," she complained. "His diet was the rule of the family. He was enraged with me if I cooked a dinner of vegetables. He called it 'rabbit food.' He'd be really mad." Susan spent hours in the kitchen only to have her husband unfavorably compare her cooking to that of his former student and patient Sheila Byrns. Felix told Susan Sheila was a better cook and more adept at presenting dishes. The comments had an extra bite because Susan suspected that Felix was having an affair with Sheila. (Sheila Byrns insists that she and Felix were never more than close friends.)

Felix was not the only one drawing comparisons. It was around this time that Susan began to compare Felix's participation in his sons' lives to those of the other Piedmont dads. "I saw these dads who were really good dads, really supportive of their kids and I started to compare. It wasn't that they were younger or good looking," she said wistfully. "They were just great dads."

"As I matured," Susan later explained, "I ceased being the adolescent. I developed morals quite alien from my husband's." For years, she said, Felix had used cocaine. Sometimes it was so obvious that his grad school colleagues complained to administrators. "I thought we were people who shared the same values," but increasingly, Susan said, she found she was mistaken.

One night, while watching a TV news story on ethnic cleansing in Bosnia, she exclaimed, "Oh my God. It's like the Holocaust!" With arms crossed, Felix blurted out, "Those people are a bunch of fucking animals!"

Someone else might have interpreted Felix's comments as an expression of outrage at those responsible for the killings. Susan, however, thinking that

Felix was referring to both the murderers *and* their victims, was horrified: "I thought, 'Do I really know him?'"

Susan began thinking Felix was not the caring, compassionate healer she had imagined him to be. Maybe he was something else altogether. While doing their finances, Susan began to consider what her life would be like if they divorced and split up the family's assets. She figured that she and Felix could live separate yet comfortable lives. Their rental properties were providing "an enormous cash flow," Susan said, some one-hundred thousand dollars annually. And that was in addition to Felix's practice and his teaching, which together brought in another hundred thousand dollars. "All of a sudden I could see my way out of the marriage," she said. She thought, "I should be able to walk away and support my children."

NOT LONG BEFORE SUSAN BEGAN CONTEMPLATING A SPLIT FROM FELIX, THE focus of his professional career had shifted once again. The mid-1990s saw the rise of yet another psychological fad: the recovered memory movement. The premise here was that adult problems could often be traced to forgotten abuse experienced as a child, and with the help of therapy the repressed memory could be uncovered. Felix, who had been swept up by both est and the satanic cult scare of the late 1980s, jumped on this latest craze.

Felix found he had a knack for eliciting abuse stories from clients. Even his therapist friends marveled at his ability. They thought he was imbued with an almost magical skill that enabled him to help patients find lost memories of abuse. Combining his efforts at recovered memories with his knowledge of est, he utilized an est process of creating an imaginary room with a TV set with as many channels as the patient is old. If the patient were scared, Felix would advise her to turn the channel to earlier times when she had the same feeling. Felix believed that his patient's unconscious would stop at a certain channel where fear would be created and often the issue of abuse would pop out.

A patient who suffered severe panic attacks when she crossed the Bay Bridge was helped by Felix's "guided fantasy." She closed her eyes and imagined being on the bridge. Her "repressed memory" returned: the rhythmic sound her tires made on the metal expansions on the bridge reminded her of the sound she heard each Sunday as a child when her mother and brothers went to church and her father drove her across a wooded bridge to a barn where he raped her. Once the woman "got in touch with" the supposed repressed memories, driving over the bridge, Felix said, was no longer a problem.

He, like many therapists at the time, appeared to disregard how easy it was to create false memories in the minds of his patients. Therapists were coached never to question the truthfulness of an abuse story. "Believe the victim," was the catchphrase of the era. With the help of professionals like Felix, tens of thousands of women and a smaller number of men across the country began to "uncover" memories of fathers and uncles molesting them as children and even infants. The memories often grew to include satanic worship—giving new legs to the satanic scare that had gripped the country.

Many of Felix's patients discovered supposed memories that they had been molested at the hands of satanic cults as children. Over the years, he built a reputation not just as an adolescent therapist but also as someone who could assist troubled women with their "repressed memories" of childhood sexual abuse. Sometimes he brought these women to his graduate school class, where they would act out the abuse they supposedly uncovered.

Given how susceptible the Polks were to such trends, it seems almost inevitable that the recovered memory idea would make its way into Susan's world. Felix kept little if no boundary between work and family. Often he discussed his patients with Susan and brandished his therapist's jargon while discussing the behavior of his wife and children. As the recovered memory narrative spread throughout the country, it also became a staple on morning talk shows and spawned a series of best-selling books. Once again, Felix was a part of a growing movement of nontraditional therapy. With Felix's encouragement, Susan began reexamining her childhood in search of an explanation for her growing unhappiness.

If a family has markers in its collective lives, Felix Polk would mark Disneyland of 1998 as the time and place where everything changed. Felix would describe what happened to Susan during the vacation as a psychotic break. Adam was then fifteen; Eli was thirteen and Gabriel was eleven.

The family stayed at the nearby Disneyland Hotel, and after dinner one evening, Susan began to cry. She was inconsolable. Images flashed in her mind that she took to be repressed memories finally boiling to the surface. She remembered hiding in a closet as a male figure whom she thought was her father, tried to pursue her. Her memories grew worse. Later, back at home in the Bay Area, Susan became certain her mother was not her mother, and she

"recalled" watching her parents bludgeon a police officer to death with a ham-
mer in a basement in Los Angeles. As therapists were encouraged to do at the
time, Felix "validated" her memories, and he told others that he believed them
to be real. Because he had believed Susan's earlier stories of their son's satanic
abuse and her being followed by silent strangers, he was much less resistant to
accepting her next story and the one after that. Helen Bolling tried to assure her
daughter she was indeed her biological mother and that she had never hammered a policeman (or anyone else for that matter) to death in a basement.
When Susan and Felix offered to pay for it, Helen agreed to take a DNA test,
which showed conclusively that they were mother and daughter. This proof
that at least part of Susan's new memories weren't true didn't seem to bother
either Felix or Susan. While Helen knew that she had never killed anyone, she
was frightened that Susan might call the police and that some overzealous officer might haul her off to jail.

When the fad of recovered memories had crested and academics began
to attack the process as a fraud perpetrated on patients by therapists, Felix
and Susan were not moved. Felix told his friend Sheila Byrns that the critics
were evil and most probably perpetrators themselves. While many ceased to
believe in the practice, the Polks committed themselves even more deeply to it.
Susan went on remembering more and more horrible events in her childhood.
Soon she was saying that when she was little her brother had violently beaten
her up. There was never any evidence to support Susan's repressed memories.
All her claims were vociferously denied by any implicated family members.

Given how critical Susan had become of Felix recently, her shift in focus to
her supposedly abusive, murdering mother, father, and brother must have been
a relief. Felix could once again be her advocate, telling her how horrible it must
have been to have to suffer so. For Felix, it was a respite but one that would not
last.

By the time he was fifteen, Adam was already noticing how calm his friends'
mothers were compared to his own. They didn't obsess about evil conspiracies
or suspect that people followed them down the street. They didn't look for hidden messages in newspapers. It was Adam who was, as he put it, "the first to
bring the issue of madness to the [family] table."

When he raised his concerns with his father, however, Felix refused to
accept it. Perhaps Felix loved his wife too much to accept that she was going
mad. Perhaps it was too humiliating to admit the truth. Maybe he thought she

was seeing the world as it actually was. Or maybe he thought that by challenging her he, too, would become her target. Undoubtedly there were many instances he supported her, fueling her paranoia. But his ability to stay on his wife's side would not last.

ONE NOT SO ORDINARY MORNING SUSAN LAY IN BED WHILE REPRESSED MEMories flooded into her mind. She was forty, Felix was sixty-five. They had been married for sixteen years and had known one another for twenty-five. She says she turned to her still sleepy husband on the pillow next to hers and asked in a hostile tone, "How old was I when we had sex? Why can't I remember what we talked about? Why can't I remember what happened?"

In the recovered memory world, a lack of memories for crucial events suggests there are repressed memories hiding in the unconscious. Felix was in her crosshairs.

As she thought of those early days in therapy, she began to think about the relaxation exercises and the guided visualizations that Felix had used on her. She began to think that Felix had hypnotized and raped her. Maybe they hadn't started their affair when she was eighteen or nineteen as she had thought; maybe he had hypnotized her and forced her to have sex when she was sixteen. The hypnosis, she was convinced, had shielded her from the truth. Until now.

Her mind began to create images of those early days in therapy. She was convinced she was pulling back the curtain on her unconscious, exposing accurate and vivid visions of what he had done to her. She saw Felix pouring her tea, asking her to count backwards from one hundred and placing a white towel on the floor of his office. Following his orders, she lay down with him and lost her virginity. She remembered stumbling out of Dr. Polk's office, she said, with "a sense of depression and sense of loss." She felt as though she had died. "How can I live with you?" she asked as he lay beside her. "How could you do that?"

Susan claims that shortly after she "recovered" her memory she *asked* Felix for a divorce, as though she needed his permission. She did not see that her subservient role and his as her master bound them together. They were so closely tied to one another that untangling seemed impossible.

Susan had finally come upon a set of beliefs that her husband could not validate or believe. He had been her champion when she accused others of horrible crimes—day care providers, her own mother and father—but now she was accusing *him* of raping her as an adolescent. How could he continue to "believe the victim," when he, himself, was the supposed perpetrator?

Although such a revelation might have been the end of most marriages, the Polk union stumbled on. Felix told friends that he still loved Susan, but she was going through a rough patch. His patients and fellow therapists continued to look up to him as a powerful man, but the influence he had always wielded over his wife was slipping. Throughout his marriage to Susan, his work had sustained him, but Susan was always what he cared about most, and now she was coming to hate him. She no longer wanted to share her bed with her husband, and with each new memory, she became more convinced that she had never voluntarily fallen in love with her therapist. She believed he had abused his exalted position as her therapist to hypnotize and coerce her into a lifetime of obedience.

In an attempt to clear up their growing problems, Felix found a psychiatrist for Susan, but according to her, Felix was nervous about her going and warned her not to discuss how the two met. That Susan was Felix's patient was a secret even in the family. They told their sons they met when Susan was Felix's student. While many of Felix's peers knew about his transgression when it occurred, over the years his younger acolytes and new acquaintances did not. A reputable therapist informed of the relationship by Susan would have felt obliged to report him, and even if charges weren't brought, Felix would have been shamed by the disclosure.

"I was terrified of Felix and I [was] sad that he hypnotized me, raped me, and that he made me marry him. But I am not allowed to tell the psychiatrist this," Susan said. "The therapist kept asking me about Felix and I was too afraid to tell him [much of] anything."

Eventually she told the therapist a little. She said that her husband was the same age as her father and that he was far too controlling. The psychiatrist told her, " I think you're headed for a divorce."

When Susan told Felix about the session, "he panicked," she said. With Felix's encouragement, Susan wrote a letter to the therapist about the good things in her marriage. Even with Susan's new memories, the marriage hadn't completely collapsed. "We weren't at daggers drawn," Susan said tellingly. "I was still trying to fulfill my role as a wife."

Nevertheless, she fantasized about having her own bed and her own room. She could no longer stand to be sleeping with him. She demanded, "Leave our bed. I don't want to live with you anymore." Yet at his insistence, she says, they continued to have sex. While once she had enjoyed making love, she now was convinced that the only kind of sex they ever had was rape. "He is sexually violent, choking me with his arm against my windpipe, biting and scratching and squeezing." She claimed that her husband had "always bitten, scratched, and raped," but as their marriage deteriorated, "there is more violence and he more frequently draws blood." No friends or family ever noticed any marks on Susan (Felix told a close friend—who was unaware of Susan's account—that Susan begged him to "hurt me, scratch me" and almost choke her to death. "They sexually teased and taunted one another," the friend said.)

Over time, Susan's "flashbacks" grew more intricate, twisted, and delusional. In one of her "recovered memories" she recalled Felix's involvement with the CIA and with the Israeli spy agency, Mossad, claiming that Felix placed her in a trance and told her she needed a code name. She chose that of one of her favorite characters: Alice Liddell, the little girl for whom Lewis Carroll wrote *Alice in Wonderland*. That too was a story of a girl who lived in two worlds written by an older man who idolized the girl. These newly recovered memories about her husband-therapist only increased her rampant sense of self-righteousness. Everything in their common history zoomed into focus. She remembered how he wanted her to deliver Adam naturally even though he was a breach baby. She concluded he must have wanted her to die in childbirth, and when she became ill after Adam's birth—she now suspected her husband had been trying to poison her.

At home, the two established a combative pattern of communication. In her low-key, passive-aggressive manner, Susan provoked Felix with cruel, biting words, sometimes calling him "a dirty Jew" or mocking what she claimed was his little penis—in front of their sons. He would respond by saying she was crazy and delusional.

For Felix to question her sanity was, for Susan, the greatest hurt he could deliver. She believed there was nothing worse than a sane person, which she believed she was, being told she's crazy.

"You'll never get custody of the kids," she recalls him saying to her. If she proceeded with a divorce he warned, "You aren't fit. You had better think about the consequences." That sounded like a death threat to her: "I thought nobody would kill someone over wanting to leave."

Susan and Felix began shoving each other around the room. Although he was four inches taller and fifty pounds heavier, Felix was obviously frightened of Susan, often barricading himself in a spare room at night. The next day it would start again. Any affection or attention Felix showered on his wife only infuriated her. Now, when he heard the clink of keys and dashed out to learn where his wife was going, she interpreted that as an effort to control her. During parties when he stood beside her at the punch bowl, she believed he was trying to curtail her socialization. She felt he was becoming increasingly vigilant, demanding to know where she was going and when she would return.

SUSAN'S CONSTANT STATE OF PARANOIA, HER FIGHTS WITH FELIX, AND THEIR increasing anger toward one another were taking their toll on their sons, who were picking fights and acting out. When they attacked another kid, broke school rules, or failed a test their mother would take them out for a special lunch and tell them they were brilliant, talented, and had done nothing wrong.

Felix believed that in many families one child is selected as the scapegoat, and in their family Eli held that position. He was suspended from school nineteen times for a range of offenses, including viciously harassing other students. Even so, neither he nor Susan believed he had done anything worse than what other kids did. Susan took Felix's theory, which was not his alone, and expanded it. As Eli was marked for failure, she believed Felix had chosen Adam to succeed. When he did well, she believed it wasn't because Adam had worked hard but because his father had intervened to help Adam. In fact, Adam remembers exactly the day he decided he wanted to play football for the best team in the nation. He knew what he must do: "Bust my ass to get good grades," which he did, only to have his mother say his success was predetermined.

Susan was developing a bunker mentality toward every aspect of her world. When the cops were called to quell a noisy party, she would accuse them of targeting her family. After Gabriel was suspended from school, she confronted the principal and told him, "Fuck you." Residents found it odd that while Susan fought, Felix would stand beside her, saying nothing. When a neighbor's gardener pruned three feet from a nine-foot hedge *on the neighbor's property*, Susan reduced their housekeeper to tears. She accused another neighbor of pitching poison meatballs to the Polk dogs. She accused Felix, too, of poisoning their pooches. There was always so much commotion; firecrackers exploding, loud parties, or family screaming matches that when the next-door neighbors sold their house they felt compelled by law to disclose to prospective buyers that the Polks were a nuisance.

The worst incident of family violence occurred in the fall of 2000, when Felix agreed to move his office out of the house. He asked Susan to help find rental space, to which she replied, "Go find your own. I'm going to the beach." After packing her beach bag, she says, Felix confronted her: "Where do you think you're going?" From there, the story gets more complicated, and according to two conflicting versions he either hit his wife or knocked off her baseball cap. Regardless, the disputed action caused the two to argue bitterly. Susan smashed their wedding plates on the kitchen floor. Felix blocked her way, she says, and yelled, "Go to your room!" She claims he "dragged" her up the stairs. Hearing the commotion, Eli and Adam followed. Susan says that her husband "had me in a corner when he yelled, 'You make me so mad I could just hit you!' " Where upon Eli slugged his mother in the mouth. She staggered back across the bed, blood spouting from her lip, requiring five stitches. In a voice tinged with sadness, Eli now says that was the worst thing he's ever done. "That's something I have to live with the rest of my life."

Adam went to call the cops, but his father chased after him in an attempt to stop him. "It was one of the craziest things I'd ever seen," Adam recalled. "They both believed something had happened and they wanted to keep it hidden." An expert on adolescence and the family was unable to save his own from emotional destruction. Adam thought both parents were nuts. He was irritated with his father for not speaking directly about what had happened, and he felt sorry for his mother, whom he knew was delusional and who could provoke almost anyone to extreme anger.

Throughout this time of rising tension, Susan began experiencing numbness in her hands and feet; symptoms that Felix suspected might be early signs of multiple sclerosis. Susan developed her own theory of what was causing those symptoms. Why, she wondered, was Felix offering her wine in the evening? She stopped accepting the glass but then, she said, he started offering her tea or coffee in the morning. When she drank the coffee he prepared, she felt drowsy. Once again, Susan suspected her husband was trying to drug or poison her.

Although medical tests showed no signs of an onset of MS in Susan, Felix continued to tell friends and patients his wife had MS but advised them not to discuss it with her because she didn't want anyone to know. He told one of his student-confidants that he believed it was the MS that "made my wife so crazy," and confided to his most trusted patient, Joel Tepper, that because of her MS, Susan "was getting her life together," because she did not have long to live.

Did Felix honestly believe that Susan was dying, despite the doctor's findings to the contrary? Was he seeking sympathy? Or was he just ashamed of his new situation and anxious to come up with a storyline? It would have been mortifying for a respected therapist to have his patient-wife dive off the deep end—especially when he had long claimed to have cured her of schizophrenia. But whatever his rationalizations may have been, the end results were obvious: Felix refused to acknowledge that Susan was delusional and that he had fed those delusions. Their fraught marriage became even worse, overtaking both their lives and the lives of their children.

Felix at age six. Not long after this photo was taken, his family was forced to flee the Nazis in Vienna.

Taken during Felix's tumultuous time in the navy, this shot shows the composed exterior that concealed his troubled mental state.

Despite the turmoil of the Holocaust, the Polk family never lost its appreciation for classical music. Both Felix's parents played piano, and long after they came to the United States, Felix and his sister, Evelyn, often played music together, with Evelyn on the piano and Felix on the cello.

Dick and Helen Bolling on their wedding day. Eventually Dick would leave Helen for another woman, but not before he fathered David and Susan.

A young Susan with her mother, Helen, and brother, David. Helen worked full time and, although she had only a ninth grade education, she taught her children to appreciate art and literature.

Susan at age fifteen, around the time that she started her therapy with Felix.

Susan at age nineteen (center), with her mother (left) and David (right). This is about the time that she fell in love with her therapist.

Susan and Felix before they were married

Felix with his arm around Susan at Sheila Byrns's graduation party from graduate school. Sheila is seated next to Susan.

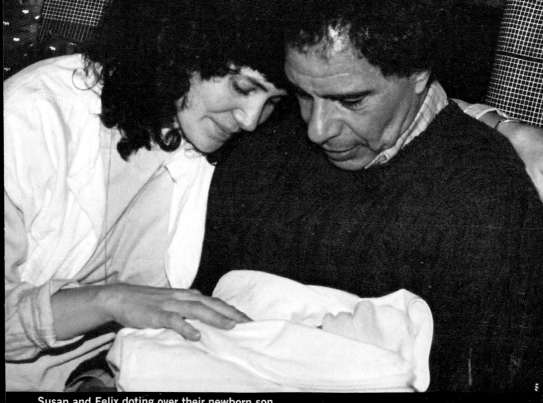

Susan and Felix doting over their newborn son

While the trial would call into question Felix's involvement with his sons, Adam and Gabe maintained their father never stopped loving every member of his family.

Susan and her young son in the garden of their expansive Berkeley home. Because Susan managed their real estate investments, she sent their sons to part-time daycare, a decision that would have major repercussions.

Felix tried to instill a love of the outdoors in his family, often taking Susan and the boys on his favorite hikes on Mount Tamalpais and in other state parks.

Felix and Eli. While future events would cloud and ultimately sour their relationship, Felix never gave up on his middle son, although Eli, like his mother, came to loathe his father.

In better times, Susan and Felix warmly celebrated one another's birthdays at home.

Susan, Gabriel, and Felix at a party for Felix's graduate students in their Berkeley home.

(from left to right) Adam, Felix, Eli, and Gabe at Felix's birthday party

Gabe, Susan, and Eli during a family trip to wine country. In the years before the turmoil, the family took frequent vacations, instilling a sense of worldliness in the boys.

Their trip to Disneyland was the beginning of the end for the Polk family, as Susan's recovered memories, which previously had focused on her parents, soon found another target: Felix.

The Polks' Orinda County estate. Susan and Felix moved to this upscale community in hopes of starting over. Here, the kids threw wild parties, while Susan and Felix engaged in frequent disputes that eventually led to murder.

A view of the pool house where Felix was killed as seen from the main house.

During the trial, Susan, in a rare admission, stated that Felix had taught her to appreciate the outdoors.

As he grew older, Felix remained fit. Here he is on vacation.

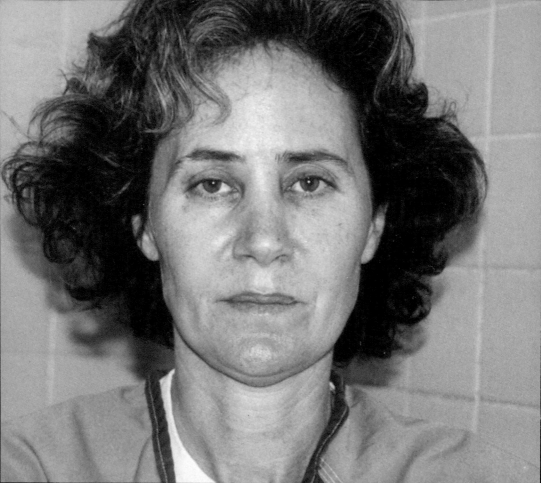

Susan's mug shot after her arrest for the murder of her husband

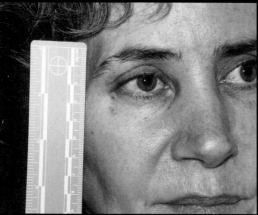

While her injuries appeared slight, Susan always maintained that Felix's death was the result of her defending herself from his attack.

A subject of contention at the trial, the footprints found by the police were one of Susan's most frequent examples that the Sheriff's department had tampered with the

When she was out on bail, Susan appeared happier and more relaxed than she had in years, spending time researching her case and enjoying the company of Eli and Dusty, their friendly yellow Lab.

Although Susan had been estranged from Helen and David for years, they became much closer during her trial, with Helen becoming one of her daughter's staunchest (and most effective) supporters both in the courtroom and on the sidewalk.

Susan's assistant, Valerie Harris, seated on a park bench with Gavel Groupies Catherine Baker and Jim Fulton (Tennis Jim).

A courtroom sketch by artist Joan Lynch of Susan (standing) questioning Detective Michael Costa (in the witness box), with Valerie Harris seated next to her at the defense table.

A courtroom sketch by artist Joan Lynch of Susan delivering her closing arguments. She displayed the photo of herself at age fifteen (in the background) to emphasize how young she

Every day as he left the courthouse with his files, prosecutor Paul Sequeira stopped to answer reporters' questions.

Gabe and Adam at the press conference after the reading of the verdict

7.

"TAKE ME TO JAIL!"

"COME HOME TO YOUR MOUNTAIN RETREAT! LEAVE THE NOISE AND CRAZI-
ness behind . . ."

Years later, the house the Polks purchased in Orinda, California, would be
marketed as a way to escape the "craziness" of quotidian life. That was something the Polks no doubt wished for as well, especially since by the time they
moved their family in the fall of 2000, Felix and Susan's marriage was already
tearing apart.

They were a family in trouble and desperately in need of a fresh start.
Gabriel and Eli had been booted out of their public school in Piedmont for
fighting and assorted misbehavior. Rumor had it that the Polks were forced out
of town, but a female friend of Gabriel's explained the real circumstances:
"Their whole family hated Piedmont and Piedmont hated their whole family."
Though the girl's mother interjected, "It was hard not to like Felix. He was
handsome, charming, intelligent. A very attractive man. A very compelling guy.
Very strong presence. I could see why she was enthralled." But by the time they
were leaving Piedmont, Susan Polk was anything but enthralled by her husband.

The village of Orinda is situated along the slopes of a mountain range and
traverses small valleys. Large, grassy regional parks ring the town. The high
school parking lot is jammed with students' SUVs and BMWs—and teachers'
Toyotas. Every year Orinda schools rate at or near the top on statewide tests.
The hamlet is sectioned by swim clubs, which dot the landscape providing war-
like competitions that fill up summer calendars on doublewide refrigerators.
Residents learn about violent crime—elsewhere—on the ten o'clock news.
Older inhabitants are only now growing used to locking their front doors.

Recently, the police issued a warning to citizens to remove keys from the ignition when they park their cars.

Decidedly suburban, wealthy, and culturally sedate, many residents consider it a paradisiacal place to raise a family. Once it was a weekend retreat for residents from San Francisco and Oakland seeking hot, dry summers and mocha-colored rolling hills. A few properties still have stables, and on some hillsides, cattle still graze. The town of seventeen thousand, a twenty-minute drive east of San Francisco, has its share of boxcar homes with basketball nets draped over stylish garage doors as well as tasteful, older homes that are designed more for living than for status. Some people who were burned out of their homes in the Oakland-Berkeley firestorm of 1991 resettled in Orinda, as did vagabond executives and their families. In recent years, the town has seen a number of column-and-cobblestone homes built for people who have more money than taste. Many built oversize homes with intimidating, tall front doors and high ceilings on vast pieces of property, protected from camellia-munching deer by iron gates along meandering country roads. Others purchased million-dollar fixer-uppers, preserved the outside wall and built homes to their specifications with enough land for small vineyards, waterfalls, and personal putting greens. This is still *Leave It to Beaver* land, with stay-at-home moms serving as foot soldiers for school snack bars, trips, and fundraisers.

With the move to their new home, Felix and Susan hoped, in that desperate way that doomed couples sometimes do, that the beauty of a new setting would make everything better. Perhaps, in their private "mountain retreat," they could bind the ruptures of a mortally wounded relationship and sooth the demons in Susan's mind.

Roger Deakins, a former hippie turned successful entrepreneur, who sold his Orinda house to the Polks, could see how troubled their relationship was. Deakins spent years lovingly constructing his Orinda house. The care and artistry he lavished on the residence would entice the Polks to plunk down $1.8 million for the estate. Deakins met Susan Polk when she and Gabe toured the house in the early fall of 2000, and from that first interaction, he took Susan to be a confident and self-possessed woman. Their second meeting, though, shocked Deakins. On that occasion, Susan was with Felix when the two dropped by to measure the living room for one of their oriental rugs. This time she appeared guarded. Her speech was lower; her body looked smaller and crunched up. On all matters, she deferred to her husband. Deakins was certain that she was an oppressed woman.

When they departed, Deakins turned to his wife and said, "What did we just see?" They'd encountered May/December relationships before, but never anything like this. Deakins was advised by his realtor not to deal with Susan but only with her husband. The orders had come from Felix through his realtor, a former patient of his. Deakins imagined that Felix was insanely jealous and didn't want his wife conversing with another man, although it could have been Felix's attempt to save Deakins from complications of dealings with Susan.

Weeks later, after the Polks had moved in, Roger Deakins returned to repair the drains. Susan Polk was there without her husband. Again she seemed bigger, taller, and spoke louder and more freely. "She was a completely different person without him," he concluded. He would not be the only outsider to describe Susan Polk as someone who appeared intimidated by her husband.

The new Polk house had graceful views from every angle, although it was more artistic than practical. The three-thousand-foot craftsman house was not ideally designed for a family with children. The land lacked the suburban prerequisite: a flat yard for swing sets, sandboxes, and volleyball courts. The house was disjointed, with only two, possibly three, bedrooms in the main building. Family members could go hours or even days without bumping into one another. Felix, Susan, and Gabriel lived in the main house; Eli and Adam shared the pool house, which was far enough away from the main household for incidents to occur that would go undetected. The sum of these pieces was a house that had the perfect setting for the minor crimes and misbehaviors of adolescents, or worse.

Spread across more than an acre of oak-studded hillside, the property seems to stand alone. The street on which it sits is so long and winding that many people who've lived in the town for decades have never ventured there. The Polk house, made of vertical grain virgin redwood, teak doors, Alaskan yellow cedar ceilings, terra-cotta floors, and Arts and Crafts lighting, is part art gallery. Even the wooden posts for the mailbox and garden hose are thick, well-sanded redwood. A pair of eight-hundred-dollar Japanese maples at the foot of the steps lends the house an Oriental feeling. Stained glass, mimicking twisted oak branches, peeks out from tall windows.

The kitchen was designed for the serious cook like Susan Polk, with a Viking range and a redwood slab against the left side of the refrigerator with circular openings for wine bottles within reach. Susan filled the pantry with her Minton china and bought only the finest kitchen equipment, including wood-handled knives and three knife sharpeners.

Although they were barely getting along, Susan and Felix shared a spacious, airy bedroom fit for an episode of *Cribs*. Windows overlooked the hills. A large fireplace was built into a Chinese pink and gray tile wall. In a poorer community their walk-in closet would suffice as a studio apartment. Below a wet bar in the bedroom was a safe for their most valuable possessions. Their spacious bathroom included his-and-hers sinks, a glass shower, and a Jacuzzi.

While all the Polks' homes had been beautiful, nothing compared to this one. Susan called it her dream house; for Felix it was the symbol of success and taste. They moved in in November 2000. Five months later, Susan Polk would flee her dream house and the sons she loved.

OF COURSE A MOVE TO A BEAUTIFUL HOUSE CANNOT UNDO ONE'S FATE. ELI enrolled in Miramonte High School where he briefly played on the school's football team. He also played rugby (on a team that had no connection to the school), excelling at the sport and becoming a leader on a team of older players. Eli had hoped that with encouragement from his coach, a rugby coach at Cal, he might go on to join the university team. Socially, Eli was an easy winner, and popular kids glommed onto him.

The Polks' new home became a party house, where kids could do drugs in the cottage by the pool. The local police grew used to being called to quell noisy parties. Soon enough they were on a first-name basis with the Polks' middle son. The cops thought of Eli as "a good kid who makes bad choices." At school he earned a reputation among teachers for being a polite doper who slept through class.

Though Eli was in his late teens, he still retained childlike qualities. He hated being away from home even on vacation, yet it tore at his soul to watch his parents bicker and fight. Gabriel, like Eli, was spending less time in school and more time with his mother, who needed her sons with her. He listened to his mother, who was fed up with the education system and had blown school off. The longer he stayed away, the harder it was to return. Both Eli and Gabriel trusted her and believed her when she declared their father was the cause of all their ills.

Meanwhile, Adam established himself *outside* his family. By 2000, he was president of his class at De La Salle High School, president of the Honors Society, and a linebacker on the school's famous football team, which would not lose a game for twelve years, the longest winning streak in high school or college sports. In a way, he did it to prove to himself that these were things *he had accomplished* and not as his mother had said, something his father had predetermined. Adam was so well liked by other kids' parents that they disregarded the strangeness of his family and encouraged their kids to hang out with him in the hope that some of his decency and drive might rub off on them.

Adam acquired distance from his family, a perspective that would play a part in the tragedy that would befall them. He hardly spent any time at home. On school nights, Adam returned at 7:00 PM, about the time his father quit work, and he studied until 11:00 every night. The eldest son was able to escape much of the day-to-day drama. Adam thought his mother was 80 percent sane and 20 percent delusional, "and that her twenty percent is completely unpredictable, there's no way for anybody to know what she's going to do next."

As the only son who recognized that Susan was delusional, Adam was also the only one who regularly spent time with his dad, eventually becoming his reluctant confidant. Eli found Adam's claims against Susan to be ridiculous, and he believed that his father had planted a little virus—the claim that his mother was crazy—in their family. For his part, Felix told friends that his house had become "the theater of the absurd."

In December 2000, sixteen-year-old Eli was expelled from Miramonte High and from the entire school district for possession of marijuana off campus during school hours and other offenses. He and his mother were convinced that the expulsion was unjust and that his father, who had spoken to the guidance counselor, was responsible.

By January 2001, disputes between Susan and Felix had escalated. In the course of an argument Felix threw a tower of newspapers at Susan, who then called the sheriff's department. When a deputy arrived, Susan complained about Felix *and* Eli. Although he was his mother's staunchest supporter, occasionally Eli, who was torn up by his parents' disputes, would agree with his father. Susan complained to the cops that both Felix *and Eli* had told her she was crazy, which she insisted wasn't true. When the deputy sheriff interviewed Felix and Eli, they each confirmed that Susan was imbalanced.

While Felix would never change his thinking, Eli, who was buffeted by the constant war, would. Susan was surprisingly vindictive. She complained that Eli was "uncontrollable," and she told the officer her son had hit her in the face months before and that he had made unauthorized charges on her credit card, purchasing *five* skateboards. She went on to announce that when she said she would seek a divorce, Felix had threatened her. She quoted him as saying; "I will do anything to stop you from divorcing me."

Before the officers left, Susan made a strange appeal: she asked that a large, stainless steel knife, which Eli owned, be removed from his room. Although both Felix and Eli agreed, it was a surprising request given what would eventually transpire.

The next day, Susan felt hopeless, sensing that Eli had gone over to his father's side. She engaged her husband in another argument. "Felix was ranting and raving," she would later write in her diary. He "threw my clothes on the floor after chasing me upstairs. He threatened to destroy all pictures of me." In his anger he smashed a Mission-style chair. After she announced again she was seeking a divorce, she claims he grabbed her and pushed her out the door. He told her she was taking the children down with her, and that he wouldn't let that happen; he would seek custody of their sons.

Whether it was Susan's warped processing of information or it was real, she said she was frightened of Felix. "He had been calling me ugly, vicious, evil, a criminal, and a swine," but while she was quick to list his accusations, she never said what names she called him. Susan grew despondent. On January 17, 2001, she caught a bus to Yosemite, where they had hiked as a family when the boys were younger. She downed a bottle of aspirin and fell asleep, awakening hours later to a ringing in her ears. She called home. Eli answered. Susan told him she loved him and that she was sorry everything had not worked out. A distraught Felix spoke to her.

Felix called 911. Susan was rushed by ambulance to the Tuolumne General Hospital, where she was placed in intensive care. Eli said that his father jumped on it as an opportunity. He told Eli, "We need to get her help! She needs to be on medicines and in a mental hospital!" Eli thought Felix was turning tragedy into a campaign to win back control of the family. Felix raced to Yosemite to be by Susan's side. She remained in the hospital for two days. He wanted her held for evaluation, but she would later say that he warned her not to explain how they met; he could lose his license and she and the boys would have nothing to live on. She briefly met with a psychiatrist who found her to be an intelligent woman disturbed by the breakup of her family and not at all delusional. But the peace between the husband and the wife he saved from suicide was only momentary.

Meanwhile, Felix told friends Susan had suffered a nervous breakdown. Felix's oldest friend and mentor, a fellow therapist, believed that despite the growing nastiness of their marriage, nothing could separate the two. They had what he called "an osmotic relationship." Felix brought out the sadistic in Susan, and Susan brought out the masochistic in Felix. (Although it could easily be seen the other way around.) It was as if they shared the same bloodstream, the friend observed, neither could live nor feel whole without the other. He couldn't stop loving her and she had no life apart from him. For most of her life, Felix had been her only adult contact, her translator to the real world.

Felix had always been so obsessed with Susan that Adam once said his father should never have had children. But with his wife on the verge of leaving, he listened to Adam, who told him he needed to be a participatory dad. Felix began paying attention to his sons. He started to show his love for them in ways they keenly felt. He went to all of Adam's football practices and games. He saw every one of Adam's wrestling matches from his sophomore year on. Felix treated Adam as if he were a grown man as well as a boy, mature before his time, which, in fact, Adam was. As the only one who was able to bridge both sides, Adam avoided conversations with his mother about her conspiracy theories and engaged her instead in discussions about films and literature.

Susan's thoughts were strongly influenced by the books she read, and so it was only natural that when she began reading about psychics she came to believe she possessed supernatural abilities. Both Susan and Felix thought that some people had psychic abilities, although it's not known if Felix encouraged Susan, especially after she began targeting her mate. She saw herself as a medium who could see into people's secret lives and even into the future. Susan's belief in her psychic powers intermingled with some of her "recovered memories," and she was convinced Felix and his closest male friends were part of what she called the "Jewish network," a cabal of secretive men who were agents of the Israeli Mossad. Afraid and angered by these imaginary activities, she threatened to contact the FBI. Felix sloughed off her threats with a shrug. Other times, he would respond by telling her, "Oh, Susan, You're crazy," which only further infuriated her.

Given the anger and craziness that was directed his way on a daily basis, it's remarkable that Felix didn't take steps to extricate himself from the marriage. It didn't make sense. There was nothing she could say or do that could change how he felt. He couldn't stop loving her. Adam watched their verbal jousting and thought that if he were his father, "I would have moved on." But neither parent could budge from their unique collaboration.

In the winter of 2001, after announcing she was seeking a divorce, Susan, who earlier had demanded Felix "leave our bed," finally moved her husband's belongings "out of my room" and into the downstairs bedroom. She couldn't sleep with him anymore. For that, she said, "There was hell to pay." He told her, "Without me you'll go down the drain."

She wasn't the helpless young thing anymore and he knew it. She knew their finances better than he. She knew that after a divorce she could support herself with assets they had accumulated during their marriage. Her rage against her husband gave her power she had not previously tapped.

On March 16, 2001, she wrote a letter "to document the unethical conduct of Felix Polk, a licensed clinical psychologist." She placed the letter in the safe below the wet bar in their bedroom. In the letter, she recounted how they met in 1972. She claimed, "During the course of therapy, I was drugged by Felix and coerced into having a sexual relationship with him. We married in 1982."

In the letter, when describing her recovered memories, she refers to them as "flashbacks." This change in terminology demonstrated a noted shift within Susan, who had devised a new way to understand what Felix had done to her. While initially, she attributed her recollections about his hypnotizing her and having sex with her to recovered memory, by 2001 she had come to a different conclusion. Given the impossibility in her mind that she might be delusional, she wrote that her husband must have fed her hallucinogens. She said that while he "most certainly (would) deny using hallucinogens, I know of no other way to account for the flashbacks which I experienced during that time period."

In later years, Susan would periodically refer to what she called her husband's "threats," and she would imitate her husband saying, "I could just kill ya," or "I'm gonna kill ya." He would say it, she said, with a little smile. What he may have said in exasperation, she may have misinterpreted, but in any case, she stuck to her insistence that Felix meant to kill her, though only her son Eli would back up her claim.

While his family life was in freefall, Felix flew to Germany to address an international conference of some five hundred psychotherapists on trauma therapy. He said nothing about the trauma of his daily existence, citing only historical examples of how beneficial psychodrama or reenacting his experience of leaving his nursemaid Katya had been for him twenty-five years before. "Since that day," he said, "I have felt much lighter in my life." He referred to some of his trauma patients whom he treated with reenactment therapy. "Maintaining a more detached therapeutic posture will tend to limit effectiveness," he told his audience, recommending a combination of mainstream and fringe techniques, including guided fantasy, hypnosis, cathartic work, dream analysis, transference, and countertransference to enable patients to "recover memories" of early trauma and deal with them. Despite personal experience with his wife's questionable "recovered memory," on the circuit he remained a true believer.

ON MARCH 28, 2001, FELIX AND SUSAN HAD ANOTHER NASTY FIGHT. AT THE height of it Susan kicked Felix, and this time he called the cops. He claimed she was a danger to herself and to him and asked that she be held for seventy-two-hour observation. Deputies said they lacked probable cause to take her in. When they tried to question her, Susan was uncooperative except to say that she did not plan on hurting herself or her husband, though she warned that if provoked, she would defend herself.

Susan yelled at the deputy that she wanted Felix taken away, and if he didn't leave, then she demanded: "Take me to jail!" She reached over and with her open hand, slapped Felix on the cheek. "Now, take me to jail!" she demanded, unafraid of the consequences. She got her wish.

After a night in jail, she was released. Felix obtained a one-week temporary restraining order, forcing Susan to find another place to live. She reestablished herself in the castlelike Claremont Hotel in the hills above Berkeley, where parents of Berkeley students mingle in the cavernous lobby and at the Olympic-size pool and spa with conventioneers and visiting professors. She kept to herself, appreciating her sudden solitude. She felt as though she were recovering from a terrible accident.

When the weeklong restraining order ran out, Susan skulked back home only to discover that Eli was still against her. On April 17, Susan and Eli argued; he wanted her to drive him to a friend's house, but when she refused, Eli grabbed his mother by the shoulders and started pushing her out the front door. Susan called the cops but refused to press charges. That same day, the distraught Eli asked Felix to move out. When Felix refused, Eli turned to his mother and asked her to go. He couldn't stand the tension. Convinced her sons were aligned with their father, Susan agreed to leave.

The next morning, she rented a house down a pitted gravel road at Stinson Beach, an exquisite beach community of wood houses tucked into sand dunes, a forty-minute drive from San Francisco. At night, she fell asleep to the rhythmic thrashing of the waves. Susan Polk, whose main role in life was devoted mother, was willing to leave her sons behind. She thought that if she were out of the picture, then Felix would have no reason to work against them, as she was convinced he was doing. And she didn't like the way her sons were behaving toward her either. She thought they had become too much like their father. She felt they had contempt for her and that they enjoyed bullying her. She liked being on her own. In her diary she wrote that if she remained at home, "I would get killed."

AS THE SUN POURED INTO HER BEACH FLAT, SHE SKETCHED, READ, AND hiked along the windswept coast. She thought about her life and in what she called a "moment of insanity," she could not recall if her father had molested her or if that was just a dream. If it had not happened, then someone must have implanted the idea in her head, creating a false memory. Her prime suspect was Felix.

When her boys came to visit she drew their portraits. And given how much she says she hated her husband it's surprising that she drew a sketch of him that bore his likeness.

In a last-ditch effort—ordered by the court on April 24, 2001, while she was still at the beach house—Felix, Susan, and their two younger sons, Eli and Gabe, met with Jimmy Thrower, a court-appointed mediator. Eli's analysis, which he would later refute, provided the backbone for Mr. Thrower's report. Eli said his mother had "a serious problem," that "she gets irrational and makes up stuff about father (i.e. , . . . having affairs, doing experiments on people in therapy). Eli says mother will just begin talking bad about father . . . Eli feels that the divorce could have been avoided if mother would have gotten treatment earlier."

Eli told Mr. Thrower that Susan was "pissed" with him for siding with his father but that "he feels greater peace with father in the home," even though he loves his mother.

In the sessions with Mr. Thrower, neither Susan nor Felix could agree on even the most basic information, such as how many hours Felix worked each week or what medication Susan had taken. Felix said that the psychiatrist she had seen had prescribed Respridal, an antidelusional medication, while Susan claimed she had been given Restoril, a sedative for panic attacks. She firmly explained that she was not in treatment, did not take meds, nor had she ever really been in treatment "other than psychotherapy with Felix." Susan told Mr. Thrower it was best for everyone that she and her husband move on with their lives so that, in Jimmy Thrower's words, "the boys aren't torn between their loyalty between both parents." She suspected the mediator would side with Felix, "due to Felix's status."

Mr. Thrower concluded, "Mother should consider a program of specialized treatment for past physical and sexual abuse issues . . . ," and, most remarkably, he recommended, "Parents may benefit from a program of anger management."

Perhaps Mr. Thrower had nothing in his arsenal that could do anything to ameliorate what was happening or what would happen. Anger was merely the end result of the tale of two Polks, and as long as they were in contact with one another, there was no hope that their combat could be managed or controlled.

While still at the beach, Susan dreamed that Felix used his hypnotic, persuasive voice to persuade her to return to him. He sounded so kind and gentle. A part of her responded. A part of her was crying about missing him. But she knew better and in the dream she turned him down. She thought there must still be a little child in her wanting to be cared for and loved. While she put up a good front, occasionally, Susan doubted herself, sometimes wondering if Felix was right and she was actually delusional. Maybe he wasn't the ogre; maybe he was telling her the truth. Maybe he hadn't hypnotized her. Maybe he hadn't raped her. But then she marshaled her facts. Susan suspected Felix was having an affair with his onetime student and closest friend, Sheila Bryns. Susan knew that Felix and Sheila celebrated the anniversary of their first meeting and that Sheila gave Felix gold cufflinks and luxurious European ties—forgetting the expensive gifts his friend had given Susan and the boys. She was convinced Sheila was in love with her husband. In her diary, Susan wondered "if it is reasonable and normal" for a therapist to receive "thousands of dollars of gifts" from a female patient. "Maybe Felix is right and I am delusional for suspecting that he was having an affair with Sheila, though I did see them kissing once. Oh well. . . . Maybe I imagined that Felix hypnotized me in therapy, and I am having delusions about him doing that. Hmmm? And so it goes."

Her self-doubt would evaporate as suddenly as it began, and Susan's anger toward her husband would continue to mount. She filed an application for a domestic violence prevention order against Frank Felix Polk, height 5'9", weight 170, gray hair and hazel eyes. She wrote: "THIS SITUATION IS URGENT, AS THERE HAS BEEN RECENT VIOLENCE AND BILLS ARE COMING DUE SOON."

In late May, she returned home from Stinson Beach, only to plan another trip; she would take Eli to Paris. She was determined "to start to live life," and to take her middle son, who, she thought, needed to heal after his violent outburst against her. In the weeks before they left she watched French movies on their wide-screen TV every night; movies that were full of intrigue, sex, and "romantic or sentimental expressions of high feeling." She planned their itinerary: Versailles, Musée d'Orsay, the Musée National Picasso, Notre Dame, where she looked forward to the artfully grotesque stone gargoyles.

But Paris didn't work out as Susan planned. On the flight over, a stewardess ordered her to wear shoes when padding up and down the aisles. The two argued. On her laptop she noted: "Stewardesses like therapists are not there to help . . . Helpers tend to help themselves."

The problems continued on their arrival in Paris. Eli slept a lot, lacking his mother's interest in art and history. It was impossible for Eli to enjoy himself. The son of a PhD was a high school dropout. He felt himself a failure. He feared he had no future and that as an adult Adam would have to take care of him. He hated Paris, had nightmares, and was homesick. Susan's response was to blame her husband. She thought he had done such damage.

In Paris, Eli bought himself a pinstripe suit. "But Eli," his mother advised, "you have nowhere to wear it to."

He bought it to wear to proms and school dances. It made Susan weep.

She also used her diary to reaffirm her life goals, most of which were never far from the theme of Felix. She vowed never to talk to Felix, never abandon Eli and obtain financial security.

When Susan tried to take Eli to a restaurant on the Left Bank, near

Montparnasse, the quarter that had housed exiled artists, writers, and poets, they got lost. Eli berated his mother for not being as knowledgeable as his father and for not doing anything right. He told her she needed to be nice to his dad and that they couldn't survive without him. He felt guilty spending his father's money when his dad, who always wanted to be with them, was not there. To compensate, he bought his father a $350 carved stone lion, a Faconnable shirt, and a wallet. Missing his friends and home, he called Felix and asked his father to make arrangements for him to fly home. Only rarely did Eli reach out to his father, but when he did, Felix obliged.

Susan stayed on a few more days. Upset with her middle son, she returned home early, her vacation having done little to lift her spirits. In June 2001, she wrote about her favorite subject, hating Felix.

"I detest every minute in his presence. I MUST LEAVE," she wrote. She thought her husband acted like a Greek God who "could toy with the lives of us mere mortals." Given the powers she attributed to him, not even a divorce would extricate her from him.

As her life was spinning out of control, she came to hate much of what she once had loved. She hated cleaning up after her family, the dogs, and the bird. During quiet moments she relaxed on the deck that overlooked distant hills, but instead of appreciating the natural beauty of the land, she was preoccupied with her burdens. She was a highly intelligent woman doing menial work, whose lament was not unlike that of many other women in her situation. No one appreciated what she did. She felt her sons only appreciated Felix.

She wanted to escape. She hated this country, hated what she saw as the smug American indifference. During the occasional moments when she and her husband had civil conversations about her feelings, he would warn her that she would encounter the same internal emotions no matter where she alighted.

Just before leaving on another trip, this one to Thailand, Susan wrote Felix that his "idea that I just remain your wife indefinitely while we are legally separated is like continuing as your property." She frostily signed it, "Sincerely, Susan Polk."

That letter sounded like a feminist lament. The next letter, though, was wilder: "Dear Felix, I can't go on living in a concentration camp. And I don't fancy being married to Dr. Mengele . . ."

She told her husband the children were old enough to decide which parent they wanted to be with. Both thought Gabe would choose her, as would Eli.

Her diary was full of vows and lists of how things would soon be different. On June 15, 2001, she vowed never to remarry or become involved in a parasitic relationship. She promised herself she would help her children, save money, buy a ski house, find a lawyer, and most surprisingly, find a therapist. She wrote how much she hated the word "therapist . . . the rapist," as she pointed out, before deciding maybe she didn't want a therapist after all.

In June, Susan and fourteen-year-old Gabriel flew to Koh Samui, Thailand, a tropical island paradise rimmed with palm trees and surrounded by warm turquoise waters. Believing the school system was corrupt, and wanting her sons by her side, Susan frequently pulled them out of school, mirroring her own lack of early education and that of her mother. She imagined that she and Gabriel would take bumpy elephant rides in the jungle and visit lost cities, but Thailand, like Paris, did not work out as planned. She found fault with her sub-par accommodations. She hated what she characterized as the duplicity of the Thai people. She despised their "constant bowing and scraping as if I believed for one instant that it was friendly and sincere." In her diaries she resolved, "never travel Asia am just not up to charade of politeness." She labeled the vacation "a debacle" and called her husband who made reservations for them at Club Med on the island of Phuket. She wasn't happy there either. She detested the "overweight Americans hanging out in packs at the bar and doing calisthenics together in the pool." Susan and Gabe booked a flight to Hawaii instead.

Gabriel called his mother a misanthrope. "He makes one remark after another about how I hate everybody," she wrote. "Why is it so difficult to explain that I don't hate everybody? I'm selective."

Later on in her diary she wrote a sad prayer: "God help me to do what I need to do: to have the courage to persevere; to remain available to my children, to proceed in the divorce in an intelligent way." She was looking for a place to restart her life. She considered her options, and came up with childlike preferences. She liked Spain in part because the people were fun and the land was beautiful. Jamaica had Bob Marley. She loved France. And she considered the Cayman Islands because she was convinced Felix had stashed his money there.

By late June 2001 Gabriel and Susan were in Kauai, when Eli, on a mission to save their vacation, joined them. The three boogie-boarded, snorkeled, and body surfed in the soft waves and warm air. "The only thing to mar it was to discover that I was over my limit on my credit card and [had] to [contact] Felix," Susan complained.

She objected when Felix reached her on vacation to help with their tax returns, insurance policy, and a loan application to help pay her expenses. Susan thought, "poor little Felix just can't find anything all by himself." When she objected to his bothering her he sounded amused. She couldn't imagine why.

In her diary she wrote: "Am convinced husband is insane." The next sentence read: "Gabe tells me [his dad] says he still loves me."

"I ADORE HER," HE TOLD FRIENDS JIM AND LISA CALHOUN. BOTH HAD BEEN his patients years before. Lisa, a hair stylist, sometimes did Susan's hair; Jim was the Polks' realtor. Many nights, Felix landed at the Calhouns for a home-cooked meal and companionship; Felix "was a gentleman about it," Lisa said. Despite his concern that Susan was eating away at their savings, "He wouldn't cut her off."

Once Susan had returned from Hawaii, Felix initiated a campaign to do whatever he could to make his wife love him. She had made fun of his "twisted yellow claws," his toenails that were cracked and blackened by fungus. For fifteen years he'd never been willing to do anything about them; now he was bleaching them. He was wearing new short-sleeved plaid button-down shirts, which Susan had always urged him to do. He bought khaki Ralph Lauren shorts. She understood what he was doing: "All of this as if he believes it were possible to make himself attractive to me. The man is insane."

She began to identify with Felix's first wife and wrote her a letter that she never sent. In it she apologized for any pain she may have caused. That Felix's two oldest children were happy, she said, must be due to Sharon. She referred to Felix's "deadly parenting," and called him "a malevolent person." Susan ended her letter with: "If there is ever anything I can do for you, I will do it gladly."

While her trips hadn't solved any problems, they allowed her time with her two younger sons away from Felix. Eli, Gabriel, and Susan, always close, bonded more. That summer, Eli and Gabriel asked for a family powwow at which they told their father they wanted to live with their mother, who was thinking of relocating to Montana. Felix told them the courts would never permit it. "Even if mom is crazy, which she isn't, I would still prefer to live with her," Gabriel told his father—according to Susan's diary—"because I love her, she's a good mom and she's fun to be with." Felix was so angry he tossed a bowl of macaroni and cheese at her and kicked the big-screen TV "which cost five thousand dollars, after overturning an antique Mission oak chair valued at over twenty-five hundred dollars." Even in anger, Susan Polk kept track of finances.

Adam, the truth sayer, arrived home later that day. He still loved both his parents, but he recognized the situation was untenable. He told his father it was time for the marriage to end. That autumn, Adam became a freshman at UCLA, further separating himself from the domestic turmoil. He thought his parents were two of the most intensely intelligent people he'd ever met. "Both of them are really well read. They can talk about literature, politics," he said, "then they just have personal lives that are really fucked up."

"It was just a bad marriage that should have ended way before it did," he said.

Felix felt he had no choice. He moved into one of their apartment units which he and Susan owned with Susan's mother and brother in the foothills of Berkeley. The separation would soon turn out to be not separate enough.

8.

ESCAPE TO MONTANA

FROM ALL THAT SHE HAD READ ONLINE, SUSAN FELT THAT MONTANA COULD provide an oasis from her tumultuous life. With her two youngest boys in tow, she planned to strike out north and make a new life for all of them. Gabe and Eli needed an escape from suburbia; in the Big Sky State shopping would no longer be a major pastime. Her boys could ski and she could hike. Although she knew no one in the state, or perhaps *because* she knew no one in the state, Susan was convinced that Montana, where the population averages six people per square mile, would restore her serenity. No one there would have heard Felix calling her crazy and delusional. She had often dreamed of a monastic life in the wilderness. "Montana was a chance to live some of my dreams," she said. "I had been living the life mapped out for me by my husband for so long. I wanted to do the things I always wanted to do: write, be an artist, do drawings and watercolors."

In September 2001, Susan, Eli, and Gabe and their three dogs set out on their adventure. Driving north through California and then Oregon, Susan was overwhelmed by a wonderful feeling of freedom. With each mile, she could feel Felix's control dissipate, as if she were escaping the gravitational force of a black hole. They had done it, she thought, escaped. She vowed they would never go back.

Driving into Montana, the air turned cool. The Aspen trees glowed golden, like they were lit from within. They settled into a four-bedroom cabin on forty-seven forested acres twenty-five minutes south of Bozeman. Susan rented the place from Christopher Harris, a fifty-five-year-old attorney and state legislator and his wife, Anna Harris, the twenty-seven-year-old Filipino mother of their three young daughters.

The log cabin sits by the Gallatin River, which flows from Yellowstone National Park and eventually surges into the Missouri River. Situated adjacent to Ted Turner's ranch, the cabin is built of fir logs and local stone. Walls and floors are made of hickory, maple, and marble. Built in 1911, the house has always been in the Harris family and is full of family antiques, including an old Victrola. Susan rented it for three months, at two thousand dollars a month. She paid in advance, explaining that she and her sons just needed to get away from California. Chris Harris thought she seemed high-strung and nervous, but rational. They trusted her; she'd impressed them with her appreciation of their cabin and their possessions.

Anna Harris, who supplements the family income by cashiering at the local grocery store, sometimes encountered Susan when she bought organic food. Anna noticed that her tenant looked haggard and tired. And while she knew nothing of Susan's history, she thought, "There was something going on inside her that she was trying to hide from people . . . She looked scared."

In Bozeman, Susan never felt the competitiveness among residents that she so detested in Californians. She attributed the difference to Montana winters, which are so harsh that, historically, citizens had to pull together to survive. In Montana, people had what Susan determined was "a whole different attitude."

"It is fall here, the soil is parched from a drought, and the trees look thirsty," she wrote in her diary.

Despite Felix's warning that moving would never solve any problems, she thought it did. Eli had been expelled from school the previous December. Gabe, who had failed several courses in eighth grade because he missed so much school, could use a change, and Susan, who had been "out of the workforce for over twenty years," could take courses at Montana State University.

"We were really welcomed," Susan recalled. The high school principal "said how delighted the school was with my children, how talented and bright they were. That was the sort of principal I dreamed of. All my children had to do was follow the rules." Both boys did well, especially in algebra, although in retrospect, Susan would remember Eli's academic performance as better than it actually was.

She would paint an idyllic tableau of their early days in Montana, but like everything else in her travels, it was not to last. Despite what would be a rapid disintegration of life there, Eli, too, remembers some of the time fondly. "We went on hikes. We talked about buying ATVs and about going hunting." Susan bought Eli his first car. He had turned sixteen only months before. Skiing was twenty minutes away. "It was my dream," he said. While Gabriel stuck it out, he found Montana boring and missed being home.

At night, with little to do, Susan and her two younger sons built a roaring fire in the massive stone fireplace, dimmed the lights, lit candles, sipped tea, munched cookies, and snuggled under blankets with their dogs, Tuffy, Ruffy, and Dusty. It was precisely the kind of lifestyle that Susan cherished, but neither of her two teenage sons would favor it in the long term.

She tried to normalize her relationship with Adam, e-mailing him at UCLA, with advice: "Devote yourself to research." On tough subjects such as astronomy, she told him to know his material and ask questions the books don't answer. She and Adam e-mailed about one of their favorite poets, Emily Dickinson. In her commentary Susan revealed some of her own thinking about how the public views people it considers crazy. Borrowing from one of Felix's heroes, R. D. Laing, she wrote that those who make the biggest contributions to art, religion, and literature could be considered "crazy, neurotic, or disturbed," when, she said, what they are really doing is holding up a mirror for the world to observe "the insanity of our sane world."

Despite the sometimes warm exchange of e-mails, she was "incredibly sad" about her oldest son, whom she believed was "gone in more ways than one." When Adam called, she wanted to say, "Just leave me alone. Don't bother me," but instead they talked about "dogs, classes, and parking spaces."

With her nascent interest in psychics she was now reading books about people said to have telepathic abilities, and she began working with tarot cards. In a humorous aside, she wrote Adam, who was convinced he could understand his mother's thinking by the books she was reading, "Am not yet collecting crystals or wearing long dangling earrings, patchouli oil, and flowing ankle-length robes. Do, however, believe in aromatherapy." She added that she was having "some discipline issues with Eli—the same old thing. Old habits are hard to break."

BEFORE SHE LEFT FOR MONTANA, SUSAN AND FELIX HAD AGREED TO SELL their house. Susan wrote Felix a three-page letter meticulously outlining her plans. She wrote she was taking the boys, the dogs, and "some pieces of furniture which are important to the boys and which will not interfere with the appearance of the house while it is being displayed for sale." She advised, "I do expect to return *after* the sale of the house for furniture, rugs, artwork, and any of my belongings which I leave behind." In a snippy aside, she promised to "handle the accounts before I leave as usual. I will have business relating to the rental properties forwarded to me in Montana as you were not able to handle it when I left you in charge." It had taken years, yet just as in his first marriage, Felix again played the role of the household schlemiel.

Like an attorney, Susan considered Felix's objections to the move and focused on the most serious one: "You don't want to lose your children." Her response provides a snapshot of how she viewed their life: She denied brainwashing their sons and told Felix his behavior, not hers, was turning their boys against him. She said she thought it was important that their sons "have a father as a resource: a reasonable, mature, unselfish father who is primarily concerned with his children's best interests rather than with using his children as leverage."

She accused him of threatening to kill her and himself. She claimed he'd warned he would quit work and stop providing for the family, and that he'd return to court to stop Eli and Gabe from joining her out of state. Undeterred, Susan promised to proceed with her plans and said she assumed Felix eventually would come to his senses.

Felix was miserable. He wanted his family back. He told Susan and the boys he'd been diagnosed with prostate cancer, though they would later learn that this wasn't true. Not even the threat of his dying would change what mattered most to him. He felt uncomfortable telling many friends how bad things were. It was easier to come up with a cover story. The fact was he had no control over the situation. He knew his wife needed therapy and medication, but no amount of coaxing would convince her that was so. Although he was an expert on adolescent psychology, he rarely could communicate with his two adolescent sons.

A close friend told him he needed to be less morose. He was still a successful, handsome man who could attract women twenty years younger than he. Felix wasn't interested. Twice he had married, and twice he had failed. No one interested him but Susan.

AS INDIAN SUMMER GAVE WAY TO AN EARLY WINTER CHILL, LIFE IN MONTANA became less idyllic. Susan caught Eli stealing money from her wallet to buy pot. She purchased a safe and even confided in Felix that Eli was posing problems again. She had thought that by taking him out of his environment, he would change. Susan and Eli argued. Their arguments escalated. One or both of the boys destroyed some of the cabin's antique furniture. Susan and Eli had one final fight—though neither one will say what the argument was about. When Eli used offensive language, Susan thought he sounded just like his dad. "If you're going to talk to me that way, you can't live with me. You can live with your father," she announced.

Eli bounded for his truck and rumbled back to California. Susan would later regret what she had done. "I should have understood," she said. Eli had been "very disrespectful in the way his father encouraged him to be," she said. It wasn't the boy's fault.

After that, Susan and Gabe didn't last long. The perfect country life tumbled apart around her. She had managed to get away from Felix and yet failed to build a life without him. But she didn't—couldn't—see it that way. She still blamed Felix. His influence had grown like a cancer into her life. It was impossible to escape by simply moving away.

In mid-November 2001, while he was in Salt Lake City, Chris Harris took a cell call from Susan Polk. She told him that due to a family emergency she was driving home to the Bay Area.

The next day, the Harrises arrived at their cabin, where they discovered Susan had been in such a hurry that she left behind toothbrushes, a prescription for one of the dogs, and unwashed breakfast dishes. The couple surveyed the damage the Polks had wrought: A lawyer's three-tiered glass and wooden bookcase was gone; the books scattered over the floor. The wooden trim on a French window in the kitchen was destroyed. A teak wooden salad bowl was smashed and left under furniture. A mahogany inner door that led from one room to the next was missing. The Harrises later found it in the calf barn. Several doors had been kicked in. A chair, part of a set, was broken. It looked to the Harrises as though a son who had been locked out had pried his way into the house. They thought there had been a terrible fight.

"I didn't think she was nuts until I saw the damage for the first time," Chris Harris said. He gave her a new nickname: "the tenant from hell."

"What happened?" he demanded, when he called Susan Polk back.

She blamed the damage on an "intruder." There had never been an intruder on the property and Chris Harris was certain there had not been an intruder now. Had the intruder robbed them of their inner door? Harris asked. Susan claimed the autumn wind had blown the door open so often that she removed it. But the door was an inner door, and the Harrises knew that no outside storm could have reached that far inside. What about the smashed chair? he inquired. Susan said one of her sons sat in it, and it just fell apart. These were not delusions, they were transparent lies. Chris Harris called the sheriff's department. He thought about suing Susan Polk, but he decided against it because he had more important matters to consider, including his reelection.

It would be several months before Anna Harris would find something else the Polks had left behind, and it would be several years before she would comprehend the importance of the discovery. While cleaning the cabin, trying to return it to its previous luster, Anna lifted a mattress in what she assumed was one of the boys' rooms and came across the pages of what appeared to be a short story. She put it aside and went back to work. When she cleaned out the bureau in the same room, she found a second story hidden underneath the lining of a drawer. Both were printed on a laser printer.

She sat down to read them and found the writing was so filthy, so disgusting, that she would never forget the plotlines. The first story, found under the mattress, told of a wife and mother who waited for her husband to leave the house each day before she had sex with her son. From that union a child was born and was raised as though he were the child of both the mother and father. As soon as the father left the house again, the mother and son once again had sex.

The second story Anna Harris uncovered was even more shocking. This one was about a wife who murders her husband in their kitchen—her weapon of choice is a kitchen knife. In the story, the husband drives home, parks in the garage, and enters the kitchen, where his wife stabs him to death.

Anna Harris showed the stories to her sister, who also read them and was equally horrified. Since her guests were from California, Anna Harris assumed the stories were some sort of "sicko movie scenarios." She recalled that the wording of the stories was adultlike.

She brought the stories home, where she placed them above the refrigerator. There they remained for several years, until one day, she became concerned that as her oldest daughter was learning to read, she might discover them. Anna doesn't recall if she threw the stories out or if she hid them in a storage bin. Whatever the case, she was never able to find them again.

9.

"THINGS I WILL NOT MISS . . ."

THE TROUBLE THAT FOLLOWED ELI TO MONTANA FOLLOWED HIM HOME AGAIN. On Valentine's Day of 2002, Eli was in a serious fight at a Jack-in-the-Box in neighboring Moraga, a town slightly less affluent than Orinda. The incident and its aftermath would begin the final spiral of the Polk family. Eli was sixteen but large and intimidating for his age. An eighteen-year-old whom he only knew indirectly confronted him. "I just got sucked into it," Eli would later say, admitting he threw the first punch. The victim's friends would say that Eli wielded a roll of quarters or a Maglite. Eli denied it. In the course of the fight, Eli fractured his opponent's nose and smashed his face. He was charged with assault with a deadly weapon and battery causing serious bodily injury. He pled guilty to a felony. Susan knew what that was like and was distraught. In a letter she wrote but never sent to her sons, she contemplated suicide. And for once, she considered—albeit fleetingly—that she was at the root of the family's problems.

She began by telling her sons, "I leave you all my love." Her sense of priorities remained as they always had been. Her next piece of advice was for her boys to find good homes for the dogs. She said she couldn't stand to stay around to discover what other terrible event might befall their family. "I have concluded that perhaps all of these events are in some way connected to me." She determined that the only way to improve matters was to remove herself from the equation. She advised her sons to marry well, to use their money wisely. To remain on guard and "forsake violence."

On February 28, 2002, two weeks after his arrest, Eli was put on an electric monitor ankle bracelet and placed in his father's custody. He moved into his father's small Berkeley apartment and began attending Berkeley High School. Susan believed that her husband, unable to win his son's loyalty, had won control over him through the juvenile system, where he had trained a number of the probation officers and over which she was convinced he had influence. She offered to trade places and live in Felix's Berkeley apartment, so that Eli and Felix could live at home. But then she changed her mind. When Felix offered to live in the pool house with Eli, so the boy could still be at home, Susan turned him down.

Eli was not the only child with problems. When the precocious Gabriel was suspended from school for cruelly teasing a girl during lunch, he asked his mother, "What do you expect? I'm acting out, Mom."

Still upset over Eli's arrest, Susan made a remarkable offer to Felix, one that shows how much she truly wanted to separate from her husband. She offered to give up her children, the house, the contents, and the apartment buildings they jointly owned. She promised not to return or have any contact with the children until Felix's death.

Her offer was ignored by Felix and his attorney, Steven Landes. They were sure Susan would change her mind, as she often did. In her diary she lamented her son's fate: "Eli is homesick of course; he wants home and Mom, his dogs, and freshly baked cookies. He has instead a bleak cottage poisoned by the smell of an angry, sterile old man."

As she was considering leaving everything behind, she began to plan another fresh start—this time on her own and out of the country. In her diary, she set down a list that said a lot about how hermetic and bitter her interior life was while she retained a sense of beauty and of the possibilities of a life alone.

She listed what she would miss most, and at the top were her dogs: Dusty, the sweet yellow lab, Ruffy, a black Rottweiler, and Tuffy, the sharpie with the corkscrew tail. At home she would miss the views and stained glass windows and her flowers. She added that she'd miss Gabe and Eli. Methodically she recorded "Things I Will Not Miss:" Californians, the scorching heat of summer, her mother, her brother, Adam, and managing their apartments.

Another list included what she would look forward to. That included "being alone," having a vegetable garden, reading, thinking, sunning, stroking a dog, walking, swimming, sailing, painting, and traveling to a country where English was not the first language.

In her fantasy, she survives without others and the difficulties they bring, or the adjustments they require. In her diary she confided that she had lost all that mattered to her. Adam hated her as much as Felix, she asserted. "Goodbye Adam," she coolly wrote. "I have lost my children." Her mother, upset about financial disputes with her daughter, cut Susan out of her will. Susan wondered why she bothered to cook and clean if family members accused her of being "crazy and delusional."

AS FELIX HAD SUSPECTED, SUSAN CHANGED HER MIND AND WANTED HER sons again. "I do everything a full-time homemaker does from preparing meals for my children, assisting them with their homework, doing their laundry, chaperoning them when they are entertaining friends, taking care of them when they get sick, getting them to their appointments, and maintaining a clean, orderly household.

"If the court feels that I am not fit to have custody of my children, I request that a Restraining Order be issued against my husband Felix for my protection, and that I be provided with alimony effective immediately as I have no other source of income." She wrote as though she and Felix had no income from their real estate investments.

Felix still wanted to be with his wife and kids, but he knew his wife hated him and he told his friend Barry Morris, "My children don't love me."

"They do love you," Morris responded. "They'll come around."

While Felix believed it was harmful for Eli and Gabe to be with their mother, he knew that both were close to her. He was becoming despondent. He didn't want to live without his family, yet he felt powerless to do anything about it. Adam had been haranguing him to intervene and return his brothers to school. The man who lectured his peers on families and adolescent acting out no longer knew how he could reach his sons who hated him. He still loved his sons and Susan. He told friends he was contemplating suicide. What he didn't tell them was that he had a blue steel 38-caliber revolver, registered to Susan on August 9, 1985, in the closet of his Berkeley office. The gun was loaded.

Seeking to break the stalemate, Felix sought custody of their sons. In his declaration he wrote, "I have *never* physically abused or hit in any manner the Petitioner. I categorically deny that allegation. I also believe that I have never emotionally abused her in any way. What I hope to make clear to the court is that for the past three years our sons and I have been living in a sort of emotional hell with Petitioner becoming more and more explosive and delusional. I have been trying to save our marriage and protect the boys at the same time. I now see that that will not be possible."

The tone of the document was stronger than the feelings he expressed in person. Steve Landes, his attorney, felt he had "never been able to work up righteous anger" about his situation. According to Landes, Susan had the power in the family, and she used it to isolate Gabe and Eli from their father.

Flaunting his credentials, Felix Polk appealed to the court: "I am a clinical psychologist with a PhD from Berkeley. I have a substantial practice and teach at the American School of Psychology. I do not, however want to be in a position where I am diagnosing my spouse and will try to avoid, as much as humanly possible, that trap.

"It is my opinion that Susan is, for the present, unstable and very angry, and not just at me. Her relationship with the boys is difficult. All the boys are experiencing difficulties to varying degrees because of her behavior. She 'goes off' on people."

Then Felix addressed the issue he never wanted to recognize. In her divorce papers, Susan had stated that her husband had had sex with her when she was his sixteen-year-old patient. "While I believe it to be irrelevant I feel I must address the opening paragraphs of Susan's declaration concerning how we became involved. It is true that she comes from a very abusive home where she was the victim of her father. However, our version of history differs. We have been married twenty years and have three teenage children. Suffice it to say that this is no brief affair or insignificant relationship."

He concluded, "This is really not about the difficulties between Susan and myself at this point. This is about the children in that, at least on a temporary basis, until we get some sort of evaluation, I believe that it would be a problem leaving the boys in Susan's care. Her behavior is unpredictable, she cannot control her anger or her delusions."

Even in the heat of battle, Felix recommended that the court authorize an "evaluation," to determine what was best for the boys. Time and again, family members with problems were referred to therapists as if the mental health profession had storage lockers crammed with magic dust.

ORINDA RESIDENTS HAD GROWN ACCUSTOMED TO THE POLK BOYS' BOISTER-ous parties. They had noticed too that Susan did not show up for her sons' soccer games the way other mothers did, and although she was a stay-at-home mom, she often didn't pick her sons up. Once when she left Eli stranded after a game, an Orinda dad phoned to suggest she watch her son play soccer; Eli was such a good athlete, he said. She seemed surprised at the suggestion, but she never followed through.

Since Susan kept to herself, few people in Orinda knew what was actually happening with the family, but in the spring of 2002, something that occurred was so out of the ordinary that residents who heard the story grew frightened. Her actions moved her from verbal attacks into more hostile and frightening territory.

Marilyn Hajjar, who had lived in the neighborhood for twenty-three years, was with her daughter, walking their poodle, otter hound, and Samoyed one airy spring day when they passed the Polks' house. Often, the Polk dogs flew off the deck and down the hill threatening the other dogs. The previous year, one of the Polk dogs had sunk his teeth into the spinal column of the Hajjars' poodle, and when she notified Susan about it, Susan claimed it had never happened and that her dogs (like her children) could do whatever they want. Given the history, Hajjar's daughter screamed, "Get your dogs!" Susan popped in her silver Volvo to catch up.

Through the car window she taunted, "What's the matter, you afraid of a little nice doggie?" Ms. Hajjar's daughter shouted back, "Get your fucking dog out of the street!"

Marilyn Hajjar then did something she would regret: she reached through the open window of the Volvo and says she laid her hand on Susan's cheek. "You need to calm down," she said. With that, Susan threw open her car door and punched Marilyn Hajjar in the face, sending her reeling. Susan pounced back in her car and began driving as though she intended to run them down. Then she halted the car, stumbled out, and punched Marilyn Hajjar harder the second time, sending Hajjar's imported frame eyeglasses and an 18-carat-gold pierced earring flying.

Susan stomped on the glasses and taunted Marilyn's daughter, "Oh, you're taking care of Mommy," and then to Marilyn, "You raised a nasty, shitty little bitch!"

The police were called; but no charges were ever filed. Hajjar says the cops told her the incident wasn't sufficiently grave to press charges.

Meanwhile Susan's verbal outbursts at home were also growing more violent. When alone with Gabriel she would rant about his dad, discussing various ways she might kill him: drowning him in their pool, drugging him, running him over, or tampering with his car. She spoke about this so frequently and with such ease she might just as well have been discussing a better brand of marmalade. She felt comfortable telling Gabriel, her golden child, because she knew that he was on her side. At one point, Susan announced to Gabriel that she was going to shove a shotgun into Felix's chest and order him to transfer twenty million dollars from his Cayman Island bank account to her. Gabe told her that wasn't a good idea.

When Adam heard about this threat, he advised, "You don't want to kill dad. It's a bad idea. You'd go to jail." His mother responded that she would never have made such a threat. But Gabe had told his big brother she had.

More and more, she mistakenly referred to Felix as her father. Felix was shaken by her error, since Susan believed her father had molested her as a child and despised him. Felix grew afraid of what she might do to him, and some of his fears began to spill over into his professional life. He told one of his grad students that things were very bad at home. He said as much to some of his patients.

On April 10, 2002, during a stormy hearing on Eli's assault case, which is still talked about in judicial circles, the dynamics of the dysfunctional family spilled over into the courtroom. The hearing was called after Eli, tethered to an electronic monitor while at his father's house, violated his home detention order several times for such offenses as being late to school. The judge in the case, California Superior Court Judge William M. Kolin, ordered Eli into custody:

"And so stand up; put your hands behind your back," the judge demanded.

Eli shook his head. The judge bristled: "You have a problem with that? You don't care? Fine." A bailiff clamped handcuffs on Eli's wrists.

Susan stormed out of the courtroom. Judge Kolin ordered her to remain. She ignored him: "I don't have custody of my son and I am not going to sit around for this farce," she announced. "You guys are disgusting," she told the startled judge, who then found her in contempt of court, and ordered *her* handcuffed.

"This is bullshit!" she hissed. Asked to apologize, she refused. "Why would I apologize when I think you were wrong? You were out of line."

The judge found her "disorderly, contemptuous, and insolent," and still Susan refused to back down.

"I hereby sentence you to five days in jail. Bailiff, take her away," he said, adding "Have a good day."

Felix, who observed the proceeding, told the judge his children were being raised by their mother in a "paranoid environment . . . They have all been affected by that." Making a prescient point he added, "Eli maybe especially is loyal and protective of [his] mother." Felix promised that he would seek counseling for Eli. "He acts out when he just has had it. It's too much stress for him. It's been going on for years."

After lashing out, Eli appeared contrite, displaying one of the more ironic aspects of his and his brother's personalities: for all of their acting out, Susan always taught them to be unstintingly polite.

"I definitely would like to apologize," Eli then told the judge. "I didn't mean to disrespect you or the district attorney."

He went on to explain that there was no reason for him to be put in custody "because I'm not dangerous and I followed the rules of home supervision to the best of my ability," he said, adding that he took "full responsibility for what I did."

Sufficiently impressed, the judge told the bailiff to remove his handcuffs.

Addressing the court, Eli's attorney, A. Araceli Ramirez, said Eli was "very troubled . . . very protective of his mother, and in fact takes cues about what is appropriate conduct from her." Ramirez asked that the young man be returned to his father and *not have contact with his mother,* who, Ramirez said, would sabotage every effort to keep Eli out of custody. The attorney called for a psych evaluation.

The judge acquiesced, but warned Eli, "This is your last chance."

When Susan next appeared before Judge Kolin on April 16, 2002, her demeanor was so civilized that the judge complimented her. She was spared the five-day jail sentence. He told her that he was inclined to order her to attend psychological counseling. Susan politely balked: "I really don't have a real positive view of therapy, and I'm really not interested in entering another therapeutic relationship," she told the judge. "I think that I was so traumatized in that relationship [with Felix], it's unreasonable to expect me to enter another one."

The judge sympathized with her plea, agreeing not to subject her to psychological counseling but only to a psychological assessment. Susan's deep concern that others believe her to be mentally healthy was obvious in her statement that day: "I do want to put in the court record that I am not on medication. I have not been in psychotherapy for twenty years unless you count the twenty years that I lived with a psychotherapist."

The following week, she was back in court, fighting for the return of her son. She told the judge that there was no documentation to support her husband's claims that "I am unbalanced, unstable, or unable to provide care for my son." She pointed out that she had appeared at every court hearing, and it was only when her husband was in charge and she was gone from the home that cops were called to their house for underage drinking parties. In addition, she pointed out that she did all her husband's billing and handled their investments.

"I don't know what sane person would turn over their investments or their billing for a practice as prestigious as my husband's to someone who is delusional," she told the judge.

Felix, who was also in court, expressed sympathy. He told the judge, "She is a very good mother." Knowing boys need their mothers, Felix sought joint custody.

As part of the agreement, the judge allowed Eli to remain on probation while staying at his father's Berkeley apartment. Susan was convinced that Felix won temporary custody of Eli because Felix had hired Eli's lawyer. And she thought Felix was "hurting Eli to get to me."

Confined once again to his father's apartment, Eli was once again miserable. He not only disliked being alone during the day, but he disliked it even more when his father was home at night. The apartment was small, and Eli slept on a couch. He missed their huge home, his brothers, his dogs, and his mother. He felt he was living with the enemy.

As the divorce proceedings continued, Susan encouraged her two younger sons to write letters to the court. Gabriel wrote simply: "I want to live with my mother, Susan Polk. I do not want to live part-time with my dad and part-time with my mom because this would disrupt my school and my life. My dad won't give me the support that I need to succeed in life. His lack of presence means that he isn't there all the time."

Eli's letter, on the other hand, was bellicose. He attacked his father as someone who himself belonged in jail. He wrote that his father took "illegal and unjust advantage of my mother's feelings, thereby seducing a young girl and making her his wife." He said his father was a bad person, bad parent, and bad husband who had lost the love of his family.

"It is obvious he will do whatever is necessary, right or wrong, to get control of not only his life, but the lives of his kids, and the control of his wife (financially, etc.)." Eli also added something he often would say: "My mother is simply the smartest person I know." He elaborated, "I learn something every time she helps me with my homework, or any questions I ask her. She is a writer, and she has a story to tell." He asked that the court grant custody to his mother "because she is the only one who could care for us like she has done all these years, and we love her."

WHEN THE WILD PLUM TREES BLOSSOMED AND ORINDA FAMILIES WERE MAKing plans to summer at their Tahoe homes, the Polks put their house up for sale. Susan wrote a "Dear Felix" letter telling him "The first open house is this Tuesday." After the sale, she wrote, she would move away from the Bay Area, "for a number of reasons, including cost of living and the damage to my reputation you have done by maligning me publicly as 'psychotic' and 'delusional.' " For a loner, she was surprisingly concerned about what others thought.

Then she did what Susan did best; she intelligently reviewed their joint properties and other matters. She laid out their rental income, property management, and vacancy issues. Those had always been Susan's responsibilities and she had always done well by them. Her mind might be reeling out of control, but she could always nail down numbers.

Under a particularly stiff headline she wrote: "WITH RESPECT TO GABE THE DOGS THE HOUSE AND THE TAX RETURNS." She wrote Felix that Gabriel wanted to come with her. She reminded her husband that he owed her a monthly payment of $9,300 (or $111,600 annually) and told her boys, "I'm probably going to lose custody of you," because, she said, "I don't have the influence your father has."

During the summer of 2002, Susan convinced Eli to break the judgeordered house arrest and come home, an act that would have tragic repercussions no one could have imagined. On his mother's advice, he cut off his ankle bracelet and hid out in their cozy Orinda cottage next to the pool. Susan was overjoyed.

His summer as a fugitive, Eli would later report, was the happiest of his life. There were no pressures to attend school. He and Gabriel slept late and hung out together, playing video games. Their mother seemed always to be in the kitchen making ice cream or baking croissants, muffins, pretzels, doughnuts, pizzas, cakes, and pies. "She would go way above and beyond," Eli marveled. They developed a lookout system. If they thought a deputy sheriff might be approaching, Eli would slide down a trap door covered with a rug in Gabriel's room. When deputies phoned looking for Eli, Susan claimed she hadn't seen him. When Felix called or came by, she fed him the same line, even though Felix was distraught, thinking Eli had run away. Adam remembers his mother just giggled.

That summer, Susan and her sons went camping down the coast of California, stopping off at Big Sur, the historic community where a group of California writers once lived in cabins nestled on cliffs overlooking the Pacific Ocean. Big Sur now possesses a state park, hiking trails, and old, tottering guesthouses, as well as luxury all-natural resorts. The trip was only marred by Eli's selection of twigs for roasting marshmallows—from a poison oak plant. Toward the end of their journey, a Berkeley police officer reached Eli on his cell phone and then Susan on hers. In a kindly tone he told her, "This isn't going to go away." Susan felt she was in a time warp—experiencing a magnificent adventure with her sons that she hoped would last forever but knew would not.

Shortly after their return, the halcyon days ended abruptly. On the first of September, Eli was caught at a friend's house. He was sentenced to nine months at a juvenile facility. Susan was devastated. Already slim, she dropped fifteen pounds. She thought juvenile hall was an awful place, though she never blamed herself for her son's predicament. Instead she managed to convince herself as well as Eli and Gabe that Felix was responsible for Eli's punishment. Gabriel couldn't understand why his dad would do such a thing. At school Gabriel took to wearing clothes and shoes just like his older brother's. Believing that his father had manipulated the system, Gabriel shattered the windows of Felix Polk's Saab with a sledgehammer.

In a poignant and ultimately important letter, Felix wrote Gabriel and told him that he would have to pay for the damage he'd done to Felix's car. "I know that you are very, very mad at me and won't talk on the phone . . . I used to think that you could see reality as it really is. In fact I counted on that for a long, long time. Now I don't know if that is true anymore. . . .

"Both you and Eli seem to have bought into Mom's horror stories about me. They are for the most part not true stories but I don't have a chance to speak up for myself. I am faced with a closed system in which Mom says what she says so hatefully about me and I have no chance to point out what is true and what is not . . . I have some real flaws and yet I am not the monster she portrays me to be."

This was Felix Polk at his saddest and best: a father who had lost his sons but couldn't stop lobbying for their love. He added that he understood Gabe was very attached to his mother, and that "you have been put into the position of having to choose a parent and that you have made that choice. I want you to know that I plan to stay around and not go away from you. You are my kid and I love you as fully as I can love anyone."

Felix wrote that he knew that there would be "many more changes like moving to another house or another school. You can count on me to be around as these changes take place. I have no intention of abandoning you or Eli or Adam no matter what you hear from Mom." He ended the letter with, "I love you! Dad."

Susan was also busy writing, using letters to express her love for her sons while voicing her opposition to the system. In the early fall of 2002, she wrote Judge Kolin, "Eli did not disappear over the summer. He was living with me . . . He came home for things like a warm meal, help with his homework, to pet his dogs, to hang out with his younger brother, to watch TV, to get help washing his clothes, in short for all the good things that a loving family has to offer . . . I wanted one more summer with my children together." She added, "We were and remain a loving family. Felix is not a part of that family."

In a comment that spoke to the defiant woman she had become, Susan wrote, "I cannot find it in my heart to apologize for my actions. I firmly believe that your order was wrong." She said she believed she had a moral obligation not to cooperate, because of her husband's history of violence toward her and her children. "Separating me from my child was wrong. I cannot ask the court's forgiveness when I cannot find it in my own heart to forgive."

"My suitcase is packed," the letter to the judge continued, "and I am planning to move out of California on Wednesday." Adam would be returning to UCLA. Gabriel "is going to try things out with his father. And Eli is a ward of the state and going wherever the court chooses to send him."

She ended by saying: "You have been unjust, Judge Kolin. I do not regret my actions."

Eli was placed in Byron Boys Ranch, an open facility in a rural part of the county where young offenders live in dormlike spaces and take courses in academic subjects, anger management, and crime victim awareness. Eli easily adapted to his environment and was well liked by the staff. But when Felix visited him for the last time, Eli, who was convinced his father had used him as a bargaining chip, ordered his father to "Get away from me!" Felix told Eli that this was something they both would have to work through.

"You can't listen to your mother. You can't live with your mother," Felix told him. "She's a sick person."

Eli snapped back, "That's not going to happen." And what Eli remembers Felix saying next reinforced in Eli's mind that his father was at the controls: "We'll see how you do in three months," adding, "Maybe I'll talk to the judge." Felix's remark, if in fact he made it, may have been that of an innocent father offering to use what influence he could to ameliorate Eli's situation. Susan and Eli took it to mean that Eli's future was in Felix's hands.

Susan believed she could not win. Felix suggested she live in one of their Berkeley apartments and he would live in Orinda with the boys. There was no way she was going to agree to that. Taking away her children would be the ultimate humiliation. "Everyone knew I was a good mom," she said. "How could I go on living the ultimate shame for a mom?"

She was desperate to get out of her locked-in situation. Her older ideas about escaping America were rapidly being replaced by a new plan to rebuild her life in Montana—without her children. She told her two younger sons she hoped that Felix might relent and let them join her. If not, she told her youngest son, "Then I would only see you on holidays."

Felix assumed that as long as Eli was incarcerated, Susan would stick around to visit her needy middle son and attend his hearings. And he figured that with their divorce wending its way through the judicial system, she would not miss the hearings on child custody or marital assets. But he was wrong. Susan took Eli's Dodge Ram and their yellow Lab Dusty and headed back to Montana to find a permanent home for herself. Though Eli wanted her to visit, he understood her need to flee, yet in the wake of her departure, he became so distraught that he often broke out in uncontrollable sobs.

Before leaving, Susan virtually ordered Felix to move back home to care for fifteen-year-old Gabriel, who, mimicking his mother, still despised his dad. Gabriel had begged his mother not to leave him with his father, but Susan was determined. It was another fateful decision that would change the entire course of the family's history.

10.

LIVE IN PEACE

WHEN THEY MET, IN SEPTEMBER 2002, BOZEMAN REALTOR JANNA KUNTZ thought her new client behaved like a frightened squirrel. She was so thin and tentative she resembled a runaway—which in a way she was. Susan Polk told Janna that she needed to escape an abusive relationship in California, although she always described the abuse as emotional, never physical.

From that meeting, the realtor and the Orinda mom, both of whom had weathered difficult marriages, hit it off. Janna Kuntz could tell how close Susan was to her sons; they were always calling their mother's cell phone. Susan talked about them a lot, though she never mentioned that her middle son was incarcerated. To Ms. Kuntz, Susan seemed to be a sad, thoughtful woman who needed to extricate herself from a bad relationship.

Despite the disaster of the year before, Susan still held hope that Montana might be a place where she could live in peace. With Janna, Susan found a $190,000 older condo tucked into the mountains that would suit her. She informed her realtor she would pay for it with the proceeds from her share of an apartment building she and Felix had just sold. She urged her realtor to speed the closing and said that she wanted to move in ASAP.

While Susan was finding herself in Montana, Felix remained distraught, telling his oldest friend and mentor that he didn't want to live without Susan. He returned to divorce court seeking custody of Gabriel and control of their house, which he said they could no longer afford. The evidence he presented in favor of his being granted custody was strong. Because of Susan, Gabriel had lost an entire semester of school for no reason, and Eli, while under house arrest, had disappeared for months. Felix argued that Susan was completely self-absorbed and not at all concerned with her sons' well-being. He pleaded with the court: "I am totally at the mercy of her vagaries."

Listening to the advice of his attorney, Felix was aggressively pursuing his interests through the courts, while crumbling emotionally. The demise of his family left him distracted. He ate poorly. He was unable to sleep. His eyes were bloodshot. He was intensely nervous and distracted. At school he walked into one class and began reading lecture notes from another. Students from outside his circle of admirers had often complained that Felix was sloppy about handing back assignments. Now, he wasn't grading them at all. He told one class that he had marital problems and that he was in trouble. He shocked one of his grad students when he told her his wife was going to kill him. "I'm telling you," he said, "It's bad. I'm afraid for my life." Then he made a cryptic remark: "A lot of things are coming out. This could destroy everything. I'm willing to risk my career on this." The former student believes that Felix was referring to Susan's insistence on telling others how they had met.

While Felix tried to maintain a semblance of normalcy, Susan and her Lab hiked in the lonely Montana wilderness. She carried her pepper spray as well as bells to ward off bears. Rumbling along in her pickup truck through the countryside she wrote her sons poetic notes about passing hawks, mule back deer, cows, and cowboys and how she observed a natural balance among the land, the fishermen, and the streams, which restored her soul. To her son Gabe she wrote that he, his brothers, and she had made the right choices and that they could look forward to many good times together.

To the incarcerated Eli she wrote a mournful dispatch: "Please believe that the greatest joy I have ever known has been in being a mother to you, Adam, and Gabriel." She knew she hadn't always acted that way, but she loved seeing how much Eli enjoyed hanging out at home. She assured him that his good life would be there for him when he returned. "For one thing, you carry all that inside you now." She told him that she, his brothers, and his dogs were all waiting for his return. She said she was proud of the fine person he'd become and that he possessed all the qualities she most admired: courage, kindness, insight, and determination to reach his goals.

She encouraged her son to define himself; his troubles, she said, were linked to his father's influence. She wrote about R. D. Laing, whose teachings Felix admired. Laing, she explained, believed that crazy-making families select one of their children to express for the rest of the family what they are afraid of and what could happen to them. She said that for the sake of the family, Felix had sacrificed Eli. She then placed her incarcerated son on a grandiose pedestal, writing: "Many good and fine men have been imprisoned unfairly: Tupac, Gandhi, and Jesus are a few. . . . You join a long list of special people who are unjustly martyred."

ON SEPTEMBER 27, 2002, FELIX POLK WAS GRANTED TEMPORARY CUSTODY of Gabriel and control of the house. Four days later, Susan learned of the devastating news in a letter from her attorney: she had lost her baby, the angel of the family and the home which was her most prized possession. Later that same day, she had another horrifying report: "Brace yourself, Susan," Felix told her over the phone, "You're in for a shock." A judge reduced her alimony and child support from $6,500 a month to $1,721 or $20,652 a year. Felix too was surprised at how much the judge reduced Susan's payments. He offered to supplement his wife's monthly payments although her finances would remain significantly reduced.

To her new friend Janna Kuntz, Susan brushed off the bad news as emblematic of her husband's behavior. But when she spoke to her oldest son, she expressed her horror that as she put it, Felix was going to leave her with nothing (despite that the couple had $2,521,000 in assets yet to be divided). Susan wondered how Felix pulled it off: "Does he bribe [the judges]? Is he a spy? I married a sadistic man but what's wrong with the courts?"

Felix remained upset about Susan and Eli. His son hated him with the same passion that Susan did, and Felix feared Eli might attack him. Anxious and depressed, Felix visited a physician friend and began taking anti-anxiety medications, Clonazepam (clonapin) and Lorazepam (Ativan).

While he was incarcerated, Eli wrote his little brother Gabe a warning that could have come from his mother. He said his father had proven that he was willing to jail one of his sons to force cooperation. Eli wrote that his life was passing him by. "Watch everything you eat, especially what he brings home to eat."

Despite Eli's warnings, Gabriel was discovering that his father was not the tyrant his mother had made him out to be. While Susan was in Montana, father and son were becoming reacquainted. Felix saw in Gabe's emotions a sea change that warmed his heart. They didn't do anything special: they shared meals, watched TV, talked sports, and talked about their family. Gabriel came to appreciate and love his father and to recognize what Adam had been telling him all along, that his mother was crazy and delusional and his father was just trying to cope. While Susan wrote Gabriel warm letters and postcards, he and his dad talked about what had gone wrong. Felix was beginning to feel he had a chance to save Gabe's life and his own. Felix was afraid he would grow old alone. Now he was beginning to imagine a future in which he might be able to rebuild his shattered world with Gabe and Adam at his side.

Every day Susan called home, and during one such phone call, Gabriel told her he didn't think his father was such a bad guy after all. Susan panicked. She had lost everything. Felix now had Gabe and Adam and he was living in their house. He had reduced her alimony to a pittance. She believed he controlled Eli's fate as well.

While Gabriel and Felix were on the phone, Susan announced that she was returning home to pick up her belongings. (She also had a dental appointment to have a prepaid crown put on her tooth.) During one conversation Gabriel overheard his mother tell his dad that when she arrived home Gabriel would live in the house with her. Felix, she declared could stay in the pool house. If he failed to oblige, she would blow his head off.

On Sunday night, October 6, Felix called his friend Barry Morris, just as Barry was watching *The Sopranos*. Morris, the family's criminal attorney, listened as Felix told him that Susan had called from Montana and announced she was going to kill him. Felix believed she had a shotgun, but he was reluctant to call the cops. He was embarrassed that his life had come to this: a prominent psychotherapist whose wife, his former patient, was threatening to kill him. Morris wasn't sure how to evaluate the threat. Was Susan, a housewife, just a little nutty or was she a delusional murderer? He told Felix he must call the cops. "This is not a joke. This is serious stuff," he advised his friend. Call them, Morris said. "I will call you back in ten minutes."

The next day, Monday, Susan signed the contract for her condo. She told Janna Kuntz that she needed to go back to California to retrieve some of her possessions and would return. She piled her few belongings and Dusty in her pickup and rode down the mountain. Janna watched and worried, afraid for Susan, though she wasn't sure why, that she might never return.

As normal as Susan seemed to the down-to-earth Ms. Kuntz, Susan's mind was wild with worry. Eli's incarceration, Gabe's defection, the loss of her house and the money had pushed her over the edge. In a rambling, incoherent letter to judges in Contra Costa County and to the FBI and the CIA she wrote about her psychic abilities, claiming she had predicted 9/11 and that her husband, a Mossad agent, had notified the Israelis but failed to contact the U.S. government. She confessed she was a medium. "It is so scary for me. Aside from the fact that I am married to a man that threatens to destroy me or kill me if I leave him, it is so scary to have been in a trance and not to remember. It is like dying."

The name on the outside of the envelope was that of her alter ego: Alice Liddell, the little girl who was the real-life model for *Alice in Wonderland*. While passing through Jackson Hole, Wyoming, Susan mailed the letter.

Back in Orinda, Felix telephoned the town's police chief, Dan Lawrence. In a preternaturally calm voice, Felix said his wife was threatening to kill him and that she would blow his head off if he called the cops. Lawrence asked if Susan had a weapon. "No," Dr. Polk said, "but she can get one."

Since she wasn't yet in California, the danger did not seem imminent. Chief Lawrence advised Dr. Polk that he could get a temporary restraining order, move out of his house, or hire a security guard. The police chief could not see spending the taxpayers' money to post an officer at the house 24/7. Lawrence suggested that if Dr. Polk decided to leave, he could call for a civil standby whenever he wanted to retrieve anything from the house.

Felix phoned his mentor and closest friend who was concerned enough about Felix's safety that, ironically, he offered him safe haven in Germany. Felix wouldn't hear of it. He wouldn't leave his sons and he didn't want to leave Susan either. He was still "hopelessly in love with her," the mentor recalled.

On Wednesday night, October 9, 2002, the showdown began. Susan approached the front door of their Orinda home. Felix feared she might have purchased a shotgun in Montana. That she didn't have it with her was a relief, but he knew she could have it tucked away in the Dodge pickup.

Susan hated what she saw. There, in the living room, were Felix and Gabe contentedly watching the big-screen TV. She knew she had lost legal custody of Gabriel, but what she hadn't fully comprehended until that moment was that Gabe truly *wanted* to be with his father. Not only did it break her heart, but it also meant Gabe believed what Adam and Felix had said: that she was delusional. It was more than she could stand.

In his calmest voice Felix tried to talk to his wife, but she was on edge. She demanded that Felix leave. The court order, granting him control over the house, meant nothing to her; she knew she still owned half the house, and she claimed he would have to give her a week's notice before kicking her out. Gabe saw his mother whisper something to his father. He believes she said, "I'm going to kill you." Excitedly, Felix rushed to the phone to call the cops—he had said if she threatened him that's what he would do—while Gabe blocked his mother in the kitchen. They didn't know what she might do next.

It was 11:19 PM when Felix Polk reached 911. "Can I talk to somebody please about a domestic dispute?" Maybe it was the medication he was on, but his voice remained inappropriately calm. He told the dispatcher his wife was kicking him out of the house. "She said, 'Leave,' which I'm not going to do." The dispatcher asked, "Is there a reason?"

"I have custody of the kids. My wife has a shotgun."

By the time Orinda patrol officer Bill Alexander arrived, the heat of the moment had passed. Susan and Felix were seated at the breakfast bar engaged in civil conversation. After some discussion, Felix acquiesced. Susan would spend the night at home, alone. It took less than ten minutes for Felix and Gabe to reach the Lafayette Park Hotel and Spa, a luxury hotel next to a graveyard in the next town over. Father and son stayed in room 304, a spacious room with faux French furniture, modified canopy beds, and a shelf of books that included Jane Howard's *Families* and Agatha Christie's *Murder at the Vicarage*.

The next day, Thursday, with Felix still gone, Susan decided to drag his bed and belongings from the den, where he'd been camped out, to the pool house. She changed the locks to the house. Despite her hope of a new life in Montana, Susan had rejoined the battle with her husband and seemed determined to see it to its end. She called her realtor in Montana and backed out of the purchase of the condo.

As Susan was moving Felix's things to the pool house, Felix was calling his former student and friend Dr. Neil Kobrin, then head of Argosy University, formerly known as California Graduate School of Family Psychology, to explain he would miss the faculty meeting that afternoon because "my wife was saying she is going to kill me." Felix said he was hiding out at a hotel. Embarrassed by this latest turn of events, he asked Kobrin not to mention it to anyone.

Felix was adrift. For once there were no directions, no books, no therapists who could tell him how to handle what was happening. The situation had spun out beyond his understanding and control.

Felix telephoned his oldest son from his first marriage, Andrew, an actor and artistic director of the Cape Cod Theatre Project, in Massachusetts, and said that Susan was threatening to shoot him with a shotgun. He telephoned his only daughter, Jennifer Polk, a social worker and the mother of his only grandchildren, and left a voice mail message saying matters were coming to a head. Susan was threatening to kill him. It was so absurd that it didn't occur to Jennifer that her stepmother would act on her threats.

Felix's friend Barry Morris and his mentor and attorney, Steve Landes, were begging him to get out of the house. "Get the hell away from there right now!" Landes insisted. But Felix couldn't leave his patients, his house, and his boys. And despite her threats, he couldn't leave Susan.

Landes had noticed for quite some time that his client was too passive or too depressed to respond to the threat Susan posed. The seventy-year-old Felix was worn down; Landes felt his client might give up. The next day, Friday, October 11, Felix asked his attorney to call the cops. Landes told him that he, Felix, must make the call, though Landes would follow up with his own.

"My name is Felix Polk," he began. It was 4:03 PM when he called 911. He told the dispatcher he had a court order giving him the house. "I want to talk about implementing the court order," he said. He asked deputies to evict his wife. An Orinda officer advised that if Susan objected, she would be arrested, a thought which caused Felix to hesitate. Nevertheless, he called Susan and told her he was coming over with two deputies and for her to stay put. Adam, a college sophomore, who had come home for the weekend, wanted to avoid a confrontation, and he didn't want to see his mother carted to jail. "Mom, let's just go to the movies instead of waiting for the cops," he said. Before heading off to the movies, Susan left Felix a note that said she did not believe he had a valid court order, but that he could stay in the cottage. To this day, Adam is haunted by the thought that his protectiveness that night may have made a difference in the unfolding drama.

On Susan's suggestion, she and Adam saw *Red Dragon,* one of the Hannibal Lechter stories—filmed as a prequel to *The Silence of the Lambs.* Susan had been reading the three gruesome stories of Hannibal Lechter and enjoying the saga. She thought the author, Thomas Harris, made Hannibal a cannibal because metaphorically he was saying that psychiatrists and psychologists emotionally consume people.

Felix spent an uneasy night in the pool house.

Sunday, October 13, at 5:30 AM, offered a break from the tension. Felix, Gabriel, and Adam left for the 370-mile drive to Los Angeles, where they were dropping Adam and Ruffy, the Rottweiler, at his fraternity house, Sigma Phi Epsilon.

On the journey to Southern California, Felix was depressed. He talked about Susan's threatening to kill him. He didn't know what to do with his life. He didn't want to live if he wasn't going to be with his sons and Susan. At other moments, with encouragement from his sons, he could envision a life without *her,* something he could not have imagined before. Sometimes when Adam recalls those hours, he describes his father as despondent. Other times, he has said his father was more hopeful than he had been in years. In retrospect, he says that both are fair descriptions of his father's shifting moods during their last day together.

When they arrived in LA, the three behaved like normal father and sons. They wolfed down lunch; and watched the Raiders go up against the Rams. Felix threw back a few beers. Then he and Gabriel made the long, dreary trek home, arriving around 9:00 PM or possibly later. As they pulled in the driveway, Gabe noticed the light was still on in his mother's bedroom.

Maybe Felix was too tired to think about returning to the Lafayette Park Hotel. Or maybe the thought of staying some place away from home seemed absurd. What were the chances? And how often could he hide? Maybe the anti-anxiety medications blunted his fear. Whatever the reason, Felix Polk made a tragic miscalculation, unless he had decided to accept his fate. He spent the night in the pool house.

The next day, October 14, a Monday, was Columbus Day. Felix planned to quit work early to take Gabriel to a Giants baseball game in San Francisco. No one but Susan ever saw him alive again.

WHAT HAPPENED THAT NIGHT WOULD BE DEBATED BY THE FAMILY, THE PUB-lic, many lawyers, and nearly four years later, by a jury of Susan Polk's peers. There are some details about which everyone would agree: Sunday night, Octo-ber 13, 2002, Susan crept down to the cottage where her husband was staying. At the very least, she was expecting a confrontation; she was carrying a hefty Maglite flashlight and a can of pepper spray.

During their final confrontation, Felix was wearing only a pair of tight black briefs. In his bedroom in the pool house he had neatly folded his jeans over a wicker chair; he parked his shoes on the floor. He read and then lay his head down on the pillow of his wood sleigh bed, where the imprint of his head would remain for hours.

On Monday night of October 14, his body was found in the sunken living room of the pool house. He was faceup on the terra-cotta floor. His arms were outstretched at forty-five degrees from his body. He was in the corner of the room near the overstuffed brown leather chair and the bamboo magazine rack. Near his bloodied left foot was the book his son Andy had given him which he had been reading the previous night, *The Company,* a popular novel about the CIA. On the book's cover was Susan Polk's alter ego, framed like a piece of a puzzle, an image of a tumbling, angry Alice in Wonderland.

There had been a terrible battle. Susan would later claim that Felix attacked her with a paring knife, "everyone's favorite knife," a four-and-a-half-inch Wusthof forged-steel paring knife that belonged in the cutlery drawer of the main house. Or wasn't it more likely she grabbed the knife from the cutlery drawer and stashed it in her pocket before visiting her husband that Sunday night? She may have surprised him, slashing him in the back as he turned away from the door. She may have stunned him, smashing him along the side of his head with what the cops in their stilted language call "a blunt-force object." Or something very different may have occurred, as she would later contend.

More than twenty times she shoved the knife in his chest, arms, hands, sides, and back. Five of the wounds in his chest and abdomen were serious. She thrust the knife into the skin just below his collarbone, leaving a five-and-a-half-inch-deep S-shaped wound, which penetrated downward into his right lung lobe, which filled up with blood and made his breathing difficult. She sliced through the soft tissue of his right chest wall, missing his heart and entering the pericardial sac, causing her husband additional chest bleeding. She stabbed him on the left side, the knife plunging into the anterior wall and into his stomach. She rammed it downward into his left diaphragm, which penetrated three inches deep, causing more bleeding in his chest cavity. She thrust it downward into his lower right back leaving a five-inch hole through his side and into the fat around his kidney.

And she waved the knife back and forth like a sprinkler system on automatic, making staple-size and larger cuts into soft tissue of his chest and back. She hacked him on the back of his arms, his upper back and even the sole of his left foot where a scratchlike cut extended from the heel forward. When he tried to nab the knife, his fingers became entangled. Subcutaneous tissue on his index fingers popped out of the skin like an oozing soft-boiled egg. Rivulets of blood flowed down his forehead; oxidized blood caked on the back of his skull. Thick puddles encircled his body, smearing his arms and legs.

There were low-velocity bloodstains in various parts of the room, the result of blood drips caused by gravity. There were medium-velocity blood spatters from Susan's hitting or stabbing Felix while he bled.

With chemical enhancement, investigators found one full shoeprint that resembled a fish skeleton and many partial prints left like fossil finds on the bloody floor. The FBI could not match the print to any shoe.

In the months and years ahead, Susan would develop an elaborate story about what transpired between them, and as she told it, there was one detail that rose above the rest, one that didn't help her argument, that didn't help prove that she had fought to defend herself. It was the sort of detail that told more than Susan Polk intended to. It was this: when it was almost over, her grotesquely wounded husband stood up one final time and gasped, *"It's me. It's Felix."* Then he mumbled, "Oh my God, I think I'm dead." He rocked back and forth, clutched his stomach, and fell straight back onto the tile and bled to death.

It was a strange line, and while it's most likely something that he said, Susan probably repeated it without understanding its full meaning. There are several possibilities, but the most probable is that Felix Polk spent his final breath trying, one last time, to convince his wife that he was her husband and not a Mossad agent or the person she increasingly mistook him to be: *her father.*

With Felix lying still in a pool of his own blood, Susan padded to the bathroom and scrubbed pepper spray and blood from her hands and face. She pulled blue towels from the rack and patted down her blood-soaked white shirt, faded Ralph Lauren jeans, and her Cole Haan slip-ons.

She walked over to her husband, splayed on the cold Mexican tile floor. She says he was unblinking. She watched his chest for movement; there was none. He was dead.

She sat on the stairs leading up to the bedroom and looked at his body. "I thought, 'Oh my God, I've killed him.' Everything that went before and led up to it, all that was secondary. His blood was on my hands. Oh my God. Is it self-defense? What if it's not?"

She sat and thought about the life they had together. Her thoughts drifted seamlessly in and out of their actual history together and the imagined world she created. She thought about Eli's incarceration and how he had gotten there, convinced her husband was responsible. She thought about her belief that Felix had prior knowledge of 9/11 and wondered if she had just killed a spy. She thought about all the times that Felix had said that she couldn't leave him. If she went to jail for killing her husband, she wondered, who would care for Gabriel? Could she call on her mother? Her mom couldn't handle Dusty their dog much less her son. She could turn to no one. She felt Felix had hijacked her life, but he alone had stuck by her and now he lay dead in front of her.

Surely someone must have heard the commotion and called the cops. She waited for them to arrive.

Nobody came.

She sat there for thirty or forty minutes. She didn't call the police. The longer she sat, the harder it was to call. "If I call now," she thought, "how do I explain the wait? The thing to do is to get Gabriel to school (the next morning). I was just putting one foot ahead of the other. Then it became I was pretending it didn't happen; how much nicer to put it off." That was what she called part of her "magical thinking."

Susan began to cover up her involvement. Bending down over Felix, she picked up the bloodied knife, the Maglite, and the pepper spray and scurried back to the main house, where Gabriel was asleep. She buried the pepper spray in the garbage can for the following morning's pickup. She washed the paring knife, which had been her kids' favorite, and "placed it in its rightful place," in a cutlery drawer, where Gabe or anyone else might select it to cut tomatoes or steak. She washed the Maglite. Climbing the stairs to her spacious bathroom, she took about ten showers and threw her clothes in the washer. She tried to sleep, but was unable to. She sewed up a hole, no bigger than a cashew, where the knife had penetrated her just-washed Ralph Lauren jeans. Then she tugged her jeans and white shirt back on, wearing the crime scene evidence.

She hadn't washed everything and sown up her jeans to destroy the evidence, she later explained, she did it "to restore a sense of cleanliness." But in her cleanup attempt, she had missed something that would incriminate her.

THE FOLLOWING MORNING, MONDAY, OCTOBER 14, SHE MADE HER SON breakfast and drove him to his continuation school. Then she drove home, found the keys to her husband's Saab and steered it to the Bay Area Rapid Transit parking lot. She thought that if Gabriel saw his father's car, "he would walk out there and find his dad's body." From the BART station, she hiked several miles home. She had two slight red marks around her eyes, but they were so insignificant that Gabe failed to notice. She acted as if nothing was wrong, a behavior which she would later explain by saying, "My husband was dead in the cottage. I was trying to hold onto semblance of normal life for a few more hours."

When she was in the kitchen, rinsing dishes, she thought she should tell Gabriel, but then she decided "to give him a few more hours of peace of mind." Or perhaps, as others would later speculate, she was waiting for her son to find his father's body in the hope he might join her in a conspiracy of silence.

11.

IN A DREAM WORLD

Orinda's police chief Dan Lawrence was dozing when the phone jarred him awake. It was the end of a long and successful Monday. He'd organized a golf tournament, a fund-raiser for the sheriff's department.

"There's been a murder in town," an officer advised him.

"Who's the victim?"

The old dread of recognition crept over him. Less than four days before, Dr. Polk had had a telephone conversation with the chief. In hindsight, he wondered what else he might have done to protect Dr. Polk.

As Lawrence spoke to the officer, Susan Polk was being driven from her family's house to the county field operations bureau in Martinez, California, where she was placed in an interrogation room. She was read her Miranda Rights and said she wouldn't be needing an attorney. Sitting calmly in a mahogany chair with dark blue upholstery and holding her gold-rimmed glasses, she looked more like an English professor during office hours than a murder suspect.

"So what has happened to my husband?" she inquired. "He is dead?"

The deputies encouraged her to tell the truth. They suggested she might have killed in self-defense. "The truth is not hard to remember," Detective Michael Costa coaxed.

She denied any involvement, suggesting detectives consider her husband's patients, though she refused to name names, saying it was not her job to find a suspect. She inquired about her son Gabriel and about "my son's dog." She told about the financial squeeze her husband had put her in by reducing her alimony, but she insisted she had no motive to kill. When the detective speculated that she might have wanted all their money she said she wouldn't kill the person with the income. Asked if she still loved her late husband, she said she had once been fond of him, and while she no longer loved him, she insisted she was not angry enough to kill him.

"I've got to tell you . . . ," the detectives remarked "you're sitting here—you know, we've been together for an hour now or so and you don't seem really choked up. You don't seem really upset that he's gone. I find that kind of— I mean granted—" but before he could utter another word, Susan Polk responded, "I'm very, very, very upset."

"You do well at not showing it," the detective said.

"I'm not in love with my husband anymore."

As a video camera stationed on the ceiling recorded her, Susan Polk argued, "Why would I kill my source of income?"

The deputy sheriffs asked Susan who could take Gabriel. She said she couldn't think of anyone.

"I did not kill my husband," she stated again. "I'm not that kind of person."

"Okay, I've got to tell you, Susan, you know, right now we have to look at you as possibly doing this . . . You have the motive . . ."

"He's my sole source of income," she responded.

"Uh-huh."

"You're living in some sort of dream world right now, where you think this is all gonna go away," the detective warned.

"I think it's been so," she admitted. "I've been living in a dream world for many years."

FIFTEEN-YEAR-OLD GABRIEL SAT IN AN INTERROGATION ROOM NOT FAR FROM Susan's, wearing only a pair of shorts. Earlier in the evening he had been read his Miranda Rights, but officers quickly concluded he had nothing to do with the murder. In one instant he had lost both parents. He told the officers that his mother "can act perfectly sane most of the time," but that she could also be "provocative and completely delusional." He told them about the near constant threats she had made to kill her husband and how after he had found his father his mother returned to the cottage, peered in and pretended to discover the body.

In Los Angeles, two uniformed police officers rapped on the door of Sigma Phi Epsilon. The cops were asking for Adam Polk. As he stumbled to the door, he wondered if he'd failed to pay his taxes.

"Your father has been murdered," one of them said. "Your mother is the prime suspect."

Adam felt as though he had been slammed with a baseball bat. He crashed to the floor. "It was," he said, "a brutal moment." For thirty minutes he was inconsolable. Then he got in gear. "What the hell is going to happen to Gabe?" he thought. He didn't have to worry about Eli just then; Eli remained incarcerated at Byron Boys Ranch.

Adam took a call from Gabe who, while in the interrogation room, asked the deputies for some privacy. The deputies left, but the video kept recording his side of the conversation: "Mom fucking shot dad with a shotgun," Gabe said to his brother. "Yeah. Fucking crazy bitch. We still have an apartment house. We still have an apartment. We get income . . . What the hell is wrong with her? I hope they give her the fucking death penalty. *(Inaudible)* a fucking gun. Well, can you come down here?"

When the deputies reentered the room, the boy inquired, "I would like to know what is going to happen to us financially." He explained that the family owned an apartment building in Berkeley. "We need a source of income."

The deputy assured him, "No one is going to take any of that away from you."

Gabriel's interest in financial matters at such a moment may have been a reflection of his mother's obsession with finances, or it may have been something he could focus on, as his mother did, when everything else had fallen apart.

After a deputy said he wasn't informed about the status of the investigation or "who is responsible," Gabriel grew anxious: "You don't have any proof yet? I am just asking you for anything, because I really don't want Mom to be walking around in the state that she is in. And I would really hate for her to meet someone on the street who vaguely resembles *her father,* so she goes out and shoots him." The deputy assured Gabe that his mother was "not free to go right now."

A crisis counselor entered the room. He told the teen that he understood what he was going through; he had lost his wife and his only child in a fire. He brought the boy a pair of socks and sweats to sleep in for the night, advising him, "This will be one of the biggest challenges you have ever worked through in your life. You will realize you will work through this. You will become stronger through it."

For one moment, Gabe was a fifteen-year-old again. He looked at the counselor and asked, "Promise?"

"You will," the counselor assured. "You will."

The boy spent his first night alone, on the floor of his interrogation room.

Within hours Adam and his roommate were driving north to sort things out.

As they drove, Adam made calls. He telephoned his half brother, Andy, on the East Coast, who then notified other relatives. He telephoned the Briners, parents of one of his closest friends, and asked if they could take his little brother Gabriel. Marjorie and Dan Briner, a responsible, decent couple, obliged even though they had never met Gabriel or his parents; they agreed because Gabe was Adam's little brother. For several years they had encouraged their son to hang out with Adam in hopes that some of Adam's intellectual drive would be contagious. Mrs. Briner assumed that her job with Gabe would be short-lived and that relatives would pick the boy up in a few days. But nobody did.

The morning after his father's body was discovered, sheriff's deputies notified Eli Polk at Byron Boys Ranch, where he had been for less than two weeks. Eli was called in to talk to deputies, unaware of the reason. "Let's get down to the nuts and bolts here," one of them said. "Your father was found deceased at your house. I know that's a shock . . . We're here to talk to you about that."

Eli's heart was pounding.

A female deputy advised, "Just keep breathing, okay?"

Eli Polk sobbed. He was allowed to go to the bathroom, wash his face, and return to answer questions.

"It's very important that you know my mother is a mellow person," he told them. "It's not my mom. I know that for a fact. I know my mom better than anyone."

He suggested that an angry patient might have killed his father and went on to name one of his father's patients (who when reached by the deputies said he was devastated by the death of his therapist who had been tremendously helpful to him). Eli told the officers that his parents were getting a divorce and that his mother had returned from Montana "to handle financial situations."

As the questions continued, Eli admitted that the divorce was "stressful" and that there had been "physical altercations" between his parents, but he characterized them as "mutual combat." He felt uncomfortable with the direction of the deputies' questions and wanted to end the interview: "I don't feel right answering any more of these questions," he told them. "I would never do anything to put my mom in jail, and that is where that's leading," he said before he rose from his seat and left.

WHEN SHEILA BYRNS LEARNED OF FELIX'S DEATH SHE WAS SHOCKED AND angered. For years, Felix had said he was scared of his wife, but he had seemed so passive. "He was telling me something important, and I didn't get it," Sheila thought. The threats had become "old hat" for her. It was painful to become involved in something that Felix was unwilling to do anything about. In retrospect, Sheila regretted not taking Felix's concern more seriously. She drove to Felix's Berkeley office and taped a sign on the door. While she had wanted to call each of Felix's patients, Felix's twin, John, who had flown to California, thought she would be violating confidentiality and advised her against it. Many of his patients had to learn about it from TV and newspapers.

Before Sheila Byrns had a chance to post the note on Felix's door, Joel Tepper went for his regular appointment. Felix didn't answer the door. Tepper thought he must have the wrong time. He tried calling Felix. Finally he reached one of Felix's colleagues who told him Susan had murdered Felix. "I, of course, felt sick," he said.

Each of Felix's friends who heard the news was incredulous. They could not believe that Susan Polk could have acted alone. Some who didn't know Gabriel thought he must have assisted her; others suspected Gabe had acted alone and that she was covering for him.

Orinda residents don't express rage, except over a neighbor's leaf blower snorting before 7:00 AM. A murder was something that occurred only rarely and always with an explanation that would reassure residents that those sorts of crimes were committed by, and happened to, other kinds of people. This crime, however, disturbed their manicured existence.

As news spread, much of the therapeutic community was horrified and a little embarrassed. A few therapists whispered that what Dr. Felix Polk had done with the young girl was so egregious that he had gotten what he deserved.

Argosy University, where Felix taught, sent out a "we regret to inform you" e-mail. For a few days faculty members and students gathered to talk about Felix. At a large social hall in the Berkeley hills, a memorial service was held. Many students, especially those closest to Felix, were in shock. A new faculty member who specialized in trauma was asked to speak to one of his classes. The night Felix's body was discovered, Susan Polk was booked into Contra Costa County's Field Operations jail in Martinez, the county seat, for classification, to determine among other things, if she was a gang member or had enemies already incarcerated. The modest Orinda housewife was strip-searched and photographed. Charged with the murder of her husband, Felix Polk, her bail was set at $1,050,000, the extra $50,000 was for her use of a knife during the killing. Within weeks, Tom O'Connor, the deputy DA assigned to her case, returned to court with Susan's defiant letter to Judge Kolin about Eli's removal of the electronic monitoring device. A judge responded by setting no bail.

When he was informed of the death of his friend, Felix's mentor felt he understood: Felix had been unable to separate himself from Susan and she from him. His mentor was convinced that Felix knew what was coming. He believed that by remaining at home the therapist had committed suicide. The weapon wasn't the knife; it was his wife.

12.

HEAVEN FROM HELL

ALL MOURNERS ARE SOMBER, BUT ON THAT WISPY-COOL NOVEMBER DAY AS autumn tilted toward winter and dried leaves skittered across the sidewalks, those who came to Christ the King Church in Pleasant Hill, California, to pay their respects to Dr. Felix Polk were painfully sad. As they entered, they heard Pink Floyd crooning, "Wish You Were Here":

"So, so you think you can tell Heaven from Hell, blue skies from pain . . ."

Haltingly, worshipers filtered down the aisles barely acknowledging one another. Gray-haired men stoically stared straight ahead. Women in tasteful tans and navys clutched handkerchiefs to blot away tears. Teenage boys, who were so muscular that their starched white collars pinched their necks, whispered softly. Before the ceremony began, the sanctuary was engulfed by the sweet voices of three young sisters accompanied by a guitarist:

> *Silence like a cancer grows.*
> *Hear my words that I might teach you;*
> *Take my arms that I might reach you.*

Throughout the honeyed ceremony, the silence held. Though mostly everyone knew, no one could bear to say who had stabbed and sliced Felix Polk and left him to die in a sea of his own blood. There were other things that went unspoken. No one mentioned that Felix's murder might be rooted in a profession and perhaps moral transgression that he had committed more than thirty years before. Many of the assembled didn't know the story of how the Polks' relationship began while those that did knew not to raise the subject.

On either side of the altar huge images of happier times were projected on the wall: Felix hunched over his cello. A virile Felix with red bandanna and dark blue undershirt cradling a baby. Felix among the trees in an old, blue Sierra Design jacket, the sort that hikers wore in the 1960s and 1970s. An older Felix, smiling with a baby from his second family in his baby-pack. Felix at the beach sunning himself like a seal while his sons frolicked nearby. And finally, Felix with Adam in shirt and tie standing beside the family Volvo, as he goes off into the world.

There were no images of Susan and no one who delivered a eulogy mentioned her. Therapists have an expression for something so glaringly obvious that goes unsaid by a patient because it is too difficult or emotionally charged. They call it "having an elephant in the room." The therapist's job is to point out the existence of the elephant. At this memorial service, even with a room full of therapists, people thought it best not to mention *her*.

"I've been a priest for thirty-nine years," Father Brian Joyce, pastor of the church, was intoning as he grasped for words. "I have dealt with a lot of deaths and memorial services. They are always tragic, but this is particularly tragic."

Mourners who knew Felix professionally assured one another that he was a great man, a man who had dedicated his life to helping others. From the altar, Sheila Byrns said that as a psychotherapist, Dr. Polk had given so much. Her voice echoed around the sanctuary: "He was warm and gentle, passionate and caring." She had known him as well as anyone, save his family.

Like many therapists of his time, he thought the old rules of placing a boundary between the patient and clinician did not apply. No one would pay a higher price for overstepping boundaries than the man whose ashes were now encased in a wooden urn at the center of the altar at this suburban church.

Even in death, he was described in therapeutic terminology. He was, Sheila Byrns declared, "the archetypal father: wise and kind, loving and demanding," though she was referring to her relationship with Felix and not that of his sons. Felix wasn't perfect, she knew, but "the most important thing about him was his authenticity," she said in her soft, smoky voice. "He was real. He told stories. He was vulnerable."

"It is hard to believe he is gone," she said. "So much of him is in me. At the same time there is this huge hole in my life there is also this feeling I'll never lose him because he gave himself so deeply."

"His life was filled with periods of stable security interspersed with tragic happenings," declared Felix's friend and onetime patient, Dr. Ernst Valfer, in his thick German accent. Dr. Valfer, a therapist, described the searing images that Felix had recalled over and over again, of leaving Vienna and his nurse-mother, Katya, at the train station. At least a few mourners thought it ironic that he had survived the Nazis but couldn't survive his marriage to the woman he had nurtured from adolescence. Dr. Valfer called Felix Polk "a European gentleman."

"Adam, Eli, and Gabe, it is possible to change this awful pain into profound, positive ways and to see this experience as a path to greater awareness of yourself," said Coach Bob Ladouceur, who coached the De La Salle High School football team to an unprecedented twelve years of consecutive victories. "With the help of others," said the other male role model in Adam Polk's life, "all will be made good."

In the years to come that rosy scenario would prove to be more wishful than predictive.

When Adam mounted the podium, he was composed. "Writing these words," he said, "marks the first time since my father's passing that I have delved into the memories of my childhood with the man I lost." Mourners sniffled.

"I close my eyes and I see him tucking me in every night and the roughness of his whiskers scraping my face and tickling me," he said. Every Sunday morning, the son said, his father blasted Mozart on the stereo, "giving me a highly cultured wake-up call."

Adam recalled long family hikes up Mount Tamalpais in Marin County, reaching the top just in time for pancakes and lemonade. Music would be a leitmotif throughout Felix's life even though he failed to inherit the musical gene from either parent. He had compensated with his uncanny ability to hear one or two notes, his son said, and be able to identify the period, the composer, and "even which movement was being aired." His father was fond of literature, reading his children Dylan Thomas's "Child's Christmas in Wales," on Christmas Eve, accompanied by hot chocolate and a roaring blaze in the fireplace.

Considering how the life of his family would later be characterized in court by his mother, his brothers, and himself, Adam's memory of his childhood was notably devoid of horror: "We were abnormally loving and caring in the years preceding the hard times."

Perhaps it was just as well that Eli, the middle brother, did not speak. That morning, he had been granted permission to leave Byron Boys Ranch accompanied by a minister affiliated with the court system. Eli came not to pay homage to his father but to be with the brothers he loved. He sat stiffly in the front row with them. He thought about speaking, but he couldn't think of anything that might be appropriate, anything that might even be kind. He believed every part of his mother's version of Felix—that he had been controlling and manipulative, that he was the grand puppeteer who had the power to send his son to juvenile hall. Eli knew that were he to say anything, it would have ruptured the loving mood. It was tempting, but he resisted the urge. Although he was the one who was always getting into trouble, he maintained the impeccable manners his mother had insisted upon.

Eventually, Eli would have his moment, his time to express his views, but that would not come for three years, and by then his audience would have multiplied into the hundreds of thousands and not be limited to a small gathering in a suburban sanctuary.

Adam recalled his father saying: "I help people. . . . The irony clearly being that no matter how many people he helped," Adam told the congregation, "his family life was in shambles.

"His greatest fear in life as he expressed it to me was that Eli and Gabe would stop loving him. Tragically, I know for a fact, he loved *everyone* in our family, even as he drew his last breath."

That was about as close as anyone could come that day to acknowledging *her*. It was a startling comment. Until the moment he died, Felix had been obsessively in love with Susan. Had he been able to blunt his obsession, he might have been able to leave. He might not have been there for their final encounter, but neither one had been willing to disengage, to do what most divorcing couples do: become embittered, file for divorce, fight in court, and eventually drift apart. He thought he was protecting her from the world. Yet in the end, she saw him as an embodiment of her many troubles and fears. He had tried to save her, but his wife thought that as long as he was alive, she could never be free.

As the service drew to a close, the elephant remained in the room. The woman whom no one would mention, the petite wife with her refined manners and excellent intellect, was sitting in a county jail cell, charged with first-degree murder of the only man she had ever loved.

PART III

A MOTHER AND HER SONS

13.

"FINALLY FREE"

GABRIEL WAS FURIOUS; HIS MOTHER HAD DONE SOMETHING SO AWFUL, SO tragic and unbearably irreversible. Her vengeful act robbed him of his childhood and forever stole from him the father he had come to love. He'd loved his mother more than anyone, but now he wanted nothing to do with her. Nothing. He refused to visit her in jail or take her calls. He tore up her letters. Marjorie Briner, the woman who would become his surrogate mother, taped them together and insisted on reading them to him until one day he announced that if she continued, he'd run away.

Although Eli and Gabe had been best friends, their reactions to the death of their father were polar opposites. Eli ached for his mother in such a way that he seemed not to be whole without her. He was heartbroken not because his father was dead but because his mother was incarcerated. Since he too was in jail, they weren't allowed to visit. When his half brother and half sister mailed him a framed photo of his father, he removed the picture and replaced it with one of his mother. In woodshop he carved another frame for another picture of her so that every morning when he awoke he would see Susan's face. Though he wanted to tell her not to change, he knew that jail changes people. He wondered if slicing off his ankle bracelet had initiated the chain of events that culminated in his father's death and his mother's imprisonment; he wished to God that he hadn't gotten caught. He wrote her love letters saying he would burn to a crisp if that meant meeting her in the afterlife. Another letter read: "Follow your light till the end of time . . . our souls will intertwine / Priceless is the sun to earth as you are mine . . ."

Whenever Adam tried to help Eli and set the record straight, his brother would accuse him of selling out. "All this craziness is still perpetuating itself through Eli," Adam said in sorrow. Their mother was a damaged person, but Eli thought she was capable of doling out good advice. "When a lie gets big enough, it becomes the truth," Adam thought. Adam dreamt about his family the way it had been—when everyone was alive and happy. When he saw friends heading home for vacation, lunching with parents, or when their moms picked up their laundry, he felt a gnawing emptiness.

He'd placed Gabe with the Briners but warned them that Susan, who at the time appeared to appreciate their kindness, would eventually turn on them. Nevertheless, the Briners did more than raise Gabe; they took care of the Polk family business, supervising the biohazard cleanup crew of their home, arranging for the installation of an alarm system, collecting the mail. Whenever Susan needed something, they obliged.

Meanwhile, Adam made arrangements for his brother's education, setting up a meeting for him and Gabe with Brother Michael Saggau at De La Salle High School. Saggau was accustomed to discussing students' academic or social complaints, not murder and its aftermath. During their meeting Adam told him he was dropping out of college to handle his family matters. Together the three prayed, and Adam asked that Gabriel be admitted to the rigorous parochial school. Basing their decision on Adam's sterling record, the needs of his little brother, and administrators' desire to keep Adam in college, the school accepted Gabe.

Although the war between Susan and Felix was over, their feud spilled over into the next generation. Eli sided with his mother. Gabriel and Adam were loyal to their dead father, although Adam tried to maintain relations with both camps, occasionally visiting his mother in jail.

THE LAND AROUND SAN PABLO BAY IN RICHMOND, CALIFORNIA, WAS NEARLY barren when West County Detention Center was constructed sixteen years ago. Since then developers had started snapping up cheap acreage on which to build "luxury homes" in developments with generic names like Bella Vista and Country Club Preserve "where nature is your neighbor." Salesmen didn't point out that just down the road they also had eight hundred neighbors in jailhouse garb, including their best-known inmate, Susan Polk.

Instead of her expansive bedroom with its Chinese pink stone wall, fireplace, and bella vistas of rolling hills, Susan slept on a flat, two-inch mattress in a thirteen-by-eight-foot cinder block cell with linoleum floor, a desk, drawer, mirror, sink, and a slit window that allowed in a shard of daylight. She shared the cell with a rotating series of inmates. In place of her massive library, gourmet kitchen, and walk-in closet, she was allowed five paperbacks, two pieces of fruit, three sets of jail uniforms, stubby pencils but no pens, paper, and photographs—but no Polaroids, since inmates sometimes sandwich drugs between the image and the paper.

The jail is one of those new-age facilities that resembles a dorm. There are over three acres of lush gardens crammed with Shasta daisies, Russian sage, canna lilies, ornamental grasses, waterfalls, and meandering stone paths, though only male inmates till the soil. Susan would never be allowed to stop and smell the morning glories. Majestic redwoods and lush ferns grow at the entryway to the women's building. Wooden doors with narrow windows replace metal bars. Inmates have keys to their cells. The setup—a deputy sheriff sits at the hub of a butterfly-shaped wing—is designed to be less adversarial. It's still a jail, though, with barbed wire topped with spiky razor rings encircling the property.

It did not take long for Susan Polk to earn a reputation at the jail. During her incarceration, more than fifty incident reports were filed against her for transgressions from smuggling in panty hose and highlighter pens to going on hunger strikes. She blocked the window of her door with towels and cardboard, and when they were confiscated, she placed newspaper over the end of her bunk to shield herself. She insisted on having a cell to herself, and when ordered to move to another cell with an inmate, she lay down on the floor and had to be lifted out. She routinely yelled at deputies, accusing them at various times of being either Jews or Nazis (and sometimes both). Forbidden to correspond with other inmates, she marked an envelope "Legal Mail-Confidential," when it was personal. Several times while being transported to court she slipped her handcuffs.

Her life, like that of other inmates, became one of regimentation. Breakfast was at 4:30 AM. There were seven head counts daily. Her exercise consisted of walking in a circle in a small concrete courtyard topped with a wire cage. But Susan didn't let her environment control her moods. In her cell she practiced yoga and calisthenics and she meditated. She tried to improve herself by reading books on deprogramming—she felt she had been a victim of Felix's mind control. And she read self-help books on trauma and recovery and the power of positive thinking.

What hurt her most about her incarceration was her separation from her sons. Though she was consumed by sadness, she refused to give in to depression, telling her boys in letters that she was on a voyage of discovery. She thought about her sons constantly and welcomed sleep because she could be with them in her dreams. In one dream she was gliding down the stairs of a beautiful Mediterranean-style house filled with leaded-glass windows. Her boys were with her.

She inhabited a space somewhere between the real world, her dreams, trances, and a gothic fairy-tale world of her own making. One month after Felix was killed she wrote a poem about his death in which Felix followed the Greek mythological character Charon, who ferried the souls of the dead. In her dream-like poem she leaves her husband at sea and "alone I wade to shore."

She wrote a childlike fairy tale about herself and Felix, which reflected her mind-set that Felix controlled her life. In the story, Felix is the old toymaker and she, a much younger puppet, is his creation. Together, they have three sons, two of whom the toymaker controls. Only the middle son escapes his grasp. When his female puppet tries to leave him, the toymaker recites the old rhyme: "Peter, Peter pumpkin eater. Had a wife and couldn't keep her. So he kept her in a pumpkin shell, and there he kept her very well."

Over the years Susan had sometimes communicated with her mother, but more often she had not. When Helen did visit Susan and Felix, she might say something at the dinner table to stir conversation but found that Felix and Susan ignored her. On occasion, Susan had yelled at her mother and told her to get out. Helen didn't blame Susan for her dinner table manners or for her accusations that Helen had abused her daughter. Helen blamed Felix. Who was it, she said, who would benefit from Susan not being well?

Two months after Susan's arrest, Helen wrote her daughter a brief note: "My dear Susan, If you would like to see me and David, please call collect. While I would love to see you your decision is OK with me. Take care. Mama." That was the beginning of a new and warmer chapter in their relationship. Helen was preternaturally optimistic. Despite Susan's being in jail, Helen thought her daughter must realize "She was finally free to think her thoughts and live her life and to do the best she could by it. Nobody was pulling strings anymore."

Initially, Adam had some empathy for his mother. She was flawed, but his dad had been too. Adam hated that she was in jail, but he would worry if she were free. When he visited they spoke through a clear partition along with dozens of other visitors, conducting personal business in plain sight. The two discussed the minutia of daily life, and his mother suggested that the boys divide the property equitably. Sometimes Susan would talk about that night. She told Adam, "Things just got out of control," a line that would reverberate in her son's mind for years.

Inevitably, Susan sometimes had problems with other inmates, although one whom she offended admitted she wouldn't fight "an old lady." Susan was kind to some of her "bunkmates," and for one of the few times in her life, she made some friends, encouraging younger inmates to make something of themselves. After being released one wrote how shocked she was that Susan would have "such a high regard for a person like myself. It actually gives me so much hope I guess because you are so educated & affluent (right word?) Our friendship not only gives me a renewed confidence but also a fear of failure. My goal is to make you proud." In a touching aside she wrote, "I came to the conclusion that I'd give one of my toes for your freedom. For the chance to continue our friendship out of confinement."

SUSAN ADAPTED MORE EASILY TO JAIL THAN GABRIEL DID TO A NORMAL FAMily. He was the angriest, most sullen boy Marjorie Briner had ever encountered, and as a junior high school teacher, she was steeped in the culture of rebellious boys. He was so unaccustomed to rules that when Marjorie awakened him for school he lashed out and refused to go. Because he had spent so much time at home with his mother and away from school, he was socially and academically behind, and it upset Ms. Briner to realize that Susan had raised her son to be dependent upon her.

Through her letters, Susan tried to mother her boys, though she was better at the practical than the poignant. After receiving a copy of Adam's eulogy for his father, she wrote Adam that she was moved by his words and that she regretted the wrong turns she'd taken in her son's life. Then she added, "It does not make sense to sell new cars, generally. The longer you keep a car the less money you lose." With Eli, she strove to keep his spirits up at Byron Boys Ranch, writing him about the books he was reading: *Call of the Wild*, *The Constant Gardener*, and *Letters to a Young Poet*.

Although Gabriel would continue to refuse his mother's overtures, she didn't give up: "What you think I did I did not do," she wrote, although it wasn't clear if she was denying killing Felix or simply saying she killed in self-defense. She wanted Gabe to remember her as she was because for most of his life he had loved her so. She wrote him that she's still that same person. "One thing is constant," she noted, "you will always have my love and high regard as long as I live."

Despite the difficult adjustment in the months after his father's death, Gabriel came to trust and love the Briners, especially Marjorie Briner. In turn, the Briners came to love him and treat him as a son. He buckled down and learned to live with the rules of the house. He dove into school, did his home-work, played rugby, and not surprisingly, given his looks and outgoing person-ality, he became popular. The Briners continued to accept long-winded collect calls from Susan, and they kept her informed about Gabe's progress—his first prom, his rugby, and his success in school.

Initially, Susan was delighted, but then she asked that they not tell her about Gabe because she found it too painful. Within six months, she was objecting to what she said was Marjorie Briner's control over her son's life, accusing the Briners of embezzling, stealing, and brainwashing Gabe. Susan blamed her split with the Briners and their friend Budd MacKenzie, an attorney hired by Felix's brother John Polk to manage the Polk estate, not on her own behavior but on Felix's "legend" that she was crazy and delusional.

Despite the rift, she didn't want to give up on Adam either. Nor was he will-ing to give up on her. When he failed to write, she sent a clever questionnaire, which read in part, "I was thinking of doing a double major in. . . . I was plan-ning to stay in LA this summer to go to school and. . . . School has been . . . I have read some good books . . ."

AT THE END OF MARCH 2003, SIX MONTHS AFTER FELIX WAS KILLED, ELI WAS released from Byron. Once again it fell to Adam to find a home for a brother, and once again, the parents of his friends took in a brother because they had such high regard for Adam. Eli stayed with one family and then another, but there was always some incident and Eli would leave. When one mother, an attorney and former probation officer, advised him not to listen to Susan because she was delusional, he vociferously objected: his mother loved him and was the smartest person he knew, he said before stomping out. For a while, Eli camped out with his little brother, Gabriel, at the Briners'. Although the boys had been best friends, now Eli saw himself as his mother's protector. According to Gabe, Eli applied pressure on him, warning his younger brother that he dare not testify against their mother. Eli was asked to leave. From there, he briefly moved in with Adam in LA, but that didn't last long either.

Nothing upset Susan more than knowing that her sons were not getting along. While she never acknowledged that she was the cause of the rift, she begged them to reconsider, pleading with them to put aside their differences and agree not to talk about what had happened. After awhile, Adam and Gabe simply could not be around Eli. Unable to live anywhere else, Eli went home to the huge house in Orinda a lost soul. He was just eighteen, living in the house where his mother killed his father. Susan tried to mother him from jail, sending him a How to Live 2.0 letter. "Make a list of what you intend to do each day," she wrote. Pay parking tickets. Seal your juvenile record. Buy a good laptop. Sell the books—she had eighty boxes of books to go to a secondhand bookstore, but, she advised, keep the first edition Steinbeck, Hemingway, and Thomas Wolfe. He should look for work at Trader Joe's or Starbucks. "Get up early every day and ask what can I do today to accomplish my goals?"

WHILE LANGUISHING IN JAIL, SUSAN WHIZZED THROUGH SEVERAL TOP attorneys, finding fault with each. For months, she represented herself, appearing among a crowd of mostly monosyllabic defendants charged with possession of controlled substances, stalking, embezzlement, petty theft, and multiple DUIs. With her cultured voice and crossword terminology, she stood out. When she nodded her head it was in a regal manner, slowly and with intent. One could almost forget she was wearing jailhouse green and gold. Judges were solicitous of the woman who would seem more at home sipping pinot gris and nibbling bruschetta. A judge might tell her she would be given one week to find counsel; she would demur saying it would take months. She spoke softly but often ignored the judges' orders and kept talking. Some judges grew irritated, then angry, others she simply wore down.

Deputy DA Tom O'Connor tried to maintain his cool while Susan stalled the proceedings, and inevitably accused O'Connor of slowing the process. She did raise one good point: for months, she'd complained to the court that she needed her computer to prepare her defense. She claimed there was information in her computer diaries that could exonerate her. But in hearing after hearing, O'Connor said technological problems prevented them from accessing the hard drive of Susan's Apple computer.

On August 27, 2003, after many delays and setbacks, the Contra Costa County grand jury indicted Susan Polk under California criminal code 187: murder, the unlawful killing of a human being with malice aforethought. The grand jury had listened to accounts of the killing and a coroner's report that listed "multiple (27) stab, incised, and blunt-force injuries to the head, torso and extremities," and based on the evidence, the grand jurors had handed down an indictment. In what may have been the first time Susan referred to a self-defense argument, she wrote Felix's sister that summer that it had been a tragedy for the whole family but that she had had no choice; it had been a matter of survival. She thought her chances were good that she would be found not guilty or at worst, guilty of manslaughter.

At various hearings and in motions she filed, Susan once again represented herself, attacking a probation report that opposed her release: "I do not have a history of criminality, violence, or mental illness," she wrote. She compared her "history as a law-abiding and contributing member of the community for all of my adult life" to that of her husband, whom she said had a "history of mental illness, domestic violence, and violation of professional ethics." She objected to accusations that she was a crazed killer like Lizzie Borden. "To be incarcerated for a crime of which one is innocent and the horror of being so is a recurring theme in literature and film from *The Count of Monte Cristo* to *The Shawshank Redemption*. The terror of being unfairly condemned gave rise to the protections which we built into our system in the fourth, sixth, and eighth amendments and the due process clauses of the fifth and fourteenth amendments," she wrote, like a student scribbling an essay in a blue book. She called the claim of twenty-seven wounds a misrepresentation.

After Susan continuously balked at hiring an attorney, the court assigned her a public defender, with the understanding that upon the sale of her house she would reimburse the public defender's office for her defense costs. Initially she worked with *the* public defender of Contra Costa County, David Coleman, an elegant African American graduate of Harvard Law. She was the only criminal client he'd ever known with whom he could discuss Voltaire. She made him feel the way few did, that he was out of his intellectual depth.

On October 1, 2003, as the discussion of Susan's bail continued, Felix's friend Barry Morris told the judge "I'm a little terrified at the prospect of her being released. I can't tell you how strongly I feel about this." Morris, whose overdeveloped muscles bristle when he speaks, told the judge, "The fact is, I'm afraid of her. I would feel compelled to buy a weapon." Ignoring the advice of counsel, the stick-figured Susan blurted out that before Felix's death, Barry Morris had been hanging out in a chat room conversing with her son Gabe, that Barry Morris was a drug user. On the other side of the courtroom, Barry Morris released an involuntary "Jesus Christ!" Unable to stop Ms. Polk's ranting, the judge ordered the court reporter to stop transcribing. But Susan continued, bellowing, "POT HEAD!"

Susan's next attorney, Jack Funk, a big, tall affable deputy public defender, admitted he wouldn't want to have been married to her but he didn't believe that Susan Polk would pose a threat to anyone. As Funk prepared Susan's defense, he began to put together a narrative that he believed could help acquit her: she was a battered woman who had killed her husband in self-defense. As Felix aged and lost the mantle of master of the universe, Susan had grown stronger. Felix had always isolated and controlled her. "It was never a healthy relationship. And it never got any better," Funk explained.

While Susan was trying to free herself on bail and cycling through public defenders, Eli remained home alone. He spent his days hanging out with friends, playing video games, smoking weed, and getting into trouble. On October 14, 2003, a year after his father was killed, Eli was driving along the freeway in his bronze Chevy Camaro with expired registration when a CHP officer tried to pull him over. Eli floored it, reaching 130 miles an hour. He'd installed a computerized device in his vehicle that he trusted would allow him to evade the cops. When his car blew a tire, it came to a screeching stop. Officers found an ounce of marijuana in his possession. He reeked of pot and having swallowed some of the evidence, his tongue was guerrilla green. He told the arresting officer he gave chase because he hadn't wanted to be caught with marijuana in his possession since he was a critical witness in his mother's defense.

Less than two weeks later Eli was in trouble again, after he shot a motorist in the neck with his BB gun, just missing the driver's carotid artery, but causing him to undergo an operation. The driver would become the mayor of the town of Orinda, and legislation nicknamed after Eli Polk would wend its way through the state legislature, making it a misdemeanor for anyone to brandish a BB gun in a "grossly negligent manner that could result in injury or death."

In response to these most recent troubles, Susan suggested her son move to Montana, where the men are strong and the weather is harsh. He never did.

ON SEPTEMBER 10, 2004, SUSAN HAD AN EMOTIONAL BAIL HEARING. Numerous witnesses testified against her including Adam, the titular head of the family. He was in a precarious position: "I love my mom. She's always known that. I . . . I don't think that she's a person who belongs in prison. I don't think that she fits into the general public of a prison . . . I don't think that she belongs in the general public right now either." He talked about his parents' marriage. "There's no arch villain in our family," he said, although his point of view would change over time. "It was just a bad marriage that should have ended way before it did," he said

While cross-examining Adam, Jack Funk, Susan's public defender, asked if Adam knew of any other time his mother had ever "threatened or attacked any other person?" He said, "No."

"And do you have any reason to believe that if your mother were released . . . that she would threaten or attack any other person?" Here his answer was not so simple: "I don't think it's a fair question to ask me because I don't know what happened in the cottage that night. I mean obviously, if she went into the cottage and killed him in cold blood, then yeah, yeah, she'd pose a danger to those other people that she's expressing similar delusions about. But if she went in there and he attacked her and she overpowered him and stabbed him to death, then no, I don't think she'd pose a threat to anybody else."

Five days later, Judge Mary Ann O'Malley reset bail for Susan Polk. After spending twenty months in jail, the forty-six-year-old defendant was set free. Susan put up eighty thousand dollars with a bail bondsman producing the remainder. People charged with murder are rarely set free. Tom O'Connor was appalled. The judge did not give her reasons for releasing Susan, but there were a couple of factors that probably played a role. For one thing, she may have seen Susan as only a threat to her late husband. In addition, she could have considered her a battered woman with a previously pristine record, who, compared to other murder suspects, did not appear to be a threat to society. Whatever the judge's motivation may have been, before releasing Susan, she gave an extreme warning that she not communicate with those people who were afraid of her, including her son Gabriel, the Briners, Budd MacKenzie, and Barry Morris.

On the day she was released, an excited Eli picked up his mother at the courthouse, and the two drove home. Had she been less of a recluse her presence back in Orinda might have stricken fear in the minds of many mothers, but few knew what she looked like and her story was not yet front-page news. That same day, Susan and Eli pushed a cart through the aisles of Safeway, just like any other mother and son. No one whispered or turned to see the woman who was charged with murdering her husband. Besides, it was fall, and Orinda moms were preoccupied buying bigger soccer shoes for tiny athletes and attending back-to-school night. Those few residents who were aware, including some of the neighbors, were upset that an accused killer was in their midst. Some complained to the cops, but there was nothing officers could do.

Susan came home to a house that wasn't completely hers. While she had been in jail a realtor had unsuccessfully attempted to sell the house and cottage ("Are you from the area?" The realtor would inquire. "Then you know the history of this house?"). The place had been staged, and much of Susan and Felix's magnificent Arts and Crafts tables and chairs had been stored, replaced by generic ones. Susan and Eli retrieved their belongings from storage, and Susan began to do what she had always had done: she swept and scrubbed, cooked and baked and she swam. When she couldn't find some of her belongings, she accused family friends who had looked after Eli of theft. She went online and conducted research for her defense, requesting that the navy send her husband's old medical records. She went through Felix's library, pulling out those books on subjects such as hypnosis that she thought might help her case. And she had her son Adam and his girlfriend over for a cordial lunch.

Despite her tactful overtures toward Adam, she also played hardball with him. When Adam forgot some of his schoolbooks at the house, she declared that he could only retrieve them if he brought her Dusty, the mellow, yellow Lab who was living with Gabe at the Briners'. Susan told Adam that if he tried to snatch his notebooks without delivering Dusty she would call the cops. He felt terrible, but with exams looming Adam thought he had no choice but to comply.

On October 5, 2004, Adam and Gabriel filed a wrongful death suit against their mother, seeking a million dollars. With legal fees and other expenses, they worried she would drain the estate. They wanted money for their schooling and living expenses and knew that their father would have wanted that too. They asked Eli to join in the suit, but he, of course, declined. In a declaration, Adam said that his mother had warned that if he didn't withdraw the suit, she would "tie up the estate" and spend all its assets in the next five years. He believed that was exactly what she was doing. In his poignant declaration Gabriel wrote: "With what dignity I have left, I beg the Court to expedite this civil matter so that my brothers and I can salvage what remains of my father's estate, and we can finally start to put together the pieces of our lives." (The lawsuit eventually would be settled with Gabe and Adam splitting three hundred thousand dollars, money from Susan and Felix's homeowner's insurance company.)

The ties that once bound Gabriel, the youngest son, and Eli, the middle son, had long since frayed. Gabe accused Eli of siding with the person who had murdered their father. In an e-mail he warned Eli that their mother's world was collapsing and that if Eli stuck with her she would drag him down, too. Gabriel told his brother he loved him but that he was running out of patience. "Man the fuck up," he advised and "handle your own shit. Love, Gabe."

Eli responded that he was disappointed Gabe lacked a sense of familial loyalty. He said he was always there for Gabe and always would be. Then he told his little brother he'd appreciate it if their contact remained private "which I'm sure it won't because I know how intrusive the Briners are . . . Love, Eli."

Gabe wanted his brother to make something of his life, but so many times Eli had been presented with an opportunity and had blown it. Felix's sister, Evelyn, had arranged for Eli to attend a school in Colorado. His plane ticket had been purchased, but he changed his mind after his mother warned he would be siding with Felix's family. When Gabe told Eli he was messing up, Eli accused his little brother of sounding like a shrink. He wrote that it was scary "to hear the words coming out of your mouth that sound so, so, so much like Dad. Are you trying to bring Dad back by becoming him????"

Both Eli and Gabe spoke of love, but they only engaged in bitter communications. Eli reminded Gabe he'd once said terrible things about his father. Gabe shot back that he'd have to live with what he said but that he'd matured since then. Gabe thought he should call his brother "Susan," because Eli unconditionally accepted everything she said. Staying with their mother, Gabe warned, would prevent Eli from succeeding in life. He signed off with: "I'm not *trying* to make you feel like shit, but in a way I am. Grow the fuck up. Love, Gabe."

Still Eli remained firmly ensconced in his mother's life. During the months she was free, Susan and Eli made the best of their numerous court appearances, bringing Dusty in their Volvo station wagon, looking like any affluent northern California family on an outing. Eli dressed in a suit. Susan tended to wear a preppy, pastel button-down shirt with khaki pants. The two sat together in court, whispering and giggling in the gallery while awaiting their cases. One might have a morning hearing and the other one in the afternoon. They enjoyed each other's company so much they reminded spectators of young lovers. During the ninety-minute lunch break they walked Dusty along the narrow streets of downtown Martinez. Observers would describe the scene as surreal.

Meanwhile the war of words between Gabe and Eli continued. In an increasingly vitriolic exchange Gabe told Eli to boil in his own anger and suggested his older brother have his mother read his e-mail. Gabe imagined that his mother would claim he'd been brainwashed. "Same old *schpiel*," he wrote.

Eli picked up on that, and after denying showing his mother the e-mail and professing his love for his little brother, he said it freaked him out that Gabe was using "Yiddish words like *schpiel*." He wondered if Felix's family was sending Gabe to Hebrew school.

Gabe sent his brother a link to webmd's definition of schizophrenia and to the *San Francisco Chronicle*'s story headlined, "Orinda man slain amid acid divorce/Wife says he coerced her as a teen" and a message that read: "Hey, remember this?? Mom murdered him. Poor Mom, poor Eli."

In his retort, Eli tried to coax Gabe home. He told his brother that things were as they always had been and that their mother was the same woman she'd always been, the exact sentiment Susan had expressed in a letter to Gabriel a few months before.

Ignoring the judge's warning, Susan wrote all three sons e-mails about family finances and about the Briners, who she thought were leading Gabriel astray. One letter talked about a dream she had in which Gabriel fell from a balcony and was drowning.

Gabe forwarded all his mother's e-mails to deputy DA Tom O'Connor. When she learned of his actions, Susan did not blame Gabe for betraying her; instead she once again put the onus on others: the Briners and Budd MacKenzie.

While Susan thought she'd done nothing wrong, the criminal courts had a different view. For violating the agreement not to contact Gabe, Susan forfeited her freedom. On April 19, 2006, she was returned to jail.

14.

MURDER TIMES TWO

MARTINEZ, CALIFORNIA, THE COUNTY SEAT, BECAME A BOOMTOWN DURING the 1850s, when seekers glided on horse-drawn ferryboats on their way to gold country. Some returned with gold while others, empty-handed, became farmers. Martinez is best known as the home of John Muir, the founder of the Sierra Club who helped save Yosemite Valley, and the birthplace of Joe Dimaggio. Despite its growth during the twentieth century, the community retains its original, small-town nature.

Residents living near the county buildings are accustomed to quick-heeled attorneys wheeling briefcases into the court buildings and jurors with badges flocking to restaurants during the noon break. Everyone in town knows not to discuss an ongoing case without first looking around for a juror. Downtown is full of so many funky antique shops that it seems there must be one for every ten residents. And on certain days Martinez's citizens are used to the TV trucks that chug into town whenever there's a big story.

Dan Horowitz ambled down the Martinez courthouse hallway trilling "Pennies from Heaven." His sparkling eyes and receding hairline were familiar though not as familiar as he would have liked. Horowitz had been on every major network and was a frequent guest on Court TV and CNN, where he was an engaging—if less than Hollywood handsome—pundit on such high-profile cases as Scott Peterson's and Michael Jackson's. A competent, compact attorney, Horowitz was wearing one of the twenty suits that a Nordstrom's salesperson had recently dropped off at his house to try on after his wife informed them he was handling *the Susan Polk case*. Today, September 19, 2005, the first day of the Polk murder trial, Horowitz, referring to the prosecution, roared: "I'm going to kick their ass!"

Together they made the most unlikely pair: the sometimes anti-Semitic Susan Polk deferring to the little Jewish lawyer with a fistful of chutzpah. Until they met, she had been determined to defend herself. But two days before her trial was to begin on August 22, 2005, Horowitz and his sidekick, attorney Ivan Golde, swept into West County Detention Center and convinced her they could provide a great defense. Some lawyers may be uncomfortable selling themselves, but not Horowitz and Golde. They knew they could help Susan Polk and that a storm of publicity was just waiting to be ignited. In response to Horowitz's request for time to learn the case, Superior Court Judge Laurel S. Brady, whose courtroom is on the second floor of the Bray Building, reluctantly agreed to postpone the trial nearly a month while Horowitz prepared his case.

On that first day of trial Horowitz's kick-ass glee was interrupted by a beep from his cell and then this overheard part of the conversation: "Thank God Susan survived! In eight weeks, Susan and I are walking out of the courtroom, and she will hug her son and find her other two sons and this horror will be over," he pronounced in a loud voice. It was obvious: this was another media call. "I remember when women who were raped were damaged goods! Now when we see crime victims, we have to love them and help them!" He continued with his wireless oratory, promising to keep the reporter informed of events. With the Horowitz spin, all the reporter would need is an intro, unless she wanted to present the prosecution's side of the case, which fewer and fewer "journalists" seemed to bother with on such high-profile made-for-cable-TV stories.

It was quite a performance, although there were only two members of the media loitering in the corridor of the Bray Building, to appreciate it. One wondered which network or newspaper he was promising to help. It turned out he was talking to a reporter from *Glamour* magazine.

Horowitz bragged that he was receiving 150 media calls a day. "Oprah's calling. I love Oprah!" he declared. "She's calling but I said, 'Susan is not some monkey in a cage.' " Then there's Nancy, Rita, and Catherine, *48 Hours, Dateline, A Current Affair,* and the local media. In the run-up to the trial, the Polk murder was becoming fodder for America's unquenchable thirst for true crime reality shows. Horowitz wasn't just a hungry pundit covering the case; he was consuming it.

Each morning he checked cable TV's online overnight ratings the way some folks do the temperature. Although hurricane Katrina overshadowed Polk, Horowitz was hopeful that as the storm receded and the trial commenced that cable news producers would come to value the Polk story "like a Greek drama." Horowitz couldn't possibly have known how true that observation would become or what the fickle gods had planned for him.

During the first few weeks, Horowitz and Golde found Susan was woefully unprepared. She had no story to present, few experts, and she knew nothing about jury selection, Golde recalled. They talked with her about how they would "tell her story" and, in a request that impressed Horowitz, she made him promise he would be gentle cross-examining her son Gabriel, the chief witness against her. Horowitz listened and said, "I like you and I believe in you."

To defend Susan, Horowitz would take a steep cut in pay, agreeing to the county rate of $105 an hour, splitting his fee with Golde. In truth, he didn't care about the money. For Horowitz and his beautiful, vivacious wife, Pamela Vitale, this trial was the next step in their master plan to transform him into one of the best-known attorneys in the nation. Horowitz and Vitale were closer than most couples. Married eleven years, she was half a head taller than he and effervescent. Despite attending college for only two years, she spoke five languages and was said to have become the youngest Pan Am stewardess ever hired. She went on to Hewlett-Packard, where she rose from dispatch clerk to an executive manager. Despite work and single parenthood, she made time to be room mother and attend her children's activities. When they were teens, Vitale slept on the couch so that her children, Marissa and Mario, could each have a bedroom. Pamela seemed an odd fit for someone like Horowitz. She was from the Midwest, he was from New York City. She wore oversize glasses, as if to hide her beauty, and into adulthood she retained an adventurous streak. In recent years, she'd given up her computer work to devote herself to the mansion she and Horowitz were building on a remote hilltop in Lafayette, California.

Several times a day Dan called her, and together they strategized how to catapult him into stardom. Horowitz did not have natural charisma. He was not even a feared or a brilliant lawyer, but he was hardworking, with drive to match his ambition. A fellow attorney said Horowitz belonged to the "throw the spaghetti on the wall and see what sticks" school of advocacy. Because he worked so fast and in so many directions he earned the sobriquet "Hurricane Horowitz."

On occasion, he would behave in ways that would give others pause. His willingness to take on a major murder case two days before the trial was just one example. The screensaver on his laptop showed off the massive Italian villa and vineyards he and Pamela were designing. The mansion, which resembled a rectangular wedding cake for 750 guests, was Pamela's project, designed for her grown kids and future grandkids, even though Marissa and Mario were living in Southern California.

Everything he did, Horowitz did at full speed. Susan saw that and appreciated it. "She's innocent," Horowitz told reporters. "She's not crazy. . . . Her IQ is genius! Her work is truly as good as a good lawyer!" He read the opening statement Susan had written to Pamela and both were deeply moved.

In the corridors of the courthouse all it took was a request from a reporter to have Horowitz reenact the death scene: Felix hovering over her with the knife; Susan on the bottom flailing and begging him to get off. Susan kneeing him in the groin and nabbing his knife. Susan was only defending herself. She had been saying that for a few years, but Horowitz's megaphone reached more ears.

One weekend, while Pamela hosted a family party at their house, Horowitz holed up at the Lafayette Park Hotel—where Felix and Gabe had gone to seek refuge—eating Trader Joe's granola and assembling his team. Golde, a short, friendly attorney with flyaway blond hair and a "hey, you guys, wait up for me" look, was already spending hours at the jail, befriending Susan and winning her confidence. His late father, Stanley P. Golde, had been a beloved Superior Court judge in Oakland and had given Horowitz his first job. Golde happily lives in the shadow of his father and Horowitz. To take on Polk, Ivan Golde put aside his other work, including, at least temporarily, the Wendy's chili finger case, in which he represented the man who sold his severed finger for a hundred dollars to the woman who "found" it in her bowl of chili. (Since the man turned the couple in, Golde was able to win for him a portion of Wendy's reward money.)

To assist them, Horowitz hired Valerie Harris, a plump software engineer with long blond hair and bangs with big eyes like a carved pumpkin. Ms. Harris credited American Idol for delivering her into the world of made-for-TV murders. After designing a fan website for American Idol star Clay Aiken, Harris attended a gathering of his fans, and there she befriended a courtroom artist who was working at the Scott Peterson trial. Valerie Harris joined her—although spectators were only allowed in if they'd won a seat in the daily lottery. Ms. Harris conducted her own investigation, tossing a dead chicken into the bay and watching it come up where baby Connor did. At the courthouse, Harris met trolling pundits Golde and Horowitz who were offering their services to any and all channels. When they took on the Polk case, they asked Valerie Harris to assist them.

Valerie Harris joined Golde, spending hours at the jail every day, interviewing Susan, and as Golde said, "fishing for jewels." Meanwhile, Horowitz went looking for a crime scene expert, a forensic pathologist and other experts, calling in all his chits from previous cases. He wrote that the seizing of Susan's laptop and what he claimed was the subsequent erasing of part of her hard drive, caused irreparable constitutional damage to his client. Rather than being portrayed as a mentally ill killer, he said her diary would prove that she was a "loving mother, sensitive and caring soul." (In fact the defense's own computer expert would later declare that everything had been retrieved.)

Despite Susan Polk's previous bail violation, Horowitz requested she be granted bail a second time. (Considering her a flight risk because she had encouraged Eli to slice off his electric monitor and because she had violated her previous bail terms, Judge Brady set her bail at a prohibitive eight million dollars.) Horowitz pushed to have Gabriel's statement to the police the night he found his father's body thrown out because, he argued, it was given when the boy was scared and brutalized and treated as though he were under arrest. Filing nearly a motion a day, Horowitz hoped that at the very least he would succeed in rattling assistant DA Tom O'Connor.

On the sidewalk outside the courthouse after a Polk hearing one day, O'Connor was indeed rattled. He had been on the case since the beginning and had assumed that Horowitz's arrival would signal much needed calm and common sense; he hadn't anticipated the media parade that Horowitz would lead. Whenever Horowitz arrived or departed, reporters gathered like guppies at feeding time. O'Connor refused to participate. Before court one morning, Horowitz offered to take O'Connor to Nordstrom's makeup counter to prepare him for TV appearances—an offer that repulsed O'Connor. Wise to the ways of Susan Polk, O'Connor was betting one of her former attorneys that the Horowitz-Polk honeymoon wouldn't last and that before the trial was over, she would fire him.

As the trial date grew closer, it became more obvious: reporters loved Horowitz. He answered all questions and called a select few with his bon mots.

Without their even asking, Horowitz gave the chosen ones CDs of the discovery in the case, a highly unusual move. Lawyers spin their facts for the press every day, but rarely do they hand over a CD of the discovery, because, among other things, the discovery has both the favorable facts as well as the unfavorable. It was a shrewd if risky move on Horowitz's part. In the thousand-plus pages on the CD, there was information that the judge had not yet decided to admit into evidence—that Horowitz wanted disseminated, such as Felix's fifty-year-old naval records, which showed he had attempted suicide, been diagnosed as suffering a schizophrenic reaction, and had been in a locked psych ward for a year.

Horowitz told reporters that Felix was "a violent monster and Susan Polk his victim." She "created an island of love" for her children, while he was "a vile, miserable man who imprisoned her." The night Felix died, Susan had walked "into a death trap" where her rageful husband wreaked vengeance on his long-suffering wife. She suffered from battered women's syndrome.

"The constant theme of this case has been 'Crazy Susan,' " Horowitz said after he and Ivan looked into some of Susan's claims of financial impropriety involving her husband's estate. "When you dig into it, it turns out she's right on the facts. . . . Once again, she's not crazy. It's people working her over trying to marginalize her," Horowitz insisted.

In the court of public opinion, Horowitz was making headway. Local and national stories publicized her plight. Susan often agreed to be interviewed; Horowitz always did. No one from the other side was willing to speak. Horowitz said the publicity led to new defense witnesses contacting him. What he failed to say was that the pro-Susan publicity could sway the jury pool as well as generate the publicity he craved.

WHILE WAITING FOR SOME OF THE THREE HUNDRED PROSPECTIVE JURORS TO be ushered into the courtroom on the first day of Susan's trial, Horowitz scanned his client's attire: a black blouse and khaki skirt she had worn the day before. Her clothes were classic and appropriate but that didn't stop Horowitz from joking: "My cousin in Manhattan can design a line of clothes for you. After we win she could have a whole line of Susan Polk clothes!" Susan smiled wanly.

Voir dire, or the questioning of potential jurors, can be an invasive and embarrassing experience. O'Connor apologized to the overflow of everyday citizens in the jury box and the gallery, "I do not mean to pry into your personal life," but then he and Horowitz did just that, laying bare the underside of American society. One prospective juror's brother was "involved in a manslaughter situation," another's grandmother was convicted of murdering her husband. A son's best friend murdered his wife. One young woman was so overcome before even telling her own story that she hyperventilated and had to be escorted from the courtroom.

Susan, now forty-seven, quietly participated in the process. She had requested that jurors not be questioned about domestic violence because she wanted as many victims as possible on the jury. She favored women, whom she was sure would be more sympathetic. She whispered her advice to Horowitz who, for the most part, took it as if he was conferring with a senior partner. When a thirty-two-year-old prospective juror named Valerie Northrop said she traveled around the world and considered herself a writer, Susan, who thought of herself as a writer too, leaned sideways and whispered she liked her and that they should keep her on the panel. Susan's voice carried and just like that, DA O'Connor eliminated the woman.

The following day, Ms. Northrop returned. She announced to the bailiff and others that she intended to write a book about Susan Polk to "champion her cause" (although it may have been wishful thinking, since none of her work had been published). With a grand flourish, Horowitz handed her the CD of the motions, something he had given to a journalist working the story. This overly generous gesture did not go unnoticed by spectators, who wondered why Horowitz would be so magnanimous with a person who didn't come across as a serious writer.

Each day, Horowitz told hungry reporters how impressed he was with Susan's advice; he was proud of her legal acumen. But after awhile, their relationship became more complicated, as it often does with Susan. When he failed to follow her directions *every time* she offered them, she would berate him in court loud enough for others to overhear.

"Don't ever say I said anything or I agree to anything without checking with me first!" she scolded in a whisper loud enough for others to hear. She said that after Horowitz had assured Judge Brady that his client would abide by a court order forbidding her to have any contact with Gabriel. Among other matters, the judge was concerned that Ms. Polk might attempt to taint the testimony of the chief prosecution witness. "I'm not willing to agree to no contact with Gabriel!" Susan hissed at her attorney. The honeymoon had been short, but Horowitz was tenacious. Susan seemed to have met her match: Horowitz would provide her a strong defense whether she wanted it or not.

By October, the air was oppressive. It hadn't rained since the spring. Like parched animals, residents yearned for the torrential downpours of late fall and early winter. Many were quietly on edge. On October 11, 2005, almost three years to the day after Felix Polk's murder, twelve jurors were seated in Judge Brady's court in Martinez, California, to pass judgment on the case of *The People of the State of California v. Susan Mae Polk*.

TV vans with giraffe dishes, symbols of a story that producers anointed as larger than the sum of its parts, were parked out front. Reporters were clotted on the sidewalk as Horowitz slid out of his silver Honda S2001 sports car to the waiting throng: "How will you handle Gabriel Polk?" one called out. "I'm going to handle Gabriel as if he's my own son because that's what his mother wants," Horowitz offered. Another thrust a mike at him: "She doesn't seem mentally stable. How are you going to handle that?" "The state of mind of Susan Polk varies from day to day just like anyone else. I find her rational, cogent, and brilliant and that's what the jury will find out."

On the first day of her trial, the only person in the courtroom who was there for Susan was her son Eli, dressed in respectful dark suit and white shirt. Because he would be called to testify, Horowitz swiveled around and said simply, "Nice to see you. Good-bye." Eli left.

When Judge Brady read the charge against Susan, she bowed her head and wept. She was so ashamed, later explaining, "Never growing up or as a young woman did I expect to be charged with murder. And then to stand in front of my peers . . ."

DA Tom O'Connor rose from his seat and strode slowly to the jury box. He leaned forward on the balls of his feet, hesitated the way someone who is confident can, and then began setting the scene: Felix was going to take his youngest son to the baseball playoffs. "Instead, Gabriel Polk found his father's motionless body covered in blood in the pool house," O'Connor intoned. When he said Gabe had been anxiously awaiting the game, Susan Polk whispered to Horowitz, "That's not even true! He didn't care about the game." O'Connor called the final struggle "clearly a one-sided battle." Susan Polk had received so few injuries that the next day Gabriel hadn't noticed anything different about her, O'Connor told the jury. The murder weapon, the clothes she had worn, "all the incriminating evidence against the defendant was gone," he declared. Except that in Felix's tightened fist detectives "found strands of Susan Polk's hair," he explained, as he looked jurors in the eye. "Thankfully, we were able to find her hair and place the defendant in the pool house that night."

O'Connor and Horowitz were a study in contrasts. O'Connor has thick, copper colored hair and a face that reddens when he becomes upset. He's as sturdy as a linebacker and likes to stand with his arms folded and his legs slightly apart. If Ivan Golde stood on top the shoulders of Dan Horowitz they would equal one Tom O'Connor. O'Connor was the kind of prosecutor that played it down the line, straight and to the point. He expected to win his case with the facts, while Horowitz would win any way he could.

The public servant had waited three years for this. His first child was born days after Susan Polk killed her husband. A second child was born before the trial began. This was personally the most painful case he'd ever prosecuted. She had spent part of the last three years publicly insulting him in court. When the two were in the same room, he often stood as far away from her as he could. He was so sick of having her berate him that once when a judge refused to admonish her, he literally stormed out of the courtroom. He thought Susan Polk was not just delusional but manipulative, nasty, cruel, and vindictive. "The defendant is nothing but a cold, calculating, callous murderer," he told the jurors. "She threatened to kill Felix Polk, and that is exactly what she did!"

Now it was Horowitz's turn. While O'Connor took large strides, Horowitz practically skipped in small, rapid steps, as though he were rushed. The gallery was full of reporters and spectators. Dan's wife, Pamela, was there too. On a projection screen, Horowitz displayed horrendous photos of Felix's body, the sort of images that can attach themselves to a person's psyche and not let go, photos of Felix with dead eyes staring out like a speared fish. Then he showed pictures of Susan shortly after she was arrested with a cabernet bruise curved around one eye. To some observers, offering these images didn't make sense, but to Horowitz it did: he thought he could immunize jurors early. He gestured at the slide on the screen and said Susan Polk had two black eyes (although there was very little discoloration to make anyone believe that.). He said his client had "defended herself against an attack by a rageful, brutal, angry man who was also her husband." Horowitz called the crime scene "gory and horrific," and said that had things gone differently, "Susan Polk would have been lying dead and not Felix Polk." In a gracious aside, he added, "We regret his death."

When he was finished with the crime scene photos, Horowitz displayed a drawing Susan had made as a child; he read loving letters her sons had sent. He humanized her. "Susan Polk was just a kid of fifteen . . . an innocent," he said, when she became involved with a forty-year-old man. "The so-called therapy," he said, "did not work." Horowitz painted a tableau of a family life in which Felix Polk dominated everything. The Polk house, he said, "was like a cult" run by its maker.

"If a witness gets to the stand and calls Felix the victim, that's a conclusion they have reached," Horowitz told jurors. "We call Susan Polk the victim." That was pure Susan; she'd been stressing that point to the judge for weeks.

Without explaining where the tape came from, when it was recorded, or what it meant, he played for the jurors the haunting voice of the dead man:

"My rage is omnipresent. I wake up with it every morning. And my son Adam doesn't have to be choking for me to do that. I am enraged. My fantasy, of course, is to kill them. And I'm a rather moral person. I want to kill them. You don't hear that too often on television either. But I won't. Not now."

The recording, which had nothing to do with the murder, was made seventeen years before, when Felix was speaking about the alleged satanic abuse of his son. Horowitz's investigator, Kent Brezee, had uncovered the tape—with a little help from Google. It was a chilling and effective character assassination.

Once he completed his opening statement and court was adjourned, reporters clustered round Horowitz to record the words "My rage is omnipresent" for that night's news. In the aftermath of the opening statements, Horowitz appeared on the *Nancy Grace* show twice, during which she pulverized him: Felix "has all the lacerations and she has none," Grace harangued. "What was she doing from Montana to California, sharpening her knife?" Horowitz wanted to say that Felix had been on top of Susan and that the angle of the knife and the blood would show that, but his point was lost in the flying accusations and the commercial breaks. He would later rationalize his appearance by saying it was good practice; no one would give him a tougher time than his pal Nancy. He said it with admiration, though the encounter neither helped him nor his client.

THAT SATURDAY, OCTOBER 15, 2005, FOUR DAYS AFTER THE TRIAL BEGAN, Horowitz had an early meeting at Millie's Kitchen in Lafayette, a popular place for hearty breakfasts. Then he went to his office to prepare for the Polk case. Several times he tried to phone Pamela but was unable to reach her. Though he was concerned, he knew she had her own schedule. That evening she was going to the ballet with a friend. At 5:55 PM he negotiated his silver Honda through their long, gated driveway, where he spotted his wife's white 1999 230 Mercedes, causing him more anxiety than alarm. His arms full with two grocery bags and his heavy computer case, he opened the door to their trailer, where the two were living while their seven thousand-square-foot castle was being built.

At the entryway to the trailer, he found his great love's listless body curled up in the fetal position, her black skirt bunched around her waist, purple panties visible. He collapsed to the ground, his bags tumbling down. For a millisecond the criminal defense attorney thought he must be viewing a crime scene photo, but he knew better. Someone had clobbered Pamela's head with a blunt object—possibly a limestone rock, which along with crumbly sandstone is common on the hillside. She had twenty-six lacerations to her head, a stab wound in her abdomen, defensive wounds on her legs and arms. Her front teeth were cracked; fingers were broken. A grotesque *T*-like insignia was carved into her back. It was rimmed in red but hadn't bled, a sign that the cut was made in the agonal phase, or final moments *before* she died. He pressed his fingers by her neck; there was no pulse.

Neighbors would later say Horowitz's cries resembled a wounded animal. "Oh my God, Pamela! No no no, Pamela!" he screamed. He'd stop and then yelp again.

Cradling her in his arms, he told her how much he loved her and screamed again. He noticed the way a husband might that the 2.5-carat diamond ring he gave her was turned inward, something she did when she felt uncomfortable around a stranger. In her face, he thought he saw the love he'd seen every day, and he imagined she had died knowing she was greatly loved.

The longer he sat with her, the more the gore of the scene receded. Describing the moment later he would say: "It didn't matter anymore you know, what was around her or the horror. I had so much time with Pamela, so I just looked at her face and it was beautiful." He called 911.

When deputies arrived they placed him in the back of a black-and-white, where he was scrunched for hours, wanting to be with Pamela but, as a defense attorney, aware that the cops couldn't let him near the crime scene. While waiting to be questioned, he notified family members and friends on his cell—before the story hit the ten o'clock news.

As the deputy sheriffs would discover, the killer had been in no rush. He drank from Pamela's Crystal Geyser water bottle before departing.

THE MURDER WITHIN A MURDER BECAME NATIONAL NEWS. MOST ASSUMED Pamela Vitale had been killed by someone connected to the Polk case. Dozens of new reporters assigned to cover the twisted tale descended on Hunsaker Canyon Road, the remote, windy hillside street where Horowitz lived.

The night of Vitale's death, investigators notified Susan Polk at the county jail. She felt terrible for Horowitz; she couldn't imagine his sorrow. She suspected that one of Felix's friends, someone who she thought was a spy, was the killer. She had told Horowitz embarrassing information about the man, which she expected Horowitz to ask about when he was called to testify. She believed this was his way of pulling Horowitz off the case.

Others suspected Pamela had been killed by a difficult older neighbor. Months before, Horowitz had filled out an application for a temporary restraining order against the neighbor—though he later withdrew it after the neighbor sought drug rehabilitation. In the order Horowitz wrote, "Most important to me is that he stay away from my wife, Pamela."

In hushed voices some reporters, even a few who knew him, speculated that as the husband, Dan Horowitz must be considered the prime suspect. Others assumed that as a defense attorney, he must have encountered violent clients who went away angry and vengeful.

Two days after Pamela Vitale's death, on October 17, Judge Brady declared a mistrial in the case of Susan Polk. The judge advised Ms. Polk to consider hiring another attorney. It wasn't known when or if Horowitz would return, and then there were the potential conflicts: deputies confiscated Horowitz's laptop, which contained the entire Polk defense. Some of the same investigators who worked on the Polk murder would be working on Vitale's, and Dr. Brian Peterson, the prosecution's forensic pathologist whom Horowitz intended to eviscerate, was also the pathologist for Pamela Vitale.

Susan, however, wasn't interested in another attorney. Despite her misgivings about him and her repeated desire to avoid delays, despite her tendency to see conflicts of interest where there weren't any—and in this case there were plenty—she said she thought Horowitz was doing a great job. She would stick it out.

Literally overnight, Dan Horowitz aged. His sparkle disappeared, and in its place were two sad, blank eyes. He lost so much weight he went from being convex to concave and had to buy new trousers. His ever present joy gave way to a look that was perpetually haggard and old. He found it a burden to have to rise each morning and no longer cared whether he ate or worked. He felt like a leaf buffeted by the wind. He had a brand-new life not of his own choosing.

For the first time, he began to think of himself as "a nothing. I totally understand that I lived through an event I wasn't a part of. It could happen tomorrow again." It was a dramatic switch for a self-described tough guy who thought he could control anything. Although he was staying with friends, every day he returned to his house, where he talked to Pamela and he raged. At night he slept with her nightshirt. When he finally got his laptop back from the police, he replaced the screensaver photo of their château with beatific images of his wife. He only wanted to be with Marissa and Mario, Pamela's grown children. Wherever he went, strangers hugged him and asked if there was anything they could do. He found that in the horror of his everyday existence there was public kindness. All except for the media, which hounded him, even in the Lafayette Park Hotel, where he had sought refuge.

Four days after Pamela's murder, after refusing almost all media requests, Horowitz agreed to be interviewed by his dear friend Nancy Grace. It made for dramatic, if embarrassing, TV. He rocked and he sobbed. Viewers were both repelled and fascinated. Horowitz showed Grace the trailer. The blood smear on the door was pixilated, a shot that Grace returned to over and over again. Dan gave her a tour of their nearly finished mansion. A psychotherapist advised viewers that it's a little too soon for "Daniel" to decide whether he would continue as Susan Polk's attorney. "He must have felt some guilt that his work led to his wife's death," she said out of the blue, drawing a conclusion unsupported by the facts. "I think he needs more time."

Grace's interview with Horowitz was conducted not during the tour of the mansion but at the lodge at Wildwood Acres Resort, a facility more accustomed to June weddings than October murders, which sits in the hollow of Hunsaker Canyon Road. In the parking lot of the lodge camera crews and reporters milled, waiting without success for a snippet from the now famous Horowitz, who had driven up in his silver sports car but was unwilling to speak to the masses. As Horowitz was inside taping his sorrow for Grace's show, one of her security guards (called "goons" by the assembled media) rebuked reporters: "Have some respect for Mr. Horowitz's privacy!"

TV reporters who knew nothing about the case were pulled off other assignments. Several days after Pamela's murder one of them caught Ivan Golde outside the courthouse: "Do you have strong opinions about what happened?" she asked. Golde looked at her quizzically. He was too polite to inquire what she'd drunk at breakfast. Instead he took the opportunity to speak about the love between Dan and Pamela.

AS AUTHORITIES INVESTIGATED THE MURDER, THEIR ATTENTION WAS DRAWN to a neighbor, sixteen-year-old Scott Dyleski. Dan and Pamela had never met Scott, but Dan had done free legal work for Dyleski's mother, an aging hippie named Esther Fielding, who dabbled in pseudoscientific DNA wellness therapy and had owned a failed bagel shop. For years, Dyleski and his mother had lived in a hut made of pallets stuffed with mud and straw in affluent Lafayette about a mile down the road from Horowitz and Vitale. For years, they had had no running water, no electricity. The land on which they lived was owned by Fielding's friend Fred Curiel, a computer expert who was building a house of straw bale they eventually would live in. Esther, a small, disheveled-looking woman whose head curled in like a tortoise, couldn't afford to pay rent so they lived there free. Some ten people, including Scott and his mother, lived in Curiel's commune with chickens and goats roaming outside and an old dog named Jazz.

Friends and housemates would later describe the earnest-looking boy with the dark brooding eyes as sweet, kind, and generous; someone who played Frisbee, took piano lessons from a ninety-four-year-old neighbor, and looked after the little kids in their communal home. But in the weeks leading up to Vitale's murder he became withdrawn, spending more time alone in his room and going out on late-night walks.

Scott's sister had died in a car crash in 2002, when he was thirteen. After that he let his black locks grow long over his eyes and adopted a Goth style of dress. He penned macabre poetry with titles like "Live for the Kill" and phrases such as "standing alone on cemetery hill the smell of corpses filling the air." He drew ghoulish tableaux of beheaded victims—the way some adolescent boys do, but he went far beyond that, taking a disturbing interest in murder and vivisection. Dyleski could explain to friends the difference between mass murderers and serial murderers and was fascinated by the story of Ed Gein, a farm boy from Plainfield, Wisconsin, who was raised by a mother in a house without electricity or plumbing. In the 1940s and 1950s, Gein began his murder spree, chopping up victims and recycling their body parts into a rug, upholstered chair, bracelet, and purse. Aware of some of her son's disturbing drawings, Esther Fielding tried to arrange for him to talk with a therapist—shortly before Pamela Vitale was killed.

On October 19, 2005, four days after the death, Scott Dyleski was arrested for the murder of Pamela Vitale. Although Esther Fielding took incriminating evidence—a box of throwaway gloves, receipts from purchases bought with neighbors' credit cards, his copy of *The Silence of the Lambs*—and set fire to them at her sister's home in Bolinas, an isolated hippie community at the edge of the ocean in Marin County, she or her son inadvertently left a trail of clues. Sheriff's deputies found an old Toyota van with flat tires, cracked windows, and mold and mildew spreading along the inside of the vehicle on the Curiel property. Inside, investigators found Dyleski's incongruously clean black duffel bag with specks of Pamela's oxidized blood on his name tag: "Dyleski, Scott." Inside the bag, they came across a Ninja-style black balaclava, or ski mask, with a single opening for the eyes, where they found Pamela's and Dyleski's DNA, and a right-hand glove that also contained her blood. Stamped in blood at the crime scene, investigators found a shoe print of an organic Lands' End no-leather shoe belonging to Dyleski.

Authorities could only speculate as to the motive. With a friend, Scott was developing a marijuana cultivation business. He'd been trying to purchase grow lights with credit card information he'd stolen from neighbors' rural mailboxes, but he encountered problems with the lighting company customer service representative, who refused to allow the caller with the childlike voice to buy equipment to be sent to one address with a credit card registered to another. Scott had given Horowitz's address as his own.

Like the murderers he studied, he may have killed just for the sake of the killing. Or it may be that he went to Horowitz's house to collect PIN numbers for the fake credit cards he was trying to set up. Scott may have spelled out his motive in an index-card-size scratch pad he'd stashed in the drawer of his room and which lodged itself on top of the drawer. The "to-do list" was a horrifyingly simple scenario for murder:

Knockout/kidnap
Question
Keep captive to confirm PINS
Dirty work
Dispose of evidence
Cut up and bury

The week following Pamela's death, Susan Polk was all but ignored. Everyone around Dan Horowitz was distraught and distracted, but by the following week, Ivan Golde and Valerie Harris were back attending to their client.

Dan Horowitz was still floating in a gray haze. He didn't know if he would ever return to the law let alone the Polk case. All he really wanted to do was become Mrs. Doubtfire, living in the Southern California homes of his stepchildren. He thought about what Pamela would have advised him to do, and he discussed it with Marissa and Mario. Two weeks after her death, Dan decided to return. He visited Susan to let her know. The meeting was warm and cordial. Susan was elated.

In a surprise move, Horowitz hired long, tall Valerie Northrop, the young, attractive former prospective juror who had declared she was going to write a book on the Polk case. In the week before Pamela's murder, Northrop had befriended Horowitz's staff and let it be known she wanted to work with them. Susan was pleased by the hire: "She's very capable, very personable, well spoken. She's a great addition to the team," Susan said, just before drastically changing her views of Ms. Northrop and Horowitz.

On November 17, 2005, Horowitz and Golde told the judge they intended to try Susan's case. Having been criticized for his appearance on *Nancy Grace*, Horowitz politely refused all media requests. He looked like a beaten man; his face was rumpled like a brown balloon with its air sucked out of it. He'd received more publicity than he had ever imagined, but for all the wrong reasons. He kept his silence. Golde spoke for him and said they remained on the case "because we made a commitment to Susan Polk. We feel she's innocent. We'll win this case."

In the coming weeks though, Susan's enthusiasm for her attorneys waned. As she sometimes did, she looked at the same facts and came to the opposite conclusion. Horowitz had failed to pursue her claim that someone must have poured water over Felix's body to make the crime scene look more bloody than it was. She pointed to a photo that showed a clear liquid near Felix's skull. Horowitz had yet to interview Eli, one of her main witnesses, and furthermore he had not helped her to file motions when she was convinced that someone related to Eli's girlfriend was threatening to harm her and Eli *while she was in jail.*

For a while, they had been a family, but as with Susan's own family, when conflicts arose she discovered villains in her midst. Ivan and Dan blamed what happened next on themselves and their own laxness. They should never have allowed Valerie Harris, the heavyset blond Peterson groupie, to spend so many hours with Susan Polk. Valerie befriended Susan, loved her really, and became protective of her. When rifts occurred between the attorneys and their client, Valerie sided with Susan. Unintentionally, she'd crossed the line, driving a wedge in their relationship. For her part, Valerie Harris believed the breakup occurred after Dan hired Ms. Northrop.

ON THE LAST DAY OF 2005 WHILE IN A PHONE CONVERSATION WITH Horowitz, Susan Polk lashed out at her attorney and announced she would no longer require his services. Horowitz, she said, shouted that she was "spoiled rotten," and "a petulant baby." But it was not up to Susan Polk to fire her attorneys. The court had appointed them and it would be up to the judge to determine if they would remain. Susan had a right to an attorney of her choice, but with a new trial scheduled in a month, the judge might not have been willing to accept her request. Susan demanded Horowitz return her files and if he failed to do so, he said she told him, "I'm going to hurt you."

Maybe Susan wanted to insure that she was free of Dan Horowitz. Or maybe she believed the horrible accusation she was about to make—she certainly sounded that way. Calling a reporter from jail, Susan confided, "I don't feel that I can be silent about this." Ever since Pamela Vitale had died she said she had "wondered whether Dan murdered his wife." She cobbled together things she claimed Horowitz had told her, things about his wife that he said he would never have said to anyone because they weren't true but especially not to his client, Susan Polk. Most notable of her claims was that Horowitz, she claimed, had told her that Pamela had had an affair.

As Horowitz came to believe, Susan simply was not satisfied with just ridding herself of him. "I think she's saying it just to push my buttons. She's taking what's most precious to me, my wife and my memory of her, and degrading them."

Either way, Susan's statements became stronger and more vicious as the trial date approached. A few days before her January 13, 2006, hearing, she began telling reporters that in conversation with Horowitz he had implicated himself in his wife's murder. She claimed he told her "I've got (Dyleski). I did a better job on him than they did on you and that little fucker is not going to get out of this."

A day or two before, Horowitz had still imagined that he could represent Susan. But after her accusations, there was no more patter. "I might have to testify against her in the Dyleski case," he said.

Some reporters listened to Susan but failed to write anything. Others, such as the *Oakland Tribune*'s Jason Dearen, put it in context: "Polk's erratic behavior and courtroom tirades have led some to question her mental stability. In the 1980s she told the *Tribune* that she suspected a satanic cult had forced her son to endure sodomy and eat human excrement. Federal and local investigations never found any evidence of those claims."

Susan wasn't finished. She told reporters that "immediately" after Pamela's death Dan and Ms. Northrop "became inseparable." That he had become "besotted" by the young woman. Like Pamela, Ms. Northrop was considerably taller than he, and as he mourned, he found in Valerie Northrop something he needed. Had she been unattractive, few comments might have been made. But Ms. Northrop wore her long black hair down her back, accentuating her pale skin. She wore her pants tight around her rump and had a flirtatious way with men. Ms. Northrop did indeed become a shoulder to cry on for the bereaved Horowitz. At the time that Susan was making those accusations, Horowitz claims he was not having an affair with Ms. Northrop. But within weeks, he was.

On January 13, 2006, three weeks before her new trial, Susan Polk struck out on her own. It was as though a divorcing family was forced one last time to sit together at the dinner table in cold silence. Joviality had long since dissipated, replaced by hostility. Susan sat between Horowitz and Golde as she usually did. Valerie Harris sat on the end of the table. Each was churchlike erect. Without an attorney to restrain her, Susan made a motion: to have Judge Brady and the entire county bench recuse themselves from her case. She accused the judges of being "biased and prejudiced against me." (Her request was denied.) She made a motion to defend herself. She thought no one could defend her "as truthfully, faithfully, and compassionately" as she could. In an insulting move, she asked that Ivan Golde and Dan Horowitz be ordered to leave the defense table. She wanted only an embarrassed Valerie Harris to remain.

Susan was not yet through with Horowitz. Getting rid of her attorney was not enough; she had to trample and smash her opponent into smithereens. That she was able to retaliate, despite being an inmate charged with murder, made her actions all the more remarkable.

Until then, Horowitz had never criticized Susan Polk, but after his firing he confided in a few reporters that he found Susan to be both manipulative and delusional and that had the case proceeded he could not have put her on the witness stand. He'd counted thirty-six conspiracies his former client had concocted. Most chilling, he didn't believe Susan's allegations against him were delusions. They were, he was convinced, a deliberate effort to destroy him. While other journalists remained sensitive to Horowitz's plight, Geraldo Rivera had no such compunction. On January 30, Susan mustered all the evidence she could to flog Horowitz on *Geraldo at Large*, and as with the satanic abuse accusations, Geraldo didn't bother getting the details right. He thought the judge was a man. He said Susan Polk had had three previous attorneys. She'd had five. He never hinted she was delusional. He said she could be "eccentric," and "erratic." He let her tell her story, egging her on at all the opportune moments:

GERALDO: Susan claims she already had doubts about Horowitz before his wife's murder. It was her attorney's statements since the slaying of his wife that really turned her against him.

SUSAN: There was a juror who was very attractive who was going to be on the jury, and he was constantly flirting with her.

GERALDO: Susan says that she heard Horowitz hooked up with the woman who now works in his office soon after his wife died.

GERALDO: So from being the faithful husband after Pam died he immediately [took up] with this former juror?

SUSAN: Yeah, and personally I feel there should be some period of mourning.

The statement seemed ironic considering it came from a woman charged with murdering her husband. She went on:

> Given his arrogance about how intelligent he was, one of the statements that really bothered me is that after the murder of his wife, he did come to see me briefly for fifteen or twenty minutes and he said, 'Everybody loves me now. And you'll win your case. Everybody loves me.' And I said, 'I don't want to benefit in any way from the death of your wife.'
>
> I have a lot of compunctions about publicly saying that someone could have had something to do with a murder, but it seems like in our country at least we have now gotten to the point where things are discussed on TV about who is guilty or who might have had something to do with something, and I hope that everyone suspends judgment until they hear all the facts.

Geraldo called her comment "eloquent."

Dan Horowitz, whose goal was to become famous, was now nauseated by the sensational media storm generated by the murder of his wife. But he couldn't shut off the fire hydrant. More than six months later, Scott Dyleski was tried for murder as an adult. Threatened with jail for destroying evidence, Dyleski's mother became an absentminded witness for the prosecution. On August 28, 2006, the seventeen-year-old Scott Dyleski was convicted of first-degree murder and sentenced to life in prison without the possibility of parole.

Horowitz would maintain a low profile throughout Dyleski's trial and beyond. He continued to work on criminal cases. Because of his relationship with Ms. Northrop his stepchildren and he became estranged. In late summer 2006, as Susan was preparing to defend herself in the murder of her husband, Horowitz and Valerie Northrop moved into the mansion that Pamela built.

15.

DEFENDING HERSELF

FORTY-SEVEN-YEAR-OLD CONTRA COSTA COUNTY ASSISTANT DISTRICT ATTOR-ney Paul Sequeira threaded his way through the mobile TV vans, with their gawky satellite poles, glancing at the media's white tent installed a block from the courthouse and wondered what high-profile case had drawn reporters to Martinez this time. On his way to the courthouse for jury selection, Sequeira, who had taken over the Polk prosecution only four weeks before, assumed that after Dan Horowitz left, the media attention would dissipate. He was, of course, wrong.

About a month earlier on the morning of February 27, 2006, Sequeira was feeling pretty good. On a bruised and blustery morning on the golf course his cell phone rang. Tom O'Connor informed Sequeira that he was leaving the DA's office for a job in the private sector. Someone would have to take over the prosecution of their office's most difficult case. Sequeira decided to handle it himself. He gathered up the Polk files and headed home to semirural Sonoma County, where he dodged his four kids and read for the next month. The crime part was pretty straightforward, but there were so many letters and e-mails—"She raised a bunch of writers," he said, and with so much correspondence to review, he could never feel he knew everything. But having been a prosecutor for twenty-two years, he felt he could master the facts. He knew O'Connor and Susan Polk despised one another but Sequeira assumed that was just personal. He thought that if he was low key he could avoid similar pitfalls; he'd let her do what she wanted and not object much. Even though he was a seasoned pro up against a neophyte, Sequeira was concerned. He didn't want jurors to see him as beating up on the frail-looking defendant. And if she put on a battered woman's defense, he worried any aggressive action on his part might garner greater juror sympathy for her.

He had other concerns as well. Susan had a list of over a hundred witnesses, many of them holdovers from the Horowitz days. Horowitz had wanted to throw the prosecutor off, and by listing as witnesses everyone who had been close to Felix Polk, that also meant that no weepy relative or good friend of Felix's could sit in the gallery creating sympathy for the victim. Sequeira didn't know whom Susan would call, when she would call them, or what many of them might say.

As for what kind of attorney Susan Polk might be, he began to worry that morning when she questioned prospective jurors. She rose from the only chair in the well with wooden feet. (In Contra Costa County, criminal defendants are not allowed chairs with wheels, which can facilitate attempted escapes.) Her red sweater and black wool skirt hung loosely on her thin frame. Her Faconnable (size small) jacket was draped over her seat. Standing before prospective jurors at the wooden lectern balancing her wire-framed glasses on her refined nose, she once again resembled a college professor. Her voice was soft but direct.

If jury pools have personalities, the first one, with many victims of abuse, was more defense-oriented. This jury pool, with many ties to law enforcement, was more prosecution-oriented. Everyone had a brother who was a cop or a brother-in-law who worked in the jails. Karen Fleming-Ginn, a jury consultant who worked on the prosecution side of the Oklahoma bombing case and on fifty other capital cases for the defense—with only six death verdicts—was advising Susan Polk.

Fleming-Ginn was looking for people outside the mainstream, jurors who've had a harder time in life and tend to see shades of gray. She knew things that few attorneys know, such as the fact that Safeway employees tend to side with the prosecution while workers at the Nummi auto plant in Fremont, California, are more pro-defense. Susan listened to her consultant and kept on the panel a man who worked at the Nummi plant. Sequeira, on the other hand, kept it simple. When he teaches young lawyers about jury selection, he tells them the most important factor is that jurors like you. Sequeira's legal buddies thought he was nuts when he kept a young guy with a ponytail down to his waist on the panel, but Sequeira felt the two had connected, and he wasn't about to go against his gut.

"Would it surprise you to know that when the Constitution was written that everyone represented themselves?" Susan Polk asked the first juror. The juror listened but said, "To me it's a very, very bad decision."

"Would you give me a chance and hear me out?" she inquired in her soft voice. "Yes," he responded.

She asked another prospective juror if it were possible that "a police officer might not tell the truth." She was spoon-feeding them issues critical to her case.

At forty-eight, Susan Polk was a quick study, but there remained so much she didn't know. Sometime during the day, she had wanted to raise an objection to a comment made by the DA, but no one at the defense table was certain how to go about it.

An imposing African American computer systems analyst with a baritone voice advised, "If I'm fighting for my life, I would want the biggest, baddest dog in the fight," a remark that elicited laughter in the courtroom.

Women called her "brave"; men called her "foolish."

To a juror who mentioned he disliked the media, she asked, "If you were accused of things you didn't do, would you go to the media?" He said he wouldn't. "After two years?" she inquired. He conceded maybe he would.

As she questioned prospective jurors, she managed to impress Sequeira. Ms. Polk did something that young lawyers rarely do: she listened. He thought she was a natural. Susan was "pleasantly surprised" by the ease with which she related to prospective jurors. "That's my community," she thought, and she found voir dire "kind of fun." She looked over at the DA and thought he seemed "a little nervous," and that pleased her as well.

In preparation for the trial, Susan Polk asked a young woman, "Do you assume I am lying and the DA is not?" The woman responded that she assumed there was "heavy evidence" against the defendant, a comment that set Susan off. Repeatedly, she challenged the prospective juror: "Can you entertain the possibility that there are political reasons why someone is charged?" she asked. "In the American system of jurisprudence," she lectured, "there is an assumption of innocence. It is not up to me to present a case, to prove beyond a shadow of a doubt that I am innocent. It is up to the DA." She wouldn't let up. On the second day of jury selection Judge Laurel Brady, a patient jurist, would refer to Susan's questioning of the woman as resembling a cross-examination. That was not a compliment.

Sometimes Judge Brady would act like Susan's teacher, advising the inexperienced pro per defendant about courtroom procedure and the law. A former prosecutor married to a retired police officer, Judge Brady was exceedingly patient with Susan Polk, but she could also be tough. Her courtroom had small touches of her personal warmth: lamps with cloudy lights and spindly plants that were past their prime. On the wall behind her in big numbers she had posted her courtroom's telephone number.

On the third day of selection, the enormity of Susan Polk's situation seemed to sink in. She told a prospective juror she intended to tell her *whole story:* "This is the one chance I have," she said as she wept.

Like Icarus and her former boss Dan Horowitz, Valerie Harris was dangerously attracted to the brightest lights. Sometimes she acted in ways that were against her client's best interest. During the jury selection process, she gave Court TV's Catherine Crier a tape of Susan Polk's interrogation the night Felix's body was found, during which she repeatedly told deputies she didn't know what happened. It made for great TV but could only hurt Susan Polk. The next day Susan tried to manage damage control. She asked jurors, if someone lied about a crime does that mean she's guilty? By the start of the second week, Susan Polk was becoming more herself—which wasn't necessarily a good thing. She peppered her questions with references to characters both real and imagined, including Thomas Paine, Jean Valjean, and Gandhi. She often ignored Fleming-Ginn's advice, eliminating a bleeding heart because the woman smiled at the prosecutor, keeping a CFO who Fleming-Ginn warned could become the foreman and would side with the prosecution. Matters only deteriorated from there.

Meanwhile, Valerie Harris was feeling increasingly inadequate. She wasn't even a paralegal. She thought Susan was much like the feral squirrels or raccoons that scrambled onto her doorstep intuitively knowing she would care for them. Susan was a wounded bird, and together they were winging a murder case.

Sequeira thought Ms. Polk was doing better than a lot of attorneys. She was insightful, articulate, and for most of the selection she had been well behaved. For a conviction, he would need all twelve jurors; all she would need was one holdout, one lone figure who sympathized with her, one individual who did not buy into his meticulously researched case. Despite the relatively smooth selection process, Sequeira suspected it wouldn't last. He knew from Tom O'Connor that Susan's good behavior would erode, she would act in ways that hurt her case.

"YOU ARE ABOUT TO EMBARK ON A JOURNEY THROUGH A DYSFUNCTIONAL relationship," Sequeira told the jurors at the start of his opening statement. Wanting to beat Susan to the punch, he told them that Felix Polk had been wrong to become romantically entangled with his teenage patient. "What was born out of dysfunction looked like a normal marriage. They had three beautiful boys, a loving marriage, and a doting mother. They lived the good life . . . he was a good provider . . . their children did not want for anything nor did the defendant," he said. "But all was not well."

As he spoke, Sequeira, who dressed up in a navy blue pinstripe suit and a serious red tie, scanned the faces of the six men and six women jury. Susan plucked a tissue from a box on the defense table and wept. Horowitz had warned her that her foe this time was more dangerous. Paul Sequeira was a very good storyteller.

"You'll hear that there was always conflict. Everywhere the defendant went there was conflict: in the schools, in therapy, with babysitters there was confrontation. When her sons had trouble at school, it was always the fault of the school and of her husband, who, Susan believed, controlled the schools."

Sequeira continued to tell his story to wide-eyed jurors: "Slowly, all the anger and paranoid delusions started turning toward her husband, Felix Polk." Some were leaning forward in their seats. Susan had thought her husband was a member of the FBI, the CIA, and later the Israeli Mossad. "She started telling their children their father was a monster." He told the jurors that she was paranoid and delusional.

"I object. There is no evidence I am paranoid or delusional," Susan asserted.

The DA was unflustered. "Was Dr. Polk the abuser?" he asked repeatedly.

"She challenged his manhood and his penis size in front of the boys," Sequeira said.

"That's complete fantasy," Susan Polk said in one of the first of her creative objections which continued to disrupt Sequeira's statement. On her ninth objection, the judge lost her patience: "I will remove you from the courtroom if you continue to object." Because opening statements allow attorneys to tell jurors what they're going to prove—but are not evidence—opposing counsel rarely raise objections. Despite her superior intelligence Susan Polk seemed to think she could craft the rules to her liking. She came up with extraordinary reasons to object, and no matter how often the judge lectured, she persisted.

"He would try to persevere because of his children. . . . Was Felix Polk the abuser?" Sequeira asked. "Hadn't Susan Polk controlled the family finances? Hadn't she traveled wherever she wanted? Is this the picture of an abuser or the picture of someone who does what she wants to do?

"Her paranoid delusions and accusations festered into bitterness and anger until she made a decision, made good on her repeated threats. Was Dr. Polk the abuser or the victim of the ultimate act of divorce and murder?" Sequeira asked. There was a rhythm to his statement that kept the gallery mesmerized. And there would be an unstated theme woven into the People's case: Felix Polk could not have controlled his wife; no one could.

Sequeira recounted Felix's "last few days on earth." And he described what happened on the day Gabe Polk found his father's body.

The DA showed the jurors notebook-size color photos of Felix's body, telling them that initially, Ms. Polk's bloodied clothes and the murder weapon were not found. "So there were lies, a cover-up, destruction of evidence," Sequeira said as he leaned on his podium and focused on the jurors.

"The victim doesn't get to come in and tell his side of the story." Here he paused. "You know what?" he added in his folksy manner, "his body tells the story." Sequeira showed the jurors a chart of a black-and-white drawing of the human body with markings for knife wounds: D is near the heart, J wound in the abdomen, K in the back, penetrating the chest wall and more.

"Why couldn't Felix Polk overcome his attacker?" Because he suffered a "significant blunt-force trauma to the back of his head." It was the old first punch theory. . . . "Ladies and gentlemen," he intoned, "that's what happened to Dr. Polk." The male juror with the long ponytail whom Sequeira's friends thought he should never have selected was leaning forward almost at a forty-five-degree angle.

"You'll see photos of redness around her eyes," Sequeira advised. "There were no cuts or wounds on her body. Does that sound like a mutual fight to you?"

Their heads down, jurors were emotionally spent. A tall woman with straw-colored hair who sat on the jury and would hold great sway, thought Sequeira presented a powerful case. Now, she thought, he has to prove it.

Although Sequeira usually has an easy rapport with his opposing counsel, Susan had made so many objections and been so obstreperous during his opening statement that he found her behavior impossible. Once the jurors had left the room, Sequeira, who was supposed to discuss handing over additional evidence, announced that he would only talk to Ms. Harris, not to Ms. Polk. "You do that, and I'll fire Ms. Harris," Susan said—before firing Valerie Harris.

Susan Polk moved for a mistrial, accusing the DA of prosecutorial misconduct because he'd said she's paranoid and delusional. His allegations "had absolutely no basis in fact, and it undermines any chance I have for a fair trial," she protested, fighting the same old prickly battles she'd fought with her husband. She argued that Sequeira's account of her life with Felix was a fairy tale. "To undo that damage is a huge task," she groused.

"Ms. Polk is paranoid and delusional to the point where she killed her husband," Sequeira shot back, shoving Susan's nose in the issue once more.

Susan Polk had been battling claims she was delusional almost every day for the last eight years, first at home, then in the courts. For her, the trial was a vehicle of self-vindication against charges of murder *and* mental illness. Her mental status was so crucial to her sense of well-being that at times it seemed she would sooner be found guilty of murder than guilty of delusional thinking. As her own attorney, she felt she could not only put on a strong defense, she could prove how sane she truly was. But she had yet to face her greatest critics: sons Gabriel and Adam.

GABRIEL POLK, HIS HANDS THRUST IN HIS POCKETS À LA JFK, AND HIS BACK erect, strode through the courtroom doors, the morning of March 8, 2006, past the defense table where his mother stood, her arms folded and her eyes focused. Mother and son were all but two feet away from one another. He did not glance at her. It was not until he had been testifying for an hour that he peeked at the woman he accused of killing his father. Only once in the last three-plus years had they seen one another, and even that was in court. In the intervening time, he'd grown so big that his mother no longer recognized him.

District Attorney Sequeira likes to start strong and end strong. It was the judicial equivalent of shock and awe. Sequeira wanted to go from Gabe to Adam, a one-two punch, and from the start, throw off Susan Polk

For a nineteen-year-old who had lost both parents in one night, Gabe sounded remarkably grounded. His voice was strong; his comments measured. He wore a charcoal suit, a starched white shirt, and a blue silk tie. (His mother, more accustomed to a courtroom than he, was more casually dressed in baby blue jersey, a wheat-colored knit sweater, and khaki pants.) His hair was clipped marine short, like both his brothers. He had starlike charisma and a handsome, angled face that resembled his brothers' and his father's when the latter was a boy. Young women in the gallery were smitten; one would begin a correspondence on his MySpace page.

Scattered throughout the courtroom were members of his support system: in the last row sat a woman with an old-fashioned blond pageboy, Marjorie Briner, his surrogate mother. Brother Michael Saggau of De La Salle High School was in the third row.

"How is it you came to live with the Briner family?" Sequeira began.

"Four years ago my mother murdered my father, and I was left without a home," the boy said. His answer was delivered without a touch of self-pity. Susan Polk, who previously had objected to the word *murder,* was so taken aback she forgot to object. She stared at her son, her eyes brimming with tears.

As he answered Sequeira's questions, Gabriel made it clear that he blamed his mother for the destruction of the family. He had missed half a year of school because she encouraged him to stay home, and by the ninth grade, he said, "I barely attended school. I was getting bad grades." His mother convinced him it was not his fault, but the result of his father's overarching influence over the schools. "It was easier for me to accept I was failing because of him rather than myself," he told the jury.

Gabe testified that at school he often engaged in fights, which he blamed on his increasingly delusional mother and turmoil at home. He said his father didn't like his not going to school, "but he had very little control over us." If his father was a party to the craziness, Gabriel Polk didn't see it.

When his father didn't want them to go to Thailand or Hawaii or Japan, Gabe said, "She didn't listen." Sequeira was building an alternative account of life at the Polks, one in which Felix Polk was hardly the Svengali Susan would make him out to be.

Gabriel Polk denied there was ever any physical abuse of his mother by his father, though he said each parent had slapped the other once and both had shoved the other numerous times.

Sequeira knew Gabriel would impress. He was not only an innocent witness but also a heartbroken kid. Sometimes Sequeira ambled over to the side door next to the jurors so that Gabe's eyes would turn toward him and face the jurors, who were riveted by his account.

Gabe explained that his mother kept telling him what an awful person his father was for "almost my whole life." For about a year and a half before his father died, his mother was discussing ways she might kill his father: drugging him, drowning him in the pool, hitting his head, running him over in the car. The jurors' eyes never moved from Gabe's face as he explained he'd grown accustomed to such comments.

He told the courtroom how he overheard his mother tell his father "I'm going to kill you," and how on October 14, 2002, when they'd expected to go to the baseball playoffs, his mother said she didn't know where Felix was. "I can tell when she lies," he said over his mother's objections. "Her eyelids flutter." Unintentionally, Gabe had given the jurors a tool—a Susan Polk lie detector test. Gabriel Polk described for jurors what happened that night when he finally walked through the narrow walkway and approached the cottage.

"What did you see?"

"I saw my father lying on his back with blood all over him."

He said he called the cops and then hid from his mother. That fact stuck in jurors' minds: he hid from his mother.

"Has anyone tried to keep you from testifying in this case?" Sequeira asked.

"Yes."

"Who?"

"My brother Eli. It happened when he got back from Byron Boys Ranch shortly after my father's murder. We were downstairs in the Briners' basement. He told me he would do whatever he could to stop me from testifying against my mother."

This was a lot for the jurors to absorb. They liked this kid. They found his story believable. Sequeira scanned the jury box, then returned to his seat. Satisfied that Susan's son had laid the framework for the case against her, he told the court that he had no further questions.

16.

BRASS KNUCKLE DEFENSE

AFTER THE LUNCH RECESS, COURT RESUMED AT 2:15 PM. THE ROOM WAS overflowing with reporters and spectators, some standing in the back, all there to observe the confrontation between the son and his mother, the accuser and the accused.

For weeks journalists and lawyers had speculated just how Susan would handle Gabriel. Her former attorney, Horowitz, who had promised Susan he would handle Gabriel with care, had planned to whisk him on and off the witness stand in twenty minutes. Susan could have taken that route: Encourage him to say that he couldn't possibly know what happened in the pool house that night and quickly usher him out of the jury's sight. Valerie Harris, on the other hand, had advised Susan not to worry about Gabe's feelings. Think about saving your own skin, Ms. Harris counseled. On another day Susan could repair the damage that she might do to her relationship with her youngest son.

Tittering in the gallery halted. Jurors and spectators stared as Susan took delicate but deliberate steps to the podium. She paused and gazed at her youngest son. "I have a number of questions for you," she said in an awkward introduction. She froze for a moment, unsure how to proceed. She turned to the judge and inquired, "Can I call him Gabriel?" She'd been wanting to talk to her son for years. At last, she had her chance but it was under the most awful circumstances. She covered her nose with her slender fingers and began to weep. "Sorry," she said, "just a moment." She caught herself.

"Would you say we were wealthy when you were younger?" Her tone had turned almost businesslike.

"I wasn't aware of our finances," Gabriel said, the words sliding easily from him, though his eyes would not meet hers. "Can you recall what our house in Berkeley looked like when you were younger? Can you describe it?" she asked.

"That's sort of a broad question."

"The jury does not know what our lifestyle was. I'd like you to tell them." She asked him about their student boarders, who had lived in their house to provide extra money for the mortgage, but he was of little help. He'd been so young, he didn't remember. Through him, Susan hoped to establish that money had never been a driving force in her life, that she wouldn't have killed Felix for that. Susan had the bailiff show him a photo of one of their boarders, but he failed to recognize the person in the picture. Making no headway, she asked what kind of car she drove. Had she ever driven a BMW or a Mercedes? No, he said, she'd driven a Volvo. Such gradations, rich with meaning for Susan, may have been lost on the more middle-class jurors. She moved on. "Did you ever see me having an affair?" she asked. "No," Gabriel said.

"Were you aware I believed [your father] was having a relationship with Sheila Byrns?" she asked, referring to Felix's close friend and former patient.

"Now I am."

Several people in the courtroom glanced at each other after that question, as the crowd wondered what she was thinking. In highlighting Felix's alleged infidelity she had provided the jury a ready-made motive for the murder.

Despite this counterproductive point, it was in line with how Susan was going about her questioning. She was more intent on proving she was a good mother than that she had not committed a cold-blooded murder. Who had Gabe had breakfast with every morning? Who had helped him with his home-work? Who drove him to school and picked him up? To all those questions, Gabe answered, "You did." When he said his father came home at night and watched a movie, read, or played chess, she asked, "Did he play chess with you? Did he teach you to play chess?" "No," said Gabe.

"Yes, you were always there," Gabe commented in a flat voice. His answer was given without a touch of tenderness. The scared kid who was afraid his mother was going to kill his father and who discovered his father's body was no more.

In the time between Felix's death and the trial, Gabriel had grown not only physically but also emotionally. Whereas Susan seemed to fall apart at the slightest mention of the past, Gabriel remained in control of his feelings. It was a difficult sight to watch, and its significance was not lost on many of the jurors. The CFO juror thought that Susan's cross-examination of her youngest was heart wrenching. She was stretching out the interrogation, he surmised, because she didn't want to let him go. "Did we go to the park? Did we walk down College Avenue to the bakery? . . . to the library? . . . did you go to nursery school?" That seemingly neutral question opened the door for the satanic day care stories.

"You pulled me out [of Temple Beth El preschool in Berkeley] because you said I was getting molested," Gabe told her.

Watching from his table, Sequeira didn't know what to think. Didn't she realize that Gabriel was not going to assist her? Did she really think she could convince Gabe to return to the fold? He reminded himself that Gabe had refused all contact with her for years. She no longer knew him. She could no longer control his thoughts, but she didn't know that.

As she spoke, Susan glanced at the jurors and she thought she saw in their expressions that she was making a good impression. She would show them that Gabe had been programmed by his dad and that his story was inconsistent.

Wanting to establish that "the decedent defamed my character," Susan asked, "Did your father say I was crazy?"

"He said you were delusional." What, his mother asked him, does delusional mean?

"It means you believe things that aren't true to be true," he responded.

"You think so of me and not of your father?" When the DA objected, Susan told the judge she wanted to "impeach the credibility of the witness." Her stark, lawyerly turn of phrase lost her some sympathy in the courtroom. She had just referred to her youngest child as *"the witness."*

Addressing the notion of Susan's "delusions," Gabriel recalled his mother saying she had been abused by her father, mother, and brother. A tiny woman in the second row bundled in a black coat and old knit cap let out a gasp. Susan's mother, Helen Bolling, misunderstood the testimony and thought Gabriel was saying *she had molested him.* She exited the courtroom babbling about what she said were crazy lies her grandson told.

While the testimony continued, Valerie Harris, who hadn't taken her firing the day before to heart, dashed about the courtroom until she located Ivan Golde, Susan's former counsel, leaning against the wall. Susan was so woefully inexperienced that Ms. Harris needed instant legal advice: what must Susan do in order to have Felix's satanic abuse tape admitted? Golde whispered that Susan had to establish a foundation that it was Felix's voice on the tape and that with his statements about wanting to kill, it showed his propensity for violence.

Anxious to crack Gabe's image of his father as the good and sane parent, Susan took Golde's advice and played an excerpt from the infamous tape, which had so impressed jurors and spectators at her first trial: "Other children were raped on stage . . . children were killed . . . baby in a plastic bag hammered to death, [Adam] remembers the blood . . . other ceremonies of blood drinking, urine drinking . . . eating throw up . . . My rage is omnipresent . . . My fantasy of course is to kill them and I'm a rather moral person. I want to kill them."

The playing of the tape for the son who no longer believed in his mother but still believed in the goodness of his dead father seemed horribly cruel. Some spectators and a few reporters found it difficult to endure, even though many had already heard excerpts. But the tape had the sort of impact on jurors that Susan had hoped for; some jurors began to wonder about Dr. Felix Polk.

"Am I a psychologist?" Susan asked. "Did I ever go around giving speeches? Your father was a doctor? A PhD . . . so he was the expert on how the mind worked . . . you think your brother Adam was abused? You think your father was wrong about that?"

"It's a complicated issue," Gabriel responded, never losing his composure. "He believed you."

She asked Gabe about being "kicked out of middle school." "It's embarrassing to talk about what happened," she said, before plunging in as though she were oblivious to the pain her questions might cause. "Yes, it was," Gabe responded. He told how he was removed for fighting. Gabe added that his opponent is now a good friend. "Oh," Susan said with surprise, "He is?"

She didn't know when to stop. She asked if it were not true that Gabe was much smaller than the kids he fought.

"Between the last four years since you murdered my dad, yeah, I grew a lot," he said, unwilling to yield a point.

Susan was hurting him and he was shoveling the hurt right back. Gabe told his mother "I believe that many other parents in Piedmont chose not to have a relationship with the three of us because of you and the way you acted."

When Susan sought more information about his adolescence, Gabriel came forth with details she would not have wanted the jury to hear. By middle school

Gabe said, "I started messing up more." Susan asked him about accusations that he brought a roll of quarters as a weapon to school. "I was under extreme stress from daily fights at home," Gabe said. His mother, he added, "was completely tearing apart our family."

Susan was shocked. She'd never heard her son speak this way. Who, she inquired, had reshaped the stories of his childhood?

"Maybe you should have believed us less and disciplined us more," Gabriel said without a note of sweetness. She had prided herself on being a fine mother. Gabriel did not agree: "You didn't do a very good job of it," he countered.

The next day Susan continued her line of questioning. "How was it that Eli became the scapegoat in our family?" she asked. Gabriel did not "necessarily think" Eli was the scapegoat but, he added, that Eli "has done things that got him in trouble." Susan persevered: "You recall Dad saying [Eli] was the scapegoat in the family?"

"Eli did hit you in the face and send you to the hospital," Gabe responded.

Sequeira looked at the jurors and thought they were swayed by Gabe's testimony. As strong a prosecution witness as he was though, some older female jurors, thought Gabriel was disrespectful of his mother and they wondered if his answers were too extreme.

IN THE MIDDLE OF THE SECOND DAY OF TESTIMONY, SUSAN TRUMPETED A line of questioning that could help her, putting forward the theory that Gabriel and Adam were motivated by money. Just before the trial started the brothers had settled their wrongful death lawsuit against Susan. They'd also filed a civil suit to have the family house, where only Eli lived, sold. Gabriel told the court that the civil suit was filed "so we could move on and go our separate ways." With her questions, Susan informed jurors that if she were convicted of murder, she would forfeit her stake in the family estate; her money would then be split among her sons. Although they didn't doubt Gabriel's account of finding his father's body, some jurors wondered if family finances might not influence his attitude toward his mother.

Susan asked her son about finding a pair of brass knuckles in the glove compartment of his car. Each time she mentioned "brass knuckles," Sequeira objected that it wasn't relevant. The third time, Sequeira raised his hands dramatically and blurted out, "Ms. Polk does not follow the rules! Ms. Polk does whatever Ms. Polk wants to do!" When she mentioned brass knuckles a fourth time, the DA, who knew what was coming, said, "I give up!"

Susan Polk asked if her son was embarrassed to have brass knuckles in the car.

"I had them because *I was afraid of both Eli and you.* . . . Eli had threatened me before. He had said he would do what he could to stop me from testifying. I was scared for my life."

At almost every juncture of Gabriel's testimony, Susan seemed to be setting down landmines and then marching on top of them. Indeed her cross-examination was proving much more damaging than Gabriel's initial testimony. She was doing so poorly that one of the victim advocates sitting in a back row was starting to feel sorry for her.

Her next set of questions was plaintive—almost pathetic in tone. "Didn't I love you very much?" Susan asked her son. "Yes," Gabe agreed.

She entered into evidence a photograph of herself and her three sons zipping along on the Space Mountain ride in Disneyland "when I supposedly went crazy," she said. The bailiff showed Gabriel the photo: "Do we look happy?" she inquired. "I guess so," he responded.

"Were you a happy child?" Susan asked, getting to the core of her questions, if not to that of her case. "I remember moments of happiness, but there's definitely bad with the good."

"Do you remember telling your brother Eli he was your best friend?" Susan asked, crying as she spoke. "Yes, at one point I remember telling him that."

"Do you miss him?"

Here, Gabriel paused. "Yes, I do miss him and you *and* my dad."

In a cryptic question, Susan Polk asked, "Is it your belief Eli had anything to do with your father's death?"

Gabriel gave a chilling response: "I wouldn't know."

It was an emotional conversation, and a difficult one to observe. When the jurors left the court during a break, the judge advised that the dialogue between the mother and son sounds "like the conversation you wanted to have with him for three years." She warned that Susan could lose the jury, but Susan was on a mission. While waiting for jurors to take their seats again, she taped old family photographs to construction paper, as though the act itself would bring back what was forever lost. She showed her son the pictures.

"You guys look happy," she said. "Yes," he answered as his mother sniffled.

She could neither win nor give up. She showed her youngest a sad little plaque from 1997, which read, *Number One Best Mom Award* from her three sons, from "about the time I went crazy and became delusional and a bad mom," she said in a mocking tone. "Yeah," Gabriel acknowledged, "we still love you," and then he added that the award "was actually Dad's idea, by the way."

After Gabriel mentioned his brother Eli's criminal record, Susan reminded him that he had been caught shoplifting when he was ten and that he had "shot your brother in the foot with a BB gun."

"I think it's getting down to spit wads and throwing cornflakes," an exasperated Sequeira interjected.

"I hope you don't feel I'm picking on you," Susan said to Gabe. "I loved you guys the same. Didn't I tell you that?" she asked. "I told each of you, you were my favorite?"

"You told me that," Gabriel acknowledged.

"Do you think I thought Adam was smarter than Eli because Adam was class president and Eli was expelled from Miramonte [High School]?"

"You appreciate Eli a lot more because he buys into your delusions and we don't," Gabriel said, expressing a family truth.

WHILE SUSAN WAS INTERROGATING GABE, CONFIDENT THAT ELI'S TESTIMONY would counter his, Eli was getting into trouble again. He violated a restraining order filed against him by his girlfriend, Jessica Provine, a striking, rod-thin blonde ten years his senior. Despite the order, the two had spent the week together: watching movies, making dinner and love. Jessica even drove him to jail, where he dropped off court clothes for his mother. Then on March 9, the two fought. Jessica called the cops, and upon their arrival she displayed bruises on her elbows and thighs that she said were from Eli. Spotted at Safeway the next day, in fact, Eli looked as though he'd put his head in a Cuisinart; he had bruises, cuts, and abrasions on his forehead, cheeks, and neck (along with what he later admitted were hickeys). Arrested for domestic violence, he bailed out of jail and started calling Jessica, who happened to be telling her story to a police officer when the call came in. She handed her cell to a deputy: "I fucking love you, that's what. Why aren't you answering my calls?" Eli asked. When the deputy identified himself, Eli disconnected. Ten minutes later, a desperate Valerie Harris, trying to stave off a crisis, played loose with the facts. She called Jessica's cell and, according to the police report, claimed Judge Brady had *instructed Eli* to call Jessica to appear in court. Judge Brady had never issued any such instructions.

Wednesday, March 15, 2006, Susan Polk was not in court when a handful of her subpoenaed witnesses gathered in the corridor. (She had subpoenaed them for this date, thinking she would be presenting her defense.) They chatted amiably as though attending a macabre cocktail party. There sat some of the main characters in the Polk drama: "Oh, you're the infamous Sheila Byrns! Where's your red dress?" one woman joked. Marjorie and Dan Briner stood nearby, proudly explaining that Gabriel had just won a national Horatio Alger Scholarship, given to students for "integrity and perseverance in overcoming adversity."

At the very moment they were touting Gabe's accomplishments, Eli, in jailhouse yellow shirt and pants, was downstairs behind a metal and glass partition anxiously facing a judge. With a mournful look, he told Judge Joni Hiramoto he was expected to testify in his mother's murder trial. "I am not a flight risk to myself or anyone else," he offered. He needed to pay bills and feed his yellow Labrador. "Excuse me," said an unsympathetic judge as she read his police report. She denied bail. Ever polite and all too experienced around the courthouse, Eli said, "Thank you, Your Honor," before turning away from the little aperture and returning to West County Detention Center, the same jail that housed his mother.

On Monday, March 20, 2006, an overcast, rainy morning, Susan Polk continued her poignant cross-examination of Gabriel as though he was the only witness and she intended to try the case on the strength of his response.

Sequeira was not enjoying his time cooped up with Susan Polk. Aside from building his case, his only outlet was to express periodic outrage that reporters found irresistible. During a break, when Susan observed Gabe talking with Sequeira, she accused him of coaching her son to cause a mistrial. In one of his most memorable lines, Sequeira responded, "I'd rather have needles shoved in my eyes than have a mistrial!"

Sequeira was not immune to Susan Polk's attacks; in fact he loved a good retort. His mother, from whom he acquired his quick wit, remembers entering his third grade class and finding him with tape across his mouth. She knew that someday he'd make a fine lawyer.

Jurors were beginning to look dazed. What medications was I on? Susan asked. Gabriel answered that he didn't know. "I was eleven."

Did his father take medications for anxiety? Susan asked. "Anybody would." Gabriel responded.

A number of jurors later admitted to feeling sorry for Susan, whom they viewed as lonely. One male juror was sure she was an innocent caught up in a bad marriage.

When Susan didn't agree with her son's answer she was becoming flip: "Pardon me? Oh, really?" She told the judge she questioned "the ability of this witness to recollect and tell the truth." Although he didn't show it, Gabriel felt his mother was torturing him with her questions.

Sequeira examined the faces of the jurors and he thought they were pissed. They didn't like Susan endlessly badgering her youngest son. The judge sent the jury home for the day and then, having lost her patience, she told Ms. Polk her questioning of Gabriel "borders on the abusive."

"She has had him on the stand for three days and not come close to asking about the week that led up to the murder," Sequeira pointed out.

"I apologize to Mr. Sequeira that it takes so much time . . . ," Susan Polk said in a mock little-girl voice. "He would like to pack me off to state prison."

"You will finish up the examination of this witness tomorrow," the judge ordered.

"I'm objecting to your aligning yourself with the prosecution," Ms. Polk retorted. Judge Brady had had enough. She ended the hearing, lifted her coffee cup, and swiftly left the bench.

On Gabriel's fourth and final day on the witness stand, the unrelenting defendant faced off against her unrelenting witness. Repeatedly he said she was delusional. "Gabriel," she said in serious tone, "have you ever believed in something that wasn't true?" He hesitated but then she added, "Santa Claus?"

"Yes."

Then Gabe slipped in a devastating line that she didn't bother to refute. Every Saturday, he said, "You tried to find codes in the newspaper that secret agents put in there."

She delicately removed her gold-rimmed glasses and folded her arms for emphasis. "After hearing your father rant and rave on the tape," she said, "you think I'm delusional and not your father?"

"Yes, I do."

She asked Gabriel to explain a letter he'd written on her behalf. "I do love you," he explained. "There's terrible memories with good memories. At different points I've hated you. At different points, I've loved you."

"Have you graduated from high school yet?" she asked, demonstrating the vast divide between them.

Because of the discipline imposed on him by the Briners, he said, he doesn't drink, he has a curfew, and when he does something wrong he's grounded. "I was accepted by six of eight schools so far, including University of California at Santa Barbara," he said, all news to his mother. "I almost had no parenting when I was with you," he complained.

Susan Polk suggested the Briners held Gabriel out of school to collect on his Social Security for one more year. He said he took an extra year at school "because my father was killed in my freshman year, not because the Briners wanted to embezzle money."

Susan seemed to derive pleasure from sparring with and trying to dominate her son. If the judge didn't stop her, she could continue for weeks. In the waning hours of his four days of testimony, Susan Polk began to ask about the time leading up to the killing. When she was returning from Montana, she asked, was that when "I threatened your father? Is that it?"

"Yes," Gabe said simply, "you did."

"Isn't it so you were really angry with your dad?"

"I was under your influence at the time," Gabe said.

"Wasn't it you, you were angry at your father and talking about killing your father," Susan said.

"I was buying into your delusions," Gabe responded. "That's something I have to live with. I broke the window on his car. I made a mistake. I have to live with that. He's dead now. . . ."

Susan launched into an eerie set of questions. "You think I am accusing you of murdering your father?" Spectators were shocked at her cruelty. "I have never ever, ever, ever said you had anything to do with it. I never told the police you talked about killing your father. I didn't talk about how you would like to gut him," she said in her perfectly modulated voice. Gabriel bowed his head; he put his fingers to the bridge of his nose to stem his emotions.

"You recall our conversation when I said *a person who murders another per-*

son is forever separated from the rest of the community?" Susan Polk asked as she began to cry.

Gabriel regained his composure: "You talked about murdering him every single day," he said. Susan began to weep. "Really?" she said, her weeping over, she gave him a cold stare. "You're going to stick with that story?"

"It's not a story," Gabe said. "It's what happened."

She had only a little over an hour left. She turned to the judge and explained, "This is the first time I got to talk to him in three years." The judge nodded. The defendant was garnering some sympathy, but then she immediately lurched into her next subject: "What exactly do you recall my saying about your father's penis?"

"You guys were arguing and you said, 'You have a little penis, Felix. You want power.'"

Susan Polk said that was no worse than claiming someone had "big balls."

"You did it in front of your son," Gabriel mumbled.

He said his mother mocked his dad for being Jewish. Susan bristled. Hadn't Gabriel thrown "the yarmulkes into the barbecue?" Gabriel laughed and said that was just another one of her delusions; it never happened.

She had kept her youngest son on the stand for four days, badgering him with queries, and yet for all of her questions, Susan continuously overlooked elements about Gabriel's testimony that could have been beneficial to her case. She never got around to asking Gabriel about the death of his father. She never played the tape of Gabe talking to Adam the night he found his father's body, when he called his mother "a bitch" and said at least they'd still have income from the apartment building. She never challenged him about Felix's computer, which, she suspected he had and which, she speculated, might have had information on it that could be helpful to the defense.

Just before Gabriel was dismissed, his mother announced triumphantly that she would recall him as a rebuttal witness. (It was said more in spite than in fact; Susan never recalled him.) With a note of humor he turned to the jurors and said, "See you later."

"I move for a mistrial!" she blurted out. Once again, her request was politely denied by Judge Brady.

The cross-examination of Gabriel had made it apparent that part of Susan's defense would involve putting her role as a mother on trial, leaving it to the jury to decide whether it was she or Felix who had destroyed the family. As Gabriel sauntered out of the courtroom with his surrogate mother, Ms. Briner, trailing, Susan seemed unaware that in many ways her son had left her forever. But she had other concerns: she was preparing to face the cops. Susan Polk knew their investigation had been sloppy and she intended to point out to the jurors the mistakes they had made. She was gunning for the sheriff's department.

17.

"DON'T DO THIS, SUSAN"

SUSAN WAS WARMING TO THE ROLE OF DEFENSE ATTORNEY. AS SEQUEIRA called cops to the stand, she tore at their statements, dissecting photos of the crime scene with particular relish. She'd spent forty hours examining them in her cell. Spectators and jurors noticed the upbeat manner with which she analyzed her husband's blood, and it made them uneasy.

When he was called to the witness stand, former Orinda police chief Dan Lawrence, a tidy, fit man, with eyes that look perpetually surprised, recalled Felix Polk telling him Susan was coming home from Montana to blow his head off. Susan found at least five reasons to object to Sequeira's direct examination: relevance, hypothetical, compound and cumulative, testifying from the podium, and the one that put Sequeira over the edge: prosecutorial misconduct. She was making this personal. The judge overruled all her objections but not before Sequeira slammed his hand on the table and declared, "I strenuously object!" He was irritated but he also wanted jurors to know how outrageous her behavior was. Susan's objections were so frequent and often so off-the-wall that at times it was difficult for Sequeira or his witness to speak.

Taking his mother's advice, every morning Sequeira would write "Keep Cool," on his legal pad. Sometimes he'd look at it and laugh; he'd gone way beyond keeping cool. After the jurors had filed out, Sequeira fretted, "God knows what they are thinking right now." He objected to "Ms. Polk's" speechifying, to her talking "over the court and getting her prejudicial material" in. He characterized her sometimes-sweet demeanor against her brutal questioning as "passive-aggressive." In fact, Susan Polk never did raise her voice, a trait that seemed at odds with her strong character.

"I object!" Susan butt in. "He's not an expert!"

"If you interrupt one more time," the judge warned, "the proceedings will stop, and I will remove you."

"I have at the beginning tried to be patient," Paul Sequeira was saying. "This is not an unsophisticated defendant. This defendant is very bright and is completely manipulative." She'd hurled so many insults at him that he said he could no longer stand having "my integrity impugned every fifteen minutes." He asked that her pro per status—acting as her own attorney—be revoked, but the judge was not so inclined.

A 1975 U.S. Supreme Court decision held that a defendant in a criminal trial has a constitutional right to proceed without an attorney as long as the defendant does so voluntarily and intelligently. If the defendant can understand what she is charged with, if she can follow the proceedings, and even if she is barely able to defend herself, the courts will allow her to try her case without an attorney.

As Sequeira spoke, Susan fidgeted over papers and craned her neck to look at the clock on the back wall. When it was her turn she accused Sequeira of "goading me. . . . Maybe he should act like a lawyer instead of like a baby!"

Judge Brady was stern with Ms. Polk: "If I rule in favor of you, it's a good ruling. If not, you call it judicial misconduct . . . I think you understand very well what I'm talking about . . . no speeches." The judge warned Susan not to make anymore "baseless accusations."

"I'm moving for a mistrial at this time!" an unfazed defendant declared. "This is denied," the judge said with alacrity. "I'm moving for replacement of this prosecutor!" Susan Polk added. "Denied," a wearied judge said. "We are in recess."

Among a parade of deputies called to testify was Sgt. Kenneth Hansen, retired from the Contra Costa County Sheriff's Department, who told jurors that when he entered the pool house he "noticed copious amounts of blood along with the victim on his back." He notified Ms. Polk her husband was dead from unnatural causes. He testified she told him, "Oh well, we were getting a divorce anyway." He said she exhibited no emotion.

Under cross-examination, Susan Polk showed Sergeant Hansen an enlargement of her mug shot and asked how she looked. "You look angry," he said.

"Are you an expert on psychology? Have you ever had to fight for your life? Do you think only men can hold it together?"

Valerie Harris had gone through two yellow sticky pads with messages such as "Don't do this, Susan," but Susan ignored her, launching into questions about unexplained footprints in the blood and water she said had been poured near her husband's head to make the crime scene look worse. When Valerie wheeled her briefcase along the sidewalk at the end of the day, she looked like she needed a good six-month vacation. "How do I stop this?" she asked no one in particular.

But Susan believed she had truth on her side, plus evidence. In a phone conversation with a reporter, she asked why would she have paid forty-eight thousand dollars in taxes days before if she had planned to murder her husband. Why would she have sent an angry letter to the judges in Contra Costa County only days before? Why after she killed him didn't she run away?

Various law enforcement officials called by the prosecution recounted conversations they had had with the victim days before he died. Sequeira played the 911 tapes of Felix asking for help, and one deputy told how Felix had called to say his wife was in Montana "trying to purchase a shotgun." Officer Shannon Kelly described putting Susan in the back of his squad car the night of the murder. Many times she asked if Gabe was okay, and when he inquired if she was comfortable she replied, "I'm not too comfortable being in the back of a police car. My husband was killed and I didn't do anything."

Kelly's testimony offered a portrait of Susan that was in stark contrast to the one that Hansen had portrayed. The discrepancy made one juror wonder: was Susan the blasé murderer who said, "Oh well, we were getting a divorce anyway?" or was she the mother who was worried about her son? During cross-examination, Susan had pointed out that an officer standing near Sergeant Hansen had not heard the cavalier remark about getting a divorce *anyway*. The juror thought Hansen's memory might be faulty; that perhaps Susan Polk was right that she never said that.

Part of each day was taken over by sparring. Susan complained to the judge that she had not been allowed to play the dramatic tape of Gabe cursing his mother and talking about finances with Adam on the night Felix's body was found.

"I'm going to stop you there," the judge admonished. "You were *never* prevented from playing tapes. You had more than adequate time," she said, "I will not tolerate any further hijacking of the court record." The silver-haired judge could be solicitous of the pro per defendant, but when pushed, Judge Brady could also be stern.

It did not take long for Sequeira to abandon his practice of writing "Keep Cool" on his legal pad. Nothing worked, but there was this critical benefit: as he suspected, jurors were feeling the same frustration he was about Susan's combative nature. Susan Polk was providing a public map of her wired mind. Without a filter, her ideas came surging forth, both the intelligent and the bizarre. By the nineteenth day of the trial, many jurors were sharing friendly smiles with Sequeira. When he cracked a joke, some, such as ponytail guy and the blond nurse seated next to him, would stifle a laugh. While they didn't frown at Susan Polk, they didn't grin at her either.

Still, Susan Polk was learning her trade. She practiced on Dr. Neil Kobrin, former head of Argosy University (also known as California Graduate School of Marital and Family Therapy). Kobrin, who wears an earring in one ear and has proud, floppy hair, was Felix's student, colleague, and later his boss. Under questioning by Sequeira he explained that in the days before Felix died, Felix called him to explain he couldn't come to school because his wife was threatening to kill him.

When it came time for Susan's cross-examination, she failed to ask about the call but succeeded in muddying Kobrin's reputation and, she hoped, raising a speck of doubt. Though she didn't accuse him of running a fly-by-night operation, she asked about why the school had five different names in twenty years, why it had rented space in various locations, and why until 1998 the school was not accredited. She was only getting started.

"Do you remember being at cocaine parties with my husband?" she inquired. He responded by saying he was unaware that Dr. Polk had used cocaine. (Several of Felix's colleagues were surprised by Dr. Kobrin's answer.) Hadn't the school had a hard time finding students? Yes, Dr. Kobrin conceded. Hadn't Felix recruited his patients to become his students? Dr. Kobrin said he had never heard that. "He recruited students from his practice and he profited," Susan asserted. And hadn't the school hired a professor who believed in paranormal psychology? Hadn't her husband believed in that too? Kobrin said he didn't know. "Did it ever occur to you that he was manipulating people around him to set me up?"

After the jurors had been released for the day, Judge Brady tried to give Susan a lesson in admissible evidence, but she wouldn't hear of it, choosing instead to argue with the jurist in a belligerent tone rarely if ever heard in a courtroom. If Susan were an attorney, the judge warned, "You would be in custody right now. To almost daily imply that the court is acting in improper manner is misconduct . . . you will not continue to do this," Brady warned.

While Susan's mini outbursts were getting in the way of her trial, they made for great drama. The gallery was filling up each day and the public was fascinated; around the country, Susan was developing a following. The *San Francisco Chronicle*, the *Contra Costa Times*, and Court TV's website were running daily stories, updating with noontime feeds to nourish ravenous readers. Having conducted so many interviews before her trial began, Susan thought nothing of turning to the media during a break in the morning session when she learned her dog Dusty had gone missing. Through Ms. Harris, she provided his picture to a local TV station. Sure enough, a reporter for San Francisco TV station KPIX stood on a street corner at noontime reporting on the trial and on the missing dog. By the end of the day, Dusty had been found.

THE NEXT MORNING, MARCH 29, 2006, AS THEY RODE ON THE INMATES' white bus to court, Susan and Eli had a rare chance to be with one another. Since both had court appearances, they were assigned the same bus from West County Detention Center, and while not allowed to converse, deputies looked the other way.

In court that day, Susan would face one of the most damaging pieces of evidence against her: the tape of her interrogation on the night her husband's body was found. She objected to the showing of the tape because, she argued, she had been tired and cold. The judge was unimpressed. "It is probably the gentlest interview in any homicide case I've seen," Judge Brady countered. Susan knew this would be hard for jurors to accept that she had lied and claimed she knew nothing about her husband's death.

Detective Michael Costa, a beefy officer with a mustache, was one of the first responding officers, and it was he along with Detective Jeff Moule who interrogated Ms. Polk that night and into the next morning. As jurors watched and followed with transcripts, Sequeira played the tape while a teary-eyed Susan sat watching herself on the TV monitor.

"What did happen?" she asks on the tape. "I'm hoping you can tell me," he responds.

A calm and soft-spoken Susan Polk recounted how she spent the day her husband's body was discovered. "What just happened to my husband?" she asked in her honeyed voice.

"Is he dead?"

Detective Moule told her that her sons "know you did it. . . . They're going, 'Bullshit, my mom just killed my father.' "

Then Detective Costa tried another strategy: "Susan, you're obviously a smart woman. You have a nice background and everything. Think this through. You're not gonna get away with this. It's a done deal. We know about how you went up and cleaned up. It's all figured out. There's scientists collecting that stuff. You're not gonna beat this. You're done."

She refused to budge.

"Did you love him?"

"I was very fond—"

"Did you love him?"

"I did for many years."

"But not lately."

"No, I didn't love him anymore."

"Did you hate him?"

"No."

"This is how you want to leave it, just deny, deny, deny, lie, lie, lie, let me live in my little fantasy world and say I wasn't involved, when everything is going to certainly tell us you were. I'm confident of that. I have no doubts about that."

Sequeira turned to the judge and recommended stopping the tape before Susan was shown undressing for a nude photo. The judge turned to Ms. Polk, who was busy whispering to Ms. Harris, and asked, "Are you all right with that?"

"I object, Your Honor," Susan said reflexively.

"To excluding taking your clothes off?" the judge asked incredulously to a courtroom of laughter.

"I'm sorry," Susan admitted, "no, I don't want that to be shown to the jury."

When it was her time to cross-examine Detective Costa, Susan went on the attack. He had told the grand jury she weighed about 140 pounds. "Do I look like I weighed a hundred forty pounds, other than when I was pregnant?" the narrow defendant inquired. "Were you trying to make it look like it was mutual combat that night?" she asked. He denied it.

She challenged his claim he had found the murder weapon, a kitchen knife, in her sink. "Do I look like the kind of woman who left dirty dishes around?" If she hadn't pissed off the female jurors about her weight, she did with that remark, but she wasn't finished. She wanted to know if the knife he found "looked like a high-quality knife or one you would purchase at Target?" Any juror who shops Target would have taken offense. "Do you have any idea what a knife like that costs?" she asked. It was a shocking exchange, highlighting how oblivious she was to the impact her statements might have on jurors.

On Detective Costa's second day on the witness stand, Susan Polk mounted a serious challenge to the veracity of his investigation, one that impressed Sequeira and made him anxious. She came at the detective with one skeptical question after another: "Did you do a background check on my husband? Did you ask my kids if he threatened me? Did you ask my kids if he threatened them? Are you aware my husband went around giving speeches about satanism?" No, he said to each question. "No? You weren't aware of it?" Susan Polk said in mock tones.

She moved onto the letter she had stored in the safe. "Did my son tell you I kept that letter in my safe in case my husband killed me? Did you investigate that he had raped me when I was a patient in his care?" she asked before another Sequeira objection was sustained.

"It was a murder investigation, wasn't it? And you didn't check these things out?"

"Not personally," Detective Costa said.

"Did anybody? Yes or no?"

"Not to my knowledge."

"You never talked to my son Adam," she said. And hadn't Eli said, "My mom wouldn't do that, if anyone did, my dad did. You never bothered to go back and find out what he might tell ya? It was a murder investigation wasn't it, and you didn't check these things out? Did anybody?" she asked in an ever so slightly raised voice. "Did anybody to your knowledge go out and check out the divorce file and go and check out Eli again?"

"Not to my knowledge," the detective admitted.

Paul Sequeira was not happy. She was doing as good a job as many attorneys. Despite her inability to sense when she was alienating people, Susan was successfully mounting a counteroffensive that showcased the flaws in the police investigation.

But it would not take long for her to stumble. Changing her direction, she began to inquire about the letter she had sent to judges concerning Felix. "Did you attempt to validate or investigate anything in this letter? Doesn't this letter accuse my husband of treason? Did you report it to the FBI?"

"Ah, no," the detective said. "No."

"I accused [Felix] of being a member of Mossad. Did you follow up on that at all? Did you make any effort to find out if I was out of my mind? Was I evaluated by a psychiatrist? Mr. Costa, doesn't this document allege my husband had information before the attacks of September 11? Does it sound like a good thing that the Twin Towers were destroyed?"

Within moments, she had gone from logical, penetrating queries to delusional ones. Her shift bolstered Gabriel's testimony. While her questions might assist the prosecution, the DA couldn't help but be suspicious. He wondered if she was playing with him. Her abrupt change in tactics was so counterintuitive, so harmful to her case, that it seemed it had to be part of a larger master plan designed to make jurors think she was out of her mind.

As she had every other day of the trial, Susan flagrantly ignored the judge's decision to sustain an objection and instead barged ahead with her questions. Once the jurors left the room, Sequeira vented in one of his most memorable rants: "I don't know what else to do," he said in an exasperated tone. "I pounded the table once. Ms. Polk keeps saying, 'I'm not a lawyer. I don't know,' but Ms. Polk does know . . ."

Susan twisted in her seat, bent down and gathered files and in exaggerated gestures, shuffled papers. "You are an extremely intelligent woman. I do not believe you do not understand me," Judge Brady warned, adding, "I would appreciate your sitting in your chair and allowing me the courtesy of looking at me."

For most of the rest of the afternoon, Susan behaved like a chastened child. She questioned Detective Costa about "the so-called crime scene."

The following morning she picked up where she left off, turning her attention to the evidence. "Isn't it so that you never found any evidence whatsoever I planned to kill my husband?" she asked. "That's true," he admitted.

The detective had told the grand jury that in the back of Felix Polk's Saab he found a dog bed. Susan Polk scoffed at that. There had only been a blanket in the back. "Were you trying to make my husband sound like someone who liked dogs?" she inquired. She was perturbed because she believed her husband had poisoned their old dogs. She thought the depiction of Felix would make him sound kinder than he was. "You slanted your report to make it sound like my husband was a dog lover." This was pure Susan Polk, harnessing her intellect to put together pieces of a paranoid puzzle. If jurors suspended their common sense, they too might believe in some grand conspiracy.

During the morning break Susan turned to her loyal assistant Ms. Harris and announced, "I don't think this is working out." She ordered Ms. Harris, who had turned her life over to Susan, to leave. And just like that, the last person who could help Susan Polk put her purse, her laptop, and a box of files on her luggage carrier and wheeled them out the door.

"Do I want to sit there with this disaster going on?" Valerie Harris said later that day. "She's toast."

Back in the courtroom, Susan asked the detective if he understood what happens to a wood-handled knife that is placed in a dishwasher. "Are you aware . . . that it dulls the finish?" she asked. The detective had taken into evidence a wood-handled knife he suspected was the murder weapon that he said he'd found in her dishwasher. Susan would *never* have done something as foolish as put an expensive knife like that in the dishwasher. For someone from such humble beginnings, she sounded surprisingly elitist, although it may have been her early years that led to her adopting a snobby air of superiority.

She chided the witness, would "someone planning to murder" select a knife that is broken (a rivet was missing) and blunt?

"I don't know," the detective said. None of it made sense to him, he said, adding, "Murder doesn't make sense to me."

Susan was trying two cases simultaneously. Her attempt to prove she was a wonderful mother and innocent victim was about to be sorely challenged with the appearance of Felix's divorce attorney.

18

WHAT KIND OF MOTHER WAS SHE?

SUSAN POLK DESPERATELY WANTED THE JURY AND THE WORLD TO BELIEVE that she had always felt steadfast love for her sons. She felt it was vital that everyone know how she devoted herself to protecting all three boys from her evil husband. Despite her best efforts, the testimony of Felix's divorce lawyer, Steven R. Landes, would turn that concept on its head.

Landes, who had spent a week in the hallway waiting to be called, told a shocked courtroom that on February 28, 2001, Susan Polk wrote her husband offering to give him custody of Gabriel and Eli (Adam was in college). In his modulated radio voice with a New York accent, Landes recounted how Susan demanded that Felix have no contact "with me by any means," including through her attorney. She did not want news about the children, their mishaps in school, or their ups and downs. "I have had enough of that news," she wrote. Nor did she want visitation rights, *ever*. You couldn't read the jurors faces but how could they not be astonished?

It was stunning testimony. Up until Landes, it seemed as though one of Susan's more sympathetic qualities had been her commitment to her children, but in a few minutes on the stand Landes, with help from Sequeira and the defendant, had been able to whittle away much of that.

"Are you surprised I was willing to walk away?" she asked while cross-examining him.

"I can't answer yes or no," he replied, complying with Susan's insistence that he limit himself to yes or no answers.

She was caught in a devastating contradiction. How could she be the brave and loving mother when she was willing to turn her back on her sons forever? The kind of callous woman who wrote that she had "had enough" of her sons' "ups and downs" hardly deserved a plaque that read: "Number One Best Mom." She had to justify her actions, but the tack she took only showed that she was willing to vilify the sons—even Eli—whom she claimed to—and no doubt did—love.

"Are you aware I have been punched in the face by at least one of my children?" she asked in a harsh, teacherlike tone. "Are you aware my children were extremely verbally abusive?"

"No," he replied.

Susan glanced at the jurors and thought they understood her direction. Once again, a line of questioning made sense to Susan, and she assumed to the jurors as well. It was emblematic of her inability to see how the jury might interpret her words.

Heading down a different path, she asked if her husband had acknowledged to his attorney that "he entered into an affair with me when I was a minor." Landes astonished her by acknowledging that he had. She'd prepared for a battle but none was necessary.

Continuing on, she accused Felix and Landes of conspiring to take control of Eli through the juvenile courts.

"Were you a boy once?" she asked. "Were you ever in a fight? Did you get prosecuted for it? Are you aware that after this, Felix didn't have to pay child support because he got custody through the juvenile courts?" Now she was back in the position of defending Eli when minutes before he was part of the reason she wanted to turn her back on her family. If nothing else, everyone in the courtroom was coming to understand how her mind worked, as she highlighted her ability to take any set of facts and mold a story where she was both victim and hero.

She asked Landes if he remembered her calling several times during the separation and saying, "Just tell me what you guys want. I just want to get out of here." Yes he did but the problem, he explained, was that she was always changing her mind.

By the end of the day, Susan Polk was not finished. Landes told the judge that six days of waiting and then testifying were a public service, but that if Ms. Polk's questioning went beyond the following morning, he would consider that "indentured servitude." The judge and jury laughed. The following day, Susan was doing what she does best: refusing to give up.

"Did you ever make an offer to me Mr. Landes?" she inquired, with the authority of a middle school principal dressing down a delinquent boy.

"I felt frankly that dealing with you on a direct basis at that time had been less than rewarding," Landes said.

Susan had told the court she would be finished with "Mister Landes" by noon. But as the lunch hour approached she warned the court she needed more time. When the jurors had left, she told Sequeira that cross-examining Mister Landes—and she enunciated every syllable—was taking longer than she had anticipated because Mister Landes was such a liar.

After the lunch break, Susan was ready to rip her husband's reputation to shreds. "Are you aware he had a reputation for being violent to his first wife?"

"No," Landes said.

"Are you aware he had mental problems?"

"No," he said.

"Are you aware he had a reputation for using drugs?"

No, Landes wasn't but, making the assumption Susan was referring to Felix's younger days, Landes added, it was the 1960s and 1970s in Berkeley, a comment that elicited laughter.

"Are you aware he had unorthodox relationships with his clients?" she inquired.

"I was aware of his unorthodox relationship with you," said Landes, who quietly sympathized with her. He knew that Susan Polk must have had problems that predated seeing Felix and that their relationship couldn't have helped. But she never asked about that.

Susan was asking about finances—she felt Landes had overcharged her husband—but she couldn't let anything go. Landes said, "I know when he was killed he owed me sixteen thousand three hundred dollars."

"You know when he was *killed* . . . ," Susan Polk said. How did Mister Landes know that his client had been *killed*?

"It is my belief whoever did it, he was *killed*," he responded, adding, "I am certain my client is deceased. I haven't heard from him in four years."

Then Susan reentered her personal Twilight Zone. "Are you aware I accused my husband of being a traitor?"

"Of betraying what?"

"Betraying his country," Susan Polk explained.

"No."

"No?"

"No."

"Are you aware I accused him of having prior knowledge of 9/11?" And here, Mister Landes couldn't help but laugh.

"So you think it's funny that more than three thousand people died?" Susan Polk asked. "Do you think a murder trial is funny?"

Mister Landes explained: "I think it was more a giggle of frustration at this point."

Not long after that, Susan completed her questioning of Landes, and the witness was excused. Like a movie critic, Susan Polk was good at finding fault. Though it wasn't obvious how she would build her own defense.

Her case was so extraordinary that she was acquiring a cultlike following. Spectators filled the gallery along with print reporters; the wackiness of early TV news stories had given way to accurate print accounts. There was no longer any need for reporters who parachuted in to embellish stories or listen only to one side. The true tale alone was fascinating enough; it required no embroidering. The drama was only just beginning.

19.

THE McGYVER ROLL

SONG WICKS WAS JUST THE SORT OF EARNEST, COMPETENT, UNEXCITABLE witness Paul Sequeira needed to analyze the crime scene and serve as a foil for Susan Polk's attacks. The young, eager criminalist reminded Sequeira of an overachiever, something Sequeira himself had never been. In high school, Wicks had loved pure science, but when a criminalist from the county crime lab talked to his class, Wicks knew that he wanted to spend his life in applied science. Since becoming a criminalist, he's investigated some two hundred crime scenes.

To prepare for the Polk trial, Wicks went over evidence with Sequeira early in the morning and for hours each evening. He was not the most experienced, but he was by far the most diligent criminalist Sequeira had ever seen. He was also nervous, having read the newspaper accounts of Susan grilling prosecution witnesses.

One month into the trial, Wicks's testimony broke the prevailing mood. Courtroom antics faded; the circus ended. Sequeira threw on the screen enlarged slides of Felix's blood-drenched right hand that looked as though it had been dipped in a bowl of red Easter egg dye until it formed a red-brown glove. One finger of each hand had been horribly mutilated. Tissue poured from the wounds. Susan objected that the photos were "unduly inflammatory, gruesome, prejudicial, and intended solely to prejudice the jury and cumulative." Her objection was denied. Jurors saw photos of Felix's skull with rivulets of blood streaming down and his dead eyes staring out. The back of his head was so caked with old blood that it looked as though he were wearing a scarlet skullcap. His feet were so bloodied he seemed to be wearing blood slippers. His thighs were encrusted with blood. His abdomen was coated. One female juror held her hand just at the edge of her eyebrow. Other jurors leaned forward. After that slide show, Sequeira showed a poster board photo of Susan Polk after the killing: even with the enlargement, all anyone could see was a red blotch near one eye.

While the photos upset jurors, Susan thought they were nothing more than a charade. All that was missing, she thought, were the peanuts and the popcorn. She said it was sad that's what our justice system had come to: this wasn't science; it was sensationalism. And she meant it.

Wicks, who was schooled in blood spatter, told jurors there had been a terrible struggle; much blood was spilled, all of it Felix's. He explained that if someone who is bleeding is hit, the force of the impact causes blood to spatter. How it lands and the size of the spatter "is indicative of certain kinds of force." Criminalists can tell by the shape of the blood splotch whether it was propelled by gravity or by impact. After applying a chemical substance to the area, Wicks explained he discovered multidirectional bloodstains, not coming from "one single event."

Under direct questioning by Sequeira, Wicks said he found an estimated twenty partial shoeprints showing someone padding away from the crime scene and out the kitchen door. Although they had not been able to match the footprints to any specific shoe or shoe size, they spanned the range of women's shoe sizes—seven and a half and eight—found in the master bedroom walk-in closet. Susan Polk believed the police had altered the crime scene, moving the ottoman and diluting blood with water. Mr. Wicks showed that while there were blood spatters on the ottoman, the floor underneath it was clean. The ottoman had landed in that spot before the fight ensued and had not been moved.

Susan was determined to cast doubt on his analysis that she and Felix had fought one another across the room. She would always maintain that Felix had attacked her and that their fight occurred only in one spot. She began her cross-examination with a charming but penetrating question: "One of the things that drew me to science," she said, "was that it was exact. How controversial is the study of blood spatters?"

He admitted it was "subject to interpretation."

"I'm guessing I'm having a hard time understanding how spatters got over the room," Susan Polk said. "I was there and I didn't see it." She continued, "The problem I have, and I'm not a trained person, the problem I have is where are *his* footprints?"

"I have wondered that," he replied. It's possible that because there was a tremendous amount of blood that the footprints might not have been visible, he said. He also said it was possible that if Felix Polk had been standing in a wet pool of blood—"I don't want to be a McGyver," he said, rising from the witness chair and falling on his hands and knees before rolling over, attempting to show that one could tumble without his feet slamming down on the floor.

Susan called him "Mr. Song Wicks," having assumed incorrectly that his last name was "Songwicks." Her mistake lent a touch of formality to an interrogation that at times was quite personal. She asked if he had used "reason and logic" or was his "focus on putting me in that room rather than figuring out how it happened." It was an odd minuet; the straightforward criminalist up against an intelligent defendant who believed things had happened that had not. She couldn't help but like him and so she participated in an uncharacteristically civil dialogue.

The next day, a Friday, the court was not in session. In her jail cell at West County Detention Center, Susan experimented falling in the way that Mr. Song Wicks said Felix had fallen. She tried it a dozen times before she concluded that it couldn't be done.

BEFORE THE JURY ENTERED THE NEXT DAY, SUSAN ENGAGED IN HOUSEKEEPING, arranging her files on the defense table and, as a local columnist noted, humming while she did so. She might just as well have been reorganizing her spice rack. The judge had given her extraordinary privileges, allowing her to keep her papers and voluminous files on the defense table overnight, every night. Each day she was allowed into court a few minutes early to reorganize her files for the coming day. On her table, Susan added a triptych of framed photos—all of young Eli frolicking at the ocean's edge. There were no pictures of her other sons.

Once the jury was returned she asked Mr. Wicks if "the McGyver roll" "doesn't sound to you like a fairy tale?" Then she moved further out. She could not help herself: "If you dilute blood, it makes it look like more, doesn't it?" she asked.

"Yes," he replied, "but it also changes the appearance of the blood."

She accused Mr. Song Wicks and other officials of moving Felix's body, diluting his blood, and Photoshopping the scene on a computer. "When you frame someone for murder, you never expect to answer these types of questions," she said in her most polite voice.

"I don't know," Wicks replied dryly. "I have never framed anyone for murder," he said without irritation. There was something appealing about his minimalist confidence. Jurors found him earnest and believable.

Certain that the crime scene photos did not depict what had happened, Susan claimed the deputies had separated the brown leather ottoman from its cover; something she demonstrated could not just happen, though as she demonstrated, she inadvertently stepped on the cover, which flew off the ottoman. A few jurors silently laughed or covered their mouths. Susan Polk was unfazed.

She would question Mr. Song Wicks all that day and into the next. From time to time, her objectification of her husband's bloody body made spectators and some jurors queasy.

After hours of her cross-examination, when the jury had wearied of her questions, the DA stood for a brief but effective redirect:

"Would your job have been made easier if you had the defendant's bloody clothing?" Sequeira pointedly asked.

"It could have allowed me to draw conclusions, if I had the defendant's clothing," Mr. Wicks replied.

"Did you find any bloody clothing anywhere?"

"No," he said.

With the redirect completed, Judge Brady excused the witness. Though Mr. Wicks had experienced an easier time than everyone else who had taken the stand, he had not come through it unscathed. Using her trademark skepticism, Susan managed to demonstrate that at least some of Wicks's conclusions were subjective, a crucial point that seemed to open the door for additional questioning.

Utilizing her flourish for showmanship, Susan was proving increasingly successful at drawing the public's attention to her plight. Everyday the gallery was filled with more and more curious citizens who came to see the drama for themselves. One newcomer likened the experience to "a reality show," prompting a veteran of the trial to object and say "this is reality." Over time there developed a clique of courtroom regulars. Alison Shurtleff came with her mother and sometimes brought along her college-age daughters. A man known as Tennis Jim, a retired GM executive, attended court during the rainy season, when he was unable to ski or play tennis. Most spectators turned against Susan, but there were exceptions. Two conspiracy theorists with long hair and straw hats posted their observations on their blog. Paul, a Filipino emergency room orderly who took a month's vacation to observe, preferred sitting alone in the last seat of the last row. He empathized with Susan, whom he believed never had a chance to develop on her own. All she would need would be one juror like Paul to stop her from being found guilty of murder.

Susan was well aware that she had a larger audience than the jurors and spectators who came to watch her daily drama. In the middle of her trial, she found time to do a TV interview with Court TV's Catherine Crier, during which she discussed who should play her in the movie based on her life. Susan suggested Winona Ryder or Susan Sarandon. Anthony Hopkins, she said, should play Felix, though Hannibal Lechter, whom Hopkins played in the movie *The Silence of the Lambs,* was nicer than her husband, she said. She would later confide to a reporter that Hannibal Lechter was a kind man whose "cannibalism is not indiscriminate. He punishes people who have values like the Nazis. He's a super moral person in a way." The *New York Daily News* picked up her remark to Crier and ran it under the headline: "Snark Attack!" The story began: "Susan Polk gives new meaning to shamelessness."

Since jettisoning Valerie Harris, Susan had begun to reach out to other possible supporters. She called reporters to ask about media coverage and to look after her yellow Lab Dusty about whom she sometimes seemed more concerned than her sons. In fact, during the trial, even her relationship with Eli grew distant. Midway through the trial, whenever Valerie Harris offered to arrange for Susan to speak on the phone with Eli, Susan Polk frequently declined. When asked by a reporter when Eli's trial was set to begin, Susan said that she didn't know.

DISTRICT ATTORNEYS LOVE DR. BRIAN PETERSON. HE SPEAKS WITH AUTHORity in a booming voice and he looks jurors in the eye. He's charismatic, funny, and engaging. If Letterman were going to interview a forensic pathologist, it would be Brian Peterson. He's as likable as Susan can be unlikable, and he's also highly experienced. The pathologist, who testified at the Scott Peterson trial, has performed 6,201 autopsies. Yet, on some matters, an inexperienced defendant can hold her own against a pro, and that is precisely what Susan Polk did.

There are only three hundred forensic pathologists in the nation. Peterson knew he wanted to be one ever since he read a Scholastic book about careers when he was a boy. He favors the subspecialty of forensics pathology, where he can hang with detectives and be on the inside of sensational murder cases.

To court, Dr. Peterson wore a bright red tie with an abstract design as though its brightness was a countervailing force against his work with cadavers. In his modulated voice, he told jurors Felix Polk died from twenty-seven stab, incised, and blunt-force injuries. Paul Sequeira walked Dr. Peterson through the autopsy while Susan Polk objected to the witness's behavior: "He's making stabbing gestures."

"If I couldn't use my hands," said Sequeira in defense of his witness, "I couldn't talk!" Sometimes Sequeira couldn't help himself. His humor in the middle of such morbid commentary was what attorneys call "an icebreaker." Behind the scenes, he wondered sometimes if he was being too cavalier and minimizing the seriousness of the situation. Despite his concerns, it seemed that the jurors appreciated his humor and needed to laugh occasionally—or at least some did.

Dr. Peterson testified that he discovered that Felix had had hardening of the arteries and that there was 75 percent obstruction of the left anterior descending coronary artery. Although Felix's health was questionable, Dr. Peterson asserted that even if the therapist had had a healthy heart, given the wounds inflicted on him by his killer, he still "would have ended up simply dead."

Susan thought much of the DA's case was fictional. She'd always maintained that she stabbed Felix five times; not twenty-seven. She said the DA was making her look "like I'm lying, but I'm not." When it was her turn to question the witness, she attacked what she was certain was Dr. Peterson's bias: "You have a bias do you not to produce evidence for the DA?"

"No, that's ridiculous," Dr. Peterson bristled, his eyebrows dipping with doubt. "I'm there speaking for somebody who can't speak anymore," he said. From then on, he referred to Dr. Polk as "my patient," a clever and effective strategy.

Susan derided Dr. Peterson's assertion that Felix died of *twenty-seven stab wounds* as something he had declared "for dramatic effect." She put up some of the most graphic slides on the screen. Did Dr. Peterson find "this scratch to be the cause of death?" she asked, "that scratch? That scratch?" To each question, he answered "No."

"Wouldn't it have been more honest *not* to include the superficial scrapes?" she asked.

"No."

"No?"

"It was the entire complex of injuries that caused death," he said.

While she was making a point, her demeanor was otherworldly and removed. She might just as well have been narrating a slide show on "My Summer in Vermont." The slides she tossed on the screen were ghoulish images—of her dead husband's bloodied head and other body parts. She ignored his eyes, which stared out like fixed marbles.

"Okay," she said cheerily, "let's look at the blood pattern, shall we?"

Sequeira thought these were the kinds of gory pictures a defense attorney would try to shield from the jury because they were too inflammatory, but Susan Polk was taking pleasure in her analysis. She was going up against the great expert and whacking away at his findings.

The trial had begun to take its toll on how she carried herself. While she was making headway against some of the prosecution's most seasoned witnesses, her appearance was evolving. She was gradually adopting the look of an inmate. She no longer wore her Ralph Lauren red, black, and cream plaid jacket or the khaki pants and black turtleneck. Instead, she appeared in jailhouse baggy sweatshirt and oversized forest green pants that fit as though she were a female house painter. Susan had stripped down to the basics; she was fighting to win.

When the trial resumed on Monday, Susan again idly threw pictures of Felix's bloodied body onto the wide screen, failing to demonstrate much sensitivity. She presented a slide of Felix with his penis covered by a yellow Post-it. At last, some observers thought, Susan had a sense of privacy, but in truth, a member of the court staff, knowing Judge Brady's sense of decorum, had placed the Post-it there.

Back for another day, forensic pathologist Peterson was sporting a jazzy purple Hawaiian motif tie. Susan was determined to challenge his allegation that a laceration above Felix's ear was the result of a blunt-force object and not caused by a fall. Dr. Peterson declared that if Felix Polk acquired the gash during a fall, his ear would also have been injured. No matter how Susan phrased it or how she tried to demonstrate that someone could fall and injure oneself at a certain spot—without damaging one's ear—the pathologist wouldn't budge. Many jurors thought Susan Polk had logic on her side. He was the expert, but she was right. By acting as though his assertion were science, he seemed to be hurting his case.

Susan was advancing on him. Dr. Peterson had explained that a stab is an injury that is longer than it is wide. After he told the court he does not guess, Susan Polk asked if he hadn't guessed at the length of some wounds? "No," he said, "I gave approximate measurements."

All Susan needed was for jurors to have a reasonable doubt, and she believed she had shown them that almost every one of the prosecution's witnesses had lied "beyond the point where it's just error." She thought the jurors understood that "when a witness is caught altering testimony or with inconsistencies," everything he says must be questioned. And Dr. Peterson's testimony made him not always believable.

As the interrogation continued, his ebullient spirit appeared to be ebbing. He would later joke among colleagues that an hour and a half into Susan's cross-examination made him wonder if Felix Polk's wounds were not self-inflicted. Susan Polk continued challenging the pathologist: "You attribute death to scratches as well as stab wounds, completely ignoring the heart condition. Was that honest reporting?" Dr. Peterson acknowledged that the "terminal event may have been the heart condition," but that what killed "my patient" was the wounds.

During a break when the jurors were no longer in the courtroom, Susan Polk thought she overheard Sequeira coaching Peterson. "Ms. Polk may think she is in control of everyone in this courtroom, including the bailiff, the clerk, and the court reporter," Sequeira bellowed. "I object," Susan Polk said. "I don't care if you object. I'm not in custody," he responded. Sequeira had been telling Peterson that over the Easter weekend his daughter fell and hit the side of her head and . . . *bruised her ear*. "I don't care what she wants, she's charged with murder," the irate Sequeira said. "She's in custody. She's not going to control me not now, not ever!"

"That is so ungentlemanly and it's not true," Susan Polk responded in her most passive-aggressive voice before she went on to accuse him of having poor manners. That's all Sequeira needed. When she resumed questioning, Sequeira let loose with an artillery of objections. Then he looked at her and shrugged as if to say that when it was called for, he knew how to be ungentlemanly, all right.

Susan Polk thought she knew how to read people in the courtroom, but she didn't. She went out of her way to infuriate people, and then puzzled over why they were upset. But with the DA, she had met her match.

Sequeira had the bailiff hand Dr. Peterson three nude photos of the defendant. Susan Polk erupted: "This is prurient! Crude! Inappropriate!" she declared, her voice rising for the first time since the trial began. "I'll stipulate," she said, "to anything." The jury was informed that there were no injuries to Susan Polk from her shoulders down.

Susan Polk contended that Felix had thrown her to the ground. Dr. Peterson told jurors that if that had happened, she would have been bruised. Isn't it possible, she asked, that she was "grabbed by my hair and pushed down?" As she spoke, jurors and spectators leaned forward. She performed a rolling fall in the well of the courtroom, her chest facing the ceiling and her legs up like an upside-down chicken.

"Is the problem here that it's just hard to believe that a little woman by myself, a hundred and ten pounds without a PhD, could defend herself and survive against a much bigger, stronger man? Is that the problem?"

Peterson responded: "I don't have a problem with that, since you're living and he's dead."

"Is that so?" she asked. For a layperson, she'd done a remarkable job. With his testimony winding down, Dr. Peterson had not landed a knockout punch. That left room for Susan's forensic pathologist to present another perspective.

She accused Dr. Peterson of twisting logic and reason. "You expect us to believe this fairy tale, that the emperor has no clothes?"

Given the leitmotif of the day, Sequeira jumped in: "Let's not get into 'no clothes.'"

The humor of the moment was about to subside. Susan Polk was preparing to meet the most combative prosecution witness: her son Adam.

20.

HIS FATHER'S SON

WITH THE WARM SPRING AIR, MIGRATORY BIRDS RETURNED TO ORINDA AND journalists flocked to Judge Brady's court to watch Susan Polk's eldest son go up against her. He would be the prosecution's final witness. Until the trial began, Susan had assumed Adam was *her* witness. But on Tuesday, April 18, 2006, a month and a half into the trial, Susan found out whose side Adam was on.

"The People call Adam Polk to the stand," Sequeira called out. And with that, the closest anyone could come to having Dr. Felix Polk testify in his own behalf appeared. Adam strode into the courtroom wearing the same tight-around-the-neck starched white shirt worn by football players who attended his father's memorial service three and a half years before. He didn't look at his mother, but with his confident athletic stride and the sureness of his voice, he didn't appear afraid of her either. In advance of Adam's testimony his mother had tucked into the triptych homage to Eli a picture of a young Adam and one of Gabe. As he squeezed behind the defense table, Adam failed to notice.

Under Sequeira's careful questioning, the twenty-three-year-old recounted his surreal childhood: how his parents believed he was a victim of sexual abuse and how his mother thought his father was a secret agent. As a child, he explained, it was difficult to differentiate what was going on in his family with what was real, but by the time he was eleven or twelve, he was the only family member to have an outsider's perspective. Despite the domestic turmoil he told the jury he managed to maintain a 4.3 grade average in high school and be a member of his high school football team.

Minutes into his testimony, his mother began objecting to the person she referred to as "the witness." Among other things, she objected to Adam's vocabulary. In describing his mother's behavior he employed the words *disturbance* and *perverse.* "He's not a psychologist," she interjected.

Built like a fireplug, Adam was 210 pounds of mostly muscle. His hair was short, his face wide and handsome. He seemed as tough inside as out. He saw his testimony as his only chance to set the record straight and contradict the lies his mother told as well as those yet to be uttered. He was on a mission: to see to it that she would go to prison for a very long time. Despite everything, he still loved her, and because of that he remained vulnerable. Coaxed by the DA to talk about his mother's attitude, Adam said that just before Felix died Susan asked, " 'Do you love your Dad?' I said, 'Yes, I love my Dad and I love you.' She said, 'Then you're not my son. Anybody who can love somebody who conspired against this family is not my son.' " As he spoke, Adam pinched the bridge on his nose with his thumb and forefinger as Gabriel had done days before.

He told jurors his mother was always trying to control the family, reinforcing the point about control that Sequeira made almost daily. When Susan Polk would erupt with objections after being told to be quiet, when she would try to order Sequeira around, he would invariably say, "Ms. Polk thinks she can control everyone in this court, but she can't. She doesn't control me!" Though they seemed like idle comments, they were part of Sequeira's grand plan, which only became visible during his closing argument.

"Did you ever observe your dad trying to tell your mom what to do?" Sequeira asked.

"Never."

"Did he control what your mother did or where she went?"

"Never."

Asked by Sequeira if there had been physical violence at home, Adam said that aside from when Eli punched his mother, and his parents "maybe touching chests" when they fought, "I never observed instances of physical violence between my mother and father."

Sequeira broached the sensitive subject of finances. Those who didn't know Adam and Gabe might think the two were treasure hunters anxious to convict their mother and collect her share of their family money. After his father died, his mother tried to control his finances, Adam said. Whenever he asked for money she demanded he first take some action, such as pull his little brother out of the Briners' house or fire Budd MacKenzie, the attorney hired by Felix's twin, John, to handle the estate. Adam said he was only looking out for the welfare of his brothers and himself. "She was using finances as a tool to control myself and others . . . I know my mom is not grounded in reality," he explained. "I did not want her controlling my life."

Adam told jurors that early in the trial (when he was expected to testify but didn't), his girlfriend received a curious phone call from Eli advising her and Adam that the trial had been postponed and that there was no need for Adam to come. But the trial had not been postponed. The war between the Polks was ongoing, in court and behind the scenes.

Adam was asked the ho-hum question by Sequeira, has anyone tried to influence his testimony today? His answer got everyone's attention: "My mother tried to influence my testimony." During jury selection, his mother sent him a list of questions with answers "she wanted." Adam told jurors he had long since quit reading his mother's letters. He handed the letter to the DA. Initially, Sequeira was excited by this revelation, but after awhile he realized that what Susan had written was not much different than what an attorney might write to a witness. He decided to raise the subject but not make a big deal of it.

While Sequeira felt confident about having Adam on the stand, he was aware that Adam, with all his remarkable successes in life, could come off as cocky. He worried that when Susan had her chance to cross-examine her eldest son, he might alienate jurors rather than endear himself to them. Would he be seen as a moderating voice in the family, the only sane one through the years, or as an operator who played both sides?

When Susan Polk rose to cross-examine her firstborn, she was wearing the oversized sweatshirt and billowy green pants she'd worn the day before. Her hair, which once was neatly combed, was disheveled. She looked distraught though she sounded strong. "I was under the impression you would support me," she said, "isn't that correct?"

"I told you I would tell the truth."

A few moments later she asked, "You're aware you are under oath?" She stared at her son as though her eyes could alter his testimony. He stared back, an equally immutable force. He'd never fallen under her sway the way his younger brothers had; she'd always known that about him. He'd been his own man even when he was a boy. What Susan failed to realize was that in the years since Felix's death, Adam's empathy for his mother had waned and his anger had grown.

While questioning her son about his lawsuit against her, Susan inquired,

"Adam, when did you learn how to lie so well?" Her questioning showed a coldness that was not there for Gabriel.

As jurors left for the lunch break, Sequeira approached Adam Polk and the two spoke. "I object to his coaching my son!" Susan declared. "I was telling him to be back by one thirty!" an irritated Sequeira shot back. "I have never coached anyone in twenty-two years."

"You're incapable of being a gentleman," Susan snapped.

"You're unable to be a human being," Paul Sequeira snapped back. "You're a pathological liar and you're treating your son like crap."

The judge told Ms. Polk that talking did not mean coaching. She told Mr. Sequeira that he could meet Ms. Polk in jail if he wanted to continue the fight.

In her convoluted way, Susan Polk was determined to show that the young Adam did as many bad things as Eli, but because Felix chose Adam as the favorite, the eldest son never suffered similar repercussions. "I am outraged that I have to impeach the testimony of the children I love," she said, although it was not apparent that in the case of Adam she meant it.

A little later, Susan continued to speak over the judge. Facing her oldest son seemed to have brought out the worst in her.

"I'm not here to be abused anymore," she complained. "I'm not here to be yelled at by the DA and not to be threatened with retaliation by the sheriff's department." The DA, she added, "behaves like a frat boy."

"Ms. Polk," the judge said, "We are not going there again!" But Susan Polk continued her diatribe. "Ms. Polk, stop!" the judge, ordered. Susan continued berating Sequeira and talking over the judge.

"We're done!" the judge declared, before giving Ms. Polk, one more chance.

While Judge Brady argued with the defendant, Paul Sequeira pressed his back into the wall as though his actions could transport him out of the courtroom. When he began his redirect he was able to get a few words out: "Eli is a convicted felon," he said. "I object!" Susan shouted.

"Okay, we're done," the judge said as she rushed off the bench and slammed the door behind her. The normally smiling bailiff hovered over Mrs. Polk like the letter C.

"Okay, let's go in back," he ordered.

"I need—"

"No you don't," the bailiff countered. "Let's go." She was put in a holding cell; a punishment the press dubbed "time out."

Upon her return she was more subdued. "You testified, Adam, that I was a controlling parent."

"I was trying to express that any sickness in the family was a direct reflection of your own sickness," he said. His mother turned to the judge and objected, "Your Honor, please advise the witness not to make speeches on the stand."

"You controlled the household. You controlled the finances. Yes, you were definitely a controlling parent," Adam added.

His answers were airtight. Adam used to say he'd never won an argument with his mother but this time he came prepared. She began to sob. It wasn't just her life that was on the line; it was her sense of herself. Susan asked, "When you were growing up, is that how you described me?" She was heaving and couldn't continue.

"Ms. Polk," the judge asked, "do you need a minute?" No, she said, she had best carry on.

He would not yield. "Who took care of you growing up, Adam?"

"That's a long period of time. It's twenty years," he answered. And once again she began to cry.

In a devastating exchange, Susan asked how old Adam was when "your father told you I was delusional."

"No," he said, *"I told my father you were delusional."* And when his father participated in her delusions it was because "everything Dad did was influenced by you." Adam had an answer for everything. Anyone who knew him couldn't help but understand, but jurors lacked the context, and in its absence, some had begun to think he had an agenda and started to sympathize with his mother.

"How is it possible for one person like me to put [fabrications] in another person's head? Wouldn't you think it would be the reverse?" she asked.

THE NEXT DAY, AS ADAM ANSWERED ONE OF SUSAN'S QUESTIONS ABOUT AN incident involving French toast, Susan noticed his lips upturned. "You think this trial is funny?" she asked.

"It's the only way I can cope with it, by finding some element of the absurd in what you bring to the table."

"You think defending myself at a murder trial is absurd?" she asked as she wept.

"Yes," Adam said, "that is absurd."

She questioned Adam about a family altercation years before, claiming he had threatened to kill her. "That's ridiculous," he said.

"It's going to take so much time to ask these questions," Susan Polk declared, "because I will not give up."

"Are you slanting your testimony?" she asked.

"I can't believe you would call my integrity into question!" he shot back. "How can you call yourself a mom?"

"Have you gone and edited your memory?" she inquired.

"You're crazy."

"Is it greed, Adam, is it just plain old greed?"

"This is why we have no relationship and never will," he groused, although that may only be the voice of youth, because Adam's role in the family is that of peacemaker.

Their exchanges were painful. At one point Adam accused her of being "cruel hearted," adding she should "never have had kids." Each remark brought startled expressions from spectators and from a few jurors. This was way beyond a family's wrestling match; each was going for the kill.

Susan asked Adam to recount their conversation after his father's death. It was the invitation he was looking for. He said she told him, "They should just take me out and shoot me. . . . I'm just going to plead guilty. . . . Things just got out of control." That phrase, Adam added, is what he thinks of every night before he goes to bed. Then he said it word by word: "Things-just-got-out-of-control."

When his mother inquired about her e-mails to him, he came back with a stinging rebuke: "I hate to say it [he didn't sound as though he hated to], I filter your e-mails to the trash."

Close to tears, Susan asked, "Do you recognize that you portrayed me as violent, angry, and a bad mother?"

"That wasn't my intent," Adam said. He intended to portray her, he said, "as someone who is extremely delusional or evil. It's up to the jury to decide."

Paul Sequeira thought Adam might be canceling his own contribution, even though Susan was not talking about the issues that would matter to jurors. She was trying to rebuild what had been destroyed. Didn't Adam remember how she had called him "brilliant, athletic, and a wonderful person?" And hadn't he told her he loved her, she asked. "It doesn't matter how many batches of cookies you make and good things you say," Adam answered, "a mother who talks about being raped or about murder and who treats her kids in a perverse manner, all the superficialities go away."

"Is it impossible for you to say anything bad about your dad?" Susan inquired. It was a fair question, and one that emphasized the central problem with Adam's testimony: it seemed dubious that Susan could have been so bad and his father so good. Those older female jurors who hadn't liked how Gabe spoke to his mother thought Adam was downright disrespectful. Adam, they thought, acted as though everything he had done in life he had done on his own, without any input from his mother. Sequeira sensed that and was concerned.

As the questions continued, Susan tried to impeach Adam's testimony with his own words. When she had been seeking bail he had written the courts: "No one could have asked for a gentler, sweeter mother" and that while only his mother, his father, and God knew what happened that night, he added, "How I view my mother is not as a murderer . . . she is not inherently a killer. I would plead with the court to release her from jail."

He said he'd written that because had he been unwilling to cooperate with his mother she would not have given him use of the family car, which he needed to commute to a summer job. "I was stuck in a precarious position of looking after my younger brother." He knew "any overtly damaging testimony" he gave could cause him and Gabe problems. Susan was making progress.

She brought up the issue of estate fraud and how much money attorney Budd MacKenzie had spent and how she believed he had undervalued their house. "I believe that's a conspiracy theory," Adam asserted, but still some jurors might have come to such a conclusion. She had never met these people and suddenly the Briners were raising her son and their friend Budd MacKenzie was managing the family finances. In a partially illuminating exchange Susan asked Adam about his brother Eli.

"Eli and you have some kind of strange relationship," Adam began. "I withdraw the question," she stammered. Sequeira wanted more: "The horse is out of the barn already."

"I withdraw the question," she insisted.

Before moving on to another subject, Adam blurted out: there was a strange dynamic. "He is your protector and you are his protector." That was a cleaned-up version of what he really thought, that his mother and brother resembled Bonnie and Clyde.

Susan Polk continued questioning Adam, lurching for what she mistakenly thought would be a soft landing: "Before I was incarcerated, was I a law-abiding citizen?"

In response, Adam cited two examples of his mother punching women in the face, one a neighbor and the other an old babysitter. Then he added, "I remember when you and Eli were eating mushrooms together . . . magic mushrooms."

By now, Susan Polk was prepared to retaliate. She tried to slander Andy Briner, one of Adam's closest friends, and the son of the couple who are raising Gabriel. The DA objected. The judge sustained the objection. Repeatedly, Ms. Polk tried but failed. Some jurors thought they were witnessing what Susan was like at home. She would never compromise and she seemed oblivious to the pain her words would cause.

"We're moving to a new subject!" the judge insisted. But Susan persisted. Adam responded:

"Everything you said is completely ludicrous. You're drowning and you're flailing. It's completely heartless."

Against the judge's orders, Susan kept on the attack.

"You will obey the basic rules of this courtroom!" the judge thundered. "Ignore my rulings and that will be the end of the cross-examination . . . This is not a therapy session between you and your children."

This very public destruction of what remained of Susan Polk's family was tragic yet mesmerizing. It felt as though she was trying to slaughter her oldest son, and in the words of one reporter, it was "beyond my wildest imagination." What most upset onlookers was her playing the entire satanic abuse tape for Adam. (She had played only an excerpt for Gabe.) Adam sat in the witness seat and stared into space as his mother tried to destroy whatever good memories her son had of his father. Some spectators found the experience unbearable, but it had the intended impact as it reminded jurors that Felix too had suffered from delusions.

The scratchy voice of Felix Polk filled the room: "Yesterday I woke up at 4:22 AM. That's pretty good for me . . . and he was choking. Now the reason he was choking was that . . . Oh, he didn't have any cold or allergies. He has allergies too but that's not the reason he was choking. He was choking . . . I believe . . . he has two ways of choking in dreams. One, uh is choking, uh, sexual meaning . . . a sexual meaning. He took part in oral copulation so there's that kind of choking. . . . The other kind of choking is the kind he has when he dreams his head is being cut off because that's what he witnessed and he's choking on his own blood. Or so we think."

During the day, Susan exhibited flashes of great anger whenever she mentioned her nemesis, Marjorie Briner, frequently pointing at the woman with the shoulder length blond hair sitting in the second row. Although witnesses were not allowed in court before they testified, an exception was made for Ms. Briner because Adam, like Gabriel, had asked that she be his support person.

"This is the woman who took care of your son! This is the woman who saved your son!" Adam said. In an exasperated tone he blurted out, "You're out of control. You're bonkers. You're cuckoo for Cocoa Puffs." His comments drew laughter, even from the judge, who shielded her mouth with her hand. That phrase, "cuckoo for Cocoa Puffs," was adopted by reporters, especially by the *San Francisco Chronicle*'s Henry Lee, who populated his stories with references to it. Lee sat in court each day silently zipping through crossword puzzles and sudoku, stopping only when he heard something he wanted to take down, which he did, in shorthand, with phenomenal accuracy.

"How 'bout when I get out," Susan Polk continued. "Do you think the Briners will be happy about that?" Susan asked, a question she must have regretted asking.

"I'd be scared for my life if you get out," Adam said matter-of-factly, although there was nothing ordinary about his extraordinary statement.

He told his mother he once had been her "biggest advocate," that he had thought, "She may just be sick. She needs our help." But he came to believe her sickness masked "an inherent evil and conniving nature." He referred to his mother's "baseless accusations" against the Briners. "I know for a fact these people are good people," he said. Her accusations against them, he said, are "the embodiment of pure evil." More than anything else, his mother's treatment of the Briners had convinced him she was capable of murdering his father. "I could imagine you walking into the room," he told her, "stabbing him twice in the back as he was falling over, climbing on top of him, bludgeoning him over the head and stabbing him to death."

Anyone else would have shut him down but not Susan, who continued to question him about fights he'd been in—this son who had been senior class president of his prestigious high school; president of the honor society, and who in a few months would graduate cum laude with a double major from UCLA. She asked about a fight he had at "Beach School."

"Beach *Elementary* School?" her son said incredulously.

At the very least she wanted to prove she had been a good mother, but Adam wouldn't give her that. He said there had been instances of happiness, but that everything had been overshadowed by his mother's sickness.

Adam proved to be just as self-righteous as his mother. She mistakenly had thought he would say things to bolster her case, but she was dead wrong. Adam's testimony laid bare a cold reality for Susan: he could not forgive her.

The following Monday, Susan would begin to build her case, to introduce jurors to her mother, her "good" son, and others who would bolster her position, but it would all be against the backdrop of the testimonies of Gabe and Adam.

Late in the day, not long before he left the witness stand, she asked Adam, "Am I to blame for everything?"

Looking directly at her, he simply replied, "Yes."

PART IV

IN THE COURT OF SUSAN POLK

21.

"GOOD MORNING, MOM"

SHE LOOKED MORE COMPOSED THAN SHE HAD IN WEEKS. SUSAN POLK'S hair was brushed, her clothes—blue jersey and khaki pants—were pressed. She strode to the wooden podium and pulled it close. She purposely had waited six weeks until Monday, April 24, 2006, to deliver her opening statement at the beginning of her defense case, a risky move since jurors tend to make up their minds early in a trial.

She could have emphasized how it all began. She might have said she'd been a poor young thing under the control of a Svengali-like therapist-husband. She could have said he molded her to his liking and that even when apart she felt she was under his control. She would hint at it in her opening statement, but that's not the battered-woman's defense that Susan Polk devised for herself.

"My story begins with my mother," she rhapsodized as she turned to smile at Helen Bolling. Her mother had "more courage in her little pinkie" than a great many men. She spoke about her mother's humble upbringing. Jurors were already familiar with the many faces of Susan Polk, or as the juror known as nursie thought to herself, "multiple personalities." Today, they were treated to sweet Susan. She told jurors her tale was one of "spies, sex, secrets, lies, betrayal, and ESP," and she likened her life to that of the actress Ingrid Bergman in the movie *Gaslight,* in which the fragile Bergman marries a criminal who systematically drives her crazy.

Susan laced her statement with literary references including Dickens and Thoreau. She said the DA painted a picture of her as a Lolita who upset her husband's peaceful life. Rather, she said, her husband was a Victor Frankenstein who molded his children to his liking. They were, she intoned, "lab rats" for a father who practiced mind control. She warned that when her son Eli testified he would appear in gold jailhouse garb and that she would be as proud of him as she would if he were wearing a naval uniform (an interesting comparison given that Felix had been in the navy). "Like me," she said, "Eli will be escorted here in chains. . . . Eli's offense," she said, "was courage, the courage to tell the truth." She said it as though she believed it.

Even if her statement was at times overblown, she spoke with eloquence, her intelligence shining through. But then two-thirds of the way through, she blew it, as she often did, telling jurors she had predicted 9/11 and that her husband, an Israeli spy, was a traitor for not notifying the U.S. government. "Don't I have the right to associate with normal people?" she inquired. "I have served my country for twenty-five years helping to thwart terrorist attacks both here and abroad." It was one of the more off-the-wall comments she would make.

A few jurors smirked.

She said she believed in fairy tales and happy endings and that soon it would be the jury's turn: "The pen will then be handed to you. It will be up to you to write the ending," she said, as if she were a character in a novel. Some reporters felt they were sitting in on a theatrical performance, and in a way they were.

Addressing the issue that everyone was thinking about, she said, "I have been asked several times, Ms. Polk, are you delusional? You heard Adam say I was 'cuckoo for Cocoa Puffs.' Who hasn't had a delusion sometime or somewhere? Who hasn't believed something that turned out not to be true? I can say in all seriousness I don't believe in little green men from Mars," she said, adding that half the country believes in extraterrestrials. "I still do believe in fairies."

Despite some of her outrageous claims, in the end, it was a pleasant introduction for what would become a wild ride of eccentric characters, including those who loved her, those who wanted to help, and those who wanted to help but might have been better off had they never appeared. For the jury and spectators, Susan's defense would supply moments of love, levity, tragedy, poignancy, and an unanticipated, unimaginable cliffhanger.

She called her first witness: "Good morning, Mom," she said incongruously as if they were sharing tea and crumpets. Helen Bolling, a tiny woman in black dress teetered up to the witness stand. With her glasses slipping down her nose and wisps of white hair poking out from under her black wool cap, she resembled an eccentric character in an Agatha Christie mystery. She said she had married only once, "It cured me!" A few spectators could be heard cooing,

"She's so cute." "I was almost a virgin when I met your father, if you know what I mean," she said, twisting toward the judge, who was stifling a laugh and couldn't help but nod in agreement. When her daughter flashed a photo of her mother as a young woman on the screen, Helen Bolling blurted out, "I'm not too bad looking, huh?" Jurors laughed too.

In what must have been an unrehearsed moment, Susan asked what kind of child she had been. "You can imagine," her mother said looking at the jurors, "she was very imaginative, very creative!" Helen Bolling told the jurors her son-in-law was "a flawed man" and had ostracized her from her family. "I didn't even know you moved to Orinda," she said to her daughter, which was embarrassing, since Ms. Bolling lived in the little town as well.

She spoke about fighting Felix over money she was owed from their joint ownership of a Berkeley apartment building. Helen Bolling said that her son-in-law told her, "If you don't like it, I'll see you in court!" She smiled impishly at the jurors and said, "I don't see him here, do you?" Sequeira thought she was over the top and assumed that the remark must have offended jurors, but in fact many were amused.

In an interesting slipup, one that Gabe had heard her make many times, Susan asked her mother, "How old was I when you took me to see my father?"

"You mean your *second* father!" her mother cajoled, "That was a boo-boo!" She said Susan was around fourteen or fifteen. Felix, she said, "had an exterior of being acceptable hidden under what was all this shit, excuse me, I beg the court's forgiveness, it's not proper language."

As she questioned her mother, Susan was girlish and warm. Susan coaxed her mother to talk about her two "near-death experiences." Both times, Helen, who is less than five foot one, had been attacked by a large man and she said her instinct was "to save myself." The implications were obvious. Helen was not just making points, she was making a positive impression on the jury. Susan was feeling good. She looked at the jurors and she thought they not only liked her mother, they liked her too.

During a sidewalk press conference following Susan's examination of her mother, legal pundit Steve Clark said Susan Polk was "doing better than any attorney could ever do. She had the jury. . . . She'd turned the tables on the DA. . . . Clearly, Susan Polk is brilliant," he said, likening her to *A Beautiful Mind*'s John Forbes Nash Jr., the mathematics genius who suffers paranoid delusions.

Paul Sequeira had to be careful cross-examining the most popular person in the room, but he knew what buttons to press. He asked if it were true, as Susan Polk had said, that Helen's former husband had "molested your daughter?"

"Absolutely not!" Helen barked. Although her bitter divorce had occurred decades earlier, Helen still grew angry when Susan claimed her father had abused her. Helen believed it was something Susan had cooked up once she was in Felix's hands.

Pushing the same line of questioning, Sequeira played an excerpt of Susan Polk's first interrogation during which she said, "My father was very abusive to me. So was my mother."

"She made that up, did she not?"

"Honey," Helen Bolling confided, "there's no way for me to know that." The sweet old lady was cagey after all. "Maybe her head doctor told her stuff." She could be foxy if she needed to be.

"Or maybe, ma'am, when she gets angry with people she makes things up," Sequeira suggested. A flustered Susan accused him of "badgering the witness."

"Ms. Polk," the judge said, "it's not even close."

Susan began her case with the easiest of witnesses; but she was gearing up for her greatest defender, her son Eli. Paul Sequeira was gearing up too, to do battle with Susan Polk's middle son.

THE NEXT DAY, SPECTATORS CRANED THEIR NECKS FROM SIDE TO SIDE IN anticipation of Susan Polk's next witness. Suddenly, the side door, the one used by defendants swung open. A large figure in dark-yellow jailhouse garb was escorted by a uniformed deputy. Eli Polk, twenty, looked as though he'd spent the day crying. Within minutes, both he and his mother were. The tension and hostility that had been there when her other sons testified was gone. Now, *spectators* were tense; not about Susan's interrogation but about Sequeira's expected cross-examination and how both Eli and his mother, who as Adam had said were one another's protectors, would respond.

"I have been accused in this courtroom of being controlling," she said.

"That's the furthest thing from the truth," Eli responded. His head was turned toward hers. Their eyes met. They were two parts of a whole. He lowered his head and answered her like a child who was anxious to please.

Susan asked if she ever bad-mouthed Felix, Eli said she hadn't. Given the number of people who had heard Susan disparage her husband, her son's response, while expected from the dutiful witness, hurt his credibility with the jury. But both he and Susan were so committed to portraying her as a saint that they ignored the boomerang effect of his words.

"Did he talk about me?" she asked.

"He came to us and said you were crazy."

When his parents fought, he said, his mother's "solution was always to go upstairs and read." Eli then recalled his father saying, "You should kill yourself," and "You're a sick puppy, Susan. Someone should put you to sleep."

Addressing the discrepancy between his words and those of his brothers, Eli stated that "each of us had a different experience." He attributed his brothers' very different view to a "financial incentive."

As Eli's testimony unfolded, Susan Polk took advantage of his easy accessibility, choosing to intersperse his testimony with testimony from other people. The following day she interrupted his direct examination to call to the witness stand Dr. Alan Peters, the psychiatrist who had examined her at Tuolumne General Hospital after she attempted to kill herself in Yosemite National Park in January 2001. With a rugged look and a Freudian goatee, Dr. Peters said he had found her to be articulate and insightful. He recalled that after her suicide attempt she expressed a hopelessness and sense of isolation in part because family members accused her of being "the quote-unquote crazy one." Although he said she was overwhelmed and "despairing," he found her to be a cooperative patient *with no delusions or psychotic behavior.*

He diagnosed her as having "disturbance of mood and conduct" and secondarily post-traumatic stress disorder. Dr. Peters appeared to be a perfect witness for the defense . . . until Sequeira got ahold of him.

With Susan Polk's mother, Helen, seated in the courtroom, where she had participated in the love fest the day before, Sequeira asked the psychiatrist about the family history Ms. Polk had provided. Hadn't she told the doctor that her mother was "mean-spirited, unbalanced, and crazy?" Hadn't Susan Polk said she was raised in "a sexually abusive household?" Dr. Peters agreed. Then Sequeira aimed for the bull's-eye: *"When she talked about fear to you, she talked more about her son Eli, is that correct?"*

"Yes," Dr. Peters said.

Sequeira continued, wasn't she apprehensive about her son, who had threatened "to throw her down a long flight of stairs?" or "punch her as he had done in the past?" Sequeira thought that nugget was "a little jewel."

The doctor confirmed that account as well.

And wasn't Felix Polk supportive of his wife coming home? And wasn't "*he* the one who saved her life by calling the police?"

"Yes," Dr. Peters said.

Sequeira couldn't imagine why Susan would call a witness who so damaged Eli, her chief ally, but she didn't see it that way. Dr. Peters had said she was not delusional. And that was all that mattered.

With the cross-examination of Dr. Peters complete, Susan recalled Eli, and late in the morning, a now dapper Eli, wearing a suit, tie, and white shirt, but looking just as depressed as the day before, returned to the stand.

"Did you love your dad?" Susan Polk asked.

"Yeah," Eli said. "He was just a damaged person."

His mother tried to tease out of him examples of his father's violent streak. Eli told the court that in 1997 when the family was vacationing in Mexico City his father "just lost it and hit me across the head . . . there was no reason for it." Other times when Eli told that story he would explain his father was angry with him for refusing to go to dinner with the rest of the family. Whenever Susan or Eli talked about Felix's violent streak, they brought up this nine-year-old incident, not realizing that it showed that Felix was rarely (if ever) violent.

As Susan's questioning of Eli continued into the following day, she spoke so softly that her words could have been mistaken for a lullaby. Eli described therapy sessions with his dad. He said that Felix had hypnotized him and his brothers—though his brothers said it never happened. "I remember not remembering what happened," Eli claimed.

He tried to convince jurors his mother was not paranoid, that someone actually had focused a camera on their house and that he'd seen it too. His father had spoken as though he were an agent for the Mossad. And he too believed his father had had an affair with Sheila Byrns, who Eli claimed had not only been his father's patient but also his [Eli's] therapist. (Ms. Byrns said she was never Eli's therapist, and she continues to deny that she had an affair with her friend Felix.) In a revealing exchange, Eli said that at his father's memorial service Ms. Byrns admitted she had had an affair with his dad when she said Felix had been inside her and she had been inside of him. She had been speaking metaphorically.

Lacking the cocky confidence of his brothers, at any moment Eli looked as though he was ready to dodge a punch or cry out in pain. At six foot two he was an imposing and good-looking figure. Unlike his brothers, Eli's dark eyes followed his mother's; his expression was of a defeated animal, lost and looking for shelter that only his mother could provide. His long face and empathetic eyebrows made mothers and girls want to help, and the jury was not immune. At least one female juror just wanted to take him in and give him what he lacked, a good home.

During another brief interruption of Eli's testimony, his former rugby coach took the stand to say Eli had been a passionate player and though younger than many teammates, a leader. Susan Polk would also bring in his former probation officer who praised his behavior, though while questioning him Susan had an embarrassing slip of the tongue. She referred to Eli as "my husband," as in: "My husband was sent to wear [an ankle] monitor with his father."

IN THE MIDST OF HER SON'S THIRD DAY OF QUESTIONING, SUSAN POLK WAS distracted by a commotion in the courtroom vestibule. Turning to the back of the room, her face lit up with childlike wonderment. "Oh my gawd!" she exclaimed, looking like a kid who encountered Big Bird. "You remember who this is?" she said excitedly. Eli nodded. In one of the most dramatic moments of the trial, an ancient woman in an electric wheelchair appeared like an apparition. Elizabeth Drozdowska, who has severe tremors, whirred into the courtroom to save the woman she called "Susie." Her arrival was unplanned and threw the defendant into a tizzy not unlike a hostess who gaily discovers her dinner party for six has turned into a gathering for twelve. Susan begged the judge to let her take Ms. Drozdowska out of turn. Eli was returned to his holding cell.

Completely shocked, Sequeira threw a dumbfounded look at Steve Clark, the pundit, as if to say, "What do you do with this one?" With her middle-aged son as her aide, Ms. Drozdowska whizzed along the edges of the courtroom, parking in front of the defense table. She raised her curled fingers in a baby fist that shook so vehemently she was barely able to complete the oath.

Once it was administered, Ms. Drozdowska began to explain how she had come to be in the courtroom that day. After hearing a TV reporter demonize

Susan, the seventy-seven-year-old got up off her deathbed—she'd had a heart attack the week before—making arrangements with her cardiologist for extra medications "in case something didn't go right." Spectators and jurors were mesmerized.

Speaking slowly, she explained she had lived across the street from the Polks in Berkeley, until they moved away sixteen years before. Ms. Drozdowska informed the jury that Susan was a wonderful mother, wife, and friend and "an outstanding citizen in the neighborhood . . . That such a beautiful person should have to go through this," she said, pausing to weep. "Okay," she said, haltingly, "I got it together." A few spectators dabbed their eyes. Several jurors wept. "I saw no meanness in the children except Eli took terrible sibling abuse from his older brother [Adam], and his older brother was the apple of his father's eye."

She recalled once hearing "a little boy screaming something awful. I wanted to cry. I couldn't say anything. I told myself this is a psychologist. He teaches at the university and he must know what he's doing. But the beating," she said, not saying who was beating whom, "was so cruel."

"Thank you for your courage and integrity for coming today," Susan said through tears.

Young prosecutors can't help themselves, but experienced ones like Sequeira know better. There would be no cross-examination. Like Susan's mother, Ms. Drozdowska had humanized the defendant. Sequeira did not want her testimony to be drawn out any longer than necessary.

In her cracking voice Ms. Drozdowska looked at her old friend and said, "I could not live with myself if I didn't come. It just breaks my heart." And with that, Ms. Drozdowska sped away. "God bless you," she said to Susan Polk. "Bye-bye, honey."

After she left Steve Clark marveled at the theatrics. No attorney, he said, could have pulled off such a scene or been as sincere as Susan was. "It's like Cirque du Soleil," he marveled, "It's incredible! You just can't explain it."

In fact, it could have been even more dramatic. Defense investigator Kent Brezee, who had been hired by Horowitz, Susan's previous attorney, had planned on sending the old woman in an ambulance and having her carried in on a stretcher.

With the dramatic aside completed, the rest of the day was spent building up Eli and bashing Felix. Eli told his mother he heard his father "threaten to kill you." He said, "He would destroy you and destroy us" and that you "had better think about the consequences to the children and dogs," something Susan often said when asked what threats Felix had made, and something that lent itself to more than one interpretation.

Question after question, Susan would set Eli up with the chance to tear his father apart, trying her hardest to assassinate Felix's character, but in the process doing damage to her witness's credibility. Susan's spoon-feeding hours were numbered. Paul Sequeira felt he had no choice but to attack her middle son.

22

THE SON VS. THE DA

"YOU RECALL OCTOBER 20, 2000, WHEN YOU PUNCHED YOUR MOTHER IN THE face, correct?" That was the first question Sequeira asked on his brutal cross-examination of Eli Polk. It was April 27, 2006, the sixth week of trial, and the gallery was full of what the *Chronicle* reporters called "gavel groupies," waiting for the anticipated showdown. At that first question, Eli's cheeks flushed and his eyes grew watery, coinciding precisely with a long string of creative objections from Susan—including her objection that the question had been "asked and answered and [was] sarcastic and nasty."

Sequeira would not be distracted. He kept his legal pad on the wooden lectern while he prowled like a caged tiger from lectern to the wall. His voice was raised, angry, and despite Susan's objections, Judge Brady ordered Eli to answer the question.

"I was frustrated with the situation and took it out on my mom," Eli explained.

"Yet in frustration you hit your mother with a closed fist, is that correct?" Sequeira inquired. "Your first response was not to defend your mother?"

"I'm not going to be baited by you," Eli replied.

"You feel intimidated?" Sequeira asked. "You're sitting in jail with a whole lot of people more intimidating," Sequeira said, a not so gentle reminder to the jurors that the defense's star witness, though wearing a suit, striped navy tie, and white shirt and acting compliant during his direct examination, was residing in county jail.

"You don't have to answer it," Susan Polk blurted out in total violation of court rules.

"I don't care if he's your son," said the irate judge. "Don't do that again!"

Sequeira moved to Susan's suicide attempt in January 2001. He cited the testimony of psychiatrist Peters who said Susan Polk was most afraid of Eli. "That's a misstatement!" Susan Polk said, though it was not.

"When your mother threatened to kill herself, it was YOU she said she was afraid of."

"You threatened to throw her down the stairs, didn't you?" Sequeira asked.

"I don't remember."

"You don't remember?"

Sequeira produced a police report in which Susan reported her son grabbed her and shoved her out the door.

Eli Polk was now blinking back tears. He said he did not recall the incident; Sequeira was cornering his prey: "You remember when you were three years old and you scored a level 12 on Tetris (something Susan Polk brought up in court to demonstrate how smart Eli was), but you can't remember an incident in 2001 when the police were called? . . . Isn't it correct you will say whatever your mother prompts you to say?"

"I don't remember the alleged incident," a sheepish Eli responded. Sequeira pounced on Eli's calling the police report "alleged."

"Deep down in your heart of hearts, do you think it happened?" Sequeira asked.

"I don't remember what happened," Eli said, sounding torn between love for his mother and dredging up the truth.

"Let's try another day and see how you do." And so it went. Sequeira with his facts lined up and Eli trying to explain why his mother had reported that her son was uncontrollable and asked the police to remove a knife from his bedroom. Or the time his mother found a scale in his bedroom: "Was it like for weighing health food?" Sequeira mocked. Susan had handed it over to the police, telling them her son was dealing drugs.

"You weren't a drug dealer, were you?"

Eli said he was not.

"I'm not saying you were," Sequeira said, setting a trap for the cornered prey.

"When your mother told police you were a drug dealer she made it up, didn't she?" he asked. "The bottom line is, Mr. Polk, isn't it a fact that it doesn't matter who crosses your mother, *her* mother, her husband, her children. She will make things up."

"No, that's not true," a saddened Eli responded.

It was hard not to pity poor Eli, and yet Sequeira was cutting away at Susan Polk's network of distortions with her star witness. While he didn't want jurors to sympathize with Eli, Sequeira felt he had no choice but to dismantle the defendant's support system, which meant attacking Eli. Jurors were transfixed.

The next morning, before jurors arrived, Susan was making one of her multitude of legal arguments and in passing she said there was nothing worse than "a sane person being accused of being crazy." First her husband, then two of her sons, then attorneys, judges, her husband's friends—all, she felt had turned on her. It was hard not to empathize.

Once the jury was seated for the day, Sequeira resumed his attack on Eli. Unable to stand quietly by, Susan was averaging one objection every thirty seconds. "Asked and answered, argumentative, improper material . . . He's being tricky, nefarious, and devious," but her constant interruptions failed to slow Sequeira.

During the course of a legal debate Susan Polk erupted as usual: "Shame on you both," she said to the judge and prosecutor. "Ms. Polk," the wearied judge asserted, "it's only 10:20. We're not going to get very far . . ."

Sequeira asked Eli about his stay in Montana in the fall of 2001 when he, his mother, and brother Gabriel moved to Bozeman.

"Things went pretty well?" he asked unassumingly. Eli had yet to grasp that whenever Sequeira said something mildly pleasant he was setting a trap. Eli agreed they had liked it.

"Isn't it a fact that again you spent time with your mother and you got angry and left Montana and drove home."

Eli denied it. He said he left because he missed his "friends, house [the DA injected here: "Your dad?"], satellite TV, skateboarding with friends."

"It wasn't all that tranquil in Montana," Sequeira said.

"Oh, yes it was."

Eli barged right into the trap. Sequeira told him to "explain to the jury" how it was that the owners of the cabin where they lived "found things in disarray," including walls bashed, doors missing. "You want to explain that if everything was so tranquil? . . . The whole time you were in Montana . . . there were no fights, no problems?"

"For the most part, yes."

The DA couldn't resist, "Tell us about *the little part.*"

"I don't remember."

Eli was a trapped animal. Sequeira's two star witnesses, Gabe and Adam, had put the jury inside the Polk home. Eli was challenging their view of Felix and Susan, and for the sake of his case, Sequeira needed to prove to the jurors that Eli was lying.

Meanwhile, Susan's creative objections continued. Sounding more like Joseph Welch's plea during the McCarthy hearings, she asked of the DA, "Has he some courtesy for this young man who has lost his father and his mother faces life imprisonment? Does he have any manners, any compassion?"

But Sequeira was not through: "Mr. Polk, you testified in detail that you believe your father was trying to get you put away, is that correct?"

This would become one of the most poignant moments in the trial. After asking Eli this question, Sequeira showed Eli a letter dated April 25, 2002, from Felix to the judge begging him *not* to put Eli in jail. Eli said he had never seen the letter. In it, Dr. Polk described his son as "friendly and genuinely well liked," and someone "who does not get into fights" but had been "enticed and goaded. . . . He is not by nature violent. . . . He is capable of being highly disciplined. . . . In my view he is very much a salvageable young man." Dr. Polk asked the court to release Eli into his custody and promised the boy would receive counseling.

Under questioning, Eli Polk insisted it was a negative letter. "You were charged with a felony, you were facing four years in CYA (California Youth Authority). Your dad was trying to keep you out of jail. You can't see that?"

Eli said he believed his father was "playing games with me."

"Couldn't you see from the letter your father was trying to keep you *out of jail?*" an incredulous Sequeira inquired.

"Objection," Susan Polk proclaimed. "He said 'no.' "

"Now she's suggesting answers to witnesses," Sequeira protested.

"Ms. Polk, if you answer questions for the witness one more time I will excuse you from these proceedings," a frustrated Judge Brady said, the most draconian of warnings she had yet issued.

Sequeira might just as well have been a deprogrammer. "You can't see the love from your dad, beseeching the court to keep you out of jail?"

At one point, Susan Polk claimed the question was "misleading, improper, and just really low."

"Ms. Polk, this is not a law school debate," the judge moaned.

At last, Sequeira made some headway: "Don't you think that your father's letter had a more positive effect than what your mother—who had made a scene in juvenile court—was doing?"

"Yes," Eli Polk acknowledged, "although it was taken out of context."

The DA moved on to questioning the son about his mother's behavior. "You're not going to say your mother doesn't like arguing," he said.

"She's not a loose cannon," Eli countered. "My mom is awesome," Eli said, as though he had forgotten he was a witness in his mother's murder trial. Susan Polk started to say something when the judge intervened: "You're not going to object to that," she said to laughter in the courtroom, but that was one of the only times that day when her objections could be stifled. As one spectator who was keeping count noted, by 4:40 PM Susan had made 148 objections—just in one day.

Sequeira told Eli that there was no one in the courtroom who didn't believe he loved his mother unconditionally. The DA then read from a letter Eli wrote on November 23, 2002, to his then jailed mother. "I am your most important witness," he wrote. "I want and need to testify."

"I would die for you, Mom. I would do absolutely anything to get you out of there."

"Lying is a lot easier than dying, Mr. Polk. You'd die, but you wouldn't lie?" Eli's answer no longer mattered.

BY MAY 1, JURORS WERE WEARING SHORT-SLEEVED SHIRTS; COURTROOM blinds, which had been drawn, now opened to the hills and blue skies, and Susan's anger with Valerie Harris had subsided. That week, Ms. Harris returned as Susan's assistant, which was good because Susan needed someone to arrange for witnesses to appear in some sort of sequence. While outwardly Ms. Harris was delighted to be back in Susan's good graces, she quietly asked people if they thought she was foolish for returning.

Valerie Harris's reappearance was hardly surprising; it underscored one of the most stunning contradictions in Susan Polk's personality: she had an uncanny ability to infuriate people, but there were always some who were dazzled by her, willing to overlook her unpleasant traits, ignore the possibility that they could become her targets, and find in her something that they needed.

During the course of questioning, Eli, who was suffering from a cold or flu, experienced a coughing spell. "Your Honor, I think he needs medicines like antibiotics," Susan said offering a quick maternal diagnosis. During redirect, Susan tried to repair the damage that Sequeira had done. She had Eli read aloud a letter he'd written when she was in jail.

"Never again will I be as happy as I could, with you in jail," Eli said. "I will always be there for you. . . . You dying is part of me dying as well. . . . We will see each other many more times in life. . . . I wake up to your face every morning. . . . I love you enough to burn all I am and meet you in the afterlife." As he read, he wept.

When he was finished, Susan asked, "Do you need to lie at all?" Eli Polk said "No," and burst into tears.

In the hallway spectators raised their brows: "Sounds like two lovers," one observed. Others said they only wished they had such a romantic lover. And one reporter said he thought *he was romantic* but he had never written anything quite *like that.*

On that afternoon, Susan Polk peppered Eli with questions to counter the DA's masterful cross-examination. Hadn't their father allowed the boys to throw drinking parties? Didn't Dad tell you you couldn't survive without him? Didn't he tell you that nothing will come of your life if you follow me?

"He told me I'd fail. You'll fail if you go along with what your mother does," Eli responded. "I certainly don't feel like I'm a failure," Eli said. Despite the fact that mother and son were both in jail, they seemed oblivious to the accuracy of Felix's prediction.

"Are you aware that I'm very proud of you?" Susan Polk asked. "Are you aware it broke my heart to see you suffer?" her face reddened and she wept.

In the ongoing psychodrama, it took awhile before her son could say, "Yes."

Susan Polk's attention to every excruciating detail, her paranoia, which Eli sometimes shared, and her insistence that every part of her family life be depicted became the subject of daily humor within the court. She could tell by the snickering that many spectators were against her, but still she thought many jurors sided with her. This notion emboldened her, and like a kid with a substitute teacher, each day she took new liberties. Judge Brady adjusted to each new outburst with more sighs, more rolling of her eyes, and more admonishments. The greater the Susan Polk blowup, the softer was the judge's response. A few spectators labeled the judge "Saint Laurel." Sometimes, jurors and spectators wished Judge Brady would take harsher measures, but it was obvious she wanted the trial to proceed without giving Susan an opening for an appeal.

For Paul Sequeira, sympathy came from outside of the court room as his family had taken pity on him. Not long after the trial began, he noticed that when he arrived home each evening, his kids were kinder, knowing that invariably he'd taken a beating that day in court. Sequeira was like a bather adjusting to hotter tub water. Initially, when Susan would call him unethical or a liar, he was outraged. Now, he only objected when she labeled him a *pathological liar*.

ON ELI'S SIXTH AND, AS ANNOUNCED BY THE JUDGE, FINAL DAY ON THE WITness stand, he wore a black shirt and black sweater, looking like a gloomy young Hollywood actor. His mother also had a change of clothes, and with her outfit of an incongruous hot pink polo jersey and khaki pants, she looked like a mom who should be at a high school gym spray-painting cardboard palm trees for the senior prom. Susan opened by asking that Eli's testimony again be postponed to accommodate two out-of-state witnesses. This time, Sequeira said he had "bent over backwards" to adjust to her schedule, allowing four other witnesses to testify during Eli's testimony. Now, he objected.

"He says he bends over backward," Susan Polk said. "That man needs a spanking!" Then she addressed her son. She told him that this would be his final day of questioning. "If I forget anything, wink at me," she said coquettishly.

"I'd prefer he not do that," the judge advised.

Susan continued to show her love for Eli and her vitriol for her other sons, claiming that Adam and Gabriel have "a book deal, a movie deal, they're pursuing right now, they received a three-hundred-thousand-dollar settlement from the insurance company." Susan was willing to fling whatever rumor she heard, no matter how flaky, to make her point. Her sons did not have a book or movie deal, and she knew that.

"How 'bout you, Eli? You ready to join their ranks and become a liar?"

"It's not even an option," Eli responded. "It's the way I am. No matter what they do to me, I'm the same person. To lose who you are is not worth any amount of money."

Spectators watched in fascination as Eli stared down the DA. What they couldn't see, because Sequeira faced the witness stand, was Sequeira's deadly stare back. "Why don't you just drop it?" Eli griped.

"Don't speak to me!" Sequeira complained.

"I can speak all I want," a suddenly brash Eli asserted as the bailiff approached, reminding him he was in custody. Eli was ordered to stand, and when he failed to move swiftly enough he was shoved out of his chair and handcuffed. Susan Polk loudly complained. A normally smiling deputy hovered over her and said, "Ma'am, you're in my custody!" Eli and Susan were quickly removed from the courtroom.

During the lunch break, an increasingly despondent Valerie Harris munched tempura and chugged hot sake. By the afternoon, Eli appeared sullen and subdued. During a line of questions Susan asked her son, "Do you recall" and before she said anything else, he said, "Yeah."

"He's psychic too!" she remarked, one of the first times she'd shown humor in court.

Then it was Sequeira's turn to re-cross. Watching him question the defense's star witness was like observing a car crash in slo-mo. Sequeira asked Eli if he had enjoyed "the high life."

"The high life? My dad is dead, my mother is in jail. That's really accurate, sir," he said.

"I object! Sarcasm." Susan offered. The judge asked if Ms. Polk was objecting to *her own* witness's testimony. She said she was because "it could be misunderstood."

Sequeira questioned Eli about his profligate ways. "There was a pot of money you were dipping into, was there not, Mr. Polk?" As he asked the question, Sequeira, with exaggerated gestures, rifled through papers, a move designed to convince Eli he had the goods on him. Eli admitted he'd spent forty thousand dollars of his inheritance *in three months*. Sequeira was shocked, but didn't show it. He quoted from Susan Polk's letters in which she wrote, " 'STOP SPENDING,' You recall that?" Eli did.

EARLIER IN ELI'S TESTIMONY, SUSAN POLK HAD ASKED TO PLACE A POLICE report into evidence. Sequeira had looked at it, and the alacrity with which he concurred and the tone in which he did made it obvious he thought she was handing over a grenade.

While cross-examining Eli, Sequeira asked for defense exhibit number 520. Hadn't Eli read what his mother had highlighted and simply agreed to her claim that the police report was a complaint against his father? In fact, Sequeira pointed out, the report was a complaint against *Eli,* and "the person who made the phone call to the police was your mother!"

Eli said the document was misleading, but the damage had been done. This incident reinforced a reoccurring point of Sequeira's that Eli was a slave to his mother's whims. "Whatever your mother asks you, you blindly go along with. You said 'Yes,' without looking at the document!"

Sequeira wasn't finished. He walked up to Susan Polk's 2003 timeline and announced "The timeline has something missing," reminding the witness that on October 5, 2003, Eli "shot a man in the neck with a pellet gun, causing him to have surgery." Sequeira pointed out that though the police recommended Eli be charged with "assault with a deadly weapon," in fact the DA's office never charged him. The very DA's office that Eli insisted had been unfair to him and his mother.

"Don't you think—and you know how tricky I am—that it would have been a lot juicier . . . and better for the DA's office . . . to make you look bad and charge you with assault with a deadly weapon?"

Eli had a curious effect on jurors. Yes, Sequeira had done a masterful job, exploding little stories Susan and Eli concocted, but he left intact what he couldn't touch: Eli's love for his mother. Jurors thought all three boys had an agenda and that none was totally truthful, but some thought Eli's motives were most pure: he loved his mother.

Sequeira and Susan's middle son continued to spar until Sequeira leaned in and asked his odd final question: "Your father is dead, isn't he?" Eli was belligerent: "I'm not answering that question."

By the time Sequeira had finished with him, it was hard to say what was left of Eli's testimony, but Susan Polk's next witness, a forensic pathologist, could make all the difference. He would support her contention that she killed her husband in self-defense and deal not with memories and emotions but with the facts.

23

THE RUNAWAY PATHOLOGIST

FOR MANY SPECTATORS, THE TRIAL WAS MORE THAN A FULL-TIME JOB. WHEN they arrived home each evening, they logged on to Court TV's website, where they counseled and conversed about the day's proceedings. In court, some scribbled like reporters. Over time they coalesced into a happy gang of court watchers, most of them turned off by Susan Polk's behavior and decidedly unsympathetic to her—but not Paul, the Filipino orderly, who believed Susan and came to care for her. The other regulars had jolly lunches together at which they dissected the morning's hearings and mimicked Susan Polk's latest outburst.

The jurors too seemed to get along. Frequently, they went out to lunch together, although one of them, the juror who worked at the Nummi plant, hung back. No one knew if his behavior reflected his desire for a smoke break or a more serious sort of break.

Susan's next witness would provide fodder for chat rooms, message boards, jurists, and journalists who had never seen anything quite like him.

Dr. John Cooper would be one of Susan Polk's most important witnesses. A forensic pathologist from Texas, Dr. Cooper had the ruddy, pressed face of a boxer. A graduate of the University of Texas Health Science Center, he received his MD in 1983, eventually going into pathology because he liked solving puzzles. He'd conducted 2,000 autopsies, of which approximately 250 to 300 were homicides. He told the court he only takes cases he believes in.

Originally, Dan Horowitz had helped Susan line up Dr. Cyril Wecht, a forensic pathologist and attorney for celebrity corpses, but in January, Dr. Wecht was indicted on eighty-four counts of misusing public funds. Susan turned to Dr. Cooper, another medical examiner that Horowitz had found, though Horowitz would later explain he had not intended to use him after he learned that Dr. Cooper was day-trading stocks rather than examining cadavers.

In a trial with an extraordinary number of dramas, none was more amazing than the testimony of Dr. Cooper.

"In your opinion," Susan Polk said as she began her questioning, "was my husband killed?"

"No," he said, to a chorus of courtroom gasps. He insisted that Dr. Polk died of undiagnosed severe coronary disease. Stab wounds, he said, were a contributing factor, although they were not severe. He said that according to the prosecution's pathologist, Felix Polk had lost 100 ccs of blood, whereas in a typical fatal stab wound to the chest, "we'll find 500 ccs of blood or 1,500 ccs of blood."

When he said, "Ms. Polk's involvement was purely one of self-defense," Sequeira objected. Harshly, the judge admonished the witness this was outside his field of expertise. Sequeira expected Dr. Cooper to say Felix Polk died of a heart attack; he did not anticipate he was going to say Susan Polk acted in self-defense and that she was innocent.

Dr. Cooper, like the prosecution's forensic pathologist, Dr. Peterson, had that charismatic connection that could help him connect with jurors. Both pathologists agreed that Felix Polk had 75 percent blockage to his coronary arteries. But there was little else upon which they agreed. Dr. Cooper attacked his adversary, calling Dr. Peterson's analysis of the twenty-seven stab wounds "excessively dramatic" and "inflammatory." Pathologists, he said, should "just state the facts." He criticized the coroner's report for not mentioning coronary disease. If Dr. Polk's heart problems had been treated, he would not have died, Dr. Cooper said.

"Are you saying the manner of death should have been ruled natural?" Susan Polk asked. Dr. Cooper replied, "That's my conclusion, now that all the information is in."

Another communal gasp wafted through the courtroom. A few jurors smiled. As off-the-wall and unexpected as his testimony was, Dr. Cooper was raising doubt in the minds of some. Add to that the fact that even Dr. Peterson had said no individual stab wound, by itself, was fatal. Susan Polk asked if there "was any evidence I incapacitated my husband" with one strike on the head with an object [as the prosecution contended]. "No, that did not happen according to the evidence," Dr. Cooper asserted. He called the head injury "relatively trivial," agreeing with Susan that her husband could have fallen and hit his head—without harming his ear.

A number of times Sequeira raised objections, the objections were sustained, but the witness plowed through. A dismayed Judge Brady called a halt to the testimony, excused the jurors, and dressed down Dr. Cooper: she said she had never encountered an expert witness who would ignore an objection a judge had sustained. "I don't understand it," Judge Brady said. Dr. Cooper tilted his head and apologized.

Susan was still steaming over Sequeira's objections: "The DA," she stammered, "I wouldn't say he's a good lawyer . . . ," and before she uttered another word, Sequeira said, "I'm done." He packed up his files and headed for the door.

"Don't leave," the judge ordered. Several years before, Tom O'Connor, the former DA in the case, had done the same thing, only he had walked out in the middle of a hearing when he could no longer cope with Susan's insults.

"You know, Judge, you can only take so much," an exasperated Sequeira sputtered.

"He's playing a game of chicken," Susan complained. "This man is having a temper tantrum. He doesn't have self-control. Maybe he should be the defendant."

As Susan spoke, her mother, who had been making noise, was ushered out of the courtroom by the bailiff. A few minutes later Helen was on a park bench in front of the courthouse as a print reporter was conducting a TV interview. To the delight of the TV reporter, Helen joined in. On camera, she said that the judge and the entire court system was biased. All of this was news to the TV reporter, who normally covered sports.

Once court had resumed, Dr. Cooper continued to fortify Susan's case, claiming that the evidence proved Felix had been the aggressor. Susan Polk had a bite mark on her hand, redness by one eye that proved he'd punched her, and Felix was found with clumps of her hair in his hand. The pathologist said that if Susan Polk intended to kill her husband she would not have wielded a knife. Stabbing victims, he said, end up in the ER, not the morgue. He considered Felix's wounds and asserted, "If you want to kill someone you go for the heart or neck vessels or some other major vessel," which, he said, Susan Polk had not done.

Susan's questioning of her expert witness was seamless. He'd given her a sheet of questions and in an unprecedented act, she followed the script.

If the jurors believed him, Dr. Cooper could turn the case around, or at least convince some that Dr. Peterson hadn't conclusively made his case. Sequeira could not let that happen.

"That's a whole mouthful you just testified to," said an angry Sequeira as he began his cross-examination. Slumped spectators and jurors sat up.

"So you wrote a report, right? You didn't? You put fifty hours into this case and you didn't?" Sequeira knew that Dr. Cooper hadn't written a report; the doctor had told him so in the corridor the day before.

"I took no notes," Dr. Cooper said, only to contradict himself a moment later: "I didn't retain them."

"You must have a case file on this case. You bring them?"

"No," he said.

"You know these things are discoverable, isn't that the case, Dr. Cooper?"

"That's why I didn't leave a lot of stuff in writing," Dr. Cooper said. That's a common trick among expert witnesses, though not something they generally admit to, at least not in court.

"That's why, so the other side can't see what you're going to say? Is that the object, doctor?"

"Yes," Dr. Cooper replied, adding that he thought "You would pull out all the stops [and prevent] me from testifying."

The judge called an early halt to Dr. Cooper's testimony and excused the jurors. She told Ms. Polk and Mr. Sequeira that she was distressed by the doctor's position that the information he relied upon, reports, notes, and materials, had not been turned over to the prosecution. When the judge asked Dr. Cooper about his files, he said, in direct contradiction to his earlier testimony, that he had some with him, but Susan's letters to him, he said, were back at his office in Texas. "I didn't form my opinion based on her letters," he insisted. If that were so, then there would be no need for him to turn them over, but the judge was unconvinced. She told him to have the letters, which the doctor suddenly was calling a "letter" faxed to him by tomorrow morning.

Every day the drama managed to top that of the day before. On Friday, May 5, 2006, before the jury entered the court, Dr. Cooper told the judge that he brought to court whatever files he had with him from Texas but that he could *not* produce a letter he received from Susan because it had *disappeared*. Dr.

Cooper suggested that he may have inadvertently left her letter on a Southwest airplane or that it may have disappeared from his motel room. To an astonished Judge Brady he said that when he returned to his motel yesterday, he noticed the door was jammed.

Susan Polk's jury consultant, Karen Fleming-Ginn, whispered to a reporter that in these last few months Judge Brady's hair had grown considerably whiter. A journalist called the disappearing letter "the Hispanic maid defense: she mistook Susan's letter for a dirty towel."

"I must admit, I'm very troubled by the turn of events this morning," Judge Brady declared. The judge told Dr. Cooper someone needed to fax Susan Polk's letters to him. He said no one was at his office—which is in his home, in Texas. His wife, he said, was gone, and only the dogs remained.

Paul Sequeira pointed out inconsistencies in the doctor's statements. "There's something new every day in court that I have never seen before," the DA said outside the earshot of jurors who were spending more and more time in the hallway wondering what "Tex," as they would later call him, was up to now. "Somebody is concealing evidence."

In her measured tones Susan Polk said Sequeira "doesn't like the testimony, so he does a little dance in front of the media." She called him "a crybaby" and accused him of "stalling, delaying, grandstanding, and being inappropriate."

"I can bring up what I want," Sequeira muttered.

"Fiddlesticks!" Ms. Polk responded.

As the judge spoke, Susan was furiously writing on a pad of paper. The judge asked her to show the same courtesy she had shown when Susan Polk spoke. "I'm taking notes rather than relying on your court reporter," Ms. Polk snapped back. The judge called her comments "extremely inappropriate" and said that unless she had proof she was not to question the integrity of the court staff. "It won't continue or we won't continue," the judge warned. Then the judge said something that many spectators had long thought: "The fact that your voice is low doesn't change the content."

The judge ordered Dr. Cooper to produce the whole file by Monday morning, pointing out that "Someone is home taking care of your dogs."

In the courthouse corridors spectators and reporters lingered, talking about the shocking turn of events. Some even speculated the unthinkable, that Dr. Cooper, like Susan's letters, might disappear.

That Monday morning, more spectators gathered than usual. They'd waited all weekend for the cliffhanger. Would the good doctor show, and would he have the letter, or would he flee and face the consequences? And what was the likelihood of that?

At 9:00 AM the pathologist was nowhere in sight.

"In all my years as a litigator, prosecutor, and judge, I have never heard of anything like this before or anything close to it," Judge Brady said, her face pale, her tone subdued. "I have never heard of an expert witness taking on such a role as an advocate and choosing not to come back . . . That is just not an option," she said while the jurors waited outside the courtroom for two hours. Dr. Cooper was a no-show.

He had sent a three-page e-mail to the judge, saying he would not be returning. "Frankly, for him to do this to you" the judge said to Ms. Polk, "in the middle of testimony is—I'm trying to think of the appropriate word—*bizarre* and somewhat inexcusable. It puts the defendant in an untenable position."

Sequeira was stomping around the courtroom and shaking his head in disbelief. He told the judge he had "been down the country road before but never seen anyone run off like a scared rabbit."

Susan Polk labeled the brouhaha "BS," but she was also concerned.

The judge knocked over her container of pens, which clattered on the bench. "Tell him to be on the next plane out here," she advised Ms. Polk, as she hastily returned her pens to their upright positions.

The court sent Dr. Cooper a succinct letter, which read

Your willful failure to appear on Monday May 8, 2006 is in violation of that Court order.

You are hereby ordered to appear in person with your file . . . Failure to comply with this Court's order may subject you to appropriate sanctions.

Judge Laurel S. Brady

WITH SUDDEN TIME ON HER HANDS, SUSAN POLK LOOKED AROUND FOR A witness to fill the vacuum. Unfortunately Marjorie Briner was sitting on a bench outside the courtroom. For a while now, both women wanted to have at the other. Susan told Sequeira that she might keep Mrs. Briner on the witness stand "for days." Sequeira's eyes drooped and his face sagged.

Perfectly poised and pretty, Marjorie Briner, wearing a suit and a cream-colored blouse, approached the witness stand. Initially she did such a good job *for the defense* that if Sequeira cross-examined her it would have been like sprinkling sugar on a jelly doughnut.

Of all her enemies, Susan viewed the woman who was raising her youngest son as the worst. "I have Gabriel and she doesn't," Mrs. Briner once explained. Various times during the trial, Susan had turned to see Marjorie Briner in the courtroom and had pointed a long, bony finger demanding she be removed. During a pretrial hearing when she wanted to identify Ms. Briner, instead of saying she was the attractive blond woman in the third row, Susan said she was the woman with *the mole on her cheek,* a comment that distressed normally unflappable reporters.

A middle school English and social studies teacher, Marjorie Briner knew how to speak clearly and loudly, and what she said was personally devastating to the defendant. After his father's death, "Gabriel was not willing to have you in his life," Ms. Briner said matter-of-factly. She told Susan she had tried to be neutral and had encouraged Gabe to have a relationship with his mother, but he adamantly refused.

Susan believed the Briners turned Gabriel against her, but Ms. Briner disabused her as well as the court of that idea. "Did you ask my permission to hold Gabriel back?" Susan asked over and over again. "He was not held back," Ms. Briner explained. "When he was with you, he was not in school."

Susan asked the witness about Eli, who after bumming around from one of Adam's friends' houses to the next, alighted at the Briners'. The witness said that she and the Polk family had tried to steer Eli back to school but that his mother vetoed the plan. While his brothers were being educated and Adam could barely afford his rent payments, Eli showed off his three-thousand-dollar suit and his thirty pairs of shoes.

"I think," she commented, "Eli is the most tragic figure in this entire thing . . . I think Eli would say anything you wanted him to," she said, adding that Gabriel calls him his mother's *"trained attack dog. . . .* That's why so many people are afraid of him."

The more questions Susan asked, the worse it got. Marjorie Briner described a friendly relationship that turned bitter after she failed to deliver to Byron Boys Ranch a "Pumping Iron" DVD for Eli at Christmas 2002. Suddenly, the phone calls from Susan Polk were full of paranoid accusations. "You yelled at me in ways no one has ever yelled at me before or since," the witness said.

Marjorie Briner had the opportunity to say what many in the courtroom had been thinking: "I think you have your version of what happens. Often it isn't reality." She said that Gabriel calls his mother's diary, to which she refers often as though it were a legal document, her "diary of real and imagined events."

ON WEDNESDAY, MAY 10, 2006, MS. BRINER'S SECOND DAY OF TESTIMONY, Susan Polk was especially testy, objecting to the fact that the DA had not turned over letters that *she* had written to the Briners. An exasperated judge countered, "They're *your* letters and she's *your* witness."

By 9:30 AM, Susan had called for a mistrial three times and had caused the judge to cover her face with her hands, sigh numerous times, and go bug-eyed. As fast as Susan would say, "I move for a mistrial," Judge Brady responded with a "Denied." Together, they sounded like two parts of a single hiccup.

Susan Polk spent the rest of the day trying to impeach Marjorie Briner's testimony. Denying she was ever unkind to the witness, the defendant put on the screen sweet letters she'd written Ms. Briner, including a handmade Christmas card with "a bunny" as the DA called it, the white rabbit from Susan's reappearing alter ego, Alice of *Alice in Wonderland*. The whimsical rabbit had long, floppy ears, a red dinner jacket, and a yellow umbrella tucked under his arm.

The two women sparred for a full day. Surprisingly, jurors were not as enamored of Marjorie Briner as spectators had originally anticipated. They respected the Briners for what they'd done, but some couldn't help but empathize with Susan. Marjorie Briner, a woman she'd never met, had supplanted her and was acting like she was Gabe's mother. She even referred to Felix's brother and sister as "Uncle John" and "Aunt Evelyn," remarks that did not go unnoticed by the defendant. At least one juror later speculated that the years of fending off Susan might have hardened Ms. Briner. Or perhaps she was just a strong but selfless mother in an unexpectedly difficult position.

At the end of the day Susan Polk told the court she wanted to call Gabriel back to the stand. Marjorie Briner said he was preparing for his final exams and would be unavailable. The defendant objected to the fact that her adversary seemed to protect *her* son. The judge called a halt to the controversy and left the bench but Susan Polk didn't stop. She called Paul Sequeira a "moral creep," a "disgusting person," and "a criminal." Sequeira responded, "You need to go to your cell."

ON THE MORNING OF THURSDAY, MAY 11, 2006, THERE WAS AN INDEFINABLE apprehension in the courtroom. Before the jurors entered, the judge asked Susan about the scheduling of witnesses. Ms. Polk took the opportunity to berate the DA and what she said was his "case of lies." The judge gave up and walked out.

"That was productive," Sequeira quipped dryly.

"You're unprofessional. You ought to be working in a third world dictatorship instead of the U.S.," Susan Polk declared.

"Actually, it might be preferable to being here!" Sequeira responded, trying to keep his temper in check. When he was in his twenties, Sequeira and a defense lawyer, an ex-marine Deadhead, almost came to blows. The pair had pulled their jackets off and exchanged words: "What are you looking at?" "What are *you* looking at, you little prick?" The bailiff squeezed in between and halted it. (Sequeira says they're now good friends.) While it had been a long time, Sequeira still struggled to hide his frustration.

Yesterday's interrogation of Marjorie Briner was so unproductive, so slow and so painful, that for the first time, a few spectators were quietly critical of Judge Brady for letting it last so long. Today would be different, and the judge reminded Susan that her inquiry was supposed to deal with the narrow issue of Marjorie Briner's alleged influence over or pressure on her son's testimony. Susan ignored the warning as she often did and proceeded according to her personal plan, trying to prove that Marjorie Briner had lied when she said that Susan Polk had blown up at her on the phone and made nasty accusations in letters to her.

"We haven't come close to the area that I deemed relevant to this trial," the judge reminded her.

"Perjury is always relevant!" Susan Polk barked back.

Soon she was spinning out of control again. The judge had had enough.

"Ms. Briner's testimony is completed," she said, before sending jurors off to an early lunch and to the farmers market, which, now that the heat of spring returned, had started up again around the corner. Marjorie Briner had been looking forward to being questioned by Sequeira, but he chose not to cross examine her, knowing that if he did, Susan Polk would have another opportunity to torture the witness—and the long-suffering jurors.

With Marjorie Briner's testimony completed, Eli returned to the stand, where he proceeded to stare down the DA while answering questions put to him by his mother. Eli's jaw muscles were pulsating, and as he grew more upset, the left side of his upper lip lifted in an involuntary sneer. His emotions and his mother's rage were palpable, even scary.

Susan asked Eli about Gabriel's life at the Briners'. He was happy to oblige. He said his little brother "was grounded a lot," had "strict curfews." His allowance was so small, Eli said, that Gabriel barely was able to cover gas for school. (The jurors already heard from Marjorie Briner that she gave Gabriel a monthly stipend of four hundred dollars, which she later increased to six hundred dollars a month to cover clothes.) "He had all kinds of chores," Eli said, glancing at the jurors and adding as an afterthought, "I'm not saying that was bad, but it was very controlling."

Susan Polk grew weepy when she asked her son his last question: if it weren't true that when she was out on bail, the two had written to governmental agencies in New Zealand about living and working there. Her face reddened. "We hoped to start over again in New Zealand," she said to Eli. He nodded without saying another word. The bailiff approached, and Eli unceremoniously left the courtroom for the last time. His mother, who was already engaged in another matter, barely noticed.

While Sequeira had wanted to re-cross Eli Polk, he knew it was just for sport. He'd looked at the judge and could tell she wanted it to end. He looked at the jurors and he thought they too wanted this agony stopped. He could tell that Eli was "not in a good state." Provoke him a little more, and there was no telling what might happen.

The court recessed for the week. That Sunday was Mother's Day. The only son who would want to wish Susan Polk a happy Mother's Day had just left the witness stand. Because he was incarcerated, Eli was not allowed to write her. The only son Susan could communicate with was Adam, and their relationship was completely fraught with bitterness. As such, it seemed odd that on Friday Adam received a handwritten letter from his mother, saying that she loved all three of her sons and that she has their pictures on her defense table. Whatever Susan's motives, they failed to stir Adam's feelings toward her. The Polks' eldest son assumed his mother was trying to manipulate him, wanting him to relay her message to Gabe and Eli.

Susan Polk spent her Mother's Day alone in jail preparing for the return of one of her most important witnesses.

24.

THE PRODIGAL
PATHOLOGIST RETURNS

ON MONDAY, MAY 15, 2006, IT WAS HIGH NOON IN JUDGE BRADY'S COURT: the return of the runaway pathologist. Dr. Cooper strode into the courtroom with his brown leather cowboy boots, a dark suit, and a dark Hawaiian shirt with splashy white flowers on it. It had been eleven days since he was last there.

"Dr. Cooper, did you find the letters the court sent you to retrieve?" Sequeira asked.

"Yes, I did, with one exception."

Now in his caged tiger mode, Sequeira began pacing again, asking Dr. Cooper if he had filed a police report once he realized a document was missing from his motel room. Did he contact Southwest Airlines? As Sequeira shot holes through the doctor's story, Susan Polk was finding more objections than there were questions. Spectators and reporters assumed Dr. Cooper had something to hide or that his client, Susan Polk, wanted him to hide, but no one knew what that was. He produced one of her letters in which Susan described how she killed her husband but there were no bombshells, just her oft-repeated account of self-defense.

Sequeira's buddies at the DA's office thought Cooper came off as a charlatan. But the prosecutor had no idea what *the jurors* were thinking. Dr. Cooper, it turned out, was like human mercury, impossible to pin down. A few deputy DAs sat along the side wall; they'd come to enjoy the Sequeira Show.

"Isn't it true, Dr. Cooper, that you ran off mid-testimony . . . ?" Sequeira asked.

"That is a complete misrepresentation," the doctor stammered.

"Didn't you write a letter saying you're resigning from the process?"

"No."

"Didn't you write that 'I am hereby withdrawing from any further partici-pation—' "

"Objection! Out of context!" Susan Polk argued, defending her prized witness. Always creative with her objections, Susan accused the DA of "wool-gathering." The judge said she would not permit an objection to every question.

When Sequeira questioned the pathologist about his disappearance, Dr. Cooper acquiesced: "I don't feel like being defensive. Make your point and I'll concede."

If Dr. Cooper were defensive or belligerent, Sequeira's style would succeed, but the witness was passive.

Still, even under an intense cross-examination, Dr. Cooper drove home his points. He claimed that Dr. Peterson described the wounds "as though they were all significant when only seven could be characterized as significant." Some he described were "mere scratches."

"We know Dr. Polk was in cardiac arrest before he hit the floor," Dr. Cooper said.

"We don't know that," Sequeira exclaimed. He then had the doctor accompany him into a Sequeira-style ambush: "Guys our age, if we get thrown to the ground we bruise," Sequeira said. The doctor concurred. "If you and I get into an altercation, and we hit the floor, we come up with some bruising," again the doctor agreed, suspecting no doubt that Sequeira was referring to the victim, Felix Polk. Then Sequeira went for the kill: "The defendant claimed she hit the ground on a hard tile surface, yet she has no bruising." She had redness around the eyes and a single bruise on her shoulder.

Sequeira suggested showing "the pictures."

"That's just dirty!" an infuriated Susan Polk objected.

Sequeira called Dr. Cooper's scenario "unbelievable." Dr. Cooper called it "miraculous."

"Didn't the defendant in her letter to you say she had a Maglite in one of her hands and that she *tapped* the victim lightly in the right temple? The Maglite could have caused the blunt-force trauma to the head," he said. (No one mentioned that when Eli had been in a fight years before, witnesses claimed he had badgered his opponent with a Maglite.)

The next day a thirteen-year-old boy in a green-and-white-striped T-shirt sat in the front row. His boatlike white sneakers were harbingers of his future height. Paul Sequeira had brought one of his sons to court. Before the public and jurors were admitted Susan Polk spotted him, and in a civilized manner, she told Sequeira he might not want his son witnessing her insults. Sequeira said he thought the boy could handle it. Now and again there were touches of Susan the good. In kidding tones she suggested that the DA probably brought him to court "so I'll be nice to you."

In fact, the morning was as mild as they came. The defendant was in control. She was doing well and her witness, who seemed like an alchemist yesterday, was resurrecting himself today.

"Why did you take this case?" Susan asked during her redirect.

"I felt if I didn't you might not get justice," he replied.

In her redirect, Susan Polk was smart and effective. The only problem was the graphic nature of her questions. What other defendant could describe so coldly killing her husband, even if it were in self-defense, without a modicum of emotion? She was in her element, periodically falling to the floor to demonstrate her point.

Denying she had been in "a murderous rage," she said a murderous rage would have occurred "if I picked up a marble rolling pin and beat him over the head with it and he fell to the ground" and struck him "ten more times and beat him to death." As she spoke she lifted her arms as though whacking Felix on the head. Her point may have been lost on anyone who was thinking about the ease with which she pantomimed beating Felix on the head.

"Don't men have a particular vulnerable area of their bodies?" she asked as the judge looked on with amusement. "So stipulated!" said a booming Paul Sequeira to courtroom laughter.

And isn't it so, Susan asked, that if a woman is on her back and kicks a man "hard in the genital area that could incapacitate him for a few seconds?"

As for her contention that Felix's head was bashed by the fall and not her hitting him in the head with an object, Dr. Cooper told jurors the injury to Felix's head could not have been caused during the course of the fight because there was no bruising. It must have occurred afterward.

Things were going along swimmingly for Ms. Polk until she ran into a roadblock. She asked if after reading her husband's medical records, "Did you find he had a history of receiving treatment for schizophrenia and anxiety by a psychiatrist?"

Many times during the trial Susan Polk had tried to insert into the record fifty-year-old information about what she said was her husband's schizophrenia when he was in the navy.

"The diagnosis was not schizophrenia per se," Dr. Cooper corrected. He said what Felix Polk experienced was a schizophrenic reaction during a psychotic period of his life "that doesn't turn into a chronic schizophrenic condition." Susan Polk folded her arms and listened. Jailed pro pers often lack the opportunity to thoroughly question their witnesses before trial. This was one of those times that Susan Polk was unprepared. Good attorneys know the answer before they ask the question.

Speaking in his soft southern accent, Dr. Cooper swiveled in his chair and faced the jurors, judiciously advising them what to consider when determining the facts. He informed the jury that two perfectly intelligent people can see things differently, and sounding personal and reasonable, he said his client was innocent.

Sequeira was impressed by Dr. Cooper's folksy manner, and he was not happy. As Susan was thanking her witness, Sequeira sprang out of his chair like a slingshot and began pacing faster than usual. He wanted to shatter the spell.

"Doctor" he said with great speed, "you looked at the jury" and said, "Two intelligent people can see things differently," informing them that he and Dr. Peterson were just experts educating the jurors. Then Sequeira pointed out that Dr. Cooper had attacked Dr. Peterson for distorting the facts. "I didn't say it in the same breath," he said. "I said it in a different context."

Sequeira mocked the doctor who admitted he had barely looked at the police report and the crime scene report and yet determined that Susan Polk was telling the truth.

"You're an expert in truth and honesty," Sequeira said.

"We all do our best," the doctor said.

Sequeira was pulling out all stops: "Are you aware of the fact that she believes she predicted 9/11, would that change your opinion?"

"My understanding is that she's got considerable psychic ability," he replied to the shocked gallery of onlookers.

Sequeira thought Dr. Cooper was another Eli—with a medical degree, a witness who was determined to help the defendant at all costs. Sequeira compared images of a blood-soaked Felix and of his hardly injured wife. The doctor insisted he was comparing "apples and oranges." How was it that Susan Polk did not sustain more bruising if she had been "drugged, knocked, pushed down and struggled?" Sequeira asked.

"That's improper English," Susan Polk interrupted. " 'Drugged' is not the past tense of 'drag.' "

"That's an improper objection," the judge volleyed.

Because Sequeira had shown slides, the lights remained off and only shards of sunlight poked through the blinds. Almost everything was stark: black and white.

Sequeira asked the pathologist how Ms. Polk could have reached around her husband and stabbed him in the back while he was over her. With Sequeira wielding the knife, the two men demonstrated, leading Sequeira to ask a question that would resonate: "You're on your back, doctor, and you're reaching around, how are you going to do that anatomically?"

It was an important visual and practical point, and one which would become a pivotal question during deliberations. Satisfied with having cast doubt on Dr. Cooper's testimony, Sequeira told the court he had no further questions. Had Susan Polk not been so confident, had she relied on a local attorney, she might have settled on a good and reliable local forensic pathologist rather than a flashy one who became an issue himself. While he was effective at proving that there existed another side to this case, her choice of experts would put a greater burden on her next witness.

25.

"I CALL MYSELF"

"MS. POLK, YOUR NEXT WITNESS?"

"I call myself," she said. And with that, on Tuesday, May 17, 2006, after ten weeks of trial, Susan Polk gathered up her notes and files and padded to the witness stand, turning as she went to see what she might have forgotten. She promised to tell the whole truth and nothing but the truth and then slowly seated herself. At last, this was her chance, and it had the potential to determine the outcome of the entire trial.

Susan, the judge, and a reluctant Paul Sequeira had agreed that rather than ask herself questions, she would be allowed to talk and testify. The courtroom was standing room only. Reporters took up the two front rows, anxious to observe her star witness, herself. Susan's mother sat in the back row balanced on a folded seat that elevated her tiny body. Her mother's old boss, Jim Johnson, a tap-dancing minister, was in the third row. The usual spectators were there, including Alison who came with her mother and her daughter, Paul, the Filipino orderly who liked Susan Polk, and three sisters who one day went out to see a movie but not finding anything they liked went to court.

Susan Polk spoke in her softest tones. The room was darkened as she showed her life in slides. There was a young Helen Bolling in wedding gown and corsage laughing next to the big, handsome husband who loved and left her. "My father is an attorney. I think he lives near Sacramento now," Susan Polk said. She did not explain that she and her father have been estranged for years. "My mother is kind of a self-made woman," Susan said with pride. She showed a baby picture of herself, explaining that her mother always put a bonnet on her to distinguish her from her brother, since baby Susan didn't have hair. There were pictures of Susan looking stiff but pretty, around the time she began seeing Felix, a beautiful profile of Susan in Hawaii, Felix hiking in Yosemite. "One of the things I really liked about him, he really liked the outdoors and introduced me to hiking. He loved Yosemite and so did I," she said. That was probably the sweetest thing jurors or anyone else would ever hear her say about the man she stood accused of murdering. There were loving shots of the two in England, with Susan's arm draped across his chest, glimpses of their wedding, and many beautiful shots of her boys. Periodically, she sniffled and wept, especially when she showed a picture of the three boys, with Gabriel, the infant, his head still floppy, seated between the much bigger Adam and Eli.

Susan had taken Horowitz's blueprint—to humanize her in his opening statement—and made it her own. As she flicked through the photos, she profiled her sons. Gabriel was the sweet child who "didn't do anything wrong. . . . He was the angel in the family." Adam was talkative. "He seemed extreme to me. He always seemed to have trouble with his big, younger brother but nobody felt that way about Gabriel." Adam was very sensitive and wrote sensitive poetry, she said. He was devoted and extremely loving. Eli was quiet and serious, and here she ran her ongoing PSA for her middle son: "It was just amazing, he was like a secret in the family," she said. When he was three, she said with pride, he rode his bike without training wheels. She was always promoting Eli as the smart one, as though a mother's word could make it so.

And she showed pictures of her beloved dogs. In an offhand remark she told jurors her husband had poisoned their old dogs. The jurors watched as she clicked to a photo of an affectionate Felix hovering over his smiling young wife with his arm reaching around her. The picture, she said, was taken when Felix threw a surprise fortieth birthday party for her, "a landmark birthday" she explained, when she began to question everything about their relationship. Sighing and periodically breaking out into sobs, she showed a picture of Adam lounging in his UCLA sweatshirt on a couch in Stinson Beach, where Susan had fled to escape Felix. Almost as if she forgave him, she told herself and the court that Adam was doing what he must to survive, but that "the real Adam is the Adam who sent me poems, called me to discuss papers he was writing for college . . . There was a side to Adam that called me names and mouthed off. . . . The other side was devoted and loving."

The last few images were of their vacation spots. Here was Susan, Gabriel, and Eli when they first went to Montana in 2001. "I thought we were never coming back," she said wistfully. Her last shot was of Gabriel in Yellowstone

National Park with what looked like snow on the mountains. She explained that it wasn't snow, but, ever the informed intellect, sulfuric deposits.

The lights flickered back on. Susan thought she would begin with a bang, reading into the record excerpts of what she believed was an exonerating letter she wrote on March 16, 2001, seven months before she killed Felix. This was the letter found in her bedroom safe. She told the jurors she advised Eli and Gabriel to read the letter if she died—Gabriel has no recollection of such a conversation.

"I did not want to just disappear," she said crying, "Sorry . . . and not have anybody know what happened." In fact the beginning of the letter, which she did not read to jurors, claimed its purpose was to expose her husband's "unethical conduct" with her as a young girl. She read this to the jurors: "When I have stated that I would be willing to leave without receiving a division of our property, he has threatened to kill me or, in his words, drive me crazy."

She skipped certain paragraphs because, she told jurors, "The way we see things changes over time. Some things maybe I have doubts about." She didn't read the jurors sections in which she complained about Eli and her mother.

She explained that she had always wanted to be a writer and had kept a diary to record what was happening and to amuse herself, à la *Bridget Jones's Diary,* though her excerpts were anything but lighthearted. She described various incidents that she said were examples of Felix's physically abusing her, but the incidents were minor and in the minds of the jurors didn't fall into the category of domestic abuse.

Her story was disjointed, but she seemed not to notice. She was inadvertently poignant when she said she had her first kiss in third grade in front of all the other kids. "It was very funny," she remarked. "The next time was Felix, pretty much."

Jurors were glimpsing a side of Susan they rarely had seen. Sequeira left her alone. The spotlight was hers and the jury was a captive audience. Some were even taking notes. It would be difficult for the DA to attack someone so calm.

Susan read long passages from her diary, including a lyrical account of a mythical place where she could be happy. As she read, she demonstrated her ability to write, a skill buried under the tumult of her existence:

I promise myself that I will not come back. I will make a home somewhere else, in a place where people wake up while we are still sleeping, where the sun feels differently on my face, the language sounds familiar, like I might understand if only I could go back to sleep, the food is spicy, foreign, and it is cheaper to live. I'd like to have privacy, no neighbors looking over my fence or through my windows. A sunny garden to grow vegetables in. A warm summer. A pool perhaps, or an ocean to swim in. A boat. A dog. Some old things, plates with a blue pattern, white lace, polished wood, clean sheets. These things should be possible.

She talked about an early appointment with Felix in which he gave her herbal tea and had her count backward from one hundred, a process designed to put her into a trance. Coming out of the trance felt to her like death. She had a "deep sense of fear and panic." What she didn't explain was that she only "remembered" this when she was forty years old. She'd been a "spunky kid," she said as she wept, "but Felix wanted someone he could control and dominate. He wanted a doll." His hypnotic sessions, she explained, were designed to override her ability to say no.

Here was her moment in the sun, and what the light revealed was a shattered mind. She looked like everyone else and seemed to have emotions like everyone else, at least for her own children and herself, especially herself, but her presentation was ultimately tragic.

She said that after Felix had induced her into a hypnotic state that, for the rest of her life, she fell in and out of trances. Because of her ability to predict events, her husband had hijacked her life. She lived in "two realities" and became her husband's medium, his "lifelong research project."

Jurors were paying attention, but when she said something emotional, they exhibited no emotion. The judge sat silently, staring, letting her go on about her life as a psychic.

In her little girl voice, she claimed that twenty-eight years ago she overheard her husband talking about the murder of San Francisco mayor George Moscone by former San Francisco supervisor Dan White—before the crime occurred. She said she warned her husband that a blind cleric would bomb the World Trade Center. She knew in advance about the plot to assassinate the pope. "My husband and his little friends wanted to let it happen," she asserted while she said she argued that the warning could be used "to sow goodwill between Israelis and the Vatican, and that is in fact what happened. There was that kind of *rapprochement*," she said.

"What's that?" Sequeira butt in, providing a much needed release. "Is that an objection?" he asked the judge. "It's not an objection," the amused judge assured him.

During a break, Susan's old friend from Felix's therapy group thirty-five years ago, Kathy Lucia, was asked about Susan's commentary. She said she hadn't known Susan had such psychic abilities, a reminder that if just one juror had been won over in the way that Susan's friend was, it could affect the outcome of the trial.

When Paul Sequeira returned to his office that day, he found a two-pound box of chocolates from Jennifer Polk, Felix's daughter from his first marriage, who lives on the East Coast and had never spoken to him. She wrote, "Keep up the good work."

IN SPITE OF THE SUCCESS THAT SHE SEEMED TO FEEL SHE WAS HAVING, Susan Polk resented the snickering she often heard from the gallery. On Thursday, May 18, her second day of testimony, she accused spectators of coming to court for the same reason that people attend "a lynching or a beheading."

Still on the witness stand, she critiqued her husband, accusing him of being a rapist, a racist, an aggressor, and controlling. She felt like "a caged bird." Living with him, she said, was "like living with a domineering, abusive parent." Sex with him, she told jurors, "was essentially rape. . . . He said that was what was attractive to men."

Whatever reputation he might have had as a loving father, attentive husband, and flawed human being was systematically dismantled and would not be resurrected.

"He was completely focused on himself, his work, and me," Susan Polk declared. She said she thought Felix's friends were "ghoulish" and "twisted." And she was convinced that they, like Felix, were members of Mossad.

The longer she spoke, the farther away from reality Susan flew. In an exchange with the judge after the jurors left the courtroom, she said she wanted to talk about her belief that her husband's friends "would come after me and the children." Then she made a most peculiar comment: "In a case of self-defense, everything I thought that was happening should be relevant." Everything she *thought* was happening. That was an odd way to put something she supposedly still believed. But she was astute enough to know that her state of mind was an important factor in the case.

The courtroom proved to be her perfect stage. The jurors were unable to respond—or exit. Some, especially those who called themselves control freaks, found it excruciatingly difficult to sit through hours both in the corridor while Susan argued with the DA and the judge and in the jury box as Susan rattled on about issues that had nothing to do with murder. Yet this was Susan at her best. Resembling a little girl who tells a story to her dolls at teatime, she read from her diary, looking into the eyes of the jurors searching for rapport. Some, she was certain, understood. But for many jurors, Susan's soliloquy was so tedious it was hard to stay awake. At lunch the nurse-juror lifted weights at a gym and at breaks she climbed up and down the courthouse stairwell, for exercise as well as peace of mind. As they sat on juror benches just outside the courtroom they befriended one another. From what their friends were telling them, Susan Polk was popping up all over the news. So the jurors quit watching and joked they had no idea what was going on in the world. But they were coming to know everything about Susan Polk.

Susan described how in recent years she suspected that when Felix offered her wine, it was laced with poison. She told them that Felix had been convinced she had MS, and how the doctor said to him, "I'm sorry, I can't give her a diagnosis of MS."

It was difficult to know what was truth, delusion, or manipulation. She belittled Felix's account of his childhood and said that when she asked his family about Katya, the nursemaid whom he said he loved and lost in Vienna, that his family said, "Who?"

A juror yawned; others stretched; they slouched; they leaned. Some started drinking Red Bull in the morning and the afternoon. Others were doodling. Courttv.com's Lisa Sweetingham observed that the jurors were listless. Paul Sequeira knew she must be boring the jurors. He considered objecting to her long commentaries on irrelevant subjects but he didn't. The more she talked, he figured, the more likely she was to slip up and help the prosecution.

As long as Susan could say something had "terrified" her, she could testify to whatever she wanted because it dealt with her state of mind. And many things terrified her. At the end of the afternoon break, the bailiff beckoned for Sequeira to return. "You can't make me!" he joked.

ON FRIDAY, MAY 1, 2006, SUSAN INTERRUPTED HER MONOLOGUE TO CON-
tinue questioning her son Adam who was in the Bay Area to attend Gabriel's
graduation from De La Salle High School, but that was something his mother
would not know anything about.

On the witness stand, Adam, in conservative suit and his trademark tight-
collared shirt and tie, sniffled and grabbed for tissues from a tissue box supplied by the court, an off-brand with the name of "Integrity." While Judge
Brady inquired about Adam's health (she was hoping he had an allergy and not
a contagious cold), his mother, who had fussed over Eli when he had a cold in
court, did not.

On the DA's slide projector, Susan Polk magnified a Mother's Day note
Adam had penned after his father's death in which he wrote, "Mom, I know
we've all had our share of troubled times, but I'll always love you. Thanks for
being there. I love you. Adam."

"Is that your writing?"

"Yes. That's my writing."

"Did you mean that?"

"Yes, I do love you and," he added because Adam is on a mission, "I will
always be there, but you need to get some help. I've stated that before."

She continued to wander through their family life, picking at unhealed
sores. In passing, Adam said his father had bought him a truck, a statement that
Susan couldn't leave alone. She asked Adam where she was when his father
bought him a truck. Not a smart move. "I'm not sure," Adam said. "Hawaii,
Montana, Paris, Tahoe. You were all over the world." When he later said she had
lived in "a lot of exotic places," Susan scolded him: "Adam, you understand
you're still under oath."

"I'm sorry," he said, "you're a world traveler."

"Excuse me? You are under oath . . . and this is a murder trial." Then she
turned to the judge. The dulcet tones had turned icy: "I'd like an admonish-
ment to the *witness* to stick to the truth exactly!"

Returning to her sugary voice, she showed Adam pencil sketches she had
made of him as he slept on a couch in her Stinson Beach hideaway in the spring
of 2001. The drawing failed to show his good looks, prompting him to remark,

"No, I don't think I look like that." As spectators chuckled, Susan quickly put up another drawing. "That looks like me," he agreed, but when he looked at the remaining illustrations, he failed to mention that they looked less like him and more like his father.

Focusing yet again on the minutia of daily life, Susan continued her defense of herself as a good mother. Did Adam recall that "every day" when he was little, he sang a Looney Tunes song so loudly that it caused his little brother Eli to spill his milk? Adam remembered it was a Daffy Duck ditty from *Quackbusters*. Was it true he sang it at the top of his lungs?

In mock serious tones, Adam, suddenly her little boy again, said, "To do justice to the *Quackbusters*, you have to." The courtroom erupted in laughter, but the laughs were truncated as Susan followed up by asking if she were crazy.

"I don't know if you're crazy or if you just contrive these fantasies to somehow rationalize and justify what you're doing and what you've done in your mind," he said.

Was he an expert, she inquired. "I spent twenty years in this situation," he answered sternly. "And you're a sick, sick person in dire need of a very controlled environment for a very long time. If that doesn't happen, then I wouldn't feel safe and a lot of other people won't feel safe."

Maybe it would have been better had Susan not recalled Adam, but she couldn't help herself. She had qualms about fully attacking Gabe, but she had no such reservations about going after Adam. She asked if it weren't true that if she died or was convicted that Adam (and Gabe) would benefit financially. Adam seized the opportunity to say that when he graduates he will be making eighty thousand dollars. "Your money means nothing to me. Seeing you put away does."

His comment hung in the air, unchallenged. He stared at her and she at him before she turned and began riffling through her papers. It took awhile before she was ready to ask another question. The ponytailed juror would see this as an epic battle between mother and son, one in which he found himself siding with the son. Susan tried to paint Felix as a controlling monster; Adam would not allow it. But other jurors simply didn't like Adam's testimony. To know Adam was to understand why he said what he did. He felt it was his responsibility to expose his mother and he didn't want to concede a single point. Jurors were right to suspect he had an agenda; he did. Another juror felt Adam had "turned his back on his mother one hundred percent" and that he would say whatever he could to get back at her.

Susan read from an e-mail Adam had written to Eli, in which he stated that his mother had killed Felix in self-defense. Susan asked why he had written that. She didn't seem to understand that every question presented Adam with an opening.

"I was willing to denigrate myself and be false with Eli to keep the channel of communications open with you." And that wasn't easy because Eli was her "stern and sometimes violent guardian."

Eli wasn't violent, she said, sauntering into an obvious trap. Adam had a scary response: "He told me he would kill himself and maybe others if you were convicted." She moved swiftly to cover other territory, momentarily returning to better days. She had Adam read from a poem he sent: "My mother sends me soaring with a gentle nudge." She quoted from a letter he wrote while she was in jail in which he said: "I wished things were the way things were." For once, Adam Polk did not disagree.

The momentary warmth, if that's what it was, would not last. Adam felt a responsibility not just to his late father and his baby brother but to society to prevent his mother from harming anyone else. He said he felt obliged to carry on a relationship with her, adding that Gabe had "asked me not to maintain a relationship with you. That would have been easier."

Susan paused and breathed deeply. "I'm alive, aren't I?"

His response was heart wrenching: "Not to him."

BY MONDAY MORNING, MAY 23, 2006, SIX DAYS AFTER SHE BEGAN TESTIFY-ing, Susan Polk, back on the witness stand, proved that she could justify just about anything. Why was it two of her sons testified against her? Adam "wanted to be a winner, and man, he would do whatever it took," she told jurors. "My husband said, 'You're gonna go down with her.' I think Adam thought 'I better not line up with Mom.' " On the other hand, Gabriel "the gentlest child of all," could be overly influenced by whomever he was around. And Gabe had been so angry with his father that "he started talking at one point about killing his father. . . . I think he thought it was a joke."

Susan said that Felix labeled her as delusional because she accused him of having an affair with Sheila Byrns. Susan not only saw them kiss and embrace, she said, but Ms. Byrns gave Felix a cashmere sweater from Neiman Marcus—Susan checked the price, expensive European ties "that could easily cost a thousand dollars," and "two sets of solid-gold cufflinks." (According to Ms. Byrns, the cufflinks weren't solid gold and the ties didn't cost a thousand dollars.) She said that Ms. Byrns and Felix celebrated the anniversary of their first meeting. Susan added, "What was delusional was what I didn't see in front of my face."

When recounting the increasingly volatile relationship she had with her husband, Susan Polk offered a curious comment. "Crazy or not, no one deserves it. . . . You don't go punching someone who is mentally ill. You don't threaten to kill someone who is mentally ill. It is not an approved technique or intervention, and I'm not 'mentally ill.' " For someone who contended she was not sick, that seemed pretty close to an admission.

When Susan Polk spoke about Eli's incarceration in 2002, she put the blame not on herself for encouraging her son to cut off his ankle bracelet, but on her husband, whom she was convinced manipulated the courts. She told jurors "I didn't decide I would kill him for it, but it was totally devastating."

She had an answer for everything, such as Gabe's story that she intended to sit her husband down and shoot him if he didn't fork over his millions from the Cayman Islands. She insisted that was just a joke. "I never ever threatened to kill my husband, ever. . . . On the other hand, he did threaten to kill me many times in front of Gabriel and Eli and less often in front of Adam."

While Susan saw her appearance on the stand as the fulcrum of her defense, the jurors were restless and irritated with her endless monologue. Ponytail thought about standing up and yelling, "SHUT UP!" but he knew that would result in a mistrial and he never wanted anyone else to endure this.

SIXTEEN HOURS INTO HER SEVENTEEN HOURS OF TESTIMONY, SUSAN POLK finally broached the subject of her husband's death. Was she averse to talking about the death scene, or was it just that she wanted to tell everything else about her life before getting to that? She'd gone over it in her mind many times in her jail cell, she'd written it out, she'd told print reporters and explained it on national TV, and when she had lawyers, she'd recounted it for them. Yet she would devote little time to it while testifying on her own behalf.

She described how on Sunday night, October 13, 2002, she visited the pool house to talk to Felix about finances. They talked about their debt, about Gabriel, and about Eli's incarceration. She says Felix told her that he could get Eli out of Byron Boys Ranch "in two months." Then they argued about 9/11. She said her husband said, "He couldn't let me leave knowing what I know. . . . 'What is it that I know?' " she said she asked. "Was it her predictions for 9/11 or was it that he had had sex with her when she was fourteen? Or was it the whole spy thing?"

"Sometimes I can be pretty sarcastic," Susan explained. "I was very strong that night. That revved him up," she said. "At some point he hit me in the face . . . I stood up, staggered back, and pulled out pepper spray," which she had left over from Montana in case she stumbled upon a bear. She gripped the spray in her right hand and a Maglite in her left. To demonstrate, she put a yellow highlighter in one palm and a blue in the other. She said she warned: " 'I have pepper spray!' He picked up the ottoman and rushed at me." She sprayed him, but "he just kept coming. He was absolutely enraged! He grabbed me by the hair and pulled me onto the floor. He got on top of me. My knees were up. He rubbed pepper spray off his hands into my face. It was oily and orangish."

"I could barely see," she said. "He punched me in the face again. I was stunned by that. I opened my eyes and I saw a knife coming down. It went into my pant legs . . . I saw the knife and thought it went into my leg."

Susan Polk held her Ralph Lauren size eight jeans aloft. She paused, squinted and put her glasses on. Then she felt with her fingers, until she found a tiny hole. "It's hard to see the cut because I sewed it up," she apologized. Her gesture did not help her with jurors.

"I thought, Oh my God, I think he's got a knife . . . It was just a flash." She said she thought, "Unless you do something right now, you're going to die." She kicked him forcefully in the groin as she reached for the knife. "The knife did loosen." She seized it. Felix punched her in the face, again. She stabbed him in the side. "He bit my hand as hard as he could. I reached around him. Before I knew what I was doing, I stabbed him in the back." She said she called to him, "You can't do this! Stop! Get off of me! Get off of me! Get off of me!"

When Felix failed to get off her she said she threatened him again with the knife. She estimated that she stabbed him about five times. And she waved the knife back and forth across his chest, as she said that her hands were clasped and her arms swayed. Felix stopped biting and stood up. She stood up. He said, "It's me. It's Felix." Moments later, Felix grabbed his stomach and muttered,

"Oh my God, I think I'm dead." And then, she said looking at the jurors, he rocked back and forth and fell straight back onto the tiled floor.

"I could see he was dead."

It was a convincing reenactment for those who wanted to be convinced. For others who'd already made up their minds, there was little she could say now to change that. At lunch and after court, spectators mulled over her account. Most were dubious, but not all. Paul, the ER orderly, thought Susan was the way she was because Felix had been emotionally abusive. Whatever transpired, he felt, was the result of Felix's initial behavior and his lifelong control over her.

Only the jurors were forbidden to discuss the testimony, but they found other common interests. Deputies thought they were the most affable group of jurors they'd encountered. But the soft-spoken juror who smoked and wore a large cross around his neck, continued to hang back from the group. He, like Paul, seemed to have his own thoughts. And Paul believed Susan's story.

ON TUESDAY, MAY 23, 2006, SUSAN WAS TALKING ABOUT KNIVES WITH THE expertise of Rachael Ray. While the bailiff grasped a Wusthof high-carbon-steel-forged, four-and-a-half-inch paring knife made in Solingen, Germany, Susan told jurors she purchased it in 2001. "It was everyone's favorite *because it was very sharp.*" She claimed that was the knife Felix had threatened her with and that she had used to kill her husband.

"Afterward, I automatically picked it up, brought it into the kitchen, washed it, dried it, and put it away," she said, in her most straightforward tone. As she spoke, Sequeira sat at the prosecution table with his arms folded. Her testimony was drawing to a close and everyone in the courtroom knew that he was preparing his cross-examination. For several days now, the DA had remained virtually silent, thinking she couldn't go on that long and then when she did, letting her run on, because he didn't want to be seen as beating up on a pro per defendant. His cross would give him the opportunity to rip into the many facets of her story.

But just as he was readying himself, Susan did the unexpected: She requested an attorney. It was only for her cross-examination, she stipulated, and it would be handled by attorney Gary Wesley, who was sitting in the courtroom smiling because he had not yet had the full Susan Polk experience. As a civil attorney and not a criminal one, Mr. Wesley, a friend of Ms. Harris's, had never handled a homicide, but he offered to read up on the Polk matter.

"You'd need months," the judge said dismissively.

Sequeira worried that the arrival of Wesley could build a case for ineffective assistance of counsel, an issue for an appeal. The prosecutor assured the new attorney that Ms. Polk "is more than a worthy advocate. Trust me, Mr. Wesley." For his part, Mr. Wesley said, "I'm just here to help," but he was one in a long line of people drawn to help Susan, who saw in her the chance for good *and* while at it, for good publicity. The judge would have to decide whether or not to allow such assistance. She took the matter under advisement and told Susan to continue with her testimony.

Susan Polk had not expected the judge to allow her to read from her diary, which she believed was crucial to her case, but in fact Judge Brady was lenient. In addition to showing "state of mind," the judge pointedly remarked that the reading of the diary informed the jury about Susan Polk's "processing of infor-mation." It was like an historical document, a chronicle of her thinking. Read-ing to jurors, Susan said her husband "referred to me as his slave, his genie in a bottle. His ideal was to have complete control over someone."

As she read, she intended to read the word *Felix* but again, said "father" by mistake. Sequeira caught it and corrected her. She seemed embarrassed but proceeded: "He told me how to think and what to believe in. I think for him, I didn't turn out the way he wanted me to." As she read, she wept and looked up at the jurors with an apology: "I don't know why this bothers me so much," she said. Then the empathetic moment passed and she let loose, accus-ing Felix of being "crazy, immoral, sadistic . . . cruel, twisted, profligate, and a disturbed man."

Susan had been wearing the utilitarian white T-shirt and jail-issued over-size green pants for days. On Wednesday, May 24, 2006, the top of her hair was pulled back with a barrette, exposing her forehead. She had the stark, lonely look of a woman in an Andrew Wyeth painting, haunting and unconnected.

As Susan spoke to the court, Valerie Harris lingered in the corridor awaiting word on Eli's trial twelve miles away in Walnut Creek. The charge of misde-meanor battery stemmed from his alleged abuse of his former girlfriend Jessica Provine. Later in the afternoon Ms. Harris heard from a spectator that Eli had been found guilty of one count of misdemeanor violation and two counts of violating a temporary restraining order. He was sentenced to nine months in county jail. He might have gone to state prison for sixteen months had Sequeira, the third highest person in the DA's office, not recommended he be sent to county jail instead.

While Eli's case was being adjudicated, Susan Polk continued to read from her diaries in her soft, easy voice, her words producing an almost soporific state in the courtroom. Listen long enough and one could begin to think like the defendant.

No one could sit through her readings and not feel sorry for such a troubled woman. Even Paul Sequeira could understand, privately wondering if Felix Polk made his wife crazier than she might otherwise have been. Whatever sympathy he may have developed for Susan was outweighed by his fury at what she had done and how she behaved in court.

At the day's end Ms. Harris told Susan about Eli's fate. Susan listened without emotion, never realizing that the man who had been her enemy for months had saved her son from a trip to state prison. But she was about to find out that he would show no such kindness toward her.

26.

CAUGHT IN HIS WEB

ON THURSDAY, MAY 25, 2006, SUSAN POLK SPENT HER FINAL HOURS OF direct testimony calling into question her husband's professional reputation. She said he practiced hypnosis at work and at home, that he led workshops on satanic abuse, and that, most improbably, he conducted exorcisms, all of which sounded absurd. Putting pages from his date books on the projector, she said it was up to the jury to decipher whether he was writing "EXERCISE" or "EXOR-CISE." She said her husband exercised regularly but did not mark that in his appointment book. (In fact, Sheila Byrns, the woman Susan accused of having an affair with Felix, confirmed to a reporter that Felix Polk did indeed conduct exorcisms for clients, but Susan never called her to testify.)

By the end of her self-examination, Susan Polk had been on the witness stand for five often painfully tedious days but spent only forty-five minutes talking about the murder. Paul Sequeira would take care of that, and every seat in the courtroom was taken in anticipation. Stunning female attorneys from the DA's office took up half a row, while a dozen reporters were scattered around the room.

"I said I wasn't scared," Susan Polk said on the witness stand as she faced cross-examination, "but I'm getting a little scared now."

"Rightfully so," Paul Sequeira bellowed.

The shades in the courtroom were drawn. A lemony shard of light illumi-nated the defendant on the stand. Not by chance, she looked like a suspect under interrogation in some B-grade movie. People's exhibit 15 popped on the screen against the wall: a darkened pool house living room with Dr. Polk's bloodied torso and legs splayed out on the terra-cotta floor.

"Isn't it a fact you let your fifteen-year-old son find your husband's body in the pool house?" Sequeira intoned. He'd thought a lot about it and knew this would grate on the jurors. He stared at her hard as if they were the only two people in the room. If she were ever going to be flustered it might be now, but Susan Polk was to be a more worthy opponent than anticipated.

"Isn't it a fact that [Gabriel] was going looking for his father and he found his father dead in the pool house, Mrs. Polk?" By calling her "Mrs.," Sequeira was not so subtly reminding jurors that she was married to the man she killed. Pushing harder, Sequeira asked if she recalled telling Gabriel that he should call the California Highway Patrol.

"I don't recall saying that."

"That would be cruel, wouldn't it?"

He recalled it for her, reading from the transcript of her interrogation the night Felix's body was found.

After he referred to the crime scene as the pool house, Susan Polk corrected him. She labeled it "the cottage." If anyone thought Mr. Sequeira would follow suit, they must not have met him. "There are keys to *the pool house,* aren't there, Mrs. Polk?" he inquired.

Susan Polk objected to the "gruesome and grisly" slides Sequeira had on the screen, but he insisted he hadn't finished.

Determined to break his momentum, she objected to some of his questions as "unintelligible." She asked that he speak slower and that he repeat his questions. He was racing at ninety miles an hour while she plunked down roadblocks. Sequeira was usually masterful, but Susan knew how to interfere and make it harder for him. This time, however, he wouldn't be stopped.

In a Solomon-esque decision, the judge had determined that Ms. Polk, while retaining her pro per status, could consult Mr. Wesley, but he could not signal her. He could only comment if and when she *sought* his advice; otherwise Mr. Wesley was to sit behind her at the witness stand and remain mum.

When Sequeira asked her about her comment to Gabriel, "Aren't you glad he's gone?" Susan Polk said he got it wrong. "I believe what I said was, 'He's gone. You aren't happy, you don't look happy.' "

Sequeira asked if Gabriel was correct in stating that before he found his father's body his mother cryptically said, "I guess I didn't use a shotgun, did I?"

"I think Gabriel was less than truthful," she said. And with that Sequeira marched over to the easel that Susan Polk often used for illustrations and with a squeaky blue marker he employed a technique he had used in other trials. He scrawled:

LIARS

   1. Gabriel

"If you never threatened to kill your husband," Sequeira inquired, "weren't you taken aback by having your son accusing you?"

"I'm sorry that question went on too long can you break it down?"

"Didn't it shock you that the first person your son accused of murder on the planet Earth was you?"

Gabriel suspected her, she said, because he had been brainwashed by his father. In response, Sequeira quoted Sergeant Hansen, who on the night Felix's body was discovered notified Susan Polk her husband was dead. "Oh well," Sergeant Hansen said she told him, "we were getting a divorce anyway."

When she denied saying that, Sergeant Hansen became number 2 on the LIARS list.

While he was up there, Susan Polk offered another candidate: her husband. Make him "number 1," she advised. Sequeira obliged but instead of writing "Felix Polk" he wrote "1. Victim." Susan balked.

Sequeira in his most casual manner asked if it weren't true that given their lifestyle of eight-hundred-dollar Japanese maples and ten-thousand-dollar Oriental rugs, that Felix Polk was a pretty hardworking guy. "Ten thousand dollars is a lot of money to walk on," Sequeira mused, mindful of the mostly middle-class jurors.

Susan Polk counseled Mr. Sequeira that her carpets were investments, and "contributed to the wealth we acquired." Then as though she were leading an investment seminar in some hotel ballroom she added, "I recommend them highly as a good investment."

Sequeira, who would never miss an opportunity to play the good ol' boy to her rich lady, said simply, "That's out of my league." But what he was really thinking was that his relatives with mud caked on their boots were richer than Susan Polk would ever be.

Moments later the civility cracked. "You have testified what a monster [your husband] was many times . . . He threatened your life. You went down there by yourself, late at night and without a witness to talk about a potentially volatile situation, that's what you're telling this jury?"

"Yes."

"You must have been scared, going in the dark, all alone to this monster."

"I object," she said, she had never called him "a monster."

"In your diary," he said.

"That's different. The tone is sardonic and sarcastic. I had moments of being terrified and absolutely panicked, but I believed reason would prevail," she said.

He let her go on for a while and then sarcastically characterized her demeanor that night: "You were being really flexible about things." As he said it, he looked over at the jurors and some, such as Ponytail, couldn't help but smile back in amusement. They were in this together.

"I tend to be flexible about some things," she responded.

"You offered to give up everything, so really there was nothing for him to get upset about." It was hard to play chess against a guy who'd been at the game for twenty-two years.

She said that after she broached the subject of 9/11 and her belief that Felix was a traitor, the conversation become more heated.

"Even though you were being reasonable?"

"Yes."

Sequeira asked the defendant to describe Felix's first punch: was it an overhand punch or a punch like a boxer? With an athlete's assuredness, he threw one punch into the air then another. He asked her to demonstrate, but she demurred.

Sequeira suggested that when Felix turned his back to lift the ottoman that she could have escaped. "You had time to go right out that door, isn't that correct?"

"I can't answer that."

Nor was she certain whether she sprayed her husband with pepper spray before he picked up the ottoman or after.

"You're asking me about something that happened three years ago and was extremely traumatic. . . . I have a hard time remembering every detail in sequence," Susan said.

Although she bought the pepper spray to ward off grizzly bears, she couldn't slow "an asthmatic seventy-year-old man . . . with an ottoman?"

"If it didn't stop a violent, abusive wife beater," she countered, "it won't stop a grizzly bear."

Only once during the cross-examination had Susan turned to her attorney for assistance. During a break Sequeira asked reporters, "What's the wooden Indian head doing sitting behind the defendant?"

Sequeira worried that because of her frequent parsing of questions, his cross-examination could become as tedious as her direct. He heard sighs from the jurors during her narration and he didn't want to contribute to their sense of ennui. Although Sequeira was scoring points, Susan Polk was fighting back.

With a long weekend looming, Sequeira planned to prepare for his continued assault on Susan Polk, play ball with his boys, and tell his wife to forget about the $139 rug from Pier 1 Imports. He joked that he had investment advice for his wife: "We need a ten-thousand-dollar rug!"

"MRS. POLK, DON'T YOU AGREE WITH ME YOU WERE MOST VULNERABLE—" before completing his thought Susan Polk interjected:

"Mr. Sequeira, I don't think I could ever agree with you on anything at all!"

"I agree with you, Mrs. Polk." It was just part of the morning jousting, but both sides meant it.

When the trial resumed after the much needed break, Sequeira slowly began to pick apart her story. He belittled her claim that she had only tapped her husband's right temple with the Maglite. "The Maglite was heavy. He was my husband. My husband and I were married for a very long time," she said defensively.

Although he was wearing only black briefs, she could not say how her husband produced the knife or when or where he found it. Was she trying to say "he kept the knife in his underwear?" Sequeira asked in a derisive voice. Had Felix Polk run into the kitchen and grabbed it? And wasn't that *her* favorite knife? "It was a good investment if you like to cook. I do," she said. It was a key point that jurors would ponder: who brought the knife to the cottage?

The DA questioned Susan about the first interview she gave—to the *Contra Costa Times*'s Bruce Gerstman, seated in the front row covering the trial. Hadn't she told Mr. Gerstman that her husband retrieved the knife from the kitchen in the cottage? She said reporters do their best, but sometimes they get it wrong. (Gerstman stands by his story.)

"I'm not asking you if you're being deceptive with the media," Sequeira said, "I'm asking if you're being deceptive with this jury."

Sequeira asked how was it possible that while standing over her that Felix could have completely missed her torso and slashed only her jeans.

"Maybe you wouldn't miss, but I survived and that's what I'm guilty of," Susan Polk responded.

He asked her how it was she could swipe the knife out of her husband's hand without cutting herself despite the fact that there is more blade than handle.

"A very astute observation, Mr. Sequeira."

"Sometimes I'm not as stupid as I look for a PE major."

"You didn't really major in PE did you?" she asked.

"No," he said.

"I thought it was drama!" she said triumphantly.

He made stabbing motions with the knife.

"I object to his standing there welding [sic] a knife!" Susan Polk insisted.

"Wielding," he said, scoring a rare point in their long-running grammatical duel.

How could it be that the knife pierced her jeans but nothing penetrated her skin? How was it that her husband was riddled with stabs and cuts and she had none? How did she hold the knife when stabbing her husband in the chest and then around his back? How could she have seen her husband fall backward and die when she testified that pepper spray made it all but impossible to see?

Sequeira bombarded her with tough questions and continued the gruesome slideshow with one of Felix's mutilated hands. Bloody tissue hung from an open sore on his index finger. Susan Polk said she suspected the photo had been doctored. "It does not look natural," she said.

"Dead people don't often look natural," he barked back.

Sequeira asked the defendant "to demonstrate for the jury" how she was under her husband but managed to stab him in his back.

"I'm not a puppet up here." She shrugged.

The issue having been raised, the judge said, she was obliged to respond.

"Mrs. Polk, please demonstrate for us how to deliver that stab wound to your husband's back!"

She made a quick gesture with a curved arm.

"Show me that again Mrs. Polk."

"No."

"He said he hadn't seen it well enough," the judge said.

"He's lying. He's looking right at me."

"This is not a debate," the judge warned.

"All I know was I stabbed him in the back. I was appalled," Susan Polk said.

"Mrs. Polk doesn't want to show us," Sequeira complained.

DURING THE LUNCH BREAK, SIDEWALK PUNDITS AGREED THAT SUSAN POLK was a fly caught in Mr. Sequeira's web. In the afternoon, Sequeira continued his assault: Dr. Cooper said the victim died of heart disease. Yet Susan Polk testified that when her husband said, "I'm dead," he "clutched his *stomach.*"

Susan spoke about Dr. Cooper in reverential terms. "So far as I'm concerned, he's a hero!" she said.

Sequeira jumped in. She had once called her previous attorney, Dan Horowitz, a hero too. "As long as everyone does what you want them to do, you say they're a hero."

She said she had been mistaken when she called her previous attorney a hero. Horowitz had implicated himself—to her—in his wife's murder, she claimed. She then ventured into sticky territory, Horowitz's relationship "with a potential juror on the case with whom he had an affair." Susan Polk wasn't finished filleting Horowitz. "He didn't skip a beat," she said, "I think people should mourn."

"Like you mourn for your husband?" Sequeira quipped.

Sequeira asked if after placing the knife back in the cutlery drawer it was used again: "Did you use the knife to cut vegetables up? You use the knife for steak?"

"I don't recall."

"You said it was the kids' favorite knife."

"Is it possible that Gabe used the knife that killed his father to eat his dinner, Mrs. Polk?"

Just because he could, Sequeira asked Susan about her attitude toward Jews. "Isn't it true you have a problem with Jews?" He asked how it was she could determine if someone is Jewish. Do Jews have a certain look, or act Jewish, or wear certain clothes? he asked. "Tell the jury how you know. Do you ask them or do you just guess?" Judge Brady was giving Sequeira a look that said, "Why are you going there?"

Susan said she didn't hate Jews, she only hates Israeli policy. Judge Brady is Jewish, she offered. The judge looked uncomfortable, but there was no stopping Susan. She was going to say whatever she wanted to say.

Attorney Wesley did not know he'd been dismissed until reporters informed him at the end of the day. He later explained that Susan got rid of him because he tried to offer advice that she didn't want.

That evening, a small gathering of spectators, some opposed to Susan Polk, some in favor, attended a wine and cheese party hosted by Valerie Harris at Susan Polk's large and vacant Orinda home. A crew from the *Today Show* was shooting a piece on the "gavel groupies" when Ms. Harris, who is to publicity what a gold miner is to gold, offered the Polk house. She would later rationalize that if people saw how Susan lived, they might be more sympathetic. The spectator known as Tennis Jim was so enthused he called his tennis partner and had her dash over to enjoy the festivities. Partiers climbed upstairs to check out Susan and Felix's bedroom. They opened the cutlery drawer in her kitchen and they tried to peer into the cottage, which was occupied by a tenant—to see where Felix died. Susan Polk did not know about the party, nor did other members of her family. When Adam and Gabe learned about it, they were appalled; Gabriel labeled Valerie Harris "a bottom-feeder." What little privacy was left in their family they felt had been violated.

The next day, Paul Sequeira paced before the witness stand. He hadn't finished scalding the defendant. Wasn't it true that "even though you were in shock, and don't mind if I use *your* words, 'Oh my Gawd!' you made a conscious decision to walk over and pick the knife off his body, pick up the pepper spray and the Maglite and leave, is that correct?" and hadn't she destroyed evidence by washing her shirt, sewing her jeans, cleaning the Maglite, and her shoes?

Susan Polk didn't deny it. She said she was afraid she would be framed and argued that detectives probably picked up one of her Cole Haan slip-ons, "dipped it in blood, and put (shoeprints) all over the place."

After another wordplay between the adversaries the judge advised, "We're getting off track." Susan Polk shot back, "I don't want to be railroaded."

"We are not going to have pithy comments today," the judge warned.

" 'Pithy' is a good word," Susan Polk mused.

Sequeira returned to his theme: the issue of control, claiming Mrs. Polk had defied authority her whole life. She said she didn't—except when it was appropriate. "If I'd been in the Holocaust, I would have defied authority," she asserted.

"What side of the Holocaust would you have been on, Mrs. Polk?" he asked. Sometimes Sequeira just couldn't help but respond with a smart-ass remark.

Systematically he outlined her inability to deal with authority. Hadn't she convinced her son to snip off his ankle monitor? Didn't she yell at the police when they came to settle a dispute with a neighbor? Wasn't it true she cursed the school principal? Hadn't she labeled her husband a traitor yet written in her diary "Fuck America" and complained about arrogant, flabby, pallid-faced Americans who made her want to "just vomit"?

Sequeira was driving home his point: if Susan always rebelled against authority, then she must have been that way with Felix and not the docile slave she made herself out to be. He read from a letter she sent Adam in which she wrote, "Fuck service, self-sacrifice, and all that blather. I agree with Aristotle, enjoy life."

"I can't say I'm ashamed to agree with Aristotle," Susan responded, before launching into a monologue that Sequeira had no intention of interrupting as her mind ranged from the Nazis to the Pygmies in Africa.

When she finally stopped, Sequeira said in a slow voice, "Are you done?"

"I could say more, but I don't want to take up the jury's time."

Sequeira said, "I'm done, Judge."

.

ON JUNE 2, 2006, ELI POLK TURNED TWENTY-ONE. HIS FATHER WAS DEAD; HIS mother could not legally communicate with him; his two brothers wouldn't speak to him, and his girlfriend helped put him behind bars. Valerie Harris asked spectators and reporters to send him birthday greetings. Sequeira kept thinking of the old Merle Haggard song, *"And I turned twenty-one in prison doing life without parole. No one could steer me right but Mama tried, Mama tried . . ."*

After Susan limped to the end of her redirect—of herself—Sequeira challenged her claim that Felix had never had a nursemaid named Katya who was like a mother to him. He read from Felix's mother's account of his childhood in which she describes "Kathy," a young employee who refused to marry the post-man because it would have meant separating from Felix.

By talking to the media, Susan Polk had provided more fodder for the prosecution. "Mrs. Polk, you testified that you were shocked and appalled the night your husband was killed." He asked about her interview on Court TV in which she joked that Winona Ryder or Susan Sarandon could play her in the movie. Unable to stop herself, she blurted out what she'd told a reporter, that Anthony Hopkins who played Hannibal Lechter could play her husband, although Lechter was "a lot nicer." She released a hearty laugh.

"Funny? This is funny?" Sequeira asked sounding incredulous. "Nothing further."

With remarkable speed Susan slid from laughter to tears. "My mom always told me when you grow up you have to have a sense of humor. I couldn't smile enough and couldn't take a joke . . . It took me years to be able to laugh at a situation." By now, Susan Polk was in the full throes of a good sob. "I could look at life as one big tragedy. Or I could look at it as a triumph . . . I don't consider myself a victim. I don't consider my husband as a victim either. . . .

"My husband tried to kill me. My husband raped me when I was fourteen. He killed my dogs. He threatened my children. The night he died he attacked me. If I can find peace of mind, is that a crime?"

And with that she concluded her nine days of testimony and was ready to begin what could be tagged as her variety show of witnesses. To talk about self-defense, Susan Polk called Laura Castro Shelley, a fifth-degree black belt, a realtor, and a onetime Miss San Bruno and Miss Fremont to the witness stand. Despite the thermometer hovering in the high seventies, Ms. Shelley wore black tight pants and turtleneck. Her jet-black hair was pulled in a ponytail in the shape of a steak knife.

When she moved to the front of the courtroom, Susan Polk let all the anger of the day slip away. She was gracious, more hostlike than hostile. Ms. Shelley saw in Susan a woman like herself, a victim of abuse. Susan asked if it were possible for a 110-pound woman to overcome a 175-pound man with a knife.

"You become *a lioness in the wilderness* knowing this could be the last day you take a breath!" Ms. Shelley proclaimed.

Susan asked Ms. Shelley to show jurors where one would plunge a knife if one were determined to kill. With startling vigor, Ms. Shelley strode to the easel, grabbed the marker and drew, fast, thick slashes across the neck and heart of stick figures. Jurors and the audience laughed nervously.

Paul Sequeira carefully rose to cross-examine the witness. He asked if it were not true that one punch to a person's nose could be debilitating. "No." What about two punches? Three? Ms. Shelley would not concede.

"Isn't it true that the more times one punches a face, the more debilitating it is?"

"No!" Ms. Shelley objected.

"When a man punches a woman in the face and knocks her for a loop, wouldn't that make it harder for her to fight back?" he asked somewhat incredulously. "Not if your life is at stake," she responded. "What about if pepper spray half blinds you?"

Sequeira cut short his questioning and thanked her. It didn't matter anyway. In her attempt to side with Susan, she transformed herself from an expert into an advocate. Some of the jurors would later say they thought her refusal to concede made her sound "silly."

Outside the courthouse, as he held his cardboard box of files, Sequeira fielded questions. Across the street, a cameraman recorded Ms. Shelley as she strode down the sidewalk, providing B-roll for a TV interview. Two days later, she appeared on Court TV.

Some of Susan Polk's witnesses were part vaudeville; others were serious and made headway with the jury. Lieutenant Roger Alma Clark, a retired twenty-seven-year veteran of the Los Angeles Sheriff's Department, was testifying for Susan Polk at no cost, because he believed in her, although he didn't believe her whole story. If Ms. Shelley had not helped Susan's defense, Lieutenant Clark would.

Clark resembled Gorbachev, minus the birthmark. He had testified in over two hundred cases—always for the defense. Susan showed him huge blowups of her face taken shortly after the incident. "It indicates in my opinion to be a person being battered . . . and is consistent with being punched in the face," Lieutenant Clark said. "Who comes out the worse does not always indicate who started it," he added, a simple truth that no doubt could help his client.

Susan was pleased with her witness. As he testified, he turned his body toward the jurors, and when Susan said something slightly off, he studied their faces. Jurors were attentive; here was a serious and persuasive witness. Based on his reading of the crime scene photos, there was not enough blood for Felix to have died from stab wounds. A human body contains twelve pints of blood, he explained. If someone loses four pints, he dies. "I can't see anything beyond a pint and a half at that scene," he said. A person who really wanted to kill Felix Polk, he claimed, would have stabbed him around the chest and not plunged randomly. Even though these were similar points to those made by Dr. Cooper, the seasoned cop's demeanor and his avuncular manner made him a more credible witness.

During a break in the proceedings he asked a reporter, "How am I doing?" then added, "She's a tragic figure." Although Lieutenant Clark was compassionate, he was not naive. He knew that Susan was prone to fabrication and he warned her not to ask him about tampering with the scene because she would regret it. But it was not her nature to take other people's advice.

Lieutenant Clark told the jurors that there were only four stab wounds "of any substance." The other serious wound was the hit to the head. "I see no evidence of bruising where we would expect to see it if the heart was pumping," he said. That told the lieutenant that the hit to the head must have occurred "just before he died. This is a result of a fall rather than a blow from an object," he said, endorsing Susan Polk's account of what transpired.

He pointed out that if Susan had been intent on murder, she chose "a pretty small knife." He also found it troubling that on the death certificate nothing was said about Felix Polk's heart condition.

As he swung his glasses around his finger, Sequeira asked if Clark had brought his files. Clark had. "That's what honest experts do," Sequeira suggested. "It wouldn't be fair to keep the file at home and try to keep it secret from the other side, would it?" An outraged Susan Polk objected, correctly accusing the DA of trying to impeach the testimony of another witness—the controversial Dr. Cooper, through Lieutenant Clark.

Clark agreed that the open wounds on Felix Polk's fingers indicated he tried to grab the knife away from his wife. And he confirmed that although Susan claimed the struggle occurred in one spot, there were passive blood droppings in other areas, proving that the two had struggled around the room.

Sequeira considered attacking Lieutenant Clark. He could get almost any witness to bare his teeth and had always prided himself on his ability to be extraordinarily irritating when it was necessary. Sequeira knew that Clark hadn't investigated homicides since he was a young detective, although he commanded an investigative task force. On his résumé, Clark had listed that he organized the office picnic. Sequeira could have a field day with that. But the witness was saying things Sequeira liked.

Instead, he let Susan do the work herself and sabotage one of her best witnesses. During her redirect she asked if Clark agreed that someone tampered with the crime scene. "That is a felony," he said sternly. "It would require the cooperation of a number of officers and I don't see it," he said. When she persisted, he said, *"Susan,"* as though he were scolding one of his nine daughters (he also has one son). "Can the scene be tampered with? Of course it can. If someone wanted to do something like that it would be reprehensible." As soon as he said that Sequeira thought, *"He's my witness."*

Susan's next witness would not be so easily turned to his advantage. Instead, she would present a very serious problem for the prosecution.

27.

THE EXPERT, THE PSYCHIC,
AND THE DEFENDANT

DR. LINDA BARNARD WAS SITTING ON A WOODEN BENCH OUTSIDE THE courtroom, looking like a gym teacher: big boned, fit, and straightforward. Sitting next to her was a jolly older woman in a traffic-stopping purple suit with yellow hair, a round face, and an infectious smile. Annette Martin, "an investigative psychic," resembles a See's Candies lady who spends a lifetime dispensing raspberry truffles to appreciative customers. Both would be witnesses for the defense. A pair of spectators who attended the wine and cheese fest at the Polk house had told Valerie Harris about their favorite psychic, Annette Martin, but they never expected her to become part of the defense and were startled when they bumped into her in the courthouse ladies' room.

Before the jurors took their seats, Sequeira complained to the judge: "I don't understand the relevance of the psychic."

Judge Brady, who had had her share of shocks in this case, blurted out "The who?"

The incredulous Judge Brady scanned the courtroom as if in search of something she could not find. "I was in deep cover as a psychic, a medium," Susan Polk explained. "This is corroborating testimony." The judge placed her painted red fingernails over her eyes. She agreed to decide whether to allow a psychic; meanwhile, she ordered Ms. Polk to call her next witness.

Both the judge and the DA were familiar with Dr. Barnard, a licensed family therapist since 1983, who carried her extensive files in a plastic milk cart on a luggage carrier. Dr. Barnard had spent thirty hours interviewing Susan, who she would try to prove was a battered wife. The lights were dimmed. Dr.

Barnard asked Ms. Polk to put "the Cycle of Violence chart" on the screen, but instead she placed "the Power and Control Wheel," on by mistake. Once corrected, Dr. Barnard explained that an abuser typically begins with a push and a shove. The second stage involves "extreme physical violence. The third stage is one of contrition, when he says he'll never do it again. The victim stays, and the cycle repeats itself."

Susan Polk asked if battered women must walk on *eggshells,* a term she often used. "Yes," Dr. Barnard concurred, "a hundred percent." She said that in upscale neighborhoods, police are less likely to make arrests because the men have the money and prestige. And upscale batterers control the family finances, she said, a point that ran counter to Susan Polk's repeated boasts that she handled the family money. Dr. Barnard explained that women try to stop the violence "through passivity." Mindful of Susan Polk's domineering personality, she had already said that a woman *does not have to be passive* to be battered.

On Tuesday, June 6, 2006, her second day on the witness stand, Dr. Barnard said that a batterer threatens the victim, children, *and* pets. Do batterers kill pets? Susan inquired. "Yes, they do," Dr. Barnard replied. Might a batterer try "to get a child in trouble through the juvenile courts?" Susan Polk asked. Barnard concurred. "Whoever is closest to the mom is usually the child who gets scapegoated," she offered. The batterer, Barnard said, justifies his actions by saying, "She's crazy, so I had to slap her." Jurors were attentive and taking notes. Dr. Barnard was the defense's strongest witness.

When the abuser is also the victim's former therapist, that causes "a double whammy," increasing his power and control over her, Dr. Barnard pointed out. Aside from Susan's monologues, surprisingly few witnesses emphasized Felix's role as her therapist, and yet that's what shaped their relationship in its formative stage. A defense attorney might have made much of it, but aside from Dr. Barnard, Susan failed to call witnesses who might have shed light on a therapist-patient relationship and what that can do to the psyche of a fragile patient. The witness said that the skills Dr. Polk possessed as a therapist could be used to help or to hurt. She added that a batterer could say, "'You're delusional' but a trained therapist who says that carries greater weight."

Once Dr. Polk sexually abused Susan, Dr. Barnard said, he initiated a campaign of "power and control" over her that lasted "for the rest of your relationship." (Dr. Barnard took Susan's word that she was a young teen when the affair began.) According to the expert witness, the shift came when Susan Polk, age forty, became "more confrontational, so everything escalated," although the power imbalance never changed. Dr. Barnard suggested that in order to protect himself against the possibility that Susan might disclose how they met, Dr. Polk may have told people, "Here's my wife and she's kind of a nut." If people knew that he had been her therapist, Dr. Barnard explained, "he would have been ruined professionally."

From her meetings with Susan, Dr. Barnard diagnosed her as suffering from post-traumatic stress disorder, ticking off symptoms that included scanning the environment for danger, an impulse to flee, flashbacks, hallucinations, recurring feelings of trauma, and hypervigilance. Playing the role of Susan Polk's GP, she seemed to have a diagnosis or a psychological justification that could explain much of Susan Polk's behavior. Dr. Barnard said a traumatic response can include having one's feelings cut off, which could explain Susan's lack of affect after Felix's death. That Susan Polk washed her clothes after killing her husband, she said, was not unusual behavior. She explained why it was that two of Susan's sons turned against her, describing how young children side with their mother, the primary caregiver, but as they grow, they side with their father, who has power. She called "mutual combat," the term the boys sometimes used to describe their parents' behavior, a myth. If the situation is that the man is bigger and stronger than his mate, then the combat can never be mutual. In addition, she said Felix's claim that he had prostate cancer or that Susan had MS was "another way to garner sympathy."

Paul Sequeira was uncharacteristically respectful of Dr. Barnard, his most troublesome witness. The DA's office had hired her numerous times. In preparation for the cross-examination, Sequeira poured over some fifteen hundred pages of her testimony in other cases. If Dr. Barnard was persuasive, Sequeira could lose.

Had she conducted psychological tests on Susan Polk? She had not. "Given the dynamics of this case, don't you think a full psychological evaluation would have been in order?"

"Obviously not," the composed Dr. Barnard replied, because a test wouldn't reveal the trauma that the defendant experienced.

Referring to earlier attempts at testing, Sequeira asked, "The fact that the defendant refused to cooperate to do a psychological evaluation (as the court had periodically requested), wouldn't that give you cause for concern?"

"He is attempting to impugn my character with extraneous material!" Susan Polk objected.

"Generally more information is better?" Sequeira asked.

"Generally, yes," Dr. Barnard concurred.

"Sometimes a woman manipulates the system with domestic violence, isn't that true?"

"I'm sure it is but most cases I've worked on I haven't seen very much."

"It is possible?"

"Yes, it is possible."

Had she read Susan Polk's letters to the county's judges—in which she said her husband was a member of Mossad? "Isn't this *a red flag* for you?" he asked, using the term *red flag* because as an expert witness, that was a phrase Dr. Barnard liked to use.

"It seemed to me that it didn't affect whether or not she was a battered woman," Dr. Barnard volleyed.

"Okay," Sequeira said in almost affable tones, "I understand that answer." He believed that Dr. Barnard's one weakness was that as an impassioned advocate she sometimes pushed it too far. "Does [Susan's background as a psychic] affect your ability to consider her as a reliable historian?" he inquired.

"People really are psychics," she said. "If she is, I'd say it's a pretty big burden to carry. It doesn't have a lot to do with domestic violence. Felix had her believe she had special abilities. That was part of his campaign of abuse of her."

THE FOLLOWING MORNING, WEDNESDAY, JUNE 7, 2006, PAUL SEQUEIRA WAS still pestering the battered women's expert. He asked if it weren't true that Dr. Barnard's conclusions were based on a history provided to her by Susan Polk. She said in some measure that was so.

He asked if Susan Polk had told Dr. Barnard her father had molested her. Dr. Barnard said she had, just as Susan Polk vociferously objected to his line of questions—she now tells reporters she doesn't know if her father ever molested her. Sequeira asked if it were possible for Ms. Polk to have suffered post-traumatic stress disorder—as a result of molestation *by her father.* Dr. Barnard again agreed. Again, Susan objected. Almost every question he asked elicited an objection or two from the defendant and a call for a mistrial.

Was Dr. Barnard aware that Susan Polk believed her previous attorney Dan Horowitz had killed his wife and framed Scott Dyleski, the neighbor boy? "Yes," she was aware of that. But she added that "I don't take anything Susan Polk or anyone else tells me as the gospel truth."

Sequeira returned to one of his central themes: "Don't you see there is a larger picture of someone unwilling to submit to authority? You don't see what's happening in the courtroom the last few days as someone unwilling to submit to authority?"

"I'm asking to strike the question," Susan said.

"This country was founded by people not willing to submit to authority," Dr. Barnard responded.

"Well," said Sequeira, "post-Revolution?"

Then he launched his A-bomb. Reading from the DSM-IV—the mental health professions' diagnostic manual—Sequeira shared with the witness—and jurors—the definition of Delusional Disorder: Persecutory Type:

> The central theme of the delusion involves the person's belief that he or she is being conspired against, cheated, spied on, followed, poisoned or drugged, maliciously maligned, harassed, or obstructed in the pursuit of long-term goals. Small slights may be exaggerated and become the focus of a delusional system. The focus of the delusion is often on some injustice that must be remedied by legal terms ("querulous paranoia"), and the affected person may engage in repeated attempts to obtain satisfaction by appeal to the courts and other government agencies. Individuals with perse-cutory delusions are often resentful and angry and *may resort to violence against those they believe are hurting them.*

Spectators gasped. Reporters were in shock. No one remembers the question that followed or the answer. While the good witness had been shoehorning Felix Polk's behavior into her "Power and Control wheels," Sequeira had defined the defendant.

SUSAN'S REDIRECT WAS BRIEF: "IN YOUR PROFESSIONAL OPINION, AM I OUT of touch with reality?" Susan Polk asked.

"No."

"After assessing me, you found me to be a reasonable person?"

"Yes, I did."

At the lunch recess, Valerie Harris was accosted by reporters on the sidewalk. They asked what she thought of the devastatingly accurate definition. "I think you can read the book and find anything you want to in it." By the time the cameras were rolling, she had a stronger response. She said, "He didn't touch the battered women's test at all."

After the lunch break came the pièce de résistance. Amazingly, the judge would allow the psychic to testify. Judge Brady called her testimony "tangentially relevant," but she narrowed the scope of the questions. The jolly psychic would not be allowed to talk about Susan's psychic ability nor whether psychic phenomenon exists but could only speak about her own work as a psychic detective. Paul Sequeira would be in the position of trying to nail Jell-O to the wall. If the judge was going to allow Annette Martin to testify, Sequeira asked, "What am I to do, challenge her on her success in predicting the future?" Ms. Martin, he advised, also talks to ghosts. (Her website says she communicates with animals and makes TV appearances.) Susan Polk was delighted. Valerie Harris, who was responsible for finding Ms. (lioness in the wilderness) Shelley and Ms. Martin, was ecstatic. "I could have kissed the judge!" she declared.

In his one-minute sidewalk press conference Sequeira was asked about the inclusion of a psychic. "It almost seems like it's entertainment," he said, shaking his head in bafflement. The prospect of Ms. Martin's testimony would be more exciting than the testimony itself. She was able to say that she'd been a "professional psychic detective" for thirty-five years. "I don't solve crimes," she explained in her melodic voice, "All I do is help [families and police departments] and bring them more information." Nearly half the jurors seemed to be taking notes.

Ms. Martin said she had worked with the San Francisco Police Department, the Montana Sheriff's Department, and the Marin County Sheriff's Department. She said she could go "on and on and on." Susan tried to inquire about psychic ability, wanting to "prove" to jurors that it exists, but each time she broached the subject, Sequeira objected and the judge warned her that she knew better.

"I'm objecting that it's dictatorship from the bench," Susan bristled.

"That's correct," a frustrated judge responded.

"You are embarrassing me in front of the jury," Susan Polk hissed.

Initially, Ms. Martin had been pleased as punch to be called to assist in the murder case, but as the bickering escalated she only spoke a few words.

Susan was infuriated by the judge constantly cutting her off: "I move for a mistrial based on the expression on your face!" she declared.

"I have my fingers on my face," the judge replied.

Susan did elicit from her witness that she had worked on "over a hundred cases," and had been successful, "I would say in all of them."

Within minutes Ms. Martin had completed her testimony, and much to the disappointment of the spectators, Paul Sequeira chose not to cross-examine the psychic detective. The Jell-O slid off the wall of its own accord.

Before leaving the courthouse, Ms. Martin confided to an acquaintance that she knew what happened that night in the pool house—but she wouldn't tell. A few days later, she made an appearance on Court TV as the first psychic to testify in a criminal trial.

ON FRIDAY, JUNE 19, SUSAN CALLED HER LAST WITNESS, LLORETTA "Ronnie" Bankus, former wife of Barry Morris, Felix's friend and one of Susan Polk's enemies. Susan had bad-mouthed Morris for years. Reporters braced for the worst.

Ms. Bankus arrived in her nurse's scrubs, fresh from the OR, with a stethoscope dangling from her neck. She may have been a footnote to the case, but she had something important to say. Susan wanted to prove to jurors that her husband had lied about her to gain sympathy from others, just as the domestic violence expert Dr. Barnard had testified. Ms. Bankus told jurors that she and her family had gone to Dr. Polk for family counseling and that Barry Morris, her ex, who also represented the Polk boys when they were in trouble, had been distraught over his brother's death *from MS*. "It was raw," she told the jurors. "You understand that?" Later, Felix confided to Barry, who by then was his good friend, that Susan had MS.

Ms. Bankus testified that Felix Polk was a charismatic Svengali who took advantage of a once meek young girl. As her therapist, he knew "all your weaknesses," she said, and for his own purposes he was willing to exploit them. On learning Felix had been killed her first thought was, "You live by the sword, you die by the sword." Ms. Bankus had reason to hate Dr. Polk; he had taken sides in her bitter divorce and treated her son, whom he also befriended, without telling her.

"Everybody says [Susan Polk is] crazy," Ms. Bankus said. She wished people would think outside the box. "Maybe there's a reason. Maybe there's a reason Susan is so angry."

Before she testified, Sequeira held an impromptu hallway interview with Ms. Bankus who told him she felt compelled to tell what she knew, while beseeching and warning him not to grill her on cross-examination. When he did the typical lawyerlike thing and told her Susan Polk had said unkind things about her son, she said she didn't want to hear it. "She shut me down," said an impressed Sequeira who decided to leave her alone.

Mindful that jurors were restless, Susan decided not to call the dozens of other witnesses she had on her list. She would save some for the next phase. "The defense rests," she said, and sat down. Valerie Harris was busy lining up other witnesses for the rebuttal phase, which was to begin immediately. The ball had returned to Sequeira's court.

For months, Paul Sequeira had scanned the jurors' faces. He knew they were exhausted. If he hadn't made his case, he didn't know if rebuttal witnesses would make a difference, and the threat of losing the jury was too great a risk. He wanted to remain in the jury's good graces. There was no doubt Ponytail liked the prosecutor, but he had said at the outset that he had a job in LA starting June 19, only ten days away. Ponytail's good humor wouldn't last much longer.

A millisecond after Susan Polk said the defense rests, Sequeira, aware that Susan might change her mind, blurted out, "The prosecution rests."

Susan Polk jerked her neck back and gave Sequeira an incredulous stare. Her eyelids fluttered. She was unprepared for the trial to come to a screeching halt; there was so much more that she wanted to say. This had been her moment. She was on trial for murder and yet the forum suited her. Everything that had happened to her, she thought, was worthy of examination. This trial gave her that opportunity in front of a jury of her peers, reporters and, yes, snickering spectators. She had had four months to make her case. Despite what she thought, the judge had given her extraordinary latitude to tell her story. Now her chance was slipping away. Soon, she would be back in the world of her own making, more alone than she'd ever been before.

JUDGE BRADY ANNOUNCED THAT CLOSING ARGUMENTS WOULD BE GIVEN that Monday. Susan was unwilling to go forward. "I am absolutely not ready to proceed," she declared. She had a litany of complaints: "I get up at four or four thirty in the morning. Many nights inmates yell and scream. Or sometimes it's the guards," she said. She needed her weekends to "catch up on sleep." She objected to the "golf pencils" she must use to write her briefs. She said one weekend was inadequate to prepare her closing argument. What she didn't say was that in addition to her being weary, she hoped the trial would last long enough to knock Ponytail off the jury.

"I have four kids," Sequeira responded, "special kids. I am harassed and awakened by my children," he said only half facetiously. In fact, he was leaving town early to look after his severely autistic adolescent son while his wife visited her sister. The trial had been more of a burden on her than anyone else in the family. He couldn't help but think that Susan Polk's weekend in jail might be preferable to his preparing closing arguments in some pizzeria with another son's traveling baseball team. While Susan imagined Sequeira had a smooth, suburban life, the reality was that he and especially his wife had to be vigilant. Unguarded their autistic son would dash into the kitchen and break all the glassware or, as he had done recently, gallop into his brother's room and smash his mirror. If allowed outside by himself, he'd run away. Susan might object to interrupted sleep but that was something that Sequeira lived with. Because his autistic son liked to sleep in snug quarters, sometimes Sequeira slept with him in the cove under their stairwell, but that was nothing he would ever explain to the court.

Unpersuaded by Susan's litany of complaints, the judge pointed out that Ms. Polk had sufficient time to schedule a TV interview for that very afternoon at the jail. (Valerie Harris swiftly scurried about to cancel the interview.) Over Susan's multitude of objections, Judge Brady scheduled closing arguments for Monday.

When Susan settled down, she, Sequeira, and the judge began working on the critical issue of jury instructions. Susan wanted the jury to be given only one choice: first-degree murder. The judge advised against it. Susan was unmoved. She was also concerned about instructions that referred to her mental state. "There is no evidence the defendant is or was delusional," she said, referring to herself in the third person. It's nothing more, than "the DA's theory." No expert, she said, had called her delusional. Two psychologists had read her letters and found her competent. Only two of her sons who she said had financial motives for "prevaricating" testified that she was delusional.

"This is putting the jury into the role of diagnostician," she protested, fighting her old sanity battle and once again losing. The instructions would read in part: "The killing of another person in self-defense is justifiable and not unlawful when the person who does the killing actually and reasonably believes: that there is imminent danger . . . (and) that it is necessary to avoid death or great bodily harm to herself." The judge agreed to add this single sentence, which Sequeira thought was crucial for conviction: *"The belief in the need for self-defense may not be based solely on a delusion alone."*

With that one line in the instructions, what she imagined to be true was rendered moot.

When the jury was brought back to court, it was the judge's turn to speak. For nearly an hour she calmly read the instructions to attentive jurors, stopping only to sip her tea. Periodically, Susan, who, deprived of sunlight, now bore a prison pallor, dabbed her eyes with a tissue that the attentive Valerie, wearing tangerine blush, handed her.

Despite Susan's request not to mention second-degree murder or voluntary and involuntary manslaughter, the judge included them. Not once during the reading did Susan look at the twelve people who would determine her fate. Shortly before noon, the judge finished her reading and dismissed the jurors for the weekend. After they left, Susan made her most unusual objection of the entire trial: she objected to the judge's drinking coffee while reading the instructions.

"I don't even know how to address this," the judge said, with lifted brows. "My mouth was dry. . . . There's tea in my cup!" she said. She said she drinks from a "wood duck cup," which she held aloft for everyone to examine. "There's nothing controversial or prejudicial," she said. "I don't make gestures with my cup. I drink from it. My staff would like to clean it some day," she said. The inside of her cup was a hearty brown. But then Judge Brady did something she had rarely done since the trial began: she smiled. The burden she had carried for four months had all but passed to the jurors.

At the end of the day, reporters, who had bonded just like spectators and jurors, gathered at an outdoor café. Some thought Susan would be convicted of first-degree murder. Others thought second. Some weren't so sure. Maybe the jury sympathized with Susan more than tough-skinned reporters did. You didn't have to like her to empathize with her.

Coming to court had become not just work for reporters but a daily drama and a not unpleasant ritual. Sometimes they had found it difficult to sit through Susan's endless monologues, but more often her outbursts and Sequeira's retorts kept it interesting. Chris Darden, a courtroom watcher and the reporters' dream source, drove by the café with copies of a handwritten statement issued by Susan Polk objecting to the jury instructions:

> "Ms. Polk is hopeful that the jury will not split the baby and find manslaughter," she wrote. "No evidence of manslaughter was provided." She objected to the clause in the instructions dealing with delusions: "The experts found that Ms. Polk is not delusional . . ."

28.

STACKING HAY

ON MONDAY, JUNE 12, 2006, THE CORRIDOR LEADING TO DEPARTMENT 31 was jammed all the way to the elevators with spectators, family members, and reporters. Some had arrived hours early. At 9:00 AM, the doors were unlocked and the crowds surged into seats. When they were filled, members of the audience crushed together in the vestibule while others, unable to fit into the room, waited outside. Susan Polk looked almost despondent until several people gave up their seats for her mother and brother who'd driven from San Diego, the only two people who had come to be with her. Helen Bolling, seventy-two, who sat on a chair near the back of the courtroom, had come to hear her daughter give her final argument in her own murder case. Next to her, separated by a few feet, sat another small woman, Phyllis O'Leary, seventy-one, Paul Sequeira's mother, who had come to hear her son give final arguments against Helen Bolling's daughter. She recently told her son he was everything she had hoped he would be, and for once in his life he was rendered speechless. Elsewhere in the audience sat Sequeira's stepmother and father, in weathered cowboy boots. Paul Sequeira had taken some thirty murder cases to jury trial in the course of his career, but none was as bizarre or as gut-wrenching as the *People of the State of California v. Susan Mae Polk*.

The prosecutor rose from his chair and told jurors that when the case started, he was "a lot less humble and a lot less gray." He spoke about the American system of justice that prevents society from tumbling into anarchy.

"If I fail to do my job and there's a lack of evidence you have to send the defendant home," he told jurors. "If the defendant is telling you the truth, if that's what happened in the pool house that night, if the victim attacked her, tried to stab her and she pulled the knife out of his hands, then she had every right to kill him dead. If you believe that to be true, that is perfect self-defense and she needs to go home as soon as possible."

He was only minutes into this closing argument when he began to address the controversial testimony of Dr. Cooper, who contended that Felix Polk died of a heart attack. Even if the jurors agreed, Sequeira pointed out, "the law says we will hold you responsible if you put a heart attack in motion by an unlawful act. You're still guilty of murder."

He spoke in plain English: "There's nothing fancy about murder," he said. All it requires is that "a human being was killed; the killing was unlawful," and "the killing was done with malice aforethought," which means "the intent to kill." For the jurors to find Ms. Polk guilty in the first degree would mean they found that her actions were "willful, deliberate, and premeditated." Premeditation does not require hours, he said. All it needs is "a cold, calculated judgment."

He spoke about his most important witness, Gabriel Polk, who discovered his father's body in the pool house. "And the first suspect on the planet Earth" whom he suspected was his mother. The "mental anguish and heartbreak must have been overwhelming," he said. "Who among us could have survived that ordeal?"

Sequeira thought it critical to address the issue of how Susan met Felix. It was, he thought, "the eight-hundred-pound gorilla in the room." That transgression alone could be reason for jurors to settle on second-degree rather than first. Sequeira wanted to frame it. In his folksy manner that jurors found so appealing he said that summers when he was a boy he stacked hay in the barn. "If the bottom layer was crooked, you can't do a good job," because the stack "will never be straight." With the Polks, "the foundation was wrong from the git-go. Dr. Polk was wrong, very wrong. No one is going to excuse what he did. . . . He turned what started out as wrong into a marriage of twenty years, but the stack was never straight." As Sequeira spoke, Susan was puncturing his argument with staccato objections and requests for mistrials. The only other sound in the courtroom was that of her mother opening a crinkly candy bag and twisting the wrapper on her lemon suckers. Sequeira continued, reminding jurors that the most violent activity in the Polk family was the punch Eli landed on his mother's lip. He called Susan Polk's accusation that Adam and Gabriel were motivated by financial gain "background noise." The issue, he said, "is about the pool house."

He characterized Susan Polk's questioning of Gabriel as "a marathon cross-examination." Then he said something startling, only because no one else seemed to have noticed: she had asked her son about "all their houses, all the friends, all the teachers," but Susan Polk had not asked her son *one question about the night he found his father's body.*

"If she had killed in self-defense," he said, "why did she tell her son his father may have been in an accident? Why didn't she sit him down and say, "We need to talk"? Why hadn't she said, "Please don't go down there" to the pool house? "Was she hoping he'd buy into some story like there'd been an intruder . . . ? Is that a caring mother, the innocent person who sits before you today?" Sequeira challenged the assertion that Felix had been the abuser. His divorce attorney called him "a beaten man," one who hadn't wanted the cops to arrest his wife. And even after he was given control of their house, he agreed to retreat to the pool house.

Sequeira was spellbinding. No one stirred except Susan Polk, who continued to interrupt, accusing him of misstating the evidence and of prosecutorial misconduct. Her objections only served to reinforce one of Sequeira's underlying points, that no one could control her. He was coming at her story from all directions. He questioned if it were possible for someone on her back to wrap her hand around the back of her assailant and stab him, suggesting that jurors try it themselves. He contrasted Felix's bloodied head and torso with the defendant's: "There are not cuts on her hands. None!" Sequeira roared as he showed the huge photo enlargement of Susan Polk's hands.

If she is to be believed, he said, then the victim, Felix Polk "hates kids, hates all races, poisons dogs, and believes in genocide. He's a monster."

Sequeira belittled the analysis of Lieutenant Clark: "I don't know how anyone can look at a picture of the scene and give you the volume of blood," he said. "Really? Wow!" But he reserved his most scathing remarks for Dr. Cooper. "He was a piece of work!" Sequeira said, speaking to the jurors like buddies at a barbecue, hoping they concurred.

"I don't want to creep anyone out," he said, but it was Dr. Peterson who "put his hands in the wounds." Dr. Cooper had to rely on the findings of Dr. Peterson to draw his own conclusions. The issue of the heart attack, he said, "is not a big deal legally." But wanting to have an airtight case, he said, "Dr. Cooper didn't even see the pictures of the heart. He never examined the heart."

Sequeira was whacking away at Susan's defense. He dismissed Eli Polk's testimony, telling jurors her faithful son would say whatever his mother wanted him to say.

As he spoke, Susan Polk was heating up, accusing the DA and judge of "deliberate sabotage of this case" and continuing her demands for a mistrial, but Sequeira ignored her. He reminded jurors that she had given differing accounts to the media about what happened the night Felix died. He pointed out that she had said the struggle had occurred in one place while her own expert acknowledged that blood drops proved otherwise.

He appealed to the jurors' common sense: why would a seventy-year-old man with asthma and a heart condition, who rose at 5:00 AM to drive his son to Los Angeles, invite his wife to the pool house if their fifteen-year-old son was even exhausted from the drive to LA? Why would he invite someone he was afraid of? Why would she go to the pool house late at night if she was scared of him? "Either way, there was not going to be a conversation down there," he said.

Why was it that the same pepper spray that can ward off grizzly bears and criminals could not slow Dr. Polk? "Where did the knife come from? How could Ms. Polk have wrestled the knife away without nicking herself?" She had given direct testimony for seventeen hours and twenty-five minutes (he was quoting from a sheet Chris Darden, a trial watcher, created and circulated called "Duration of Testimony") and yet she devoted *only fifty-four minutes* to what happened that night. . . . "She destroyed key evidence," he said, and that showed "consciousness of guilt."

"She hated him for things that happened many, many years ago when she was young. That didn't give her the right to kill him in 2002." The trial had exhausted him but the prospect of its winding down and nailing the defendant buoyed him. He stood facing the jurors, comfortable in the task before him. Sequeira had summed up what many in the courtroom felt. For members of the audience who sided with him, his closing argument was cathartic. But he wasn't finished. Susan Polk would give her final argument, but as the People's representative, Sequeira would have the last word.

IT WAS NOW SUSAN POLK'S TURN TO STATE HER CASE. THE TRIAL HAD exhausted her. She looked strained, severe. Her brown suede dress with capped sleeves hung loosely from her bony frame. Her hair was pulled away from her forehead. Before beginning, she felt compelled to inform the judge there were misspellings in the jury instructions.

Moving her favorite prop, the easel, to the middle of the room, she placed a larger-than-life-size photo of herself on it. The image showed Susan as a beautiful young girl with thick dark hair falling four inches below her shoulders, wearing a tiny green-and-white checked top and miniskirt that emphasized her budding figure. She didn't have to explain: that's what she looked like when she met Dr. Polk. What she said was that's what she looked like when Felix Polk "drugged and raped me."

Without straining herself, the fit Susan Polk lifted the heavy wooden podium and hauled it across the floor, a move that did not go unnoticed by jurors. She pulled her gold rim glasses from her nose and looked but didn't seem to see the jurors. "In a case of self-defense," she said, "the burden of proof is on the prosecution. . . .

"If you find the evidence shows my husband may have been aggressive or that he died of a heart condition not brought about by my actions, then you must acquit," she said. Next she set about pummeling those family members who needed to be pummeled for her to win her case. Accused of being crazy for years, she slapped that label on her husband. She said he could not be trusted because he was a schizophrenic, he claimed their son Adam had multiple personalities, he claimed she had MS, and "he became involved with me when I was fourteen."

Susan attacked the prosecution's claim that she had a motive: "I had no financial motive to kill my husband," she said. He was earning $175,000 a year.

Mixing her wild theories with her reasonable points, she told jurors that deputies poured water on the scene, stamped her shoeprints in the blood, and added postmortem wounds to her husband's feet. The controversial wound on her husband's head, she said, lacked bruising, which proved he received it when his heart had stopped pumping. She said Dr. Cooper "exposed the naked truth."

Valerie did what she could. She had spent the weekend conferring with Susan's most important witnesses and with attorneys who pitched in to help. She wrote a final argument that Susan Polk dismissed as not sounding like her. She still believed she knew better than anyone else. She told the jurors her account of her husband "was thoroughly corroborated in my letters and diary" and in the divorce papers and by her witnesses. She spoke about myths and legends, likening her three sons to princes, with Adam and Gabe seeking their fortune, while Eli found greater wealth in his gift of compassion. She accused her oldest and youngest of lying and hanging her out to dry. She denied ever threatening Felix.

She accused the DA of turning the case into "a witch trial" and claimed that she stood charged with the heresy of delusion. "Are dreamers delusional?" she asked. Was H. G. Wells delusional? Was Captain Nemo the subject of a delusional mind? "Was the idea my husband was a spy outside the realm of possibility? There was no evidence presented that my husband was *not* a spy. No evidence presented I was *not* a psychic."

She didn't say she was delusional but she said, "Do crazy people deserve to be treated with violence? The presence of a delusion doesn't preclude self-defense nor is it relevant . . . Crazy or not," she said, she knew "he is going to kill me." And that "pure and simple is self-defense." Fate determined whether she lived or died, she said. "I chose to live; that is my crime."

At many points throughout her final argument, Susan asked what kind of man would "have sex with a fourteen-year-old? What kind of a man would kill my dogs?" What kind of a man, she asked, would say she had MS when she didn't, or claim he had prostate cancer when he didn't? The kind of man who would call her crazy and delusional.

Attorneys would have done a better job. But none would have done a truer one. By her going pro per, the jurors came to know her better than they could have otherwise. But would that help Susan or the prosecution? The next morning, Tuesday, June 13, 2006, Susan completed her final argument. She told jurors that the reason her husband stabbed her leg and not a vital organ is "common sense," it's because her legs got in the way. She said it was only common sense to believe that her husband was the aggressor. She stretched her skinny arms out like a scarecrow and said, "I could not have thrown him on the floor. . . . Please use your common sense." In the distant way she does, she talked about the blood flow patterns on her husband's head, pointing out that the blood streamed down his face because he was hanging over her.

Valerie Harris never lost sight of the fact that Susan Polk was in charge and that she thought she was the smartest person in the room. Susan believed she was resonating with jurors. Valerie passed her a note telling her to pound home reasonable doubt and tell jurors to "stick to your guns. . . . Don't compromise with my life. . . . When you hit your pillow at night you have to sleep with a clear conscience." Susan brushed the note aside.

She said she did not provoke the fight "other than [talking about] 9/11 and calling my husband a Mossad agent."

"Pure and simple," she said, "I didn't imagine he was on top of me; I didn't imagine he put a hole in my pants; I didn't imagine his rage and anger and threats to kill me; I didn't imagine my diary. I didn't imagine he threatened to harm the dogs. I didn't imagine being raped at fourteen. None of that was my imagination." She didn't plead with jurors so much as she defended her dissertation. She didn't beckon them to empathize, so much as she told them what they needed to know to exonerate her. Her manner was somber and assured. And with that, Susan Polk had said all she would say to the twelve citizens who would determine her fate.

PAUL SEQUEIRA HAD BEEN WAITING FOR THIS OPPORTUNITY. FROM THE beginning, he'd fertilized his case with the theme that Susan Polk balked at authority.

Sequeira replaced Susan's image of the beautiful girl in the green-and-white outfit with the larger-than-life-size booking photo of the defendant's face looking like a hardened con, with cold eyes and unyielding lips. He did what he had to do: he dealt with the accusation the defendant made that she was fourteen when her therapist raped her. "The problem is just like everything else in this trial," he said, her account could not be believed. Initially she had told everyone she was sixteen when they had sex. "But sixteen wasn't good enough, fifteen wasn't good enough. Now it's fourteen! Now she was being *drugged and raped*." Mrs. Polk had to make things "sound worse."

He asked jurors to consider who had the power in the family. Who controlled the money? "Not the victim," he said before making a point he had been weaving into his case from day one: if someone is going to be controlling—as Susan claimed Felix had been—doesn't the other person have to "submit to some kind of authority?" he asked. Jurors knew as well as anyone that Susan Polk could never submit to authority. She would not listen to the judge in juvenile court, criminal court, or this court, he said, "but she was controlled, right?"

"I object. That's a misrepresentation of the facts," Susan Polk insisted. "I move for a mistrial again."

When she was traveling in Europe, Thailand, and Hawaii, "did he chase her down? What did he do?" Sequeira asked, "he made travel arrangements for her" when her arrangements "weren't good enough for her."

In "the greatest irony of this trial," Sequeira continued, "Felix Polk saved her from suicide." She called her husband whom she accused of abuse and he called 911. The man who she claimed called her a "sick puppy who deserved to die" saved her life. And the doctor who interviewed her while she recuperated in the hospital said the number one stressor in her life was not her abusive husband but her son Eli. "It's Eli!" the DA declared triumphantly.

"Objection! That misstates the evidence," Susan Polk declared. She raised so many objections that the judge warned, "You do it one more time, I'm going to sanction you. Mr. Sequeira, continue please."

"There were two sets of rules in the world," Sequeira said, "one for Susan Polk and one for the rest of us."

He belittled her claim that cops had tampered with the crime scene. If the coroner's office really did cut the bottom of Felix Polk's feet, "couldn't they have cut a toe off for me?" he asked facetiously. "Wouldn't that make it more dramatic? If they were going to make it up, couldn't they do a better job?"

Using the projector, Sequeira exhibited the most grotesque image of Felix Polk's profile, with syrupy blood dripped across his face and his eyes staring blankly. Susan stoically glanced at the image, without emotion. "How did he get the head wound while he was still alive?" Sequeira said. "The pump stops. The blood stops," he said. Felix Polk must have been alive when, Sequeira argued, Susan slammed him over the head with an unknown object. If, as Mrs. Polk alleged, her husband's last move was to fall backward and hit his head, then the blood, Sequeira indicated, would not have spurted from the wound.

Sequeira zeroed in on the knife. He approached the judge's bench and wrapped on the wood: "Knock-knock!" he hollered. "Hey, can I come in? She's standing there with a butcher knife!" he said, as his eyes moved from one juror to the next. The paring knife he said "can be concealed. It fits neatly in the back or front pocket. It got down there because she took it down there!"

He'd been waiting for this moment when Susan Polk no longer had the ability to respond. He reminded jurors that when Susan said she washed her clothes and the knife, he asked her what she had done with the Maglite, which she had also *washed*. *"Oh, really?"* he said, offering up another zinger: "What did she have to clean off? She had to clean the blood off!" he practically shouted.

According to Sequeira, her motive was buried deep in her persecutory delusions. But, he added, she knows what she's doing. She knows right from wrong. These delusions make her dangerous; especially dangerous to her husband, who was not the monster she made him out to be. "The defendant did more carnage on his character in this trial than what she did that night," he thundered.

He knew he could have laid out the case for premeditated murder, but after talking it over with his boss, Sequeira decided not to lock in "the good jurors," those who were leaning toward first degree. If he did, Sequeira worried that he might end up with a hung jury, a not uncommon occurrence in situations like this, when jurors become so recalcitrant that they hang between first and second. He would settle for second-degree murder.

Quoting from Susan's conversation with Gabriel years earlier, when she said that "a person who murders someone *is forever separated from the rest of the community,"* he eyed the jurors and said, "You folks, you represent community standards." Then he lowered his voice: "I can only ask you to do the right thing. . . . Justice for Dr. Polk and his children is now in your hands."

As he made his way back to his seat, Sequeira's eyes scanned the last row, where his little mother sat. She mouthed the single word, "Good."

Moments later, the twelve jurors filed out. Dazed spectators ambled out of the courtroom. Valerie Harris corralled Susan's mother and brother. On a yellow legal pad Susan had written a note imploring them to stay for the verdict, but Susan's brother, David, had business in San Diego. He told Ms. Harris that he had two certificates of deposit that were maturing and he had to take out the garbage at their rental properties. Close to tears, Valerie Harris offered to find someone to take out the garbage and said CDs could be rolled over with a phone call. They debated staying.

In the courtroom later, Susan looked dolefully at her mother and brother, her eyes begging them to stay. She wrote a second note to her brother: "Dear David, you look really, really nicely dressed and well groomed. You also look well taken care of. Love, Susan." In fact, he looked pale and wasted, as he had for many years. Still he was not inclined to stay.

Minutes after the hearing ended, Helen Bolling's silver station wagon streaked by. She and David hadn't bothered to inform Susan or her assistant; they were heading home. In conversation with Valerie Harris later that night, David said they would return if Susan got out of jail.

29.

SOMEONE ON HER SIDE

ON TUESDAY, JUNE 13, 2006, THE FIRST DAY OF DELIBERATIONS, TWELVE jurors waited to have the evidence brought in. As they waited, they gushed about all the things they'd not been able to say. They talked about how impossible Susan Polk was. How based on her diary entries she would have hated them for being happy Californians. Juror Kathy Sommese, the blond nurse, kept track: during Sequeira's closing argument Susan requested a mistrial *twenty-four times*. They joked that they needed to see more pictures—of the family dogs.

Just as jury consultant Karen Fleming-Ginn had predicted, jurors turned to the CFO, Pat Roland, to be foreperson. Because his kids attend the same school as Gabe and Adam did, he declined. Lisa Cristwell, his seatmate, an organized, charismatic professional, stepped in.

Under Cristwell's leadership, the six men and six women systematically considered their options. They began with self-defense and examining the physical evidence: the crime scene photos, Song Wick's drawings of the room, the medical examiner's drawings of the wounds, Susan Polk's interrogation tape, and, among other items, the white stitching on Susan Polk's jeans, looking for traces of blood. None of the facts, they were concluding, suggested that this was a case for self-defense.

As Sequeira advised, they reenacted the struggle between Susan and Felix, with Sommese on the floor, and Jason MacDavid (Ponytail) hovering over her. They drew on a board the medical examiner's description of wound X, the cut on Felix Polk's back. Brandishing a marker, Sommese tried to "stab" MacDavid in the back. Her arms couldn't reach far enough.

All twelve voted against self-defense and moved on to manslaughter and murder. They listened to Felix's 911 calls and read transcripts. While looking for other evidence, Lisa Cristwell came upon Felix's letter to Gabriel, after the boy, blaming his father for Eli's troubles, had smashed his father's car windows, As she read it aloud, Lisa Cristwell choked up. Felix was not a horrible person; he was a father who loved his son, not a monster who controlled his family. Some jurors were already at murder one. That moved more jurors over. Most of the men agreed that Susan Polk's account didn't make sense. There was no way Felix would have told his wife to visit him at the cottage to talk about finances after a grueling day driving to LA and back. Still, some male jurors empathized more with Susan than the women. As he watched Susan, juror Pat Roland, the CFO, thought "she was a lonely lady getting lonelier by the minute." To most of the jurors, the fact that she had been Felix's patient when she was a girl did not seem relevant. And while they knew her to be delusional, they followed the instructions and put that aside.

They debated what premeditation meant. For hours, the group talked to Scott, the Nummi worker, who wore a big cross and went out for smoking breaks and who Karen Fleming-Ginn, the jury consultant, had said from the start, would be pro-defense. He believed firmly Susan was not a murderer but the victim of a bad marriage, and he told others he could only agree on a verdict that would allow him to sleep at night. Over the months, he had grown attached to the defendant. In his eyes, she had not planned on killing Felix but must have engaged in "a sudden quarrel." He was the only juror who saw the events that way, and his solitary position made him uncomfortable. When Ms. Cristwell asked him to point to the facts that supported his thinking, he trembled and was inarticulate. She knew he was an emotional wreck. Each time he said he felt Susan Polk was not guilty, other jurors said he couldn't rely on his feelings but must depend on the evidence, which he failed to do. Often, he kept his chair away from the table, as if separating himself physically from the debate.

By Wednesday, June 14, the second day of deliberations, jurors were discussing "malice aforethought." The strongest personalities believed there had been premeditation and favored first-degree murder. They took a vote: five were for second degree; seven for first. "Well, there's a hung jury!" one of the quieter jurors remarked. Though they were more divided than they had thought, the group was always civil with one another. Together, they vowed that if it took another week, they would not be a hung jury. They didn't want another twelve people to suffer the way they had, and some had such strong affection for the DA that they said they didn't want Paul Sequeira to have to retry the case.

Some jurors were stumped because there was no proof Susan Polk had brought the knife to the cottage. And in all her voluminous diaries, she never once wrote that she was going to kill Felix. While Gabriel described his mother's frequent comments about killing Felix, some jurors were not convinced. Even those who voted for first degree thought Gabriel was so young when it had happened—he was fifteen—that Marjorie Briner and others might have made him angrier than he might otherwise have been. They didn't believe everything he or his brothers said; the truth, jurors thought, was somewhere in between. As for Susan's words, most jurors simply discounted what she said, since many believed she was an outrageous liar.

On Thursday, June 15, the third day of deliberations, while everyone was discussing first- or second-degree murder, Scott, the nervous loner, said he wanted to reexamine manslaughter. Everyone knew that Jason (ponytail) Mac-David had a new job in Southern California the following Monday. He was willing to postpone his move to LA and live at another juror's house, but Jason was frustrated. He told Scott, "We know it's murder. You want us to come to manslaughter but we're not. If you think with eleven to one we're going to go for manslaughter, we'll have a hung jury."

THEY WERE DRESSED UP—ON DRESS-DOWN FRIDAY, JUNE 16, 2006, THE fourth day of their deliberations. One female juror wore a blouse and hot pink sweater; another wore a buttery colored jersey. Some carried plastic grocery bags stuffed with grapes and other snack food. It looked like brunch for twelve. The night before, as they left the building, jurors asked the bailiff to snap a group photo. All signs, reporters assumed, that a verdict was imminent.

At 10:31 AM, the court e-mailed the media: "The verdict will be read at 11:00 AM."

Susan Polk, wearing a black Calvin Klein sweater set, Anne Taylor khakis, and black mules, was brought into the courtroom. Her hands trembled. Sitting at the table beside her was Valerie Harris. They sat in silence.

All along, Susan Polk had remained hopeful. She was convinced of her innocence, and after looking in jurors' eyes, she believed that some were with her. The door to the courtroom swung open. Susan Polk was startled to see her somber sons Gabriel, nineteen, and Adam, twenty-three. The two took seats in the front row. On either side of them sat Mr. and Mrs. Briner. Susan stole glances at her sons and dabbed her eyes. She knew they had come to see their mother go down.

Neither Susan's mother nor her brother drove up for the verdict. Eli, the one family member who wanted to be there for her, was in jail. The courtroom was packed with journalists, the regulars, Sequeira's boss, the law librarian, legal interns, and the public; the only person who seemed to be on Susan's side was seated at the table next to her. So many people cut in line that Paul, the orderly who sat in the last row, was unable to squeeze into the courtroom.

At 11:28 AM twelve solemn jurors filed in. Lisa Cristwell handed the verdict forms to the bailiff, who handed them to Judge Brady. Her face frozen, Judge Brady leafed through each. Scott, the juror who preferred being alone, wore wide black sunglasses and stared out the window, refusing to look at Susan or anyone else. One female juror wept. The judge handed the twelve pages to her clerk, Nancy Chertkow, a tall, attractive woman with blond hair piled in a twist atop her head. At 11:31 AM, she stood and in a clear voice read the following declaration:

"The People of the State of California Versus Susan Mae Polk . . . On count one, we the jury find the defendant not guilty of first-degree murder . . ."

Not guilty!

What did it mean? Susan Polk, along with nearly everyone else in the courtroom, including Sequeira, wondered if she had actually beaten the rap. Sequeira knew better, but he couldn't help but worry. Did the jurors so sympathize with Susan that they couldn't convict her *of anything*?

A moment later, Chertkow kept reading, "We the jury find the defendant guilty of second-degree murder."

Paul Sequeira let out an audible sigh, joyously shoving his chair away from the table. Susan's nose blushed pink, and her eyelids fluttered. Not unlike when she was informed her husband was dead, she showed no emotion—but Valerie Harris would later say the defendant was shocked.

Upon Susan's request, jurors were polled. When it was his turn to speak, Scott's voice was softer than the others. Susan stared intently at each one. For once, she was silent.

At 11:40, the jurors filed out. After most of the spectators had left, Susan Polk stood to return to her holding cell. "My life is over," she told Valerie Harris, who embraced her and said, "There'll be another day."

THE JURORS HADN'T EXPECTED TO RESOLVE THEIR DIFFERENCES SO QUICKLY, but when they arrived that Friday morning to continue their deliberations, Scott broke the deadlock. He told them that he saw the evidence. "I know it's there. I will go to murder two. I will *never* go to murder one." They took a vote: it was unanimous for murder two. No one expected that. Had Scott not been part of the jury, they likely would have settled on murder one.

Susan seemed to always have someone on her side: first Felix, then Gabe and Eli, then Eli, more recently Valerie Harris and, in the gallery, Paul the orderly, in the jury, Scott. Despite the overwhelming evidence, the brutality of the murder, and the web of deceit, someone was always drawn to her either because she filled a need in them or because they may have understood how Felix's transgression could have warped a young girl for life. Though in this case, that would not be enough to save her.

At a well-attended press conference on the first floor of the courthouse, Adam Polk read a statement from Felix's East Coast relatives, including the older children, Jennifer and Andy, from his first marriage. Felix's sister, Evelyn, had written her own message that was not read. In it, she said she regretted that twice in her life when her brother needed her, she had not been able to help: when he was a little boy at boarding school crying out at night for Katya and when he was hospitalized in the navy and begged her to help him escape the ward. This time, she said, she would help resurrect his good name.

The family letter said, "Felix Polk was a beloved father, brother, uncle, cousin, and nephew to his family. We as his family are devastated not only by his loss but by the violent manner in which he was taken from us. It has been painful to stand by and listen to the many lies about Felix. He was not a violent man. He did not abuse his children. He was not the controlling and manipulative individual that Susan portrayed him to be.

"Felix was a loving and good man, and much loved in return. Though justice has been served, there is no triumph here. Felix is no longer in our lives and we miss him terribly. . . ." It was signed by many members of the family.

Eight of the jurors attended the press conference. Sequeira was terrified. His advice to jurors, if they ever ask and none did, was "to get the hell out of here." The more they said, the greater the risk that the defense might find misconduct.

They said they did not let Susan Polk's offensiveness affect their verdict; they were guided by the law and the facts. There had never been any proof that Felix Polk had physically harmed his wife, though they believed he had been emotionally abusive toward her. Susan's "lack of injuries was huge," Lisa Cristwell said. The only evidence of physical abuse was what Eli had done to Susan. They said they could see his mother coaching him while he was on the witness stand. Gabriel, many concluded, had been hurt the most and was the most convincing witness.

As they filed out, Paul Sequeira stood just outside the door and shook each one's hand and thanked them. He looked like a relieved father of the bride. Then he told the press that while he had dealt with "many heinous criminals, I can't say I've ever prosecuted a more hateful person." It was the most difficult case he'd ever had. He was sure it was the most difficult case the judge had had as well. Had he been her, "I would have banged my head in[to] a wall," he said. Sequeira said he was sorry that Felix Polk's character had taken a beating but that resurrecting the victim was not his job.

Asked about Susan's future in prison, Sequeira said, "The parole board will only let you out after you acknowledge your guilt, say you're sorry, and go through some therapy in prison. I'll let you figure out if any of those three things are ever going to happen."

After the press conference was over, all the jurors and the alternates celebrated with a festive lunch—all but Scott, who did not attend.

Paul Sequeira, tie off, collar unbuttoned, was heading to his son's baseball tournament in Bakersfield. Adam Polk and the rest of his family were flying to Los Angeles, where on Sunday he was graduating cum laude from UCLA with a double major of English and philosophy. Susan Polk, who didn't know her son was graduating, spent the rest of the day cooped up in the holding cell next to Department 31. Late in the day she was hustled onto an old white bus with painted windows, just another inmate on her way back to the West County Detention Center.

Eli, who learned about the verdict from an inmate who'd ridden the bus, cried uncontrollably. Offered the chance to see a counselor, he declined. Helen Bolling said she didn't know when she might see her daughter again. She said,

"I'll write her a letter and tell her to keep her spirits up. Sometimes life does this to you, if you know what I mean."

On the sidewalk in front of the courthouse, Valerie Harris waited until the cameras were ready. She handed her own digital camera to a spectator who agreed to photograph her as she was questioned by the media. Then she headed for the white tent down the block, where she had an appointment to be interviewed on *Catherine Crier Live*.

Later that day, Susan was moved to a jail in downtown Martinez and put on suicide watch. After a few days she was released to the maximum-security building at West County Detention Center, where she would spend twenty-three hours a day in her cell, awaiting sentencing. After recovering from the shock of the verdict, she remained hopeful that she had a good shot at an appeal.

In the months following the verdict, Susan Polk spent her time doing calisthenics, yoga, meditation, writing letters—and reading nearly a book a day. Valerie Harris supplied her with the books, crossword puzzles, and sudoku. She was rereading one of her favorite authors, Charles Dickens, and devouring Dean Koontz's Odd series about a young fry cook who can commune with the dead. Uncharacteristically, Susan refused to talk with reporters. She was doing what she has done for much of her life: isolating herself and reading her way into a fantasy world. For awhile, she maintained her relationship with Valerie Harris who said Susan "is in a really good space. She's the nicest Susan in the whole universe!" Recently, Susan found fault with Valerie Harris and refused to communicate with her.

Deputies at the jail relented and allowed Susan to correspond with Eli. The two conversed about the books they were reading and about what Eli would do when he was released from jail in late October 2006. Recently, Susan contacted one of her old attorneys and asked that he work to shorten Eli's probation so that he could realize his dream of joining the military. Nothing more has come of that.

Shortly after the trial ended, the phone service at the Polks' home was cut off. The court appointed a referee to prepare the Polk house for sale. The realtor will have to advise potential buyers about the murder that took place in the pool house. After the verdict, Susan went attorney shopping, an acknowledgment of sorts that defending oneself is not always the best defense. Nineteen criminal defense attorneys in Contra Costa County claimed they had a conflict of interest or were busy and were "unable" to represent her. In late August 2006, Linda Fullerton, a top-notch criminal attorney based in Point Richmond, California, agreed to take her case.

Once she is sentenced, Susan will be shuttled to the Central California Women's Facility in Chowchilla, the largest women's prison in the nation. Known as a tough place to do time, its population includes "the seriously mentally ill, violent predators, and people who've never been in trouble before but did something stupid," said Dr. Linda Barnard, the expert on domestic violence who testified on Susan's behalf. The women are constantly watched. Prison guards control their lives. "If you piss them off, your life will be hell," Barnard said. The best way to survive is to keep a low profile, something Susan has never done. If she becomes a disciplinary problem, she'll be put in "the shoe," a special housing unit consisting of very small cells with slots in the doors for food to pass through.

Like all the other inmates at Chowchilla, she'll be required to hold a job—she's rarely had one—either in administration, as a groundskeeper, or sewing upholstery, for example. Because Susan often misreads people, she's likely to make enemies. Dr. Barnard fears that Susan "will become easy prey for someone to exploit." With no recourse, she'll unravel. At Chowchilla, one-on-one therapy is not an option.

PAUL SEQUEIRA, WHO MAKES A HABIT OF ATTENDING PAROLE HEARINGS FOR people he's put away, will be there when Susan comes up for parole. If she outlives him, a statement he'll deliver at her sentencing will be reviewed by parole board members when she appears before them years from now. Sequeira admits that Felix put the terrible events in motion. "He took advantage of her. He stole her innocence and brought her into a world she didn't want to be a part of." But that did not give her a license to kill. "In her twisted way," he said, "she created a huge fabrication and she felt entitled to murder."

POSTSCRIPT

AFTER A STINT OF WARM DAYS DURING WHICH PLUM TREES SPROUTED POP-corn-like petals and pink magnolia blossoms began to undress, the air on February 23, 2007, in Martinez, California, snapped cold and wintry. Camera crews on the courthouse sidewalk shuddered while the faithful lined up inside in front of Judge Brady's court as they had done so many times before.

Four and a half years after Dr. Felix Polk died, his wife would be sentenced for his murder. This would likely be her final act, her last moment in the spotlight. Would she plead for mercy like an ordinary criminal or would she remain defiant? In the courtroom the audience divided up like guests at a wedding. On one side were Felix supporters, on the other, the few who supported Susan. The rest of the seats were filled by spectators and reporters. Every spot was taken.

It was a veritable who's who, a cavalcade of characters, from the Susan Polk trial. In one row sat Elizabeth Drozdowska, Susan's ancient neighbor who returned in her wheelchair to defend her. Next to her sat Susan's daffy mother, Helen Bolling, more vocal than ever. In the same row but on the other side was Sheila Byrns, Felix's old patient and friend whom Susan was convinced had had an affair with her husband. Next to her sat Felix's adult daughter, Jennifer Polk, who'd flown in from the East Coast. Then Gabriel and Adam Polk and Gabe's foster mother Marjorie Briner. Against one wall of the courtroom, three of Susan Polk's former attorneys were lined up: Peter Coleridge, who represented her while she was out on bail; Ivan Golde; and Dan Horowitz, who with a fashionable haircut, jeans, and new, small framed glasses looked like he'd been reborn.

Susan sat at the defense table wearing what one spectator dubbed "a farm-fed-salmon-colored" sweater and tan pants and looking too small and brittle to have caused such havoc in the lives of so many people. She shared the table with her new attorneys, Linda Fullerton and Paul Feuerwerker, who earlier had filed an appeal on her behalf. Before the hearing began, Susan's head turned as she stared longingly at her baby, Gabriel, and then at Adam. Both were dressed in suits and ties, young men on the move. And on the other side of the room, Eli, in an oversized Warriors jacket held hands with a pretty but severe-looking woman with pale skin who bore an eerie resemblance to his mother.

Susan's attorneys argued that there had been judicial error and jury misconduct—that jurors, they claimed, had talked about the trial and known of news accounts. One argument was considered more serious: during voir dire, after Sequeira knocked a number of women from the jury pool, he was unable to explain why he had eliminated one woman in particular. The judge's solution had been at first to call the woman back, but when the woman cried and begged not to be put on the jury, the judge merely gave Susan Polk another preemptory challenge. Susan's attorneys argued that the law requires the jury be dismissed and a whole new pool of potential jurors be brought in. Another issue on appeal was Susan Polk's behavior. If the jury viewed it as harmful, Ms. Fullerton argued, then she should have been given backup counsel.

Late in the morning, after listening to the entirety of the defense's case for a mistrial, Judge Brady rejected all the defense arguments.

The rest of the day was set aside for victim impact statements and statements on Susan's behalf. Together, they brought the case into focus. Elizabeth Drozdowska, Susan's old neighbor who had had a heart attack and a stroke and whose body constantly trembles, made a simple case for her: "Susan Polk would never be the person you've seen here," she said, had she not been psychologically kidnapped by Felix as a child. As a caregiver held the microphone to her lips, Ms. Drozdowska said, "Dr. Polk used his professional skills to seduce her and control her. . . ." As Ms. Drozdowska completed her statement, Susan's mother burst forth with "That's the absolute truth! I know it to be so! Hallelujah!"

The old neighbor was followed by a video message on a TV set delivered by

Andy Polk, "the oldest and first child of Felix Polk," as he put it. With a receding hairline and a pleasant, determined face, he spoke about what a wonderful father Felix had been and how Susan was "the lowest form of human being . . . a dangerous sociopath, a violent person."

"She will pay! She must pay!" Andrew Polk declared. Then he did something that Sequeira and his pals who were in court had never seen before. Andy Polk said Susan had stabbed his father twenty-seven times. He wanted the impact of that not to be lost on anyone, and so he slowly and purposefully counted to twenty-seven. With each number he held his right fist in the air plunging it downward, as if he held a knife: "One, two, three, . . . " His father, he said, "died the way no man should have to die, alone, he bled to death." He regretted that his stepmother could not be given the death penalty, he said. "May she now be the center of her own hell and burn there."

Susan heard from every one of Felix's five children. Andy's sister Jennifer, Felix's only daughter, who during her high school years had lived with Susan and Felix in Berkeley, said that until recently, she believed that people were basically good "at the core." An attractive social worker of forty, Jennifer has soft features and the sort of warm face that like her father's puts people at ease. "Susan taught me there are some people who are evil," she said as she stood at the prosecution table and directed her words to Judge Brady. "It troubles me that I have to share this earth with her."

Then it was Adam's turn. He, too, stood before the prosecutor's table. Like his half brother and half sister, he tried to resurrect his father's good name. Sturdy and muscled, he looked as if the blows he'd taken in life had made him only more resilient. His father had been a kind and good father, he said, inspiring his love of literature and music. As he spoke, his mother watched, turning occasionally to take notes. He told the judge and his mother about the impact his father's murder has had on his life: "One day I was a sophomore in college," he said. "The next day I was head of a family." She had robbed him of his carefree years. "You took my dad, and I don't know if I can ever forgive you. My father will never see me get married, never share a beer with me, never watch the Giants with me. He will never see Barry beat Hank's record," he said. Softer in his denunciation than his older siblings, he told his mother, "I still care about you, sincerely," he said.

Susan smiled, but it disappeared when he added, "I hope you get the help you clearly need." When he talked about having graduated from UCLA, Susan's lower lip jutted forward, the closest she would come to a mother's approving smile. Adam said that he believed his father "loved you even as you murdered him. If he were here today he would want you to get the best head doctor and get fixed." Gabriel's comments were the most heartbreaking: He stood at the prosecution's table and turned toward his mother. "Mother, Mom," he said, "the words are not hard for me to utter." In the eight months since his mother was convicted of murder, Gabriel had become a freshman at the University of California at Santa Barbara. Although his eyes were sunken, he was fit, as though he spent part of every day working out. He said Susan had given birth to him, she had raised him and "given me so much. Then you took it way. I was fifteen and you left me with no home. No family." Now twenty he said, "You may have been done with my father, but I was not." The center of her face turned a shade of pink; she began to cry.

When it was his turn, Susan's mortal enemy, Paul Sequeira said, "She felt she was smarter than anyone else," and she felt entitled, entitled to kill. He spoke about the more than fifty disciplinary actions against her from her four-plus years in the Martinez County jail. After today, he said, she will become "old news. She will just be another killer with a number in the department of corrections and the world will not revolve around her anymore." Then he liberally quoted again something she had once told Gabriel, that a person who kills another "should be forever separated from society."

He was followed by the few people who came forward to ask for leniency for Susan Polk. Susan's mother, Helen Bolling, her black wool cap askew on her snow-white hair, hung onto the wood podium and focused on the judge. In her right hand she waved an anthology of children's writings from the Mount Diablo Unified School District published in 1969. Twelve-year-old Susan was the only student who had three pages of writing in the book. "That in itself is an achievement," she said to the judge, "wouldn't you say?" The judge did not respond, and Helen Bolling continued:

"The hunter walked quietly through the forest searching for another victim." Helen was reading from Susan's short story about a hunter who killed a lion for its pelts but who regretted the killing when he realized the lioness had had cubs. As she read, her daughter watched, occasionally smiling. Back when Dan Horowitz represented Susan, Helen had tried to convince him to use the story in his opening statement, but he thought any essay that talked about a killer was unlikely to help his client. Helen Bolling had reached back thirty-eight years to talk about her daughter's "tremendous compassion," unaware of the story's irony. Then Helen did something that witnesses are not allowed to do: she moved over to her daughter and placed her hand on Susan's shoulder. No deputy moved in, nor did the judge object. "She never had a young womanhood!" Helen shouted in her small voice. "She did not kill him willingly! She was trying to save herself from death. . . ." She asked the judge to "have compassion, since she was imprisoned since she was fourteen years old."

When Helen was done, Eli, ever his mother's protector stood up to defend her again. He looked distraught, his empathetic eyebrows lifted like a church steeple. He said his mother was the real victim in this case and that he had loved his father. "He's my father," he explained, but "my mom is the best person, the most caring person I know." Turning toward the audience, he found his brothers and said not in a vindictive voice so much as a sad one, "I don't know you guys anymore." Then he talked about how lost he was without his mother. He said he couldn't start his life again until she was released from custody. "There is an emptiness eating away at me every single day of my life."

And then it was his mother's turn to fight for herself. In a highly unusual move, she insisted she speak from the witness stand—so that she could address her adversaries. To her son Adam, she said she could show no remorse. "I cannot express remorse for surviving." To Adam and Gabe she said, "I can only say this, I forgive you. I love you," then she added, "I'm sorry the way things turned out," but she blamed it all on their father, whom she said she had failed to transform "into a better human being."

To all of Felix's children, she said that she was "sorry" she dragged Felix's name through the dirt, but she didn't sound at all apologetic. Sequeira and the other DAs scattered in the courtroom had never seen a performance like this.

Her eyes swept the court as she proclaimed, "Shame on you all!" In her denunciation she included the court staff and the judge—whom she now icily called "Mrs. Brady." She said, "I would rather die on my feet than live on my knees. I'm not going to beg for mercy!"

Susan Polk would not give her adversaries the satisfaction of knowing she would be punished. "I hate to tell you this," she told the court, and she didn't sound at all regretful, "I enjoy every day in my cell." She said she writes letters and reads and that if she spends the rest of her life in prison, she'll write poetry, write about what happened, and "do things I want to do."

She quoted from a jailhouse library book, *Boy's Life* by Robert McCammon, an adventure book that includes the story of a killer who lives unnoticed among his friendly neighbors. "Men and women are still children," she read, and they would "like to return naked to the swimming hole if just for one day." Perhaps she was referring to her childhood cut short, although there were those in the courtroom who thought she killed her husband so she could return to the days before she'd met Dr. Polk.

To her son Eli she said as she looked down and wept, "Don't wait for me. This is the springtime of your life."

"I'm going to be okay," she assured. At least she wasn't going to be sent to a mental ward: Her fate in prison, she said, "is better than being hospitalized in some sort of coma."

Susan scanned her legal pad on which she'd composed her notes. She ended her speech as she had begun it, with bitterness: "I don't even hate you, Sheila," she said to Ms. Byrns, who smiled nervously at her. "I'm sorry for you," she said, before rendering her final punch: "You were his patient too!"

Then Susan slowly left her bully pulpit for the last time. Her attorney would make an impressive effort to beg for leniency for her client, but Linda Fullerton was no match for the record that Susan Polk had amassed.

Swiftly and without emotion, Judge Brady sentenced Susan Polk to the maximum: sixteen years to life. The defendant showed no emotion. The judge said Ms. Polk would be given credit for the 1,376 days she had already served—which meant she might be eligible for parole in twelve years, when she is sixty-one. The judge ordered her sent to state prison "forthwith."

AFTER THE CROWDS HAD FILTERED OUT OF THE COURTROOM, DEPUTIES placed Susan Polk in belly shackles and behind her back clamped cuffs on her wrists. In the judge's chambers, the exhausted staff nibbled pieces of cake in celebration for surviving the tortuous trial of Susan Mae Polk.

When the TV crews had long since packed up and only print journalists remained, Paul Sequeira exited the courthouse. He told the small band of reporters that Susan Polk "deserves to be in prison the rest of her life." He said she still shows no remorse and remains defiant and that "she will be until she draws her last breath."

ACKNOWLEDGMENTS

Although the Polk family remains divided, I found sources on both sides. I'm indebted to many people, none more than Adam Polk, whose insights guided me. Eli Polk also spoke to me at length about his own struggles and his family. Susan's mother, Helen Bolling, who calls me "sweetheart," offered me Susan's early writings and her own observations. Initially, Susan Polk refused to talk to me, but once she relented I accepted many lengthy collect calls from the jail in Martinez, California. Then, just as quickly as she began cooperating, Susan Polk shut me down. One day in the courtroom she spotted me conversing with one of her enemies and that was all it took, but by then I had asked her nearly every question I had and I was yet to hear another thirty-one hours of Susan Polk on the witness stand.

To bring Felix alive I spoke with his friends, colleagues, students, and patients, as well as his twin brother John, his sister-in-law Barbara, and especially his sister Evelyn.

Susan Polk's fictional world made finding the truth a sometimes-Sisyphean task. I verified what I could and failing that, weighed the likelihood that something happened as she said it had.

The most controversial aspect of the story is Susan's assertion that she was between fourteen and sixteen when she and Felix had sex. It wasn't until I had interviewed her many times that she explained she had fallen in love with her therapist when she was eighteen or nineteen, but that when she turned forty she had a flashback that her husband had hypnotized her and had had sex with her when she was sixteen or younger. I don't believe that account nor am I a believer in recovered memory, but I have little doubt that Susan Polk believes that's what happened.

For their assistance, solace, and gallows humor, I am grateful to have had such capable partners in crime as Lisa Sweetingham, Bruce Gerstman, Henry Lee, and Chris Darden, as well as Jason Dearon, Matt Fields, Will Harper, Falguni Lakhani, Demian Bulwa, Chris Weicker, and Rita Williams.

I'd like to thank my many sources, including: Lloretta Bankus, Linda Barnard, Sam Barondes, M.D., Helen Bolling, Kent Brezee, Marjorie Briner, Sheila Byrns, Lisa Calhoun, Paula Canny, Lieutenant Roger Clark, Steve Clark, Nancy L. Davis, Roger Deakins, Karen Fleming-Ginn, Danny Goldstine, Cynthia Gorney, Laura Grandin, Thomas Gutheil, M.D., Marilyn Hajjar, Chris and Anna Harris, Valerie Harris, Mary Herget, Sergeant Ken Hansen, Sergeant Todd Kidder, Janna Kuntz, Steve Landis, Dan Lawrence, Jimmy Lee, Kathy Lucia, Budd MacKenzie, Tom O'Connor, Phyllis O'Leary, Stephen Pittel, Ellie Rex, Karen Saeger, Brother Michael Saggau, Stephen Sarewitz, M.D., Gary Schoener, Paul Sequeira, Jerrold Shapiro, Alison Shurtleff, Lee Steinbach, Joel Tepper, Cathy Thielen, Patricia Topsmiller, Ernst Valfer, Song Wicks, Robert Wilk, and jurors Joe Kermode, Jason "Ponytail" MacDavid, Pat Roland, Kathy Sommese, and jury forewoman Lisa Cristwell, and Susan's many lawyers including: David Coleman, Peter Coleridge, Jack Funk, Ivan Golde, Liz Grossman, Dan Horowitz, and Kim Kupferer.

Many other sources insisted on anonymity either because they sought privacy or because, reasonably or not, they feared Susan Polk.

I could not have a better ally than Sterling Lord, my agent, editor, and friend. Kate Coleman suggested I do the story. Danelle Morton whipped up the title. And Jeremy Larner offered worthwhile insights. When I was dissatisfied with the shape of my manuscript, I was fortunate to find Ethan Watters, who helped reshape the first part of the book. At William Morrow, the unflappable Matt Harper guided the project through pressurized days and nights. I appreciate the help of computer czar Russ Boynton, photographer John Blaustein, and attorney John Pelosi, who meticulously examined every part of this book except this sentence. A special thanks to Jim Spalding for his encouragement and understanding.

For always bringing me back home, I thank my friends and family: Jake Wood on drums, Rachel Wood on customer support, pastries, and unsolicited fashion advice, John Wood and Cindy Lopez for landscaping, photography, and baby Dylan, Bill Wood for conversation and animal rescue, Henry Krumholz, M.D. for a lesson on the human body, and especially my sister, Susan Pogash, who near the end of the process swooped in and edited the manuscript, finding the sorts of glitches that had they remained would have sentenced me to Ambien for life.

INDEX